MW00681452

Escaping from Reality Without Really Trying

40 Years of High Seas Travels and Lowbrow Tales

ROBERT JACOBY

CLOUD BOOKS

Copyright © 2011 by Robert Jacoby. All rights reserved.
Published by Cloud Books

An edited version of the chapter "Cape John" was first published in *The Oregon Literary Review*.
The excerpt "What Will Entertain People" (a selection from "Off to see the wizard") was first published in *Alice Blue Review*.

More at: WWW.ESCAPING-FROM-REALITY.COM

ISBN-13: 978-0-615-43489-6
Library of Congress Control Number: 2011902734

Book design by Brion Sausser.
Manufactured in the United States of America

Author's Note

The interview sessions for this book were conducted in Fall 2006 over the course of 10 days and nearly 40 hours of interviews. The narrator kept every Certificate of Discharge from the ships he sailed with, from July 1967 to June 2006. And we sat down in a room, and he told his stories. He is a natural-born storyteller with an eidetic memory.

The original title for this book was *Idiot's Despair*. In the Greek city-states, the word "idiot" meant someone who was consumed with self-interest and ignored the needs of the community. To the Christian existentialist philosopher Kierkegaard, "despair" meant the losing of the self to life's extremes—anesthetized, or unlimited.

I wrote a dedication as an introduction to *Idiot's Despair*:

> *In every man there lives an idiot,*
> *at least in part,*
> *struggling to be complete.*
> *And every man despairs for want of extremes in his life.*
> *To the idiot in every man.*
> *To that over which you despair.*

This book is for the idiot in every man.

Here is the new dedication:

> This book is for dreamers, doers, and adventurers; retired pirates, armchair pirates, pirate wannabes, and even the parrots on the pirate's shoulder looking out on the action and squawk-

ing to be *in* on the action; young men, old men, middle-aged men, workaday malcontents, and all the women who love them and want to keep them sane and sound; and anyone who wants to read adventure stories you *think* can only be found today in the movies.

The views and opinions expressed in this work are solely those of the narrator and do not reflect those of the author, the compiler and editor of the work. Reader discretion is advised.

Now, go grab a cold one. You're gonna need it.

Contents

I was sitting in a bar having a couple of drinks, that's how it always starts...

I saw people going to work, coming home, bitching about work, whether it be the money, the conditions, whatever, constant complaining. They'd get their 2- or 3-week vacation, what did they do? They either stayed in that house, fixed the house up, put some money into it, rather than spend it, then they'd go back to work, maybe take a 2-week vacation, maybe a week somewhere, and they couldn't wait to get back. So basically, if you were going to work, work to keep the house, keep the house for a roof over your head, and then on your vacation, you still worked to keep the house over your head, you really never had escape.

I couldn't do that. I mean, I can't worry about a payment on a house, I can't spend my entire life working and worrying about a house. There's a bigger world out there. There's more girls in this world than the ones that live across the street.

The television was always the idiot tube, but it was an escape. It was an escape for the people who worked for a living. It was easier than going to the show. You could select your own programs, or your parents or your guardians selected what you watched, which was OK. But if you screamed loud enough you'd get what you want. Cuz it was a control issue. They wanted you to watch what you were *supposed* to watch. It was what *they* thought was good for you. They were always doing what was *good* for *you*. "Now, this hurts me more than it hurts you."

Any freedom was totally stifled by school, religion, parents. My aunt and uncle might give me a little, you know, "Hey, go do something. Go do what you want." Other than that, it was, "You gotta go to work. You gotta do this. You gotta play football."

Well, I don't have to do anything I don't want to do. I'll sit here. What are you gonna do? Shoot me? Go ahead.

You know, it's so strange. I never saw in any school about this is your Bill of Rights and your Constitution, we the people. Basically, everywhere you go you're being dictated to as to how to do things. I mean, I can't get any relief. My rights are being abused. "You don't like the way we do this? We've been doing this for 3,000 years." Well, does that mean if Admiral Nelson on his flagship was shitting off the stern, that means you're gonna go do it, too?

I understand that everybody wants it better for their children. I guess it's supposed to be right. But does anybody ask what the child wants? I mean, very seldom is there options. I mean, I made it so far in the Merchant Marines cuz I say yes, and then I go do whatever I want. But then I didn't, in my youth, I didn't. I'd ask why?

"*Whadya mean 'why'? Because I said so, that's 'why.'*"

You know, the *ultimate* authority.

High school was terrible, from parochial to public to not going at all. After awhile, I refused. It was idiotic. They would just come into school, and you might as well have had a TV there and they could tape whatever they're gonna say for that class for the day, cuz that's what they did every day of their life, every year. They taught that same class. Drugs were just coming into fashion. Girls were being girls. That's when I first noticed people's opinions, like you had to have a girlfriend, or you had to have a boyfriend. And automatically, I said, what? You know, I got this church over here with the Ten Commandments, now I'm in public school and they're telling me what to do. I have to have a girlfriend? They all had it figured out. They were gonna go to college, and you had to go to college, too. They had it all figured out already. I'm talking high school. And I said, "Excuse me. I don't think so."

I wanted a life of adventure.

Anything what was different. Not necessarily to see the world; meet people of the world, kill 'em. Sit around and drink. What I hated about it was I was always told how you can't do that.

They'd say, "You can't do that."

"Well, why can't you do that? Because you're saying I can't do that?"

"People don't live like that."

What do you mean people don't live like that? Let's get out of the box here. I'm talking east side of Cleveland and a home in Euclid, you know, which was the *ultimate*. God forbid you moved to somewhere in the suburbs. *Oh my God*. And: "They've got three wonderful children. Don't you think you'd like that?"

No.

Let's face facts, I'm not a father figure. Or, maybe I am. But how would the world like four or five of me running around? I mean, it's bad enough there's one of me.

I'm not saying that's right or wrong. But the hypocrites in Washington or the UN are no better than I am. At least I'm heads-up about it. Hey, look, I don't want to do nothing anyway. And as for nepotism, yeah, I'm gonna help my blood relatives. I'm not gonna sit like Kofi Annan and say, "My son had something to do with that Oil for Food deal in Iraq? I never knew!" Give me a fucking break. And Bill Clinton: "I never had sex with that woman." Now we get: "Well, it depends what you call sex."

At least I'm honest.

"Where were you?"

"I was in a bar getting a blow job. She only charged five bucks. I think I'm in love."

It's just a terrible suppression, really. When I moved down to Florida that time with the girlfriend. "Yeah, we can go to Florida." I called my friend who lived in Florida and said, "You gotta come down. I need somebody to drink with."

He said, "What are you doing with her?"

I said, "Well, we're probably gonna get married." I said, "She wants what I want. We're gonna get a sailboat and sail around."

It never materialized.

But like my friend told me: one wrote the book, and they all read it.

And that is pretty much it. No matter what's *said*, what's *done* is another thing. No matter what they say, it's pretty much they want the white picket fence, the house, and the kids. Most of the women in my life have always assumed: "He *says* that, but he really doesn't *mean* it."

Excuse me, I really *do* mean it.

Or they think they're gonna change me, or I'm gonna change. I'm *not*. I didn't want that when I was 15, 14, 13. I *never* wanted it.

I remember in high school, one of the many guidance counselors who were gonna steer me into the social way of life; I was going to be, you know, an *asset* to the community and the world.

He says, "You gonna play football for us?"

I says, "I don't think I'm gonna be here that long."

He says, "Well, girls really go for guys with football letters on their sweaters."

I says, "I'll get lucky or unlucky, as the case may be, eventually."

Let's stop and think about this:

"Why are you going with him?"

"Oh, he's got a football letter."

How fucking materialistic is *that*? And it's totally acceptable. And shallow. So the girl feels it's OK, but then it becomes, "You *used* me."

Well, wait a minute: What did *you* do? I mean, come on.

As my uncle once said: there's always three sides to a story. And somewhere between lies the truth.

The state of Ohio said that I had to go to school; they didn't say anything about learning anything. So I stayed to sixteen and a half, and I left.

My mother tried to buy me, tried to get me to go into the system: she needed control. She never had control over my father, her husband, who got killed a couple months before I was born. So she never had something she could control, dominate.

As I got older, I got freer, because the system was actually becoming freer for people, through the communication system, through the news media. People knew more and more about what was going on in the world, reading the paper. I mean, *they* opened the paper and read the obits. I read the paper to read what was going on in the world. And it was almost like they didn't want me to. You know, their world consisted of the obituaries, so my world is supposed to be that, too, or what happened three blocks away. Basically, it was always a control issue. And the only way to break free was to leave.

I remember telling a girl who hated me—and the more they hated me, the more I used to try to put the make on them; the ones that liked me, I really didn't care about much—that I had a whole list of places I was gonna go. I think she said something to the effect of: "I'll blow you if you can get to any of these places."

I'd like to catch up to her now, even at 61. I kind of liked her.

I exceeded those places that I had written down.

I tried it, working in the steel industry.

It was terrible.

I remember an old black guy, short and fat. He drove the tow motor. In the steel industry at that time, every 20 years, you got a 13-day paid vacation. He was working on his second one. He'd already had his first 20 years in. What he did was, he would sit on that big tow motor that he was driving, and he'd use a lever to hook up the scrap in a truck-bed container, and he'd pull that over to the scrap yard. That's all he did all day. Most days he got 2 hours overtime. And that's all he did.

And people were envious of him cuz he got 2 hours overtime and he didn't have to do a whole lot.

I'm sure his wife and the kids were happy, the loved ones back home, you know: "*Give me that money! Did you work overtime today?*"

"Here you go, honey."

If that's what you want, God bless you, far be it from me to pass judgment.

I thought it was insane. I was becoming part of the system and didn't want it. I might as well have been on the dark side of the moon.

I lasted 6 weeks. I was glad they laid me off.

Everybody said, "Oh, don't worry kid. We'll get you back."

I said, "Don't worry about it. Thank you, though."

"See if you can work a double today. It's your last day. Go tell 'em you want to work a double."

I said, "Oh, no, I don't want to push the issue. I don't want to force anything on anybody."

The rush hour traffic, the coming home to the same dumb shit. "Save your money." Save your money for *what*? Save your money so you can get your 2-week vacation at the end of the year and blow it? What ever happened to *now*, or *me*?

I've always had a million dollars worth of good advice, it's just nobody gave me the million dollars. No, seriously, it's like that. To me, it's totally absurd. I mean, how many bosses do you have in this life?

It's ridiculous that children are nurtured to be independent, and when they do become independent, they're condemned for it. When the whole theory is to get them up and get them functioning, but it's still the control issue. "I'm gonna get you to the point where you can function on your own, but I'm still gonna tell you how to function. Don't drink, don't smoke. What are you drinking that for?"

I've been in fistfights in bars just over a: "What are you drinking that for?"

"Cause I feel like it. That is OK, isn't it? I'm sorry if I'm offending you." So I finally have to knock 'em out, you know? People will tell you what to drink, when to use the bathroom.

"Hey, she'll blow you."

"Well, so will a million other girls. What the fuck do I care?"

It ain't like the first time. I'm not the first one she'll blow.

There's some bars I actually quit stopping in, not because I had problems in there, but because I got tired of people asking me ignorant, stupid fucking questions.

"Gee, we got it good here in America, don't we?"

I said, "Ever been anywhere else?"

"Well …. I see it on T.V."

"Well, what else do you see?"

Fucking dumb shit you see on T.V.

The news media today is terrible. Very bad reporting, overseas reporting. I've seen *numerous* inaccuracies in their reporting, and they don't give the whole story. People would rather, I think, turn on a personality they want to see on the news media no matter what the stories are gonna be, how long they're gonna be, and they're actually waiting for the commercial so they can get up to use the bathroom.

Anyway, I happened to run into a guy at a bar, we're helping his dad clean the place. The doors were open to air it out. It'd been closed for a year.

This Jim Pierce came in, and somebody asked him, "Haven't you shipped out yet?"

I heard about it, and read about it, the Merchant Marine, and I though it was a great idea. I went down and got a seaman's card. I went to the Lake Carriers Association. Then I went with Jim Pierce to Philadelphia, to the union hall. I paid the dues. And that was it. I was on my way.

An opening to a career I could really adjust to

⚓

My first job out I caught a job in the steward department because I was told that was the best way to break in. It was the *American Veteran*, an old freighter built at the end of World War II, and United States Lines being the largest company the union had under contract, most people worked for. I caught it in Philadelphia. One of the guys quit. I got on, got the job out of the union hall. They went to different ports loading, discharging cargo, now a thing of the past. It's easier just to centralize the cargo and truck it in, truck it out. Containerization. Modernization. But these were old freighters, and they would go down the coast, picking up and discharging cargo from New York, go over to Europe, basically do the same thing. The majority of it was government cargo for the military in Germany and Belgium.

Everybody said, "Stay, stay, stay," you know, "try to stay on as long as you can. Get your sea time in with the union," right?

I made the trip, and the steward department just wasn't for me. It's better known as the stupid department. You didn't have to worry about any gear. You were always inside the house. But there was no real freedom there, either. I was steward's utility. I would get the food from the galley, put it in the plates, and then people would come up, and the messman would come back there and I'd give him the food or he'd give me the orders, I'd fill them up and give them to him, we'd work together, get the food out to the crew. It was hectic, like a restaurant would be.

The captain on there was Peterson, used to call him Port and Starboard Peterson, cuz he had one blue eye and one green eye. Port wine is red. That's a little saying we had. So your port side would be

9

red, your starboard side would be green. So that's what they used to call him: Port and Starboard Peterson. We also used to call him The Sponge—he drank all day and night. The only thing he cared about was keeping his ice bucket filled. He was pretty easy to get along with.

But he was another malcontent for the simple reason that his father had sailed with the United States Lines during World War II and had been interred, a POW, for about 2 years by the Japanese. Technically, he was an enemy alien civilian, in China, I think.

When he got freed after the war, he came back to U.S. Lines, and he told them, "You owe me 2 years' pay."

They said, "No, we don't. We just owe you a job. We don't owe you any money. Here's your captain's job."

Well, now you got a real malcontent.

And Kenny, his son, Port and Starboard Peterson, had come out of school as a third mate, got a job with U.S. Lines, they put him on *The United States* passenger ship. He was the youngest one to ever sail captain with U.S. Lines.

I'll tell you why.

His old man liked to drink. And the captain usually carried $10,000 in the safe, cash money for payments, pay the crew, we always got paid in American money. Peterson absconded with about $20,000—for some reason, there was $20,000 instead of $10,000 in the ship's safe. Took the money and made a run for it.

U.S. Lines freaks.

He says, "You owe me the money."

They says, "We're charging you with theft. You stole $20,000 from us."

Kenny runs up and says, "Wait a minute. If you don't charge the old man, just leave him alone, let him pension off, retire, I'll pay you back at such and such percent interest."

The company looks at it and says, "Hey, that sounds fucking good."

So he was the youngest captain to sail, but what they weren't saying was that he was paying U.S. Lines back, and they kept promoting him up so they'd get their money back. Even though it was a good interest rate, they wanted their money.

Anyway, you'd think, being my first trip, it would be eventful, but it really wasn't. It was kind of mundane. We loaded on the east coast and then went to Zeebrugge, Belgium to drop the ammunition off there, and then over to Bremerhaven, Germany, which was kind of wide open then. We went down to Hamburg, Germany, went to Two Mark Alley.

Two Mark Alley. Every place in Europe has an alley, whatever they want to call it, where the girls sit in the windows. It was kind of a trip, really. Notoriously terrible area. There's a barricade in front of the street. You have to walk through the sides to get in. The girls sit in the windows in every array of undress, and it's just a trip. It really is. Talk about a culture shock. You knock on the window, and they open the window and you talk to them. One of the guys off the ship was trying to trade his portable radio for a blow job. It was hilariously funny.

I mean, it was total freedom. And there was no recrimination. Like an old girlfriend of mine once told me, "You know, you don't try hard enough." I said, "Well, I don't feel like trying at all." I mean, how do you try when you can have any woman you like when you walk down the street and just pick one out and you never have to talk to her again? You never have to see her again. There's no drama involved in this. Yeah. Yeah. My kind of way.

It was an opening to a career I could see I could really adjust to.

American Shipper

When we got back to the States I quit, went back to Philly, registered as ordinary on the *American Shipper*. Home sweet home for 10 months.

At the time you registered at whatever rating you had, and I had what we called entry ratings, ordinary wiper and food handler. I registered as an ordinary seaman. Mainly, I wanted the weekends off in port. Money didn't interest me that much. Still doesn't to this day. We got $311 a month. Five days for every 30 vacation pay. That was what? '67. At sea I got the weekends and the holidays. If I was off watch for dockings or undockings, if they called me, I got overtime for that. It wasn't enough to live on, if you were trying to raise a family. You saw guys who were, you know, they wouldn't go ashore. They'd try to work every overtime and get every hour they could.

But I remember two guys: Bill Harris and Joe Char.

The bosun, Joe Char, half Hawaiian, half Chinese. Very good, very good. Rum-dumb a lot, you know, but he was good. He told me they had what they called able seamen, able-bodied, AB, what I am now, and they had the bosun, a carpenter, two deck maintenance, able seaman that worked a straight 8 hours, plus you had two ABs and a watch and an ordinary on watch, for three watches. I would have to work with whoever the ABs I had on watch.

The bosun kind of took to me, and Harris, too, I assume because I was willing to learn, maybe they saw some of them in me and, you know, "Hey, kid, we gotta do this."

The bosun, Joe Char, told me, "I'm gonna put you to work with Harris."

Bill Harris—Harry—he was out of Sheep's Head Bay. During

World War II they didn't have a training center for merchant seamen, so the government started Sheep's Head Bay in New York for unlicensed, not officers. Harris went there. I guess he wanted to get out of the war, cuz if you went in the Merchant Marines you didn't have to go in the Army. But you had to keep sailing.

And Harris was good. I mean, he was fucking good. The bosun Joe Char said, "I'll keep you working with Harry. If you learn anything, you'll learn it from him."

And, more than less, I was willing to work, and all the ABs were asking, "I wanna work with Ronnie," you know, or "Give me Ronnie."

The bosun says, "Look, I only got one fucking Ronnie on here. He's working with Harris."

Harry drank three fifths a day. I know that sounds strange. Really. I can look back on it today, and at my best I couldn't drink three fifths. I could maybe do two. I'd get just so fucked up doing two fifths.

We'd turn to at eight o'clock in the morning, the bosun would gather up the day workers in port. He'd say, "OK, Harry, you take Ronnie, go do this. Splice wire."

Back then you spliced wires, before everybody got involved in it, the wire splicing, the wire would part again and kill somebody. Finally the insurance companies said, "Fuck that, get new wires." Because even though the splice itself was good, once a wire parted, and you just said, "Ah, fuck it, you know, just cut that end off, we'll make another end and we'll splice it." Well, when the wire's bad, the wire's bad. It was killing people. And the insurance companies were paying through the nose.

Anyway, Harry'd be up by six. He had false teeth, and he'd go *cluck, click, cluck* all the time with them, and smoke. Smoked Camels, just fucking smoking all the time. He'd been there since World War II, he'd been on the North Atlantic for fucking years, I mean, since his *birth* he'd been out there. He knew every fucking bar on the east coast and London and France and Belgium, and he had kids all over Europe, too.

We turn to at eight o'clock, 0800.

Bosun says, "Ronnie, you work for Harry. Harry, take Ronnie, go back and splice the wires or something."

Harris saying, "Now, look, Ronnie, you dumb son of a bitch." He's gonna use psychology on me. "You fucking idiot, *this* is how this is done."

I says, "OK, Harry."

He says, "You always gotta wear a hat." He'd always have some stupid fucking hat on. And I'm talking cold. This is *November*, in the North Atlantic. In New York, in November. *Anywhere* in November up north, right? He would come out with a fucking jacket on. I'm freezing to death. I got fucking tons of clothes on. He'd come out with that fucking little stupid hat on, little watch cap. "Always gotta wear a hat, Ronnie, or you'll get a head cold."

I says, "OK, Harry."

Jacket was open, shirt open, just a cloth shirt, buttoned. No T-shirt. Pants, dirty, usually no underwear. Fucking boots, shoelaces hanging, no socks. I got cold looking at him. Never wore gloves. Never wore a watch. His fucking hands were so calloused and hard. He would get what we call fishhooks from the wires, sharp, broken wires. They'd cut into his hands. He'd chew them out with his teeth. Never wore gloves all those fucking years. Just swollen and shit.

He was the best fucking able seaman I've ever seen.

People tell me, "Oh, you're a good AB."

I'd say, "You think I'm good? You shoulda saw me 30 years ago, and you shoulda saw a guy named Bill Harris 40 years ago."

But it'd be eight fifteen.

Harry says, "What time is it, Ronnie?"

I says, "Eight fifteen, Harry."

He says, "OK, I'll be back in a minute." He'd go get a drink. He'd let me finish up the work. He'd be back in 5 minutes. He'd walk back to the room, have a drink, come back.

This went on all day.

He had a shot every 15 fucking minutes of his life. He had a shot every 15 minutes, and he was the best fucking AB I've ever seen in my life. In 10 months of sailing with him I saw him make one fucking mistake, and that was on the turning of the turnbuckle. He got it the wrong way. I couldn't believe he did it.

We were turning it, and I says, "You know, Harry, we got it going the wrong way here."

"*What the fuck you know, kid? Jesus Christ, Ronnie.*"

"OK, Harry, but I think we're going the wrong way."

"*Don't tell me what the fuck to do!*"

"OK, Harry."

Half hour later: "You know, I think you were right."

That one time.

He drank Christian Brothers brandy, and he had a bottle of scotch, and a bottle of anything else. That wasn't counting beers in between.

He'd go ashore: "Come on, Ronnie, we're going ashore."

I'd say, "OK, Harry."

Liverpool, Dublin, Glasgow, back to Liverpool, he'd been running there since '43. He had kids in London. He knew every fucking bar to go to.

There was a guy, Owen Matthias. I know he's dead now. He grabbed me to go work with him. "C'mere, home boy."

I says, "What the fuck's a home boy?"

"That means you're homie. That's me and you: tight."

His hands were like Harris's, from being on that North Atlantic. He'd been on that ship 23 years. Twenty-three years. It was a steady job and that's all he wanted. Depression-era mentality. His hands were so fucking swollen, he sometimes couldn't move them from the arthritis.

He says, "Home boy, you going ashore?"

We started running to Le Havre-London-Le Havre, France.

I says, "Yeah, I'm going in."

"Do me a favor?"

I says, "Yeah, what do you need?"

He gives me this tube of hand cream, like a Ben Gay, but the French version of it. It had something in it that you couldn't get in the States, some kind of narcotic or something that was bad in America. Like: oh, you're using drugs. Oh, you're one of *those*. He gave me an empty tube.

I says, "I can't fucking read this." I got a hard time with English. I would take it to the drugstore on the way to the bar, get a tube of this for him. I'd show the tube, give them the francs. I get back to the ship.

Next day I says, "I got that for you, Owen."

"Thanks, home boy, you have enough money?"

I says, "Yeah, Owen, thank you."

"Do me another favor?"

I says, "What do you need?"

He says, "Open the tube and squeeze it into the palms of my hand."

"Well. OK."

He couldn't move his fingers to even take the cap off. He would actually slam his hands together, and just keep going back and forth like that, until it finally gave him relief. He said it was the only thing that would work.

Anyway, Harry wanted to go everywhere. Everything was within walking distance back then. It wasn't like it is today, you know, you gotta take a taxi to get a drink. He knew all the girls that were left over from World War II. They used to give you blow jobs in the back of the bar for 10 or 20 bucks. They were all married. Their husbands knew what they were doing, but they didn't care as long as the money came in.

Harry knew every-fucking-where to go, and he'd get in arguments with 'em. They wanted too much fucking money and all that, they were all drunk.

Those old guys left over from World War II, they always wore suits. Sometimes with a tie. I mean, I'm talking able seaman, ordinary seaman, professional ordinaries, guys that never advanced—they couldn't read or write, but they always wore suits.

We're in London and Harry says, "I'm going to see my little girl-friend tonight. You wanna go?"

I says, "I'm gonna go look around a little bit, Harry. I'll go with you tomorrow." I wanted to go see Madame Tussauds House of Wax. I was actually doing stuff like that. I says, "I've seen it on TV; I always wanted to go see it."

I took off to go see it. Then I kind of wandered a little bit and got back to the ship halfway early, got some sleep.

Back then there were three men in the room: an ordinary seaman and two ABs. And a bosun with the carpenter, two men were in the room. Now it's one man in a room. That cut down on the homicide rate 50%, you know, guys killing each other. It's called the fire ax brigade: "*I remember what you did 3 years ago!*" Three years ago, right? They wonder about some guy going crazy. People remember, something triggers it.

Next day Harry comes in the foc'sle, in my room, and he says, "You going in tonight?"

I says, "No, I'm gonna take a break. I'm staying in tonight, get a decent night's sleep." I didn't want anything to drink.

He says, "Do me a favor."

I says, "What's that?"

He has the suit on, with a white shirt, no T-shirt. We're fucking cold, right? Not Harris. He's fucking one shot every 15 minutes. He can gulp fucking antifreeze. I mean, we'd be out there freezing in the fucking day. He wouldn't have socks on, shoelaces were dangling. We used to do shackles, horseshoe shape with a pin that goes through, the big wires, the eye that goes through, you wire them to the deck. One time Harry was over there bullshitting, standing there. He couldn't see one shoelace, it was dangling; we tied a fucking shackle onto it. He started walking with the fucking shackle. It was nuts.

Anyway, he says, "I can't get my zipper open."

His hands were so fucked up he couldn't get the zipper up. He pulled the zipper down and tore the fucking bottom of it out so you couldn't line it up with the little teeth. He tore it out. Two safety pins held the bottom.

Harry says, "Do me a favor, Ron. Get this zipper up for me, will ya?"

"Harry, me and you are OK, but, you know . . . ." Jesus. So I'm sitting on the bunk trying to line it up to get the zipper up, he's standing there.

There's a knock at the door, Harris opens it, and at the door is the chief mate next to the captain. They see this and go, "Hey, we didn't see anything. Whatever you guys . . . ."

I says, "*No—mate!*"

He says, "Alright, he's trying to get that zipper up for you. Oh, OK." He says, "You guys working tomorrow?"

It's a Saturday.

I says, "Yeah, mate, I'll be out there."

Harry says, "Yeah, we're working."

"Well, goddamn it, don't go out and get all fucked up tonight, I need you guys tomorrow."

"OK, OK."

I get the fucking thing up for him. "You're all set, Harry."

He says, "Come on ashore."

I says, "No, Harry."

He says, "Meet my old girlfriend from World War II. She's working at the bar now."

I says, "Harry, I'm not going again tonight." I wanted to go see something. "I'll tell you what." I says, "I'll go with you tomorrow night, Saturday night."

So he turns around and goes ashore, and he comes back, and he's got this fucking wallet. He's showing me the next day, we're out on deck.

He says, "Look at this, Ronnie, my daughter gave me this."

I says, "That's nice. She gave you a wallet."

"Here, look at it."

So I'm looking at it. It's an old used wallet. I says, "Harry, that don't look like a new wallet." I says, "Harry, she stole this wallet."

He's pissed. "*Gimme that! That's not important! She gave it to me!*"

OK.

God, what a life.

He says, "You fixed that fucking zipper?"

I says, "Yeah."

He says, "I went to the fucking bathroom in there." He says, "I zipped it and it came down too far. I'm trying to get it up." He says, "Some English guy came in there and was looking at me, and I told him, 'I wish Ronnie was here.'"

So I says, "Give me the fucking pants. Before we go out, just give me the fucking pants."

He comes over, gives me the pants.

He says, "When we gonna go?"

I says, "Just let me take a shower." I says, "Seven o'clock, we'll get outta here." This is gonna be a fucking trip.

I take the pants. I fit the zipper up, without him in them, and I take two safety pins, and I stick it so he can't pull it down that far.

I says, "Look, Harry, I got you so much here, that's as far as you're gonna get, then you've got another one I put under there. Don't just rip it out."

"Alright. Thanks, Ronnie, thanks."

So we're gonna go.

We hit the bar. There's this old crazy broad behind the bar.

"This is my old girlfriend."

She says, "And this is my daughter."

I says, "Harry, is this your daughter?"

He says, "No."

I says, "Whose daughter is it?"

He says, "I don't know. She don't know."

She had about five kids by five different guys. She probably just told Harry that was his kid. I can see this is gonna be a fucking operation that night.

"Do you want to meet any of the girls, Ron?"

"No, not really. It's alright, Harry. It's OK." You know, I'm gonna get the fuck outta there. Time to get away from that fucking operation. I was better off going ashore on my own.

And we had a wiper, a kid that worked in the engine room, called him blondie wiper. He looked like Alley Oop out of the old comic strip. He was mentally not all there, and he walked kind of hunched over. The fucking guy could eat, though. He would make fucking Dagwood sandwiches and have it gone in three bites. He lived with his mother in New York. He was a wiper, and he had other endorsements—*higher* endorsements—but he couldn't handle the job. I mean, he was fucked up.

Then you have a captain, that's master after God. He's in charge of everything. Then, on TV, they call it the first mate. There's no such thing. It's the chief mate. Then you have a second mate, and then one or two third mates. Their job descriptions change radically from ship to ship. In the engine room you've got the chief engineer, first assistant engineer, second assistant, and one or two third assistant engineers.

Then you have unlicensed personnel for the deck department. You have a bosun, who's actually the foreman. He's a straight day worker, and he runs the deck gang. He communicates between the chief mate and the crew. The chief mate will tell the bosun what he wants done, and the bosun will tell us.

Then you've got six able-bodied seamen. Sometimes you have one man on watch, some you have two, sometimes they put ordinary seamen on up to three. The AB is above the ordinary. The ordinary sometimes stands watch and sometimes is a day worker. Sometimes the ABs are day workers. It varies from ship to ship.

Anyway, this blondie wiper comes on board for the Liverpool run. First thing he says in the mess hall is, "The only reason I'm making this trip is my girlfriend in England had a baby and I'm going over to see her."

I says, "That's nice." I'm not saying too much. I'm letting the older guys tell him what a fucking idiot he is.

We get over there, Liverpool. So Harris is out, I'm out, the bosun's out, we're getting all fucked up. This blondie wiper, the next day, we had an AB in there named Jimmy, who was originally from England. He was a heavy drinker. At breakfast the next day, we're all in the mess hall trying to eat. I'm hung over, fucked up and sick.

Nobody asked him, but blondie wiper's saying, "Oh, yeah, I went over and met my girlfriend last night and saw the baby and everything. Jimmy, my baby looks just like you."

The bosun just kind of looked at Harris like, "This kid's a fucking idiot."

The next morning at mess he says he brought some clothes over for the baby and his girlfriend from the States. He says, "Yeah, I gotta call my mother." Now, we're talking about somebody in his late 20s. "I gotta call my mother, though, because my girlfriend wants a TV set. She wants me to buy it for her, but I gotta call my mom first and ask if it's OK."

Everybody did a double take on that.

And we were loading scotch whiskey. That was an old scotch run. Old man Kennedy used to get a dollar a bottle cuz he did the deals during World War II. He was ambassador there. He used to get like a dollar a bottle, on his end. But we're loading it there, and we were stealing it. They had me down there stealing it, too, giving it to 'em.

Harris says, "Hey, Ronnie, go down there in the cargo. Put your big jacket on and go down there."

"OK."

Bosun says, "Don't forget, Ronnie, put your big jacket on. Get it, get it, Ronnie."

"OK."

I'm out there stealing bottles of scotch. Constantly. It was considered part of the pay for the crew. Any part of the cargo was considered part of the crew's. I mean, you weren't supposed to do it, but it was an unwritten rule. I think we had more in our rooms than we had in the cargo.

But this electrician, he's wandering around all gassed up. The first engineer, he's putting in his overtime, you gotta write your overtime down, and they use a red pen to cross it out. And the electrician's writing overtime, and the first engineer is writing it out with a red pen, "Drunk in the bunk." You know, when the guy's supposed to be working overtime. "Passed out in the rack."

We're in one night, drinking, and here comes the electrician all fucked up. You gotta imagine this: little wiry guy, bald head, in his 60s, he'd been shipping awhile, too, no teeth, wire-rimmed glasses, a little stubble, same fucking clothes he's always been wearing. He gets a drink and sits down at the table. He's got some fucking problem with the bartender.

He says to the bartender, "You just aggravate me so fucking bad."

The bartender comes out from behind the bar, takes his drink, says, "You've had enough. I'm sorry, you can't have any more."

The electrician gets up and says, "Now you're gonna make me do something. You're making me do this, and I don't want to." I'm thinking: this fucking idiot isn't gonna attempt to jump this guy? Out of his fucking pants he pulls a bottle of scotch that he stole off the ship. "I'll show *you*. I'm gonna drink *this*."

They took that bottle away from him, too.

Blondie wiper's on board every night, still talking about his girlfriend and the kid.

Finally, at mess one morning, the bosun says, "Hey, you got a girlfriend and a son here, and you're on board *here* every night?"

He says, "Well, yeah, you know, her husband's a Norwegian seaman and she doesn't know when he's gonna come in."

Just another deep fucking thinker we got here, you know. God, they should have had DNA testing back then, it'd probably saved a lot of grief.

This was the run that I ran into Sing Lee Chung. I spent a couple of nights with her. Sing Lee Chung, Liverpool Eight, England. She's Oriental, and I was in love. For the first time, anyway. One of the old ABs on my watch, and this other ordinary, we went ashore together, picked up these three girls. That's why I didn't want to go with Harry that one night. We were at some club and they picked us up, or we picked them up.

We went over to their place, and I ended up with Sing Lee Chung. She lived in an old row house.

We pay for the taxi, we get there, and I'm gonna go freak out with her, see, but she says, "They've got the upstairs. We don't have a bed down here."

So I says, "Fuck that."

I went up and took one of the mattresses from upstairs and brought it downstairs. Her and I were freaking out, and we had to get up in the morning to get back to the ship.

I gotta jump ahead 40 years, and I mentioned this to one of the British security guards, he's from Liverpool.

He says, "What was that address, Ron?"

I says, "Hartington Road, Liverpool Eight."

He says, "Ron, there's nothing after six."

I says, "Mate, there wasn't much there 40 years ago, either." Ended at six, you know.

He says, "It's all black and Oriental."

I says, "That's what it was then."

We get back like nine o'clock in the morning. We missed breakfast, turn to late.

So we see the bosun, Joe Char. "You gonna log us?" You know, take our pay for being late.

He says, "No, I don't think he's gonna log you guys. I was talking to him." He meant this chief mate, Anderson, and Anderson liked to drink. "But," he says, "he's pretty much blaming you, the AB," he's pointing to the old AB, "for leading these kids astray."

"Blaming *me*? Fuck, *these* two don't need any help!"

So Anderson wanted to see the old AB. He didn't want to see us.

About that time Harris walks by, all fucked up. "*What'd you do with these two? You ain't no fucking help here!*"

The chief mate's all gassed up, he calls the old AB up there, blames him for everything. "*What the fuck you doing taking these ordinaries out, taking them ashore and getting them all fucked up?*"

This AB comes back, "*I'm never taking you fucking guys out again!*"

I was waiting for one of the other ordinary seaman in London on a weekend. We weren't working. We were at the old India docks. We're gonna go look around London.

Here comes the chief mate, "What are you doing?"

I says, "I'm gonna go ashore."

He says, "You know, back in the '40s, I was third mate here." It was along those old India docks, the Canary Wharf they call it now, they've got condos there. "Ships as far as you could see up and down the harbor here." He says, "I saw a guy way down there, with a bag over his shoulder, and he's running up and down the gangways from ship to ship. I could see him 20 ships away. He just keeps coming."

He says this guy, Indian or Pakistani guy, comes running up the gangway with his bag and he says, "I have recommendation. I need job. I have recommendation."

He didn't know anything about unions or hiring halls, we couldn't hire foreigners, you had to be an American citizen to be on an American-flag ship.

"Let me see your recommendation."

He gives him this envelope, it's all fingerprinted and dirty. He opens it up, and it says, in English, "Don't give this dumb son of a bitch a job."

I says, "What did you do, mate?"

He says, "I folded it up, put it back in there, gave it back to him, and said, 'I'm sorry, we don't happen to need any help.'"

This was '67, and that was '47—20 years *before.*

I says, "Mate, that poor guy's still running around with that recommendation to this day."

The mate had a bigger sense of humor than me.

Then back in Liverpool we see the girls again. And Sing Lee's saying, "You'll come back and see me?"

"Oh, yeah, I'll come back." I was in love. Right.

We're securing the ship. Everybody's drunk, everybody's raiding the booze, the electrician's wandering. Fucking *cold.* Heat was a fucking pipe going up through the middle of the foc'sle, and the heat just blew out. We had to put rags over it, all that dust we're breathing. No wonder we're all fucking dead from the asbestos. The bulkheads were just asbestos against the steel. You just put more lead paint on it when it would crack. It's no wonder we're all fucking dead.

They had a day-working oiler, but this guy was a day D-mac, they called him, a deck engine mechanic. And the electrician was a day worker. Well, they had 'em in the same room. They used to fistfight. These are two old guys, all drunked up. They used to fistfight with each other. One burned the other one's mattress, and the captain made him pay for the mattress. The D-mac went on a drunk, the electrician took his TV, but he didn't take the adaptor. The electricity's different there. He plugged it in and it blew out. You had to see this to believe it. The D-mac was just standing there, all wiry, all fucking skin and bones: "You motherfucker." Looking at the broken TV like it's gonna change anything. "You motherfucker."

Those old ships, they had these Kidde smoke inhalators on the bridge. There was the wheel, big handle, you know, like you see in the movies. Off to the left, it wasn't a column like you have today; near the end of the bridge on port side is a console. If you stood in front of it you could see that it was pipes halfway to the top. It looked like an old organ. These things would check each hatch in the ship, and it would suck air out. I mean, we're talking ancient here. They have a little string on it where you could see the air blow up, and if there was any smoke, it would let you know. I think the cycle was every 20 minutes, it checked the entire ship. Really antiquated.

Anyway, it wasn't working right. We're on the way back in the North Atlantic, and you're gonna hit bad weather in the North Atlantic. Fucking bouncing all over, cold, miserable. Everybody was fucked up. We'd be out there trying to secure the ship; I'm talking about the old batten down the hatches, pull the tarps, swing the booms in. Everybody's fucking drunk. And the ones that weren't were bitching cuz they weren't drunk, bitching at the ones that *were* drunk. "You dumb motherfucker, you!"

The old man calls the chief and says, "Something's wrong with this fucking smoke inhalator. Get it fixed!"

So instead of the first assistant going up there, he gets the electrician to do it, and he's all fucked up. He takes this whole fucking thing apart. He's gotta have a drink, too, you know? But he couldn't drink like Harris could, and keep functioning.

I come up there to steer, just to practice.

He's got this fucking thing all laid out on blankets. The fucking glass is out. These tubes are laying with screws, bolts, nuts, panels, everything.

We hit this storm.

Now this fucking shit that's on the deck is sliding all over, just rolling all over.

The old man calls down, "*Send somebody up here to put this fucking thing back together, or I'm throwing it all over the fucking side!*"

25

The first engineer had to put it all back together.

We got to New York to pay off. If you got logged, you had to see the Coast Guard; they came on board, before you could get paid. There were more people in the log line than there were in the payoff line. We're talking 42 people.

And the Coast Guard's saying, "And what did *you* do?"

The electrician had a bunch of logs. He had some warnings, and he had to make a Coast Guard hearing.

I says, "What are you gonna do now, man?"

He says, "Oh, I got a ton of these in the fucking drawer. I don't care."

Last I saw him, he got his suitcase, same clothes he had on for the entire trip, he was going to New York to look for a drink. Fucking unreal.

It pretty much stayed that way for the entire time. We made that run and kept going back and forth for 10 months.

We had a captain on there, Glen Albright. He used to like to brag: he started out as a messman, and then World War II started, and for some reason he swung a deal and he got into some kind of maritime school for officers. He got a third mate's license. Then: "Yeah, I worked my way up from messman to captain."

He didn't say anything about how he married one of the presidents of U.S. Lines' daughter. He didn't mention that. He was alright, I guess. Glen Albright. We used to call him Not So Bright. He had a sign on his desk: The Master's Word is Law.

I never had a problem with him, though. He liked me. But I performed, too, cuz I was trying to become an able seaman. So I applied myself for once in my life.

We had a pilot, these guys would take the ship out or in, to every port. When we used to leave Le Havre, France, they would take us out of port, and then the pilot would want to get off. Albright would keep the pilot on board to get to London. The company would have to pay the pilot, cuz he wanted the pilot on board to cross the English Channel. You know, all the help you can get is all the help you get. But, normally, you didn't do that. The majority of captains that I had in this 10-month run, other than Albright, never took that pilot. They would just fight it out through the fog. Post a lookout, put the fog horn on, and go to hand steering. You did that whether you had the pilot or not.

And he drank a lot. The company used to put like 12 bottles of booze on there for the passengers; we could carry up to 12 passengers on those old freighters. If you carry more than 12, you have to have a doctor on board. But the company would put 12 bottles of booze on board for the captain, if you drink at the captain's table, or the captain would buy you drinks. Albright used to take the booze for himself and drink it. Never shared. I remember that now, never did give me a drink. He'd come up to the wheelhouse on the weekends. Didn't want any talking up on the bridge. Wouldn't have any radio or anything. But he would come up like on Saturday or Sunday, on a nice day. He would go up there during the day, and he would take a chair and sit there and put the radio on and take his sunglasses and just sit there and look out. And *he* had the radio going. But we couldn't.

But he got offered a vacation, so we had different captains come on there. There was "North Pole" McGinty: he'd take you so fucking far north you thought you were gonna freeze to death.

But, Albright, you gotta jump ahead now to '77 or '78. I came on board in Sunny Point, North Carolina, it was loading ammunition. The captain was getting off, and I says, "Gee, maybe we'll get this Captain Albright."

The bosun, who'd been on there for awhile, he looked at me and says, "*Albright*? He was on here about 6 months ago."

I says, "Really? I sailed with him 10 years ago. I always wondered what happened to him."

He says, "They had to take him off on a stretcher. He was drinking himself to death."

They had to carry him off on a stretcher.

It's a shame. You know, if you lose your nerve, you lose your nerve. I can understand that. I haven't yet. It doesn't scare me. I don't give a fuck. I'll steer a ship down Ho Chi Minh's throat. I could care less. But you run across a lot of guys that just—for some reason, they're still out there and they're still trying to do it, and they're so fucking scared, for whatever reason, I don't know. But it's like anything else. They lose their nerve. It's almost like a cop or a fireman that's scared to go out and do it. They actually become a hindrance to everybody else, because now you have to push them out of the fucking way. It is a shame. The pension's not enough for them, because they're like everybody else. They were in over their heads.

He'd been there so fucking long, the wife, the pressure, the company. But this Captain Albright was an example of been out there too fucking long, couldn't, wouldn't, retire. U.S. Lines gave him a job as port captain. Maybe they saw that he couldn't do it anymore. But that went to his fucking head, too. One time, the longshoremen, he went to get his car—he was fucking with the longshoremen—he found his car up on top of a container box. They had picked it up and put it up there. You know: "Just leave us alone, things are functioning. Just sit there and let us do what we do." But he couldn't do that. Some people can't handle that: to just sit there and do the fucking paperwork and collect the check. He had to fucking *apply* himself, and he was his own worst enemy, and you couldn't tell him that because he was captain.

Years later, I heard a story from somebody he had given a ride to up near where he lived. He was getting off the ship, and his wife picked him up and this other guy, too. The wife was driving, Albright was in the front seat, and this other guy was in the back.

They pull into a gas station, and this was when they come out to fill up the gas, and the guy comes out and says, "Oh, Captain Albright! How are you?"

"I'm fine. And you?"

The wife says, "*Captain.* Phhht."

You know. So here was another man: the only authority he had was on the ship. And he's losing that. At home was just run-of-the-mill. It was a shame. He drank himself to death. I'm not saying it's right. Maybe he should have got divorced. What he ended up doing was obviously wrong, for him.

Anyway, this ship was being sold, so I had to get off. The company taking over was selling off all these old ships.

Harris and all them wanted me to come up to New York. Now don't get me wrong, hey, I love those guys, they were great. But I knew if I went to New York and I started drinking with them . . . .

They were saying, "Hey, Ronnie, we'll get you a job, you can stay."

I says, "Guys, I appreciate that, I really do. But I'm gonna go to Baltimore."

I knew I had to get away from New York. That would have been another trap, exactly what I had in Cleveland, if I go there. I'd probably get hooked up with some bimbo. And New York—this is no offense to New York, I'm not trying to offend anybody in any of this—always reminded me of fleas on a dog. That's the only way I can see that city. It was just massively too big, overrated, and like I said, I had no reason to ship out of there. I didn't want to meet anybody there. You know, I mean, when you could walk into a bar in Europe or somewhere, walk in, and at the time it was 5 or 10 bucks and I'm talking about normal white women, as far as you can go with normal white women. Whatever "normal" is. We're talking 10 bucks apiece. What the fuck do I need some girl in New York telling me how the fuck to live? I mean, the less English they understood, the better off, I felt. Really. Those who knew sign language, we got along fine.

American Pilot

I was back in Cleveland for 4 or 5 months listening to the same dumb shit I'd wanted to get away from in the first place. I got enough money to get back down to Charleston where they were shipping from, the ammo dump, Sunny Point, North Carolina to Vietnam. Went down there because shipping was good, because of the Vietnam War, loading ammo to go over there. They needed an AB on the *American Pilot*.

This had been a U.S. Lines ship, one of the old ones. The company, at this time, had sold these ships to get out from under them. Matter of fact, Kidde bought them—the smoke inhalator people. They bought 'em and just got rid of all the dead weight and said, fuck it, we're going into containers, that's where the money's at. And they started these paper companies to run these things. Amercargo Incorporated was the name of the employer. It wasn't U.S. Lines anymore.

I made one trip on here. It was my first trip to Vietnam.

We had this really stupid fucking chief mate named Lowell. The captain was Lang; he was on his last leg. Assorted mixed nuts, as usual. You got that on those old ships, cuz nobody wanted the old ones because you had three men in a room and it was gonna be a long trip.

This guy, Lowell, was the real character on this trip. He stuck out because he was such a fucking idiot. See, the company, U.S. Lines, when they sold these old ships, one container ship would replace five of these. They basically told these captains, if you want to keep the same job, you go with the company. If you stay with us, you're lucky we're gonna find a third mate job for you. It's happened over the years with these companies when they do that. I call it the Night of the Long Knives. They'll get rid of their people and, you know, "You want a job, go with them, we don't have anything for you." Lowell went with them, and the captain went with them. They gave him their choice. You know, get off the ship, and don't work for this Amercargo company, but we don't know if we have a job for you with U.S. Lines. Well, most people aren't gonna give up their chief mate or their captain's job. They're gonna go just to keep their pension, and everything went by how you sailed at, whether you sailed captain or chief mate, you had your time, you got a higher pension. Lang stayed. Lowell had shipped in the SIU, the Seafarers International Union, not the NMU, the National Maritime Union, that I was with. And U.S. Lines was NMU. But when he got himself a license as third mate, he didn't want to sail on SIU ships because he knew everybody. He figured he could fuck more people by going with this new company, you know, nobody knew him. He started out as third mate with them, and he was working his way up.

He had just gotten married, and he was in his late forties. He married this French-Canadian girl, but she came out of an orphanage. He was complaining then that she had wild ideas, and he couldn't stand it. I guess she was spending the money, you know, cuz you're gone, and it happens to a lot of guys. You're gone, and she's just doing whatever she's doing. You think you'd take it into account. I would. "OK, yeah, I had some good years, now I'm losing my job." Fuck it. I mean, maybe that's not the time to get married. He did. Maybe it wasn't the right girl. Obviously. The one time I saw her I remember she looked pretty good, but that doesn't mean a whole lot. So that was working on his mind, plus he was losing his job, technically, with the company he was with. He was just a fucking trip.

You would think that he would pay less attention because he's on his way out. Well, he couldn't break the habit of just being a real asshole. Right from the beginning everybody's a fucking idiot but him. He'd insult you all he could. I didn't know it at the time, then, but I found out sometime during the trip this was his second or third trip under this new company. I found this out on the way back, which isn't really getting too much ahead of the story.

On one of the other trips they had a Puerto Rican ordinary seaman on there, and they were going to Vietnam, back and forth with ammo. And you could always go to see a doctor. You used to ask for time off in port. They didn't have to give it to you, but most would give you half a day off, or take off early. They get to Vietnam, and this Puerto Rican ordinary seaman wants to go to the doctor. Well, he wanted to get the day off is what he wanted. They could never deny you a doctor. That was the first thing Bill Harris told me. If you ever want time off, go to a doctor. If the doctor gave you a "Not Fit for Duty," they'd fly you home. Even if you weren't injured on board, just sick, and the doctor says you can't work, they had to fly you home, give you unearned wages, until the ship came back to the States, or you got "Fit for Duty" back in the States, plus $8 a day. No taxes.

So this ordinary wants to go to the doctor. Lowell, trying to fuck the guy—cuz he wants a day off—got with the agent and said, "Make sure the appointment's in the afternoon." He got him an appointment for like two o'clock in the afternoon. They're on day work. So he tells the ordinary, "Your appointment's at two o'clock." So, OK, you turn to from 8 to noon, then you're off at noon, clean up, then go to the doctor. You'll be there at 1.

Well, the ordinary goes out and gets all fucked up that night and says, "I ain't going back to work. I'm just gonna go to the doctor. Why come back for 4 hours?" So, the ordinary just doesn't come back. At two o'clock he goes to the doctor, but he comes back with a "Fit for Duty," not a "Not Fit." So he comes back at like 4 in the afternoon. So now he's got the entire day off. So Lowell goes to Lang—and they're buddies cuz they shipped together—and he said, "I'm gonna log this guy." Put him in the book, you know, the paperwork to justify taking his pay.

And Lang, I guess just for old times' sake, says, "Yeah, OK."

So he tells the ordinary the next morning, "You're getting logged." For eight o'clock in the morning 'til noon.

Now, the base pay was still about $311 a month, so, what's that, $10 a day? So this guy's logged for what amounts to about half of that: $7. So the ordinary gets a big fucking attitude.

Lowell gets an attitude. "You're getting logged. I'm gonna take you to the Coast Guard." You know, the leader thing. "I'm in charge here." You know: "I might not have any control over my job or my wife, but I'm gonna control *you*." If you met Lowell you could see that's what it was. You had people out there like that. That not so much those were the rules and they could be overlooked or bent or, "We can work something out here," or "Hey, look, you owe me 4 hours, work 2 hours overtime somewhere, don't write it in, and we'll call it even." It was always an option, but not with Lowell. He's an idiot. He logs the guy for it.

Now the whole trip the guy's frustrated about it, right? They go through Panama. I guess this guy got hold of some of that cheap fucking booze down there in Panama, and they're coming up to Wilmington.

Now this guy's getting fucked up. Lowell's taking a shower in his room, officers always had their own room. This guy attacks Lowell with an ice pick. He stabs Lowell four or five times, punctures a lung. Lowell beats the fuck out of him. They call the police, take him away, go through his gear. They take Lowell to the hospital, punctured lung. They find out this Puerto Rican ordinary's just gotten out of a mental institution.

Well, now Lowell's gonna press charges, fucking murder or something, but the guy's obviously insane, so he's gonna go back to the nuthouse.

All over half a day's pay. Seven fucking dollars.

Anyway, Lowell took one trip off and comes back. Needed the money. But that just goes to show you what kind of person he was. So when I get him, he's primed, ready to go—I don't know this at the beginning of the trip.

We get down to Panama, and he's already fucking with everybody: "You guys don't know shit. I know everything. Doesn't anybody follow orders around here?" Just being a real fucking asshole.

We get down to Panama, I'm on watch on the gangway, and two of the Puerto Rican ordinaries come back from being ashore. But now I get the taxi driver coming up after them screaming and yelling they owe him money.

I says, "Look, partner, I can't let you on board."

Lowell happens to show up. "What's going on here?"

"This gentleman says the guys owe him money."

"Well, he ain't coming on board."

I says, "Yeah, mate, I told him that." I could see where this guy could get stabbed. I says, "Yeah, mate, I told him that. He can't come on board."

"Well, I'll stay here," he says, "you go get those ordinaries and get them up here."

So I go and I says to them, "You gotta go talk to this guy." They speak Spanish.

They says, "We don't owe him any money."

I says, "I don't care what you guys owe him or not. Go talk to this fucking guy before there's a real fucking scene."

So they go and they're yelling back and forth in Spanish.

And Lowell's all, "Yeah, I straightened that shit out." He's a tall skinny guy, kind of round faced, a little bit of a lisp, almost drooled. Sunglasses. Somebody'd fart and he'd say, "Speak again to me sweet lips." He'd show up behind you when you were working on deck and point—"You didn't tie this down properly"—or some fucking thing.

Before we left Panama, Lang and Lowell had gotten together and bought Panamanian beer, and they were selling it to us for a dollar more than they paid a case, which was illegal, technically. But they figured they'd make a few bucks on it. We weren't supposed to have it, anyway.

So we go across. Had one guy, Crotcher—Crotch—this guy was so fucking ugly, divorced, from Ohio, needed the money, trying to make a living for the ex at home. He was pretty much an idiot all fucking trip. His son used to write him letters with poetry, which he wanted to show us all the time. Another guy, Joe Birdie, played cards all the time. We had this Danish guy, third mate. He was always in the fucking card games. I used to have to go wake him up, he'd be sleeping on watch. "Vat? Vat?" We had another AB, Womack. Drank himself to death.

Now this poor guy, Womack, was one that if he drank three drinks he was fucked up. No matter how much more he drank, he was still as fucked up. But he never got *more* fucked up, you know. He'd get all fucked up and walk up and down the passageways like cuckoolamunga. Poor guy. And he had married. He was going with the sister and he married the other sister who was a bigger alky than he was, and he had a daughter by her. I kind of felt sorry for him. He was just an aggravating, fucking drunk type. Lowell hated him. Everybody pretty much hated the guy. It's just personalities coming out.

Now they're gonna stop selling the beer. Because, you know, Womack was fucking up. They wanted to log him.

Somebody said, "Wait a minute, you sold him the beer, now you're gonna log him? *Come on.*"

So, they're gonna send us to Quy Nhon, about the middle of South Vietnam. We get there, and we're going from the inner harbor to the outer harbor, every night we drop the anchor, they'd unload us, and then they'd get us out of the inner harbor because of mines. The Viet Cong would swim out and put mines on the ships and sink them. Or they could hit us with a missile. We were too close to the shore and all the ammo.

They put GIs on there to guard us, too. One day this white sergeant had come out with these two Puerto Ricans, our GIs.

Lowell—as goofy as he was, always looking to stick his nose into things he didn't need to—looks at them and says, "Get those people off my ship." He thinks they're Vietnamese.

The sergeant looks at Lowell and says, "You want these two men off your ship?"

Lowell says, "Yeah, that's right. I'm the chief mate. I want them off my ship." He thought they were Vietnamese, he didn't know they were Puerto Rican.

The sergeant says, "You want them off, get a hold of President Johnson, cuz he's the one who told them to be here."

Lowell goes off mumbling.

That was the time the GI shot the shark. We hung cluster lights, over the open hatches, so you could work at night, like you see in these old pictures with the hatches and the booms and the cargo coming out. Well, we'd hang 'em on the side of the ship to keep divers away—I don't know, I think they just lit us up. We had the GIs on there, and they're wandering around. I was on gangway, midnight to four or midnight to eight, and I'm standing there. I happen to look over the side, and here's a fucking shark with its mouth open, head halfway out of the water. The smaller fish had come alongside the ship to pick off the bullshit that was on the side of the ship. The light attracted him. Well, the shark was just coming around like a vacuum cleaner, you could see these fish are just going into his mouth.

The GI come walking by, I says, "Hey, do me a favor."

He says, "What's that?"

I says, "Shoot that fucking shark, will ya?"

"Nah, I don't wanna shoot."

But I aggravated him enough. I says, "Give me the rifle. I'll shoot him."

"*No, no, no.* If anybody shoots him, I'll do it." He says, "If it comes by again, get me, I'll shoot the shark for ya."

I says, "OK."

Here comes the shark, just going around the ship, he's sucking up fish.

I says, "There he is. Take a shot at him."

It was an M14, a .30 caliber. He puts one in the chamber, leans over. I'm watching. One shot, and you could see just a little spurt of water. The shark never moved. It just went right down until you couldn't see it anymore. Killed it dead. That was the entertainment for the night.

We'd go ashore during the day. We went in one time, me and Joe and Crotch. Even the Vietnamese broads didn't want to fuck him. You'd just go in the back, get a blow job off one of the Vietnamese broads for like five bucks. This poor guy, Crotch, though, he's trying to give them five bucks, and them broads look at him, he's ugly. It was 10 bucks. No. I think they had him up to 20, and they still wouldn't take the fucking money. I felt sorry for the guy. He couldn't get them to blow his ear.

They had what they called the cowboys, the South Vietnamese

militia. Had an assortment of guns. No clue as to what they were doing, just walking around. So we end up walking around with them for
awhile. It was just all kind of fucked up.

We're back on board the ship, and one day these two Navy guys
came on with some orders for us to leave. We had to have official
orders to leave the harbor. Even though you discharge all the ammo,
you just don't leave, they tell you where we're gonna go and what we're
gonna do. Both these Navy guys are clean. I mean, *really clean.*

This third mate from Holland had on a pair of boots, cut off
shorts, and a khaki shirt and, well, he's standing there, I'm standing
there in my jeans and shirt and boots, and the ordinary's standing
there.

I'm kind of stuck in the middle, I'm able seaman here. I says, "Can
I help you gentlemen?"

One Navy guy says, "We have your sailing orders."

I says, "Alright, fine. Who do you have to see?"

He says, "I have to see the captain."

I says, "Well, OK, I'll have somebody stand by, and I'll take you
up."

The third mate says, "Vat? Vat? I'm third mate here." You know,
now I get *another* fucking ego trip. He don't want to be anything until
he can see what's going on, *then* he wants to jump in. "You should see,
I'm third mate. Look, I have khakis on, he has no khakis."

This Navy kid, he's *clean*, I mean, we're talking about somebody
who's intelligent, was in the Navy cuz he wasn't gonna get killed, was
working for MSC—Military Sealift Command—through the Navy,
was gonna go out to these ships and do his time and go home and get
out and go do something normal with his life—he's looking at him.
"Well, look, I'm sorry. I don't know what a third mate looks like, I'm
just trying to give these orders here."

"You should know because I look like third mate."

I just wanted to punch him right in the fucking mouth.

*"You should see that I'm third mate. Look how different I am from
everybody else."*

Oh, God! Why do we create these fucking headaches, you know?

I says, "Excuse me, he'll escort you up to the captain."

He says, "Can't you do it?"

I says, "Don't. Please. Go with him. I gotta work with this fucking guy."

That's the way it was, every day with some dumb shit. Everybody's a fucking hero, or an officer, or something.

So they ordered us back to Subic Bay, Philippines, to await orders. Now this is when they buy more beer, sell it to us for a buck more a case. Make money. And we were gonna go all the way back to Panama, with beer.

We're going back, and now they wanna clean the ship up. Now Lowell's gonna put the overtime out. And, see, there was an unwritten rule that if you don't put any overtime out on the way over, nobody wanted to work it on the way back. Nobody liked Lowell. So we told the bosun: we don't want to work.

So Lowell says, "*What's wrong, you guys don't want to work?*"

"Well, mate, you didn't give us any overtime on the way over. Why should we . . . ."

"Well, yeah, I guess I can see that, but you know, we really gotta get this—"

Now he's the nice guy. You know.

The bosun was a pretty good guy, black guy, telling us, "Goddammit, let's try to keep this ship up, even if we just paint over the rust."

So, yeah, we'll go out there. We're painting the stack. The smokestack was always where you had the company colors. In Sunny Point when I first got on board, it was still U.S. Lines. They still had the blue, white, and red. The owner finally shows up in Sunny Point, like the third or fourth trip, right, maybe the fifth under this company, says, "Why do you still have the colors of U.S. Lines on the stack?" He owned like three or four of these ships.

The captain says something to the effect: "Nobody ever told us to change it." Which was the truth.

The owner looks up there, and he looks back at the captain, and he says, "What kind of paint do we have? Which color do we have the most of?"

The captain says, "Well, I believe, red."

He says, "OK. This company's colors will be red, white, and red." We just painted the blue out. That's how the colors got the way they were.

On the way back they wanted that painted again, you know, put another coating of red. It made it look good, so when you got back to the States, the owner or company officials would show up and they'd say, "Boy, that ship looks clean." I mean, not that nothing *worked* right. But it *looked nice*.

When we made Panama, we didn't transit right away, we stayed over both times, went to the dock and waited for the next date of transit. They had a policy, if you had ammo, you had to tell them. You went by on your own, you didn't go through with a convoy, so there's no chance of another ship hitting you and fucking blow up.

I'm on my gangway again. Here comes this American guy coming up the gangway with a suit on and an attaché case or some fucking thing, and he got to the top of the gangway, and I says, "Excuse me, can I help you?"

He says, "Yeah, I'm a third assistant engineer."

I says, "I'm sorry, I didn't know we called for a new third." You know, out here.

He says, "Oh, I am. I'm the third assistant engineer."

"I'm sorry, I've never seen you before."

"Yeah, you have. I made the trip."

Here comes Lowell. He couldn't stand it if he wasn't fucking with some thing or some body. If you wanted to find Lowell, stand still 5 minutes, he'd find you and fuck with you about something. So here comes Lowell. "What's wrong?"

I says, "This gentleman says he's the third engineer. We didn't call for a new third that I know of. The third didn't get off or anything." I says, "I've never seen him before."

He says, "Yeah, that's the third engineer."

I says, "You're telling me that this guy...."

The guy says, "I'm the third engineer."

I says to Lowell, "Is it OK for him to come onboard?"

He says, "It's fine."

I let him go.

I says to Lowell, "I never saw this fucking guy before."

He says, "I know. He goes from his room to the engine room, gets off watch, goes to his room. When he eats he goes right from his room to eat then goes right back."

We had about 90 days on that ship. He'd been on there and I never saw the fucking guy. That was the first time he'd gone ashore. He went to call his wife on the phones that were down there near the dock.

We're on our way back to Sunny Point, and now Lowell's gonna save the company some money. We gotta get the booms up for our cargo. The day before, we rigged them. It's called "stretching the gear." You stretched it, getting ready to top it, but don't top it. Because Lowell said the Coast Guard was gonna come and they were gonna inspect it. So he just wanted the boom stretched, and our pay stopped. We were getting in at like ten o'clock at night. As soon as we tied up, our pay stopped at midnight. Even though we were working under contract, we shoulda gotten the next day's pay anyway, because of the shipping commissioner. He was gonna try and save that, see? Fucking prick that he was, Lowell.

"That's it, ten o'clock, everybody's pay stops."

So we tie up at 10 at night. That's it. We're off. Everybody's packing, getting showers. I'm sleeping in. They're gonna pay us by noon and we're outta there. We get up the next day and eat breakfast. Got our free world clothes on, ready to go.

All of a sudden Lowell comes running through. *"We gotta get the booms up, we gotta get the booms up! I'll pay you for today, I'll pay you for today!"*

We says, "We don't wanna do it."

"Come on, you fucking guys."

We says, "You've been fucking us all trip, you prick. Now we're fucking you. We ain't doing it."

A couple of the guys, Womack, too, he'd been out all fucking night, gassed up, he's sick.

"Come on, you motherfuckers."

So the bosun, he's a good guy, he says, "Look, it's all we gotta do is put them up in the air. We'll do one boom at a time. I'm staying on here, I gotta put up with this, you guys are getting off."

"For you, we'll do it." We all went out. We were gonna do one boom at a time.

Well, now we had to take the screen, a wire mesh, down from the stack. The actual smokestack was inside, and you had a dummy stack on the outside. You could go in and climb up there on the walkway. It was enclosed, and you had all that soot, acid, steam. They'd blow the tubes every once in awhile to blow this shit out, and it would just cover everything. This screen was there to keep the sparks from coming out when you were loading or discharging ammunition. It was just a round cut-out piece of screened metal. It had to be 8, 10 feet in diameter. They weren't gonna work the cargo until the inspection, and they had to take this metal screen down. Somebody had to climb up in there, maybe two guys, and throw line down.

So the bosun says, "One last job guys. Can somebody go up there and take that fucking thing down?"

I says, "You know, bosun, I'll go do it for you, but I need help."

He says, "Womack! Give Ron a hand."

Womack's all fucked up from the night before. Fucking idiot. We climb up there.

Womack's whining, "*This is fucked up!*" He's no help. He's starting to cough and shit. "*I'm choking!*"

Lowell's down there, screaming and yelling. He's gonna direct the whole scene.

We get up there, and I've got the heaving line, the line to throw down to lower this thing. Well, this soot and acid and shit is fucking my eyes up.

The line gets hung up, and all the soot's breaking loose, and the shit's flying on us from the screen.

Womack's whining: "*I'm sick! I'm sick!*"

I says, "You were drunk last night, right?"

The shit's hitting us in the eyes, and the smell—it's sulfur, you know—that *smell*. I'm trying to free up the wires. I get Womack to free up one of the wires. I free up two of them. We're climbing over this and under this and we're filthy with this soot and oil and shit.

I get the heaving line tied on, and I says, "OK, be careful, I'm gonna throw it off, and I'm gonna hold it here with the line." Well, the line got fucked up, and I had too much line going at one time. I shove the thing over.

They're yelling from down below, "The line's caught!"

I yell, "It's coming!" Fifty feet of line went out; this thing's 30 feet high. *Boom!* The thing hits the fucking deck and bounces. *Boom!*

The chief mate's *screaming*. Bosun's trying to catch the line. I didn't hurt anything, I just got it hung up, that's all. Fuck it, it went down. It's just a piece of metal.

But Womack, he sticks his head over the fucking side and throws up, all over the bosun and Lowell.

We come down. He threw up on Lowell and the bosun. I didn't know it. We get down.

Bosun says, "God*damn*, Ron."

I says, "Fuck, bos'. The line got hung up, you know."

He says, "Well, it didn't hurt anything. But god*damn*, Womack threw up on the mate and me."

They go take a shower.

We got off there. We all quit and fucking went back to Charleston. It was just all fucked up.

Lowell says, "Aren't you staying on, making another trip?"

I says, "No thanks, mate."

He says, "Everybody's quitting!"

I can't imagine why. Why would you leave all this? It was funny. We finally got our money. I went and took a shower and got out of those clothes and put my free world clothes on again. We all bailed out. That was my first trip to Vietnam.

I mean, it was a lot of fun.

The way I always kind of look at it: everything's important and nothing's important. If you're gonna have a drama, have it over something that's worth the time. Some people take it more seriously than others, like a Lowell. But we all end up the same.

Every union puts out magazines. They got "Final Voyages," the obits. Years later, I was on some ship, and I happened to get a Masters, Mates and Pilots newsletter. I don't know why, but I picked it up to look through there, and I see "Final Voyages," the obits section. I see "Lowell." Died such and such a time. No mention of "survived by wife and children." This is Lowell: born and died. Nothing in between. No kids, no marriage, no "survived by." Just: Lowell. That was it. Poor guy. I don't know what his mission was in life or what he expected to get out of it. He was part of the pensioners when I saw that he died. I don't know where he lived; it didn't say where he lived. It was just "Lowell." So much for 60 years of existence. Lowell. Survived by no one. It fit the whole thing, like, "OK, I'm totally in control *now*." You know. "I'm *dead*. I'm totally in control."

I can jump ahead a few years on Womack. I was sitting in Charleston where I shipped out of. Who comes in the hall but Womack. He looked the same. I happened to mention I was on the *American Pilot*. He didn't remember me.

He left next door to get a drink.

I can't remember who I was talking to. I says, "Yeah, I was on the ship with him." I says, "Poor fucking guy. He had two beers and he'd run up and down the passageway yelling cuckoolamunga."

The guy told me, "He's living down here now with his mother and his daughter." He said the wife drank herself to death, or he divorced her, or both. He was living with the mother, and they got custody of the daughter. I guess the wife was an alky worse than he was.

Jump ahead a few more years, and I know he died because after that, this is in the '70s, I walked in the hall again. The union official was Duke Duwarky, a black Portuguese, he was agent down there. I came in the hall looking if something comes up.

Duke says, "I'm glad to see you. I never hear complaints about you." He says, "You make me look good. I'm gonna get you a good job."

I says, "Thank you." I says, "I don't drink when I'm down here. No girlfriends. I'm away from the loved ones." I says, "I'm here!" You know, I got a little flop house room, and I'd get a little radio, and I'd go to the Book Bag in Charleston and I'd buy a book I wanted to read. I'd pick up anything that was out of the ordinary. History, politics, novels. Whatever would catch my eye. Anything I ever read had something to do with history.

Guys would find out what I was reading, or see what I was reading. Skip ahead to this one trip to Australia, I was reading *The Egyptian Book of the Dead*. I was off watch, back on the stern, reading, nice weather, you know. The mate and the bosun happened to be coming by one day, and they saw what I was reading, *The Egyptian Book of the Dead*.

And the mate says, "Watch him." Kiddingly.

But, there in Charleston, I'd go to my room and sit and read. This is what I want to do.

I don't want some guy: "Hey, man! Check out them bimbos over here! Man, she really likes you!"

I says, "I'm sure she does. I'm sure she'd like anybody who's gonna pay the freight."

Which, I'm not saying is wrong. I mean, everybody's looking for somebody, and like I said, it gets to be the domination thing. And I can't deal with the drama-domination. I can't do it.

I seldom voiced my opinion when I first started. After I got so many good reports, though, it got where they would call me to keep working for them, like the bosun and Harris, they said come to New York, we'll talk to the union for you, we'll get you back on. That was nice of them. But I'm giving up my freedom again. Which is the exact reason why I wanted to do this, for freedom, to come and go as I please.

But anyway, I sat and talked to Duke.

He says, "That fucking Womack!"

I says, "Don't tell me: he was drunk."

He says, "How do you know?"

"I was on a ship with him. The poor guy has two or three beers and—"

"That fuck! He got on here, he got off in Norfolk, they fired him for being drunk. He's supposed to be taking care of his mother and that daughter of his. Norfolk calls me down there: 'Is that the best you fucking got? He can't even make it through coastwise.'"

I says, "Yeah, the guy's got a problem."

Jump ahead again, and I came in there, and there was a girl that worked there in dispatch. She and Duke were real good. Somehow or another, Womack's name came up.

She says, "He's dead."

I says, "Dead?"

He caught a ship in Sunny Point, North Carolina. I guess it was running to Europe. He was at dinner, and he said he was gonna go ashore and have a couple of beers. Everybody kind of knew him, said, well, this is the end of this. He didn't end up going ashore. Next day when they called him, he was dead in his room. Had a heart attack and died. Poor guy.

I says, "Man, his mother and the daughter are gonna be in big trouble. They don't have anything!"

She says, "Not only that," they came in there to see what kind of death benefits they could get, and they couldn't get anything because he had a heart attack. You can't sue over that. You could have if he like fell down, you know, hit his head and got killed or slipped or something. He couldn't get anything except a burial, which I think was $1,000 from the union. At the time, you didn't get any vested pension. They didn't give anything to the wife or kids. Rotten fucks.

I can't remember how much money it was in the bank, but the mother and the daughter—she was like 14 and going to school there—thought they had this money in the bank. Well, Womack, every time he'd come into Charleston, he'd go to the fucking bank and draw the money out to go drink. Nothing much left from that.

It was another sad story with two drinkers. I mean, the daughter and then the mother got stuck, too.

You know, typical merchant seaman. That was common. Very, very common. I mean, the escapism, even if you were married, it was even more of an escape. I've been escaping as long as I can remember. And this was the greatest escape I could find. I just kept escaping. Sometimes life threatening. But I always got out of it, one way or the other.

As my uncle once told me: "Never lose your head trying to save your neck."

You just aren't happy...

🔗

Here's a good one. Cargo ship going to Vietnam.

Captain was Hopewell. I had the 12 to 4 watch with an old third mate, white-haired guy, drunk all the fucking time, but he was one you didn't know drank until you saw him sober. And a guy named Dan, an American Indian. Haines was the second mate on there, re-tired Navy. The chief mate was a guy named Spydell. He'd been ship-ping since the '30s.

Back down in Sunny Point, load the ammunition, easiest runs to get. They were old ships, and nobody wanted to be gone for 120 days. Guys preferred coastwise tankers, you made more money. The vaca-tion pay was more on tankers, base rate was better, overtime was bet-ter, better food cuz you're always in and out of port, you could keep in touch with your loved ones. But, you got 10% of your base for haul-ing ammo. In the war zone, there was a certain area that you hit, it worked out to a certain longitude and latitude, but it ended up being about 100 miles off the coast of Vietnam that you doubled your base pay, as long as you were always in that zone. I think the most I ever got was about 70 days in the zone.

We had one crazy black guy who was a story unto his own. His name was Belew, and he was just a crazy fucker. He got fired in port there, because he was just being crazy. He had been an enforcer for the union up in New York and had met an Irish girl, an immigrant, married her. She drove him nuts. She just literally took advantage of him, you know, she'd fuck his brains out when he'd come back from a trip, and then she'd throw him out in the street. He couldn't even make the coastwise. They brought him onto the ship, and he's threat-ening everybody, so they fired him.

We get outta there, and they told us we could pick the crew up in Panama, because the NMU had a union hall there of Panamanians. Well, they tried to get American citizens, but a lot of 'em were just Panamanians. Only one of 'em even knew what the fuck he was doing.

We go ashore down there. And it was me and Haines, even though he was second mate, I was standing watch with him.

I says, "I'm going back to the ship."

He says, "I'm gonna have another couple drinks."

He ends up getting in a fistfight, and Hopewell's gotta go get him out of the can because we're getting ready to go through the canal. Automatically, I knew I gotta keep drinking with this guy.

We had this bosun on there, Pasatti, an old crazy Greek. He and this Belew were partners at one time or another, and they were just miserable fucks. Belew got fired, and the bosun didn't, and according to Hopewell the bosun was the only one who had any real experience.

We had this guy Roberts, he was a snitch. If I ever run across him, I'll break his fucking face. I never have in 40 years, always promised myself I'd do it. He's always sucking up to the bosun, whining: "*Hey, bos'—*" Sneaky motherfucker.

We had an ordinary seaman, Scotty, who was kind of a big, burly kid. I heard later he committed suicide. He was ordinary seaman, dumb and easily led.

One of the guys in the engine room was Mitchum. Called him Mitch the Bitch. He loved it. He had big scars on his face from all his fights. He was one of these guys who could drink and stay drunk, and work, too.

Then there was a guy named Brady, he came from the west coast, that's how hard it was to get a crew, they flew him in from the west coast. He was an old Irish agitator, been in the British Army, and then he got out and came to America for a new life.

Had this ordinary seaman named Benny, a Filipino, he was fucked up on pot all the time. The whole crew was fucking out of it.

Had a guy named Ray Vote, AB, and he was on the 12 to 4 with this Scotty. This Ray Vote, he was 5 foot, layin' or standin', living with his mother in Miami. As soon as we leave port, the slop chest opens up, we get cigarettes, candy bars, clothing, if you need it. Ray buys a whole fucking box of candy bars. First watch he goes up on the bridge at midnight, he takes the whole box of candy bars with him, and in his 2-hour watch he ate a box of fucking candy bars. Wondered why he was sick all the time.

We get down to Panama, now everybody's gonna go to the doctor, they're sick, fucked up. We're at anchor and we're waiting to go through. Ray goes to the doctor.

Doctor says, "Jesus Christ, you're 300 pounds overweight. No, you're not 'Fit for Duty,' how the fuck did anybody pass you?"

He's gonna go home, and he's gonna get paid, right? Until he gets "Fit for Duty."

Well, we're out at anchor. There was some hang-up about getting us through with the ammo. They wanted to run us through in daylight, and they had too many ships or something. Sometimes you waited days before you went, because they wanted to run you through in daylight, alone, because of the ammo, in case you blew up. They estimated if we detonated, we'd take anywhere from 12 to 15 miles with us. We got paid 10% extra for that. And we're supporting the war effort. We're good Americans. Yeah. They had little fucking medals for us, but you had to mail for them. Not many did.

Guys are starting to get hold of that fucking hooch down there. Me and Brady are going ashore. The steward was from England, a little short guy with a little cigarette holder thing, glasses, a little wiry guy. I walk into a bar and here he is, got his hands in his pockets, and he's looking at this fucking pinball machine saying, "I don't have it, I don't have it." I knew he's fucked up. Found out later there was a girl standing in front of him trying to get him to go out with her, and he's saying, "I don't have the money." Well, she had left, and now he's still standing there all wobbly, talking to the machine.

Anyway, the bosun—never bathed, dirty—he had one of those old pocket watches, but the glass face was missing out of it. He'd be out on deck, and we'd have our coffee time, ten to ten fifteen, and then three to three fifteen, then he'd knock us off about quarter to five for dinner. Well, we'd be doing something, working with dirty, greasy wires and shit, and he'd take that watch out—try to work us to the minute, right?—and he'd put that fucking watch down somewhere, and he'd be working as hard as we were: "*You don't know what the fuck you're doing, I'm gonna do it!*" We had these leather-palmed gloves, and they were greasy, so wherever he put the watch, whoever happened to walk by would take their hand and grease it all up and put it back down. He'd run back to look to see what time it was—"*Baaaa!*"—and he'd clean it on his pants and put it back. Somebody would come by and do it again. "*Who's fucking with me now!?*"

Anyway, it was coffee time, and when you went into the mess hall, there were two tables to the left, and three tables on the other side where the portholes were; the door opened against the wall, so there's a straight pathway to the pantry and the coffee on the countertop. The coffee was there with two of these old metal percolators. I mean, the big heavy ones.

The ordinary seamen on the 12 to 4, that was his job at two thirty to go make coffee. Then you went in there at three o'clock and had your coffee, you know, 5 minutes to 3. Well, this bosun: "No, no, three o'clock, that's when you start."

We get in there, get our coffee, we're sitting around.

This AB comes in bitching about something, something's fucked up. I'm talking, we're under 10 days out *maybe*.

Bosun says, "Ah, never mind, that'll change later."

Well, the AB's got the big coffee pot, fucking 2 foot high, and he's pouring the coffee. He says, "This is our coffee time. We don't need you to tell us what the fuck to do now."

Bosun says, "I'm the bos'!" He jumps up, runs out of the fucking mess hall, right?

And I'm thinking: what the fuck is gonna happen *now*?

We're just sitting there, this AB puts the coffee pot down, and he's still got it in his hand, and he's drinking the coffee, he's trying to talk to one of the guys about some beef they got about the ship, something's not right.

Dan was the delegate, and Dan's telling him, "Just write it all down, that's the best thing we can do," which was the way it always was. All the beefs you had, all during the trip, as soon as you got back and paid off, nobody cared anyway, we never got nothing anyway.

All of a sudden the bosun comes in with a fucking 2 by 4, he's all dirty and sweaty and shit, ain't bathed in a week. "*You can't talk to me like that!*"

This AB still has the coffee pot in his hand. We're talking 2 foot high, maybe 3. This thing was fucking big. And as he turns around, Pasatti tries to hit him with the 2 by 4. As he swings at him, he puts the coffee pot, his right arm, up. The board hits the arm, the hot coffee grounds go into his face, and Pasatti slips in the coffee that hit the deck. They were kind of tussling there, but he slips on the coffee grounds and he falls, and this AB still has the coffee pot, and he smacks the bosun in the fucking head.

Boom! Boom!

Guys are yelling and climbing over tables to get outta there. I'm watching all this, you know, hey, I don't give a fuck who kills who.

And he's *beatin'* him. He's busting his eyes up, fucking him up, and I'm thinking: I just hope he fucks him up enough to get him off the ship, you know, I'm tired of working for this asshole.

Finally somebody broke it up. The bottom of the coffee pot, where the metal is, the heavy part, was halfway up into the fucking pot.

Now the captain shows up: "*What happened here?*" This Hopewell. "*What's going on now?*" Like, "Can't you guys play nice?" Real fucking cunt.

They send the AB to the hospital there in Panama for merchant seamen, for guys in transit who get sick. He had coffee grounds in his eyes, he's burning.

Captain says, "What the fuck happened here?"

I says, "They got in an argument, the bosun left, come back with a 2 by 4, tried to hit him."

"What does it look like to you?"

I says, "Looks like the bosun tried to kill him. The bosun came back with the board. He initiated it."

Hopewell didn't like that, so I knew I was on the blacklist. I didn't give a fuck.

That night, Dan and myself went over to the hospital to see this AB. He was fucked up. I mean, they were still trying to clean the coffee grounds out of his eyes; he was burned up bad.

Somehow or another he had called the Canal Zone police, which were American at the time. This happened in the Canal Zone, technically. We had just got there, and the Canal Zone cop shows up a little later.

The AB says, "I want this man arrested."

This copper didn't know what the fuck to do. So he called the head of the Canal Zone police, this old cop, been down there for 20, 30 years, and he says, "Yeah, go arrest him."

They went to the ship and arrested Pasatti, took him to court that night. We went to the court, with the AB. Pasatti got fined something like $300, and they put him on probation in the Canal Zone.

Me and Dan went back, and the bosun says, "What are you guys goin' with him for?"

"Hey, bos', you can't run around trying to fucking kill people."

So we're still waiting to go through. We went to shore a couple of times, picked up some bimbos. You just assume all these Panamanian broads are bimbos, and we're walking down the street and Brady's half fucked up, I'm half sober, and Brady puts his arm around this one broad, and she got indignant. She was some kind of school teacher or something, she wanted to punch him out, and Brady's all, "I'm sorry, I'm *sorry*."

Later on that night was the first time I went to The Blue Goose. It was up on a hill. You had to take a taxi to go up there. The Blue Goose. I'd always heard about the place, you know, when I was in the North Atlantic: "If you go there, you gotta go to The Blue Goose." There were four or five of us, the bosun was with us, too. It was a big building. The place had swinging doors, just like in the old west, and sawdust on the floor, I guess to clean up the blood or the cum or whatever the fuck it was, and they had a jukebox. You walked in through the swinging doors, there was a bar to the right and about 12 barstools. Then there was an entrance to go upstairs. To the left there must have been 20 tables with four chairs each. I look over, and there was at least three girls at every table, if not four. And they were all in bikinis or bras and panties, or bras or panties or with a shawl wrapped over, every array of undress you can imagine. And they could've all been movie stars. Make a seaman blush. An idiot's delight. You forgot all about the girl back home, the loved ones, all that bullshit.

So right away we sit at the bar, and then the girls start coming up. "Hi. Let's get a drink first."

You go over to a table, and it's 5 or 10 bucks for a short time, or just for 20 minutes, anything you wanted to do, they didn't give a fuck. You went upstairs. I'm talking to one of the girls, and I'm serious, they were Panamanian, Colombian, all over South America. Panama was one big whorehouse. I mean, you'd be walking down the street and there'd be some girl from Argentina hitting on you. They came up from Colombia, they came up from Argentina, and the older they got the cheaper they got.

So one of the girls comes by, and she's always bumming quarters for this fucking jukebox. The Panamanians used U.S. dollars, they always did. You give her a quarter, and she'd go over and play the jukebox, and she'd switch the songs around, but she'd always play "Love is Blue." They later banned it in the States cuz people, girls, committed suicide, some girl in France jumped off a fucking bridge over it. They banned it in Europe.

Anyway, I says, "What the fuck's wrong with her?"

She fell in love with some seaman, and he was gonna come back, never did, and that was their song. It's not really a bad song. I can listen to it, I can handle it, don't have no effect on me.

Anyway, she says, "You wanna go upstairs?"

I says, "How much?"

She says, "Whatever you got." It's 5 or 10 dollars.

I says, "OK."

When you went upstairs there was an old woman used to sit there, and she would charge you 50 cents for a short-time towel, and that's how she made her living. Yeah. She took care of the girls, cooked for 'em and that. They lived there, downstairs. Upstairs was for the whorehouse. But she would sit there and she'd have clean towels, you know, cum on 'em that she'd have to wash. I'm sure she cut back on the soap to show a profit. And she would give one of 'em these towels for 50 cents. I think back about it today: if it was ignorant, dumb, or stupid, I did it. But at the time, you think it's great. I guess it probably still is great. If I could go do it again, I would.

Anyway, we go up there, and it's just a square room with these wooden slats together, and a bed in there. Where the slats had parted they had taken toilet paper, shoved it in there. No real ceiling. You could hear people in the other room.

We go in there, and she says, "OK, take your clothes off."

I says, "OK."

She's taking her clothes off, and you can hear people in the other rooms doing whatever they're doing. "*Unh, unh, unh.*" She's taking her clothes off, so I start pulling the toilet paper out between the slats.

She says, "What are you doing?"

I says, "I'm getting a little extra."

So, put the toilet paper back, her and I are freaking out, and I says, "OK," she gives me the towel, "Thank you," we're done.

We go back downstairs, get another drink, and I'm bullshitting with her, and the bosun's still sitting there, he's sitting there with this big fucking bleached blonde. You could see the blonde was getting aggravated, cuz he don't wanna go upstairs, he wants to sit there and bullshit.

I'm thinking: I'd like to freak out with her. Maybe he'll leave her alone and I can slide in there, you know?

Anyway, it came time to go, we had to get outta there.

Next day we're *still waiting for transit.* Now we're on day work, right?

The bosun's filthy dirty as usual, never bathed. "Yeah, you shoulda seen the one I was with last night, that big blonde."

I said, "Bos', you didn't even go with her. I was waiting for you to leave so I could fucking freak out with her."

"*Ahh, whadya mean, 'I went with her, don't try to lie.*"

Fucking screwball.

I think we went up there one more night, and then we made the transit. Hopewell was worried he wouldn't have a crew by the time we got ready, cuz they had to call for another AB again, we were short one. And it was pretty much the same thing. I mean, I can see where guys can leave their wife and kids and just stay down there. I'm very serious. I really am. I mean, if you saw the place. The girls spoke Spanish, broken English. Kind of brought the whole scheme of things into focus with the girls I'd seen in Liverpool, London, Germany. There were so many women in the world, how could you stay with one? I mean, that's a choice, obviously. But how could you marry the girl next door and listen to dumb shit your whole life when you could spend 10 dollars and never have to see 'em again if you didn't want to? I says, man, this is beautiful.

Anyway, we make the transit, about 12 hours, and now we're on our way across the Pacific.

They had us clean up and paint our rooms. Basically, it was just painting over the fucking asbestos that was breaking off. Roaches in there. Three of us in a room. Bosun in a room by himself. So we had this light green paint, almost pea green. They had these big cluster lights for these lamps to put in the hatches or hang over the side. They had these bulbs, and these bulbs were big. Brady came by for some reason, and he sees this cluster light, and he sees the 5-gallon can of paint; we're going in there painting with this lead paint over the asbestos.

Brady says, "Hey, wait a minute." He sticks the light bulb in the paint. "Hey, green light." He just takes it, puts it down. It dries up.

Well, the bosun sees it, this dumb motherfucker, and he says, "Oh, man, this is a good idea." You had to know this guy: "*A green light!*"

He always kept his door locked. He opens up the door, turns the light on. And all he had was a wire coming out with a fixture and a light bulb. He unscrews that one and puts this one in. "Oh! It's green! Doesn't that look better?" He goes outside and locks his door.

Well, I'm going back and forth because I got the next room over, right, next foc'sle over, and I'm cleaning that one out, we're gonna paint it, we're throwing out all the wood and shit people had built up in there over the years, like it's their own cell. I'm going back and forth, and I walk by his door, and I smell something burning.

"What the fuck's burning in there?" So I'm trying the door. "Fuck, it's *locked!* Something's burning in there."

We got fucking ammo on board, you know, I'm going to get a fire ax. Here comes the bosun: "*What are you doing? Get out!*"

I says, "Something's burning in there."

"Ain't nothing burning in there."

I says, "Open the door!"

Opens the fucking door. Here the light bulb is just *smoking*, it's getting ready to *ignite*. He left it on. Turn the switch, right? Turn the switch and almost instantly *died*, you know. Whoa, man, who fucking did that, huh?

He unscrewed it, threw it over to the side.

Oh, somebody took the 2 by 4 and coffee pot and put 'em on the stern with the trash to be dumped. Back then you threw everything out anytime you wanted, over the side. I threw it all over the side. Somebody put it back there, that was evidence, you know, so I threw it all over the side.

We were going to Da Nang. Panama to Da Nang was 9,999 miles. I remember that, because they said we're going to Da Nang, we're not going to the Philippines. Second trip we did the same thing. Because, when we came out of Panama, I was now on watch with the second mate Haines, and he said he had to figure out the miles to Da Nang.

I says, "It's 9,999 miles."

He says, "How the fuck do you know that? I'm second mate, you're not."

I says, "Cuz that's what we did last time; Panama right to Da Nang."

He says, "Well, I gotta check on it."

And it was 10,028 he got.

We went right to Da Nang, and we were discharging the ammo there, into the barges. Somebody opened fire on us, the shells actually hit near us. We were gonna put in for harbor attack, which we never got, they said it was an accident, probably an American shooting at us, who knows, somebody on drugs.

Matter of fact, you can back up to the *American Pilot*, we went to the dock that time in Da Nang, we went from Quy Nhon to Da Nang, and we had a harbor attack there, too. They had us dock the ship, and a rocket hit the dock a ship away from us, and we put in for a harbor attack and didn't get that, either.

And, basically, nothing really went terribly fucking wrong there. You know, you could go there and sit around at the bars, nobody said too much to you at Da Nang. We went in a couple of times. You went to a little military check point. They didn't really want you taking American money in. You had to hide your money, you know, cuz you could sell it on the black market, and the VC would get it.

They did have a place there in Da Nang, called Mama Lee's. She ran a little beer stand, and you'd find a bunch of women there, their husbands had been killed in the bombing, and she had a little whorehouse with a bunch of young Vietnamese girls. Mama Lee's. She's kind of famous, really. Her brother was the chief of police in Da Nang, and she would change your money. She would take the money and fly to Hong Kong, because the Vietnamese money was worth nothing. I think they were giving us 400 for a dollar. When she took the money to Hong Kong to change it with the money lenders, they'd give her 800 for a dollar. I mean, she was making money. I heard later on after the Vietnam War she opened up a place in Hong Kong. Anyway, she had a whorehouse there with a bunch of young Vietnamese girls, and women hanging around, and kids and shit. It was just a little fucking stand, like an ice cream stand we have here in the States in the old times with the push cart. She'd sell beer outta there and had tables set up, and then if you wanted to go to the whorehouse, she'd have her driver take you over there.

Anyway, I had the 4 to midnight watch, and they were discharging the ammo. It was the second mate, Haines, he always had the 4 to midnight. He was a drinker, Haines, retired Navy. He turned around, and right away at four o'clock we both started drinking. And he was drinking more than I was.

I says, "Fuck, one of us has gotta sober up here." So I tell him, "Go on, get outta here, I'll take care of it."

Well, when it got to a certain level on the ammo that has come off the ship, the mate on watch would have to sign for it. I had to go find Haines to get him to sign this paper. Here he's fucking passed out in the officer's lounge.

"Hey, man, get up. Pass out somewhere else. Sign this."

"*Get the fuck outta here.*" Real cooperative.

Then the other time I had to go find him he was passed out on the port side of the ship in a lounge chair, trying to hide.

I'm like, "Don't hide from *me*, I'm the one on watch with you." I says, "Here, sign this."

He's looking at it all blurry-eyed. "You sure about this?"

"Yeah, it's good. Don't worry about it."

I says, "Look, I gotta get the third mate up now," the one I usually stood watch with. I says, "Go up to the bridge, get in the chart room, and just *stand* there, and I'll tell the third mate that's where you wanna be relieved." I says, "I'll sign for the paperwork, he'll have to take the next load, they're not gonna be done with any more until like 0200."

He stumbles off. "OK."

So I go wake the third mate up, old guy, white hair. He drank, too, but you didn't know it, he was still acting sober. Haines, you just knew he was fucked up. I get him up at 11:20.

I says, "I made a pot of coffee in the officer's mess for you, and the second mate's in the chart room, relieve him up there."

"Oh, OK."

So I go back down to the gangway. I was about ready to get relieved by the AB, and here comes the third mate.

He says, "Who's been feeding the second mate?"

I says, "Feeding him what?"

He says, "He's drunk."

I says, "He didn't appear drunk to me."

He says, "What?"

I says, "He signed all the paperwork for the ammo going off."

He says, "You're telling me you've seen him, and he's not drunk, he was out here on deck?"

"Yeah."

"You've seen him?"

I says, "Yeah, not drunk. He didn't appear intoxicated to me."

He fucking storms off.

I says, ah, what the fuck you gonna do?

I crash, eight o'clock in the morning, I had to go back on. So I eat and turn to on the gangway, it was my gangway watch.

Chief mate comes down, says, "The old man wants to see you."

I says, "Yeah, OK, I'll go up. OK if I leave the gangway?"

He says, "Yeah. He wants to see you and the second mate."

I says, "Yeah, OK."

He says, "You know what's wrong?"

"Yeah." I can figure.

Here, the third mate, when he got off in the morning, he told the old man, "Fucking second mate was drunk, and Ron swears to God he wasn't."

So here's me and the second mate, Haines. By now he's got 8 hours' sleep and got off the fucking sauce, he's OK.

Captain says, "Gentleman—" this is Hopewell, *hated* us "—the third mate, when he relieved last night, he says the second mate appeared to be intoxicated."

Second mate says, "I wasn't intoxicated."

Captain turns to me, "How about you, what do you think?"

I says, "He wasn't intoxicated. I was on watch with him all night. He signed the paperwork, and he was out on deck."

Captain says, "You're saying he wasn't intoxicated?"

"I'm saying he wasn't, and I'm saying that he was out on deck with the cargo."

"Alright. OK. I looked into it."

Second we get out there second mate says, "Hey, thanks."

I says, "Yeah, OK."

Then he says, "Weren't you drinking?"

"Yeah, but one of us had to stop."

He says, "Yeah, dirty fucking third mate. Next time I catch him drinking I'm snitching on him."

I says, "OK."

He says, "By the way, we're off at 1600 today, aren't we?"

"Yeah."

"Well, it's on me, we're going ashore."

"OK."

1600 rolls around, second mate comes in. "Ready to go?"

I says, "You wanna get cleaned up or anything?"

"What the hell we need to be clean for?"

So we're heading down the gangway. I found out later that the chief mate and the captain were standing there watching the second mate and I go down, because the chief mate, Spydell, he liked us, he told me. He said Hopewell looked over at him and said, "Ahh. There they go. One lies, and the other one swears to it."

We went in that night, and we're sitting there drinking, and you could see the ship sitting out there at anchor.

Haines says, "Who's your next of kin?" He meant on the life insurance for the trip.

I says, "I think I put my aunt and uncle down for the $10,000."

He says, "It's my wife. You know, if that ship blew up right now, they'd think we were on there, they wouldn't find any part of us. You think we could get away with it? The $10,000? I don't know if my wife would give me the money, though, if she collected it."

One time, Mitch the Bitch comes back all fucked up and goes down to the engine room—I think he was the 4 to midnight fireman down there—and comes out on deck, he's the fireman and never supposed to leave the engine room, you know. Engineer on watch can never leave, either.

He comes out: "Hey, motherfuckers!"

I says, "Hey, Mitch, I'm tired of that shit."

He's, "Ah, fuck you, too!"

So I hit him, and we get into it. And it's just that fucking whiskey strength he has.

I had him between a rail and a ladder way going up from the main deck to the next deck. I punched him and I got him in there, and they break us up, and they send him back down to the engine room.

Second mate Haines was on watch, and I think he's the one that broke it up. He comes over to me, says, "He hit you," you know: "He started it."

I says, "OK."

That's when they sent him down to the engine room. He fell back down there drunk and fell down on these valves. We got him in the basket, and I'm gonna put the knot in the basket and pull him up by these ladder ways to get him up.

He's strapped in: "You motherfuckers! Leave me alone!"

One of the guys says, "Don't put it there, put it around his *neck*. We'll just pull him up by his neck."

We got him up and the Navy took him.

He came back later all fucked up going back down to the engine room.

Then we went up to Sasebo, Japan. It wasn't expensive yet, this was about '69, it was still cheap. They had saki town for the Japanese, seamen town for the seamen, and skivvy town for the U.S. Navy. We had a couple days there.

We had this little British steward. Soon as we got to Sasebo, he says, "I gotta go buy food." We had all these Panamanians we picked up, so we were short on food.

Well, we're coming back on the launch, and I looked at it, it's like 500 pounds of rice.

I says, "What's this 500 pounds of rice?"

He says, "That's the main staple diet for Panamanians."

I says, "Well, *my* main staple diet is *steak*. Why the fuck didn't you get 500 pounds of *steak*, you little motherfucker you."

Brady and I were bouncing around, and we went in one bar and started playing tic-tac-toe with the Japanese girls, trying to get laid without paying—forget it. It was that kind of place where people come in, their ears were deformed, stuff like that from the war yet, from the atomic bomb.

I nodded over to one of them and says, "What's wrong with him?"

She says, "Oh. Bomb."

We were playing tic-tac-toe with them and dicking around, laughing with them and that, and "Oh, don't go, don't go yet."

Well, we're not getting laid. So we went over to this other bar, and it was dark in there, and the bartender's a Japanese kid, but he spoke real good English. We were partying it up with them, and we said, "Where's the bathroom?"

"Around back."

Well, you had to go in the alley to take a piss, you know. *That* was the bathroom.

We're fucking around in there, and some old white broad came in. She was actually Russian who had married a Japanese, and was selling flowers. Brady bought the flowers, and there was some Japanese girl had just come walking by, she was selling trinkets or something. Brady gave her the flowers.

"Oh, thank you," she said. Some school kid.

I'm thinking we're gonna go to jail.

We took her around with us, the old white woman, the Russian. I can understand Slovenian, I can understand Russian, if I'm around it. We took her around to the bars, but we had to let her go because she had to go home or something. It was really late, and we went to this one area, it was a park, and there was just a tent there, and Brady knew there were hookers there. And we go over to get a beer, and they're selling sushi, fresh fish, which everybody knows about now, but back then you could only get it in Japan, really. And who comes in, just like in a movie, a Japanese guy with a white karate outfit on, and he's got the flat wooden shoes. He comes in, and we're like, oh, fuck, we're gonna die. But we're friendly to him, you know, just hoping this guy don't lose it.

Well now, this guy, he's ordering sushi, so now we gotta have some. Brady had some, and the guy's motioning for me to have some, too.

I says, "No, thank you, but no, thank you."

He grunts, *"Sushi!"* Like I insulted him or something.

So I figured I'd better eat the sushi or get killed. So I just did it, I took a beer and swallowed it raw.

Brady picked up some hooker and went up to these little rooms up there, and I stayed down there in the tent. Then we got back to the ship. I mean, we had to get back, and we got like 4 hours sleep, if that.

And Brady gets through with his watch and he says, "C'mon, let's go do it again."

I says, "I'll go, sure."

And the chief mate is still telling me, "Why don't you get that bosun and beat his fucking brains out? I'll give you overtime."

Brady and I go back, and we stop at that one bar, that little hole-in-the-wall joint where we took the piss out back.

I ask the guy, you know, are we OK, cuz I don't want to cause the guy any trouble.

He says, "Trouble? I thought you guys were hilarious. I'm gonna buy you guys a drink."

We got back early. They were securing the ship, lowering the booms, pulling the tarps. We were going back empty. Here comes the bosun, he went ashore with a suit on. He comes back with Roberts; him and Roberts are buddies.

Well, Roberts has this flute he bought for his son. His wife writes him a letter that she needs a new coat for the kid or something; he takes up with this hooker, you know, right, he can't be fucking bothered. And we picked up a white guy in Panama that had hurt his back and got off the ship, another one of these company ships. One of the AB's, Woody, was from North Carolina. He bought a pair of shoes, and he was really fucking happy with them, and he was just a real fucking idiot.

Roberts came back with the bosun to secure, and he turned around and he left his fucking flute. He was so in love with his wife, he missed the ship.

Bosun says, "Roberts ain't coming back, he's gonna stay with this Japanese girl."

I don't know how the fuck Woody got in this, but they were recruiting because we were losing people. And the bosun comes back, and we're already starting to secure the ship. He doesn't even bother changing clothes. He's got a white shirt on, jacket, suit pants, shoes.

He just takes the fucking jacket off, throws it down, rolls his sleeves up, and starts working, getting all dirty. And we're still fucking with his pocket watch.

Anyway, we're getting ready to leave, and the bosun's out there all raggedy and dirty. Roberts misses the ship. It was just all fucked up. Hopewell's screaming and yelling. Haines is out of his mind.

We finally get secured, and we get cleared by the Army, got all the ammunition off, and we're gonna go directly to the Panama Canal. Roberts is gone, so somehow or another, Woody gets on watch with us. He's got this fucking flute that Roberts had bought for his kids— his loved ones that he missed the ship for to stay with the hooker— and we're going through Sasebo to Panama, it's gonna be 30, 35 days.

By now it's pretty well calmed down, booze is out of the system, we're in a routine, working a little overtime, and the chief mate wanted me to do some extra work. I was on the 8 to 12 watch.

He says, "Ron, you wanna turn to in the afternoon? 1300?"

"No, not really, mate."

He says, "No, you're working for me."

I says, "Yeah, alright."

He says, "Meet me up by the lifeboat. I want you to do something."

Spydell used to slide me overtime. He always wanted me to kill the bosun. I went out at 1300, and he was up on the lifeboat, he wanted something done, so I'm working with him, and it was just about 2 hours, just about coffee time, three o'clock, and we were done.

Spydell says, "Why don't you go and have coffee. Finish up the day. Put down 4 hours, 1300 to 1700; five o'clock. Go work with the bosun for 2 hours."

I says, "Mate, I'd just as soon have the 2 hours, you know, I really don't like working with the bosun."

About that time the bosun's on deck. We're up on the lifeboat. You can hear him screaming, "*You fucking guys!*"

Spydell looks over at him, looks back at me, and he says, "I know what you mean. Just write down 'til 5. I'll pay you."

We get off at midnight, have a cup of coffee, read for a while. There's three guys in a room. Woody would sit up on his bunk, and he'd play that fucking flute. This is from Sasebo, right? This is *every, fucking, night.* The only thing he knew was some ancient Peruvian death chant.

Finally, I guess we're about a week from Panama, I says, "Woody, you ever learn anything on that fucking flute besides that ancient Peruvian death chant?"

He says, "No. What's wrong with it?"

I says, "Well, I don't know what's wrong with it, but we got about 5 days to the canal." I says, "You got 5 days to learn something else, because if I hear that fucking thing after we get through the canal, I'm gonna wrap that fucking thing around your head."

Never heard it again.

He was gonna give it to his son, though: "Here's a flute from Japan."

Fucking screwy.

We got to Panama, let the Panamanians off cuz they didn't want to have to pay their way back. Now we're shorthanded, so they gotta stand the extra watches and pay us. And we gotta go to Wilmington, North Carolina before we go to Sunny Port for all these repairs. Shit's just falling apart.

One night at Sasebo they sent me up to the lights, they had cluster lights up there, they would shine down onto the hatches, for the booms, and one was tied up there, and they wanted me to change the light bulb. They sent me up, probably hoping I'd get killed. The bosun had me go up there, and the chief mate was out there, Spydell, and the bosun's standing right underneath me. You had to unscrew the metal cage, then the glass cage, then unscrew the bulb. So I had the bulb up there with me. I'm trying to reach around, to feel it.

The bosun's screaming up, "*Can't you fucking do anything right?*" He's trying to direct me, you know, I'm 60 feet above him.

I hear the chief mate saying, "Bosun, I wouldn't yell at Ron that way when he's working above me like that."

We had some bad weather, and I hadn't tied it secure enough, and the whole fucking thing went; electric wire ripped out, the fucking thing was *gone.*

We were going through the canal, and somebody's gotta stand by the bow when we transit. I came up there for some reason, and Benny was there, that stupid fucking ordinary that smoked pot all the time. We had to lower the gangway, so the bosun called some of us to help out.

The bosun says, "Alright, Ron, come out with me, we gotta lower the gangway."

Spydell says, "You're not leaving that stupid fucking Benny here with me! Take Benny and leave Ron here!"

So I'm up there, and Spydell says, "Why the fuck didn't you beat his brains out? I'd have given you overtime for it."

I says, "Mate, we're getting to the end of the trip. Who cares?" I says, "If he'd have fucked with me personally," you know, I says, "Yeah, I'll fuck him up. But other than that, he got married and he's just trying to make a couple bucks, you ain't gonna get any better."

He says, "You know, many, many years ago, when I was AB and we had a bosun like him, and I was painting stack, and the bosun walked by, I accidentally dropped the brush and hit him right on the fucking head with it."

I says, "That's good. That's good."

We dropped off the Panamanians, picked up some booze, and we're on our way back up. You got three men in a room, your little desk in there, the chair, and me and Dan picked up a bottle of gin, we were off watch.

Spydell came by, he saw the bottle. He says, "No, no, don't put the bottle away. I've been known to have a drink."

"Well, mate, if you want one."

He says, "You guys gonna stay out here and make the next trip with me?"

Dan says, "Fuck no, man, I'm getting the fuck outta here. I don't need this! This is insane!"

He says, "How 'bout you, Ron?"

I says, "Mate, I'll stay for the coastwise, but after that, I don't know."

He says, "You stay here, I'll take care of you. Ron," he says, "I'm telling you, you stay here with me, I'll take care of you. Second mate wants you to stay. Cap'n hates you, but he's getting off."

I says, "Mate, I'll keep it in mind, thank you. I'm not quitting at pay off, let's put it that way."

So we're drinking.

Chief mate Spydell says, "Did I ever tell you the story of how I got my license?"

I says, "No, you never did, mate."

We got the bottle open now. He's an old drinker.

He said he got his license just after World War II and moved up quickly. The companies had all these government ships, and he made captain in 1947. And he loved it; says, man, this is great, captain of my own ship. Well, 1950, the Korean War breaks out. Greece is gonna donate sea salt to the Korean people, but they gotta have an American ship down there to pick it up and take it around to Korea. So it's an old Victory ship left over from World War II. He gets to Greece to load this sea salt.

The agent comes on board, like they always do, and he says, "Captain, I'm going to take you out to dinner tonight."

He says, "Thank you."

Over dinner the agent says, "Captain, you look like a reasonable man. How would you like to make one million dollars?"

This is in 1950.

The captain, Spydell, says, "Yeah, well . . . ." He drank then, too, you know; a couple more drinks, he's a little more interested.

This guy says, "Myself and my friends are willing to put this money in a numbered Swiss bank account for you, and we'll give you the number, you can check it's there." And he says, "If you'll run that ship aground, we'll get the salvage rights."

Spydell tells us, "Man, I'm thinking about this, I'm really thinking."

Agent says, "Think about it. You're gonna be here 2 or 3 weeks getting the sea salt. You think about it."

And Spydell tells us, "I thought about it. You know, 1950, captain of my own ship since 1947, just married, and I'm thinking about that million dollars in a bank account and what I could do with it." He says, "I could have got away with it." The charts were left over from World War II, and he says, "I could have done it."

Which, you *can*. I mean, *anybody* can make a mistake up there, right? Even if you got a good AB and a good second mate, you can override everything. You'd lose your license, but you'd get a million dollars, as long as nobody got killed.

He says they're getting ready to sail, and the agent comes back and says, "Captain, I got the number. You never called me back."

He says, "I can't do it. I'm just married, master of my own vessel, I got a great future ahead of me with the company, I can't do it, but thank you."

OK, no pressure.

Takes the trip, takes the sea salt there.

He's telling us this in 1969. So that was almost 20 years difference, right?

He says, "I wish somebody would make me that fucking offer *now!* That fucking wife I got, I'm fucking *nowhere*, I'm shipping out of *nowhere*, I gotta deal with all these crazy people!"

Poor fucking guy.

It was funny.

He says, "I'd like to have you with me, Ron."

"Well, mate, if you cut me in on the million, I'd probably help you out on something like that."

Then Haines comes down. "You're still planning on making the trip, ain't you? You're coming on the 4 to 8 with me."

I says, "Yeah, I'll come on there with you."

We get to Wilmington, and we're out of everything. In Panama the steward had bought two cases of apples, but we had no food. The freezers had gone bad coming back, we had to throw all this food over the side, and we're eating rice all the way back, and the fucking steward, little raggedy motherfucker: "Oh, I'm buying food in Panama." He bought two cases of apples. We're fistfighting over the fucking apples, so we had to eat rotten food.

They gave us some kind of beef over rice. I had a plate of it.

Brady happened to come in, sat down across from me, says, "Give me the same thing Ronnie got, but give me half an order."

Messman comes back a minute later with a pile of it, it was spilling over. "Chief cook says you can eat all you want and leave the rest; there's no half orders."

Brady gets up, picks up the plate, and dumps it—*psshhh*—down on the deck. Walks out.

It was like that, you know. It was that kind of trip.

So we tie up at Wilmington at the Old Molasses dock for repairs. They call all hands to the dock about ten o'clock at night, and here's Mitch the Bitch, alright, we're all sitting there waiting to get called out, so they had a phone in the crew mess, that's where we wait to go tie up or let go, whatever. And it's pretty cold at night, we're sitting in the mess hall drinking coffee, waiting to get the call.

Mitch happens to be sitting right next to the phone. The phone rings. Mitch picks it up. "Hello. Crew mess." I guess they were calling for us, right, and he put his hands over his eyes and says, "No, I don't see nobody."

Everybody's, "Ah, fuck, Mitch, you're gonna get us all fucked."

Everybody's getting off. I'm the only one *staying*.

He hangs up.

They're all, "Ah, fuck, we gotta get outta here."

So we go and tie up.

We're gonna pay-off the next day. Barely have enough fucking food. I'm staying on, and chief mate Spydell's telling me, "Ronnie, you stay here, I'll take care of you. Make sure you stay. I want you on watch with me."

I says, "OK."

We're paying off, and it's just a fucking zoo. Brady's bitching he can't get transportation: "What about my taxi?" We're like, "It's the end of the trip, Brady," and he's, "Ah, you motherfuckers, there's nothing out here, you fucking union." And Hopewell's, "Hey, come on, it's the end of the trip, I'm getting off, too."

Well, here comes the Coast Guard, and they're looking through all the log books. "*All this fucking happened? We wanna see everybody!*"

So they got Mitch, they gave him a warning for fighting with me.

Chief mate and second mate stuck up for me.

Coast Guard says, "They're sticking up for you." Then they says, "What about this fight in Panama?"

I says, "Yeah, the bosun beat the guy with a 2 by 4, and the guy beat his brains out with a coffee pot."

They says, "Who did this?"

I says, "Well, bosun started it, he hit him first, he got the board and came back. Sounds like 'intent' to me."

The bosun got a letter of warning. He's supposed to show up at a hearing cuz of the fight.

The Coast Guard just couldn't handle it. "*All this fucking happened?*"

We were trying to get our money, *I'm* trying to get *my* money. Nobody's there. The steward agreed to stay a day or two. There was nobody left. It was like a ghost ship.

But I'm staying on.

Hopewell had called Customs, Immigration, and told them he had a bunch of druggies on there, cuz that 4 to 8 watch that he had, José and Benny, smoked up all the time, they were up on the bridge all fucked up, trying to steer. José's trying to steer. Well, if it goes to the right, you give it left. If it goes to the left, you give it the right rudder, you know, to catch it. Well, he had it just the opposite; if it was going to the right, he's giving it more right, trying to catch it, he's all over the fucking place, almost ran us aground, motherfucker.

The Coast Guard's just in awe. "All this shit happened?"

So Hopewell called Customs. They were waiting for guys to come off, and they were searching the gear.

Spydell told me, "Give everybody a hand."

I'm helping everybody get their stuff, and here's Customs, plain clothes, flashing a badge.

They says, "What of this stuff is yours?"

I says, "None of it."

They says, "What do you mean 'none of it'? What are you doing with it? Possession is nine-tenths of the law."

I says, "I'm helping everybody get their stuff. I'm the only one staying on board. The mate told me to give these guys a hand getting their gear out. They're putting it by the gangway, and I'm helping 'em get it off."

"So you're just standing here? None of this is yours?"

I says, "None of this."

Benny comes up there with his broken English.

They says, "This all yours, Benny?"

"Yeah, yeah, yeah." He's got a suit carrier, one of those that folds over. So they cut it open. And you could buy corn cob pipes and pipe tobacco that they had on the ship. Well, Benny's buying it, putting pot in there, and smoking it, right? So they find the pipe.

"What do you smoke in this?"

"Oh, tobacco, tobacco, tobacco!"

They're sniffing it, you know, "You motherfucker, we know what you're smoking."

He had a deck of playing cards. You've gotta remember, this is '69. So they open it up, and here's a dirty deck of playing cards he bought somewhere. "*What are these? This is disgraceful!*" Right? This is '69, you know, *pornography*, you're *importing* it into the United States. "This is *trash*."

Benny's flipping out cuz they're going through every fucking thing.

I says, "Well, I'm outta here." I go back, and Spydell says Hopewell's getting off. He says, "Go take his bag off for him."

I says, "You know, *mate* . . . ."

He says, "Yeah, I know, but *listen*. You're on *constant* overtime." He says, "You're the gangway watch, you're everything. I'm giving you overtime straight through." I think an AB was making $440 a month then, and then there was still about 5 for 30 vacation, and I wanna say the overtime rate was less than $8 an hour, $6 or $7 an hour, but, "You're constantly on overtime, right through to today."

I says, "OK."

So I take Hopewell's shit ashore. He had rented a car. Hopewell says, "OK, thanks."

I says, "Yeah, OK, Cap'n."

Usually they piece you off with five bucks or something. Hopewell didn't give me nothing. So I come back and here's the second mate. He's staying.

He says, "How much did Hopewell piece you off?"

"Nothing."

"That cheap motherfucker. That goddamn Hopewell." He didn't like him, either. He says, "Fuck, I'm telling the mate."

I says, "No, he's giving me overtime."

"Oh, OK, OK." He's about half in the bag, too.

So the steward's left, one or two of the cooks, a couple of the guys in the engine room. I mean, they couldn't even find a fucking crew for this thing. We got nothing on there, nothing to eat. We got stores coming. It's like ten o'clock at night! You know. We're all gonna chip in, there's a couple of cooks, the steward goes up to the cooks, a couple of guys in the engine room that were off, and we're all out there trying to get this stuff loaded. The fucking boom blew on us, short circuits. We gotta pull this shit up by hand.

We get it all on.

I says, "It's twelve, one o'clock, mate, I'm going to sleep."

He says, "Don't worry, I'm taking care of you."

I says, "OK."

"I'll write it in for you, you don't have to keep your overtime sheet."

"OK."

Next day I get up, and here we're starting to get the new crew; bunch of rednecks out of Charleston. Pretty good bunch, really. Charles "Chester" Matthews, bosun, right? Charlie Matthews. Charlie had sued every company, got off every fucking ship, bribed every doctor he could bribe. Charlie was a trip. He had actually come on earlier when Customs was there. He took a plate of food out for his wife to eat from our food. They went through the food, poking, making sure there was nothing in there. Packets of heroin, coke, whatever.

But now we're gonna ship. They'd done the repairs. We're gonna ship up to Sunny Point.

So we get this mate, Shepherd, he was steady second mate, but they made a mistake and called Haines' job steady, and Haines wasn't

gonna give his job up. So we get up to Sunny Point, and now Shepherd's really pissed off—young guy, you know—cuz he was working
for U.S. Lines and figured he'd get the chief mate job. Well, he had to
take a third mate job, Spydell ain't gonna get off, either. We had this
captain, a real nice guy. He'd come from U.S. Lines, too. They were
trying to get rid of the old captains.

We're up in Sunny Point now, and we got the new crew, and Charlie was strictly padding his overtime. Charlie was something. Charlie
had done so much shit in his time, it was unbelievable. He'd married
a Filipino girl. She was hooking and he was tending bar, and then he
came back to the States. He was suing these companies over everything, you know, anything and everything he could do.

We're at Sunny Point, getting ready to load again, and it's kind of
confusing. Plus we got some drinkers. I'm 4 to 8 now, and I took the
wheel going up. We get there, and we tie up.

Spydell calls me and says, "You gotta go to a hearing against the
bosun in Wilmington." He says, "You're on the payroll, don't worry
about it. Plus," he says, "I'm giving you overtime. It might be a day
or two, but I just want you to stay there, I want you to save your hotel receipts or whatever." He says, "I'm authorizing this. You tell that
fucking bosun I know he stole that fucking drill."

He stole a drill; we had an old one and a new one. He leaves us the
old broken one. Who the fuck's gonna steal a drill?

I says, "OK, I'll tell him."

So I get off that night, go to downtown Wilmington, the old Hotel
Wilmington, get a room in there for the night, and the next day I go
down to the Coast Guard station. We're waiting, I'm with the pros-
ecution.

The Coast Guard guy's looking through the books. "*Goddamn.*" He
says, "How'd all this take place?"

I says, "Well...yeah."

I go to the hearing, and he never shows up. So the hearing commissioner finds him guilty. There's some little talk about it. He says,
"What do you have to say?"

I says, "He coulda killed the guy."

"OK. We'll take care of this. Thank you."

I think I was gone 2 or 3 days. When I came back to the ship, the bosun's the first one to get me, right?

He says, "Hey, you're on pretty good terms with that chief mate, aren't you?" Old Charlie had been around a long time.

"Yeah."

"Go find him. We can't find him any fucking where."

Here he decided to go on a drunk. He's back in the mooring lines, in the stern of the ship, where the mooring lines used to get stowed, that's where everybody went to hide to go to sleep, and I knew that, you know, so I go back there, and sure enough that's where he is, all fucked up.

I says, "Come on, mate, get up."

So we get the new captain, he tells Spydell, his wife had come down from Philly to visit him. He says, "Mate, OK, for today, I'm overlooking everything. Why don't you go home and sober up and come back tomorrow?"

Well, he don't come back tomorrow.

So the captain tells the second mate, Haines, "You have chief mate's license?"

Haines says, "I only got second mate."

Well, the third mate, Shepherd, who got beat out of the second mate job, *he's* got a chief mate's license. So they promote him from third to first.

Now the captain says, "I gotta fire him!"—the chief mate. So the captain takes the second mate and goes to the hotel room, knocks on the door, and Haines tells me later, the wife answers the door, she says, "Yeah, he's on a drunk again." Haines says she was so fucking ugly he doesn't blame him for drinking. Captain fires him right there.

We're getting ready, they're loading ammo, and I'm standing watch and working out on deck, we turn around and who do they send back? Belew! He got fired the first time! He had problems with everybody. Now we got him *again*. I'm on the 4 to 8, he's on the 8 to 12, and we got these guys out of Charleston. They were nice guys, but they were seamen by no stretch of the imagination; they were making a lot more money doing this than they could in Charleston.

We're getting ready to sign to go foreign, and chief mate Shepherd calls me up there and says, "Where's your overtime sheets for this coastwise from Wilmington to Sunny Point?"

I says, "I gave them to the chief mate."

"You didn't get them back?"

"No."

He says, "You made like a million hours overtime here! You had to work 24 hours a day, and I understand you were gone for some of that for the hearing."

I says, "I submitted it. I don't know what happened to it."

He says, "Well, I'm gonna pay you, but I don't see how the fuck you can—you know, one day was like 26 *hours* you had overtime, you only got 24 hours in a *day*! I'm gonna pay you all this, but I don't know . . . ."

I says, "I don't know, either, mate. I mean, I submitted it, I worked it. Gangway watch, I was up 24 hours."

He says, "You never slept!"

"That's right."

So he paid me, and we signed on to go foreign. We had the usual alcoholics and drunks and shit, this crazy Belew's back. Gonna have to stab him, wouldn't wanna fistfight him.

We're out there securing. I got this watch partner, Andy, nice guy, just kind of fucked up. I got this old crazy ordinary from Charleston, Rufus.

We're making the trip, going down to Panama.

Haines is saying, "Oh, man, I wanna go back down there."

I says, "Man, you got fucked up down there last time. Don't do it again." I says, "You can't *constantly* keep getting all fucked up."

"Yeah, yeah, yeah, right."

We get down to Panama. We didn't have as much time. During the day I stayed on board, and at night I went up to The Blue Goose. I stayed there and came back and didn't get in trouble; just freaked out with one of the bimbos.

I worked overtime on the way over, making a few dollars.

We get to Subic Bay, Philippine Islands. Subic Bay, Philippines was kind of like a staging area. They didn't know where they needed ammo. There was really no such thing as an ammo dump in Vietnam. Any ammo that came into Vietnam got sent out as soon as it came in. It *left*. Trucks came in and picked it up and got it out of there. There was no such thing as a "dump."

When we first got to the Philippines, it was almost like repelling borders. You know, we had to put the hoses out and shit. Nobody had to spray them, but that was when they were really selling beer, and you had to lock everything down. Well, somebody left a porthole open in the purser's room. The Filipinos had crawled in there and stolen the fucking typewriter. It's the only thing they could get.

We had these brass plates in the deck for soundings, they're brass and they screw into the deck and then you unscrew them and you put the sounding rod to see how much water or fuel you had down there. They'd stand there and talk to you, and as they stood there and talked to you, they were barefooted, they'd have their toes going, unscrewing it, fucking steal it later. It was all fucked up. Everybody's drunk.

This guy came on board, I'll never forget his name: Dex Lee Golden. He wanted an AB job. He was in the monkey house, that's what they called it, for American seamen in the Philippines that missed their ships.

He says, "Captain, I need a job."

Captain says, "Well, yeah, we could use an AB." I think we were short.

He turns around and says, "Captain, I need $100 to get my gear out."

Captain says, "I can advance you $100."

Well, he's out there bumming cigarettes, anything he can get, you know. He's gonna go ashore so he can get his gear and come back. He takes off, we never see him again. That was 1969.

Now, jump ahead about a year. I'm reading through the union magazine. One of the columns in there, *Notices to Mariners*: "Dex Lee Golden, please contact your mother, Mobile, Alabama. I'm three-fourths dead, been trying to contact you." He's probably still over there, laid up with some bimbo.

From the Philippines we went to Quy Nhon, South Vietnam. We had this one wiper, he was giving shit to Haines all the time, and Haines was, "I'm gonna fire on that guy," and I'm holding him off, you know, cuz we just got off those Coast Guard hearings.

Haines and I were going ashore. There was this American that had this bar there. Chuck Metzger. Most of the Americans were going there. He *lived* there. We had to sneak in. Where the launch would let us out, you had to walk around to get to what we called Gonorrhea Gulch, and when you got to the gate to go to into Quy Nhon, they had a strip out there—Gonorrhea Gulch—a bunch of bars and whorehouses, little hole-in-the-wall joints. Now, technically, you couldn't get outside that gate. The GIs wouldn't let you out. But they knew we were getting around. Finally, the GIs gave up, and they'd just tell us to get in the truck, and once we got in the truck, we could get out. Or the Vietnamese would pick us up and take us across the harbor.

Captain was always screaming about there wasn't enough security. So he puts the Army patrol boats that were coming around.

So the Army guy says, "You want security? We'll give you fucking security."

Cuz we were sneaking onto boats to go ashore, right?

Next morning, I'm on watch, I was on 8 to 4 that day. Here comes the garbage boat. They grab that one, punch him out, fuck him up. He's all, "You tell captain. You tell him we garbage." Vietnamese, you know: "We garbage boat. We garbage boat." About that time they stopped another bumboat coming out. Here's the chief mate coming back late, you know, where he'd been ashore all night getting fucked up. I'm standing there by the gangway, I can see the mate, and I can see the Army's got him, they got the bumboat.

Captain says, "Is that the chief mate on there?"

I says, "Looks like him, captain. I'm not sure, though."

"*Goddamn.*"

And that's the way this went.

We used to get out that way, me and Haines, and we end up at

Chuck Metzger's. Just about every fucking night we were in there. He turned around, and that one wiper, he's all gassed up. Well, Haines fires on the wiper, *boom*. The wiper falls back. They were on the side of the bar, it was only about a half bar, and then there was a table there. But the bar was just kind of built up and out, and there was a cooler back there with some grill work. The wiper falls back and hits his head on that.

I says, "Aw, fuck, you killed him."

"Whadya mean I killed him?"

He's laying there, eyes rolling.

"I think he's gonna fucking die here."

"Whadya mean? He ain't gonna die."

I says, "Well, we can't drink here anymore."

We get outta there.

We're walking down the street. Some Vietnamese, middle-aged guy, is fucking with Haines. He's trying to sell us his sister, his daughter, something; he's trying to make a living, you know.

I says, "Naw, we don't want any. No, partner."

Haines picks him up and throws him through a fucking door there, an old abandoned building.

I says, "Aw, fuck, you're gonna get us in more fucking trouble."

"Aw, whadya talking about, don't worry about it."

We end up at the Hollywood Bar, running out of money. This Vietnamese broad's showing she's got milk in her tit, she's pushing on it, showing us. I'm fucking with her.

Anyway, we had enough money left, and we didn't have to be back. We were on days, and then we had 4 to midnight. So even if we went back, we wouldn't have to go to work until four o'clock the next afternoon.

Haines is in worse shape than I am, so I counted the money.

I says, "Let me have your money."

Basically, we had enough money for one girl and one room. He's all fucked up, so I give him the girl. I figure I'll just go up there and go to sleep.

They had some problem that night. Everybody was screaming

and yelling in the street. The VC were coming, or something. I go get Haines.

"Come on, man, get up! We gotta get the fuck outta here!"

"Where we gonna go?"

I says, "I dunno, but we're not staying here."

Instead of going down, we go up. We're going *upstairs*. So now there's a bunch of Vietnamese asleep. We're walking over these Vietnamese, and we're trying to see out in the street, but they got these wood slats over the windows, so Haines is smashing through the wood to put his head out.

Nothing happened, though. We went back, went to sleep. Up in the morning, back to the ship, stand our watches. We're gonna be there 2 weeks. This is still Quy Nhon.

That wiper was OK. He's grumbling, "The second mate hit me."

Anyway, I go back. Haines didn't go. I end up at the Hollywood Bar again, and there's this GI there, all fucked up. The MPs came. They're getting him outta there.

They says, "There's gonna be trouble here tonight."

I says, "Oh?" You know, VC are coming or something.

They says, "You can't stay here, but we can't arrest you, either. But you can't stay."

I says, "What am I gonna do?"

They says, "We'll take you over to Meechow's."

I says, "Where's Meechow's?"

"She owns a whorehouse over here. We figure she's VC, but we can't catch her." You know, *everybody* was VC, I mean, whoever happened to be there, that's who they were, c'mon. You know, the VC are in charge.

Went over to Meechow's, and they hit the horn. Here comes this woman out.

MP tells me, "Here, just give her this money. Don't give her any more."

I says, "OK."

Go in back, it's all dark. Go into this big room where people are sleeping.

She tells me, "Pick a girl."

Well, there's no light on, I can't really see, so I says, "Oh, fuck this," I just turn the light on.

Broads are sleeping all over the fucking place, two in a bed. I pull the curtain back on one bed, and there's a broad sleeping, so I just kick the bed.

"Hi, honey, it's me!"

I crawl into bed with her. I leave the light on. So I hear this scream about the lights. I can see they've got to have all the lights off. So somebody gets up and turns the lights off. I'm freaking out with her, but I gotta take a piss, so I'm trying to find my way around in the dark. I find the light switch, turn it on. I'm out in the alleyway, taking a piss, and here somebody's screaming again. They turn the light out on me. So I get back in and turn the light on again. More screaming.

Dumb motherfuckers.

I get outta there in the morning, I go back to the ship, I'm all scrubby and shit.

Haines says, "Hey! You went ashore without me!"

I says, "I just went in."

"Well, we're going back!"

I go in again by myself and ended up at the Peace Hotel. It was the UN Hotel at the time. I acquire some girl, or she acquires me. We're in the lobby, trying to get the room, and this one American comes by, all scruffy.

I says, "Goddamn, man."

"Oh, man," he says, "I did a year and half in the bush."

I says, "You look like you did a year and a half in a garbage can."

We end up in a fight. I insulted him, or he insulted me, or we insulted each other. We were both breathing. That was enough to fucking get it going.

I found out later he had married a Vietnamese girl and was living at the Peace Hotel.

We're fistfighting. I finally get the better of him. I knock him down, and they had these big fucking oriental elephant statues.

I says, "I'll fix you!"

I pick up the elephant like I'm gonna hit him with it, but I fall back with it. I go *backwards* with it. He's on top of me now. *Boom*. We're punching each other. *Boom*. I finally get the best of him. I get 'im in a chokehold. *Boom*. Hittin' 'im in the face. *Boom*.

Next thing I hear, these two GIs are coming. "*Hey, what's going on?*"

So I figure they're gonna help *me*, right? Bu they're his *buddies*. They got pistols, .45s. I'm holding on, trying to fend the one off, the other one's hitting me on top of the head with the butt end of the .45. I can hear *GONG* inside my head, like a fucking bell—*GONG*—but I'm fucked up, I'm gone, I'm steaming.

I'm thinking: I'm fighting this one off, and I got this one, but I can't—*fuck*, I gotta let go of *somebody*, and I'm not gonna do it.

After about the third fucking *GONG* I bit this guy on top of his head. He screamed like a wounded banshee. I let him go, and I get into a corner. Now I'm gonna have to fight all three.

I don't care.

They're saying, "Wait a minute! Wait a minute!"

"OK, OK."

You know, we're OK now.

They're saying, "What the fuck you doing with him?"

I says, "I didn't do anything."

"This is our friend."

I says, "Fuck it. You put them pistols away, I'll fight all three of you."

"No, no, no."

Now the hotel people are coming over. Fucking give them some money for the elephant I broke.

The girl grabs me to go up to the hotel room. So we go up there. Literally, I passed out. My fucking head. Get up in the morning. She smells like 10 gallons of get away, stay away, and don't come any closer. I says, ah, man, I'm all sweaty and beat up, my fucking head's throbbing.

She says, "You come back to village with me."

I says, "I'm not going back to the village with you, I'm getting back to the ship."

So I go downstairs and I says, "I owe you any money?"

"No, no, you pay, you pay, it's OK, you come back, you come back."

"Well, thank you."

I get out there, and I still got money! I get a kid to take me back on a motor scooter, back to Gonorrhea Gulch. I says, fuck, I ain't got any cigarettes, I need something cold to drink, and my head's fucking throbbing. This one place is open in the morning, right near the railroad track. There was a gate, you crossed over the railroad track, and the Vietnamese weren't allowed to come over the railroad track, and once we went on the other side of the railroad track, we were on our own. This was about the only place that was open in the morning.

I'm hot, sweaty, dirty, bloody, fucked up. I go in there. Mama-san opened up already, and she got one hooker left over from the night before.

"Oh, I be number one for you."

I says, "Look, here's some money. Get me a pack of cigarettes, and get me a Coca-Cola or something cold." Comes back with the Coca-Cola, cigarettes—Salems. I remember that: Salems. Better than nothing—I'll smoke menthols.

I'm trying to smoke these cigarettes and trying to get my head together; mama-san sees the cuts in my head from the butt end of that pistol, right? Dried blood.

"Ewwwww." She's screaming and she points, tells the hooker.

Now that I think of it, I should have taken the cold can and put it on my head, I didn't think of it. I'm drinking and smoking a cigarette.

Mama-san disappears. She comes back, and the next thing I know, I feel this cold rag on my head, and boy, did that feel good. But I have cuts, and my head has bumps, I'm open, you know, we're talking nice gashes here.

She's putting this cold rag on.

I says, "Aw, man, does that feel good."

They're talking and that.

She's wiping it down.

And I'm smelling this . . . this is the *douche rag she used in the morning!*

I says, "You're gonna give me an infection!"

"No, no, no, no!"

They can't get an infection, they've been living in it for *thousands* of years; I *can* though!

I says: time to turn myself in. I'm going across that fucking railroad track.

They says, "You stay here."

I says, "No! I gotta get back."

I get back, and for some reason the launch wasn't ready, I couldn't get back. One of their little boats came by. Technically, you weren't supposed to come back on their boats, you had to come back on the launch.

I says, "Fuck this. I ain't waiting."

I get back, and I'm sitting on top there so they can see it's me and not somebody coming out.

I climb up the ladder.

Bosun's there, fucking old Charlie Matthews. He says, "*Goddamn!* What happened to *you*? You just aren't happy unless you go ashore and get all fucked up."

I says, "Yeah, I had a pretty good time."

I had to go on watch. I go in there and make the showers and the heads. I stood in that shower with the cold water. I gotta get rubbing alcohol or some peroxide or something and put it on my head. I get some clean clothes, get some coffee in me and whatever food we had left over from lunch, I had something, and 10 minutes to 1600 I turn to.

Here comes Haines. "What the fuck happened to *you*? You went ashore again and didn't tell me!"

"I got in a fight at the UN Hotel."

"You look like you got the worst end of it."

"Well, I was fighting three of them. They beat me with the butt end of a .45."

"Three of 'em were beating on you, huh? We'll go back tonight and fix them."

I says, "*We* ain't going nowhere tonight. *You* do what *you* want. I'm going to sleep tonight at midnight when I'm off. I'm fucked up here. I'm too beat up."

The next day we take off.

Haines says, "Let's go back and get them fuckers."

I says, "I'm going ashore with you, but we're not going back and get them fuckers. I'm lucky I walked out of that one." I'm glad I didn't drop the elephant on *my* head.

He says, "We'll go back that way."

"OK."

We go back, and we're going from bar to bar again, and we end up in this little hole-in-the-wall, and they had the rooms upstairs, and we had enough money that time, so I says, "I get the girl tonight, you just go to sleep."

I'm up there with her freaking out, and the next thing I hear is a fucking explosion. I'm on my back, and plaster from the ceiling is falling and hitting me in the face. I'm spitting this out of my mouth.

I says, "What the fuck?"

She jumps up and runs to the balcony; she doesn't try for the door. She opens it, *naked*, and I'm naked, and she starts screaming out there. I don't know what she's screaming—I didn't know Vietnamese that well—but the only thing I was thinking was she was telling them where we were. I assume we're under attack. I get up, go to the balcony, and I push her. She goes two stories down. "Ahhhhhhhhhh."

Hey, sorry, honey. If you're still alive, you know, occupational hazard.

I get my pants on and I put my boots on and my T-shirt, I get everything else in my pockets. I ran and I got Haines in the next room.

He's like, "What the fuck's going on?"

I says, "We're outta here."

"How come?"

"We're outta here."

We take off and go back to Gonorrhea Gulch, spend the night there, and in the morning we go back to the ship.

We thought we were going back to the States, but they sent us to Nationalist China to pick up broken-down vehicles to take back to the States. Then we went back to Sasebo, Japan to pick up some worn out military vehicles. Their time was up. They couldn't sell them there or scrap them there, they'd take them back to the States for scrap or sale.

We turn around, we stop back in the Philippines. There's three of us in a room. There's Andy, myself, and the ordinary, this Rufus. Andy turned around, and he filled up his sea bag with beer. He's fucked up the whole time, and he just stayed fucked up, you know, just happy. I mean, he's just falling down in his bunk, just drinking *constantly*.

Anyway, I'm laying in the bunk one night after watch, and I'm trying to sleep, and the ordinary's above me, and Andy's over in the other bunk. I'm half asleep, and I hear Andy get up. I figure he's gonna run out in the passageway, use the head. I've got my arm hanging out.

Next thing I know, I hear pissing, and he's *pissing on my arm*!

I jump up. "Andy, what the fuck are you doing?"

He's all fucked up, puts it away, and he falls right back in his bunk.

I get up, go take a shower, change all my linen. Go to sleep. They call us 3:20, be up there 10 minutes to 4 for the four o'clock watch. So I get the first lookout. I go up. The ordinary leaves me at 5. I come back from my hour standby. I go up at 6 to relieve Andy. He's not saying anything, you know, he's, "Uhhhhh." He goes down for his hour standby, and by then it's seven o'clock. He's just sitting around down there. I come down to eat. I don't see Andy. I go back in the foc'sle to lay down.

Andy's sitting on his bunk.

I says, "How's it going?"

He says, "You know, Ronnie, I had a hell of a dream last night."

I says, "You weren't dreaming."

He says, "You serious? I got up and pissed on you?"

I says, "You fucking-A did, man."

He says, "Goddamn, I'm sorry, man. I never had a watch partner like you. You know, you never say anything, you just . . . you know." He says, "Man, I'll change your linen, I'll go get the linen."

I says, "I already took a shower, Andy. I changed my linen." I says, "Me and you are OK, but if you want to do me a favor, slow down on that fucking booze. And when I come in here and I take a shit in the middle of this floor, don't say nothing to me, either."

In Nationalist China one of the ordinaries got off on a medical, and we get this old man. We're talking 1969. He had to have been in his 70s. He was a freelance photographer/writer. He'd been in Nationalist China so long he was wearing his jacket inside out. He had one of those old cloth jackets with the insulation in its sleeves so it looked like it was padded, like the Chinese wear. He just turned it inside out. He had a beard, all scrubby. He turned himself in as a destitute American to the American Embassy. At the time they'd give you a couple dollars a day and something to eat if you stayed out of trouble, you know, they wouldn't put you in jail. Why he didn't go back to the States, bum a ticket to go back to the States, I don't know. Now they gotta get him out of the country. They says, "Just stick him on there. Get him back to the States. Get him the fuck out of here."

We had this Filipino kid, Ronny, he's on the 8 to 12 watch, me and Andy are on the 4 to 8, right, and he's in there with that fucking crazy Belew and this other guy named Balloo, little skinny white guy's drunk all the time, too.

So, they send this old man down to our ship. He goes up, sees the captain. He's got this fucking duffel bag on his back, he's carrying all his worldly possessions. He's got cameras and shit in there and his writing material, portable typewriter. I'm on the deck doing something, or ashore; I hear all this later from Andy.

Captain says, "OK. You're on the 4 to 8 watch. Just go down there, and they'll tell you what's going on."

This old man comes in the room. Andy's sitting on the bunk, probably drinking beer.

This old man says, "I'm the new ordinary."

Andy says, "Yeah, OK. My name's Andy, and I'm the AB."

He says, "Where's the other AB?"

Andy says, "He's ashore, or getting a blow job, or something. Who knows with him?"

So he comes over and he's got this bag with all his stuff in it. He throws it on my bunk. He says, "I'm an old man. I don't want to have to climb up to that top bunk. So I'll just take this bunk here."

Andy says, "That's Ronnie's bunk."

He says, "Yeah, but I'm an old man. I can't climb. You can't expect me to climb back and forth up there."

Andy says, "Can you fight?"

"No."

Andy says, "The guy that sleeps in that bunk can. You should just get your shit out of his bunk."

I don't know any of this yet. I come back from where I was. Well, he's in there. Rosencort is his name. I used to call him Rotten Crotch. Little filthy old man. He's in the top bunk. He starts going on and on and on about whatever he's doing.

I says, You know what? I ain't putting up with this for the rest of this trip. I tell Andy, "We should get rid of this fucking old nut."

I go get Ronny, the kid, "Come on, you're going on the 4 to 8."

I tell Rotten Crotch, "You just got transferred." I says, "You're going on the 8 to 12 with the drunks."

We're still in port.

The chief mate comes and says, "Did you switch the ordinaries?"

I says, "Yeah."

He says, "You don't have authority to just give somebody a change of watch like that."

I says, "The second mate said I could do it." I put it right off on Haines. "He said, you know, if I felt there was gonna be a problem, get rid of him. So I got rid of him."

About that time Haines happens by. "It's fine with me, yeah, OK."

So they says, "Alright, this time, but don't do it again."

I says, "OK."

So I stick that Rotten Crotch on the 8 to 12, and he's just totally useless. Well, that whole watch was. Matter of fact, the 8 to 12 third mate told me, "*We get all the fucking bums! They put all the bums on my watch!*"

I says, "I don't know how that happened."

Now they're really fucking drinking. Belew started to go crazy. I mean, just literally started to go crazy.

We get to Hawaii, and we're getting ready to dock, we're up on the bow, Haines, myself, and a couple of the other drinkers. I'm looking down on the dock.

Haines says, "You see any wild women down there we can get?"

I see these big fat Hawaiian women down there.

I says, "Hey, look at that, Mr. Haines. They're waiting for us."

He says, "Is that the best you can do?"

I says, "We're not ashore yet."

This crew turns out to be part of Rosencort's crew. He had gotten in touch with them somehow, and he turned around and went to U.S. Public Health, and they gave him a "Not Fit for Duty." So the company had to pay his way from Hawaii back to the States, give him unearned wages until he got "Fit for Duty." He gets off, right? Well, skinny Balloo, the little white guy that was all drugged up, he cut his finger or something. We were about 3 or 4 days in Pearl Harbor. He cuts his finger. He goes to Public Health, comes back "Not Fit for Duty." What a fucking operation. So we only got this big crazy black guy, this Belew, from 8 to 12, right?

So we're trying to secure the ship, we're getting ready to leave. One of the firemen—they stayed down in the engine room for the full 4 or 8 hours—he comes flying out of the engine room swearing to God that Indians are chasing him. He's drinking that rotten Filipino gin. He goes crazy, right? He runs out on deck yelling, "Indians are chasing me!"

Belew just starts beating him up.

We're out there all dirty and greasy. There's only so many of us left, you know. Charlie Matthews had gone home on medical, too. Yeah. Charlie decided he didn't need it anymore. He went home from Nationalist China. He went to a doctor. He was slick. And they promoted the day man to bosun. We're trying to get the fucking ship secured. Like four or five of us. There's nobody left.

And Belew's beating up on this fireman out on deck. Then he starts, "Don't nobody fuck with me!"

So I'm thinking, well, I'm gonna have to stab him. You know. I'm gonna have to stab him. It's the best I could do. And I told him: "That's it." I says, "I'm gonna cut you. I'm gonna stab you. Cuz I don't think I can whip you."

I don't know what he was smoking or what kind of drugs he was on or if he was just natural, because he had a history of being a nut. They said in New York he used to get all drunked up and that white girl from Ireland that he married, she'd throw him out. He'd climb up on light poles and start screaming and shit. He was an old enforcer for the union back in the '40s and '50s. Big, black, burly Jim Brown type. I'm not even gonna try to fight this guy.

Somebody goes to the old man about him beating this guy. The old man calls up the Department of Defense police, and they're coming up the gangway.

Captain says, "He's fired! I want him off the ship."

Belew says, "I gotta get my gear."

In the meantime, my watch partner Andy's drunk. Second mate Haines comes back drunk, too. I lock both of them in my foc'sle, I just put Haines in my bunk and I lock the door so nobody can get in there.

Now Belew's running all over the ship with these Department of Defense police chasing after him. "Get your butt in gear! We're getting you off the ship! You're fired! You gotta get off! The captain fired you!"

He's screaming, "I gotta get my gear!"

So he goes in his foc'sle and starts tearing it up.

The Department of Defense police go in there, grab him. "Get the fuck out of here!"

Now he wants to go in my foc'sle. "I gotta go in there and get my gear!"

I says, "You ain't got any gear in there." I'm not about to let him in there cuz I know Haines is in there passed out, and I gotta cover him. I gotta cover Andy, too. I says, "You ain't got nothing in there."

"Yeah, I do! Open the door!"

I'm thinking: I oughta just cut your fucking head off. I says, "I'm not opening that door."

Finally, they just converge on him. Three or four in front, three or four in back. You're gone, partner. Walking him down the gangway, he's screaming, "Ghost riders in the sky! Ghost riders in the sky!"

I go back, they're starting to secure the ship. Now they're looking for the second mate and Andy. I says, Aw, fuck. I sneak back around and I get in my room, open the door, wake them both up. "Get the fuck up, both of you. Get the fuck out of here, man."

"Whoa, what happened?" Andy's all gassed up.

"Just go up there, man, so they find you. We're leaving! They gotta know you're on board!"

They go up. We finally get secured. We're shorthanded. Everybody's drunk. "Hey, don't put that poor fireman off." He's all beat up, you know, laying in his bunk. He shoulda went to the doctor.

They start yelling for me from up on the bridge. "Come up here!" I go up there.

Captain says, "I need you as a witness to this, Belew going crazy, beating these people up."

I says, "Sure, captain, no problem whatsoever."

About that time Haines staggers in, all fucked up, says, "You can't log that man, captain!"

Captain says, "What the fuck is this? I'm not logging him, I'm getting a statement from him. Get out of here!"

"Oh. OK." Haines is all gassed up, he stumbles out of there, shaking his head.

We leave, what's left of us, we're going to San Francisco. It's just a fucking zoo.

The next day, I'm up on the bridge. Haines is sober, thanking me. "Covered me again, huh?"

I says, "Yeah, you cover me, I cover you. No problem."

He says, "I really appreciate you locking me in your room."

I says, "That's OK."

"Boy, captain's really pissed!"

Can't imagine why, right? Why would the old man be pissed?

So, the captain comes up, and the radio officer gets a message from Hawaii, from the Honolulu, Hawaii police department, where they found Belew washed up on a beach. How the fuck he got away, I don't know. To this day the only thing I can think of is the Department of Defense police must have said, "You're on government property. We're putting you out." Cuz the captain paid him off, gave him his papers, said, "You're out of here!" And they must have just got him to the gate and threw him out in the street and said, "You're off government property, we don't care about you." Because the Hawaiian police found him the next day washed up on the beach, passed out. He was declaring himself a destitute seaman.

He says, "The captain owes me money. They never paid me off, they *threw* me off."

The captain tells the radio operator, "You wire them back and tell him I don't owe him a *goddamned* thing! I paid him off! He's on his own!"

I laughed about that. Who knows, he might still be there.

Anyway, we got to San Francisco, and that fireman got off on a medical, he's all beat up. Had a few delusions there about Indians chasing him around the engine room. I think they put that off on too much heat down there. I don't think they mentioned the gin.

We fucked around there a little bit in San Francisco and Oakland. Didn't really get into anything. It's the States. I was really never happy in the States. Well, we're going down, gonna go through Panama and go around to the east coast. We get to the canal. They didn't even let us stop. Just took us right through, we were empty. We went up to this place in Rhode Island, and then we went down to New Jersey with some more vehicles. That's when Haines and I got off. He got off on vacation, I just quit.

He says, "Oh, man, whatever you do, stay in touch." He says, "I'm gonna get chief mate's license, and then I'll be captain. You'll go with me."

Oh, God. You know. Right.

He says, "I'll take you with me."

"Don't worry about it, Mr. Haines. Don't worry."

"You stay in touch with me."

I says, "OK."

Never saw him again.

Mallory likes it

Mallory Lykes. Ships were all named after the family. We used to put "Mallory Lykes it." You know? "Mallory Lykes Tom," "Mallory Lykes Dave." "Mallory Lykes it." Just fucking around.

I was in the hall, and they always said never let a crowded hall scare you. At the time, this Lykes Brothers was out of New Orleans. They had built some ships, but they weren't profitable enough, and they had nothing else to do, so they gave them to the government, because they'd gone to containerization to try to make money.

So they signed these over, and it was about the newest ship I was ever on. I couldn't believe it. Booms automatically winged in, hatches opened and closed like an accordion. Real nice.

The crew was what we called Lykes Brothers stiffs. They all sailed out of the Gulf, and they stayed with the Lykes. But I got on. Very authoritative people. Masters, Mates and Pilots union, and MEBA engineers, but very authoritative. MEBA: Marine Engineers Benefit Association, something like that.

This was supposed to be quick: load ammo at Sunny Point, go right to Saigon, drop the ammo off, and come back. They said you were lucky if you got 60 days out of it.

I says, "That's alright."

It turned out to be a 4-month trip.

We get to Vung Tau and go up to Cat Lai. Vung Tau's at the mouth of the river going up to Saigon, and Cat Lai was an anchoring area up near Saigon. We start discharging ammunition.

We turn around, we take the launch into Saigon, going in, getting fucked up.

They couldn't stand it, you know, they were all good Christian-ites,

Lyke-ites, and company-ites, and all those "isms" all rolled into one. *Hated* me.

Then we go up to Newport Docks, the new docks there in Saigon, and we discharge the rest of the ammunition. Right there at Newport, we go outside the gate.

There was a bar there, Bluey Browns. He's Australian. He had married a Vietnamese woman and had a kid or two. He opened this bar. I mean, it was a fucking shack with a cooler in it. There were about four or five of 'em outside the gate. Bluey was a junkie. He had shot up in his right hand, you know, mainlining heroin, which was cheap over there. His right hand had swelled up and got infected, had a bandage on it. He had constant problems with the American MPs. He had somehow managed to get a .45 Army automatic, and he'd strap it on behind the bar, but since his right hand was fucked up, he had it switched over like left handed, like out of the fucking movies.

I says, "Where's your head out here?"

"Just out through the back." And he says, "Say hello to the alligator."

I says, "Yeah, OK."

I walk through these curtains, and I see these boards, and I start walking. Then my eyes take a little bit to get adjusted to the dark. It's a swamp back there. He just piled the beer cans up, and then he put boards across the top and it got so high, and when you got to the end of the boards, you took a piss.

I'm thinking: what the fuck? You come back here drunk and just keep walking and they'd never find you again. I'm talking 40, 50 feet he had out there already. You just walk out there and take a piss. Don't walk on the boards, they'll never see you again.

We were empty and supposed to go back, and they sent us to Nationalist China to pick up some more vehicles to bring back. We got to Nationalist China, and we were getting ready to load the vehicles, and something happened in Quy Nhon, South Vietnam. They needed ammunition. They changed it around and they loaded us with ammo to take back to Vietnam. It was the same old Quy Nhon. Changed from the UN Hotel to the Peace Hotel. I went by and took a look.

Gonorrhea Gulch was the same. I think they had some different girls there, though. Other ones must've died from VD or TB or something.

We turned around and we dropped the ammo off. Went back to Saigon to load more vehicles. We actually went into Saigon, right across from the floating restaurant they had there. VC blew it up four or five times. We stayed there about a week.

That's the first time I got logged. We were in Saigon, I got fucked up one night and ended up with a bimbo at the Majestic Hotel. There were a couple of hotels in there. The Caravel was a whorehouse. That's where all the news commentators stayed, you know, the fucking rear echelon. I don't think they ever got anything right. At the time, they were making all the girls at the bars in Saigon "waitresses." There was no more "prostitution."

I ended up there overnight, and I got up late. I got back to the ship about 1 in the afternoon. I knew I was getting logged a day's pay.

I come back, the guy on the gangway says, "Man, you're back. Everybody was worried about you."

I says, "Well, I heard the captain was putting out a draw, so I came back." You know, what I say off the top of my head. So I go see the bosun.

Bosun says, "We thought something happened to you."

"It did. I passed out and I couldn't get up."

"Well, you're logged for the day."

I says, "Yeah, OK, I'll just take a shower and go back."

He says, "Yeah, go ahead. Show up tomorrow."

I made a point of getting back that night. I slept on board, and then the next day it was like I was gonna be fucking inquisitioned. I mean, Jesus Christ, "You missed a day," you know, "Oh, God, you're logged one day's pay."

I says, "OK." First time I was ever really logged.

We ended up in Cam Ranh Bay. Got stuck over there for a little over 2 months in the war zone. We were there discharging ammo, and there was really nothing there. It was supposedly the most secure area in Vietnam: Cam Ranh Bay. You could go to the seaman's club, or there was a village there, Suchin Village. It was off limits to everybody, but I managed to sneak in, knowing I'd have a good time, cuz the Vietnamese are very open about—you know, they were there to make money. They didn't care about sex.

I snuck in a couple nights. One night I snuck in, and I'm drinking, going from bar to bar, and I turned around and here are some South Korean troops, allied troops at the time fighting the VC. I'm walking in the middle of the village and run into this Korean. He spoke very little English, and he was fucked up, and I'm fucked up, but we're communicating because we both want another drink.

We're walking along, and somehow we got orientated towards his pistol, his .45. So we're walking along, and I says, "Let me see that," you know.

"Oh, here." Gives me the pistol.

So I pull the slide back, put one in the chamber. *Boom, boom, boom.*

He says, "That my gun!"

I says, "Here, you wanna try?"

He takes it, fires off a couple rounds. So we're wandering around shooting up the village, just out of our fucking minds.

And he's saying, "You come with me, you come with me."

We went to this whorehouse.

He says, "You meet my officer, my lieutenant."

I says, "OK."

So we get in there, and these South Koreans are sitting around. The Vietnamese girls are hanging on them, drinking beer and that.

"This is my lieutenant."

"Hi. How are you?"

We don't even know what the fuck we're doing, right. We're fucked up.

The lieutenant tells the Vietnamese girl, "Bring beer, beer, beer."

She says, "*You no pay, you no pay.*"

Boom, he punches her.

"Get my beer!"

"OK, OK." She goes off.

We get all fucked up there. I end up in a room where the girls lived. She locks me in the room cuz I was all fucked up. I wake up in the morning and I gotta get back to the ship. I get up with a hangover, I turn around, I'm almost breaking the door. I'm trying to pick the lock. They got me locked in, there's no lock on the inside. I says, "Who the fuck locked me in like this?"

Finally, they come and let me out.

I says, "I gotta go."

I have to go completely around the harbor to the piers. I'm walking down the road trying to hitchhike. Here come two GIs in a deuce and a half truck.

They says, "Hey, man, where you going?"

I says, "Trying to get over there." Pointing at the piers.

"Come on. Get in."

Jump in the back, and they let me out, right by the ship, and it's like seven thirty, and I gotta be there at 8. I'd go in the logbook, get fined for not being on time, and I know on board they've already checked my room and saw I wasn't in there to call me for the watch.

"He's out there fucking up again." *Hated* me. They fucking *hated* me. They were all establishment officers, you know, working for Lykes Brothers.

So I turn around, and I'm walking down there, hung over, and here's a guy, midnight to 8, standing there, and all of a sudden I come walking up, like 15 minutes to 8.

I says, "I'm here. I got ya."

He says, "What happened to *you*? They sent guys to get you. They couldn't find you. You weren't in your room." Like mother hens, squawking: "*You weren't in your room.*"

You know, hey, I'm a big boy now. I get up and put my pants on all by myself. I says, "Let me go get a cup of coffee. I'll be back and relieve you." I'm just all fucked up, same fucking clothes I slept in, all drunk. I get a cup of coffee, come back out. "OK, I got ya."

They all come looking, the officers, "Oh, you're here? You're here?"

I says, "Yeah, I'm here. I got it." You know. Is there a problem? Motherfuckers. About ten o'clock I get my coffee break. I run up to the room and take a shower and change clothes so I could function.

That day goes by, I'm off at four, and I says, "You know what? I ain't fucking with this anymore." I says, "I'm gonna sleep in tonight."

Next day I get up, and there's a guard tower at the end of the piers. Next morning I'm bright-eyed and bushy-tailed, had a decent night's sleep.

This U.S. Army GI comes down from the guard tower, comes up on the gangway, and says, "I couldn't get a cup of coffee from you, could I?"

I says, "Sure, not a problem." I says, "Stand by here a minute."

So I go and get him a cup of coffee, bring it out. We're starting to bullshit.

He says, "Man, thanks, I appreciate that. We don't have anything up there, it's just a shack up there." Really, it was just a pole coming up out of the end of the pier with a shack on top of it. It didn't look like it was supported in any way but this pole. We're talking 50 feet up in the air.

"Yeah," I says, "maybe tonight I'll go over to Suchin."

He says, "Yeah, but be careful." He says, "The other night, there was some Korean in there shooting up the town with his .45."

I says, "That was me."

He looked.

I says, "Yeah. I was in there the other night . . . ."

He says, "Goddamn."

I says, "Well, the Korean shot a few rounds, too." I says, "We just shot up in the air."

He says, "Jesus Christ, everybody heard about that. Fucking Koreans shooting the place up."

I says, "Yeah, fuck it," you know, what are you gonna do?

I went back in and ended up getting fucked up again, but this time I didn't get in any trouble. I ended up with one of the bimbos. It was a Sunday, and I didn't have to work on a Sunday, so I just didn't even bother going back, I just stayed with one of them hookers. Girl of my dreams.

Un-fucking-real.

It turned out to be a long trip, really. Bounced around over there, and I can't remember all of it.

We came back through the Panama Canal, and the canal had been on strike. The pilot's association there, the U.S. Army, ran the canal, and they were going on strike. And they were gonna show the U.S. Army. Well, they showed them alright. We were backed up about 2 or 3 days. Then they started moving out again. The pilot that came on board said, "Yeah, we showed them." It took the Army about 3 or 4 years to get even with them, but they did. At the time, you had to be a captain and sail on your captain's license to get a job down there. Three, four, five years later, all you had to have was a third mate's license to apply cuz they had taken away the subsidies and everything else.

I got off in Norfolk and was happy to go. That was about the end of that. They were happy to see me leave, and I was happy to go.

Green Ridge

This was a fun trip. I caught it at what we called a pier head jump. Somebody had quit. It was getting ready to sail, and we had this old captain on there, Kunopke. He'd actually started sailing before World War II. He was a real fucking trip. Just an old crazy violent Mobilian captain who sailed the South China seas. I heard later they finally had to retire him when he punched everybody out and wouldn't do what anybody said.

Coast Guard told him, "Don't bring that ship in."

He said, "Ah, fuck you, I'm gonna be home for Christmas."

Got fired.

But he was good to me.

Usual assortment of nuts. The bosun was just useless. I mean, he should have been a typical bosun—foreman—cuz he couldn't work. Just fucking useless.

It was a C3, not a C2. Had bigger rooms, and they were a little newer than the C2. This is Cargo 3, built by the government, and given to these companies.

We went down to Panama with a load of ammo to go to Thailand, and we go through the canal. We get down there, and they never signed me on. At the time you had to have a shipping commissioner sign you on.

So the captain says, "Whatever you do, stay ready. When we get to the canal," he says, "I'm gonna take you over to the shipping commissioner and get you signed on."

I could technically walk off any time. I could say, "Captain, fly me home." I says, "Sure, captain."

"Also," he says, "I owe you transportation from Charleston to the ship. I acknowledge I owe you that, but can you give me some time to pay you?"

I says, "Sure, captain, not a problem."

"Well, you're gonna be easy to get along with."

"I never argue about money." I'm here. Make the trip, you know, make a few dollars, then I'm going home.

Had some real screwballs on there. The ordinary seaman with me used to walk around with a bottle all the time. Jim Mock. Out of New York. And a Chinaman, Ty. He'd started sailing in the British Merchant Navy when they had a Hong Kong crew on board. He wasn't born in Shanghai, but that's what he told everybody just to simplify things, and he ended up in Hong Kong working on the British ships. He'd come to the States and started shipping again. There's another Chinese guy there, Old Man Lee. He used to walk around with a radio all the time, rubbing it like a little kid. Had a guy named Ed Crummel, useless, crazy, heavy-set guy, teeth missing. And we had an ordinary seaman, black Filipino, used to call him T.T.

We're going across, and there's no overtime, but T.T. used to wake up the chief mate in the morning, 7:20, cuz he was on day work, and ask for overtime. Chief mate said no every day. Twelve to four was me and Mock and Ty. And 8 to 12 was Old Man Lee, and Benny and Rudy. They were both Filipinos, good guys.

We're going across, and the old man used to come up and talk to me. I had my first motorcycle, a Triumph. I had a picture of it, showing the third mate I was on watch with.

Captain used to come up, and I showed him that, and he says, "You have a motorcycle?"

"Yeah, I do."

He says, "I always wanted to have one of them."

He used to just come up there and talk to me. We used to do a little work on the bridge, a little painting or cleaning or something. Or he'd come up and bullshit with me.

On the way across, they put night lunch out for the officers and the crew, cold cuts. Well, one night, Crummel got up, he got called at 3:20 to turn to at 0400. And for some reason, the old man got up and happened to go down to the officer's mess. Well, here's Crummel taking food out of the officer's night lunch, these cold cuts.

Captain says, "What are you doing?"

He says, "Well, captain, there's nothing to eat, and I was hungry."

Next day the captain comes up at four o'clock just as I'm getting off the wheel. He says, "I want you to do me a favor."

I says, "Yeah, captain, what do you need?"

"When you go on watch at midnight, I want you to check the officers night lunch, and the crew night lunch. If there's no night lunch in there, get me up."

"Get you up at midnight, captain?"

He says, "Yeah."

I says, "Can I ask why?"

And he explained why. He says, "I don't trust that fucking Crummel, sneaking around."

So I checked, and there was night lunch. In other words, Crummel couldn't find what he wanted in our night lunch, so he figured he'd go up and get the officer's night lunch. That's the way the guy was.

We stopped in the Philippines, and sailing those foreign voyages, according to the '36 Seaman's Act, they had to give you a draw on your pay, if you wanted it, like half of what you had coming to you, minus Social Security and taxes. They had to give you a draw. Well, when you go to a bunker port, only for fuel, they don't have to do that. But the old man, he's a good guy, he says, "I don't have to give you a draw, but anything you guys want, I'll give you."

I ended up getting a draw. I'm gonna go ashore and get fucked up and have a good time. I turn around, and everyone's getting loaded. We're only there like a matter of 12 or 15 hours, but we got it done.

Now we go to Sattahip, Thailand. It's a Sunday afternoon. And, technically, we were off until Monday, we were gonna have gangway watches or day work.

Kunopke called the entire deck department up there and says, "Look, we gotta paint the entire ship while we're here, the hull, everything." He says, "Everybody's gonna be on day work." But not *really*. What he was gonna do was, for $6 a day, we could have from Monday 'til Friday—$30—we'd be off. And they would hire the Thais to do the painting. Now the bosun and the day man, the day working AB, they couldn't get that deal because they needed them there to give out the paint and supervise. So one could have 3 days and the other one could have 2 days. So they agreed to that.

Well, I think we were making $440 a month plus overtime on weekends and holidays. The old guy's were saying, "Wow, that's too much money." You know, to lose. "I'd rather work."

Six dollars a day not to work, you're still making money, you know, right? I don't believe it.

So the captain says, "What do you want, Ron?"

I says, "Five days, captain."

"Sign here. $30."

"OK."

He says, "You want a draw?"

I says, "Yeah, captain."

"How much you want?"

"Would it be possible to get a hundred and a half?"

He says, "Yeah," you know, you're not signed on, you're not saying anything about the transportation. Here, it's *yours*.

I says, "Thank you, captain."

So me and Mock and Crummel are gonna go up to Bangkok, and we catch the bus. Talk about a Mexican bus ride. Mock's got a bottle of whiskey, right, he always had a bottle of whiskey. So he goes to take a vitamin pill and wash it down with the whiskey, and he coughs. One little Thai kid was looking at him over a back seat. When he coughs the vitamin pill pops out and hits the kid right in the head, and the kid's looking and the mother's looking. Not so much difference that can make, considering the babies and ducks and chickens and shit they had all over the fucking place.

We get off the bus, and we're right at the Mosquito Bar, which was kind of an American hangout in '71. Ed's just gonna go in there and get all fucked up. I think Mock was, too.

I says, You know what? I'm not hanging around with these guys. I just want to go exploring.

I get in a taxi, and I think a baht was like a nickel. You got like 20 baht for a dollar. I changed my money somewhere.

To make a long story short, I end up at this fucking Bronco Bar in Thailand. That's a good place to start. I go in there, and the girls start hanging on you right away. Well, I think it was $20 for the girl and the room. The hotel was next door. So I ended up freaking out with them one night. They used to put on little shows at the bar.

So, next day, I get up. I'm looking for something to eat and that, and the girl says, "Come on, come on."

So I go next door with her. I take a shower, but I got the same clothes. I turn around, go upstairs above the Bronco Bar, and this is where all the girls that didn't get any work stay, and they're all walking around naked, and there's a cat up there to keep the mice down.

They're asking me, "You want coffee? You coffee?"

Yeah, they're going to get me coffee. So I'm sitting up there reading, they got me an American newspaper, *Herald Tribune*. I'm sitting there reading the paper, all these hookers are walking around naked, and I thought I'd died and gone to heaven. It kind of reminded me: gee, if they could only see me now. In those schools I was at. Or any of them fucking super-straight structures I was in. With the fag priests.

Oh, God! What a fucking zoo!

One thing leads to another.

Evening comes, I'm back in the bar having something to eat, they give me some food. I'm back in the bar drinking. I end up with another girl. I never left the place. Monday morning we were on the bus, Monday night was there, Tuesday night was there, Wednesday night was there, Thursday during the day—now I'm broke. But every night we're doing the same thing. I'm staying with them up there. I'm having a good time just watching them walk around naked.

One of 'em says to me, "You like show?" Cuz I was going with a different girl every night.

I says, "Yeah."

"You want go show? American movie?"

"Sure, that's fine." I think there are like six or eight girls up there. I says, "Why don't we all go?"

"You take us all?"

"Sure."

It cost like a buck, you know what I mean? What was playing was Dustin Hoffman in *Little Big Man*. We get in there, and it's perfectly fucking quiet. There's like four girls on one side of me and four girls on the other side of me, and we're getting this cold corn in cups for like a nickel, you know, right. They're getting all this stuff, but it's costing me nothing, I mean, I'm spending *nothing* here. And I personally think it was kind of a funny movie, the clichés were there. But the girls are seeing all these people get killed, and they're crying, and they're taking this seriously.

Another funny thing, years later, after I meet a cop friend in Cleveland, I was talking to him in the late '70s, and he told me he was in Bangkok on R & R from the service in Vietnam. And this is another strange thing in life. One night, when I was staying there, two Americans came in to the Bronco Bar, and I didn't talk to them, and they didn't talk to me. They had a couple of drinks and left. And I'm looking . . . .

Years after that he says, "Yeah, I was in Thailand in '70."

I says, "You stopped in at the Bronco Bar?"

He says, "I was everywhere, me and another guy."

And I'm looking at him, and to this day, I think that was him. You know, strange how you cross paths. I mean, I can't prove it, but I think it was him. It's like I see these things in the corners of my mind.

Anyway, Thursday I'm out of money. I tell the girls I gotta go.

"You no go! You stay! You stay!"

I says, "I'm out of money. I'm broke."

"That's OK, you stay anyway. Free, free."

I says, "No free." They were real good about it.

It's something to do.

I had gone through the money, and I had enough to get back to the ship on the bus. I went back to the Mosquito Bar. That's where the bus came to Sattahip. We got off there. I couldn't find Ed or Jim, and I figured maybe I could borrow some money from them. They weren't there. The bus came. I get back on the bus, and it's about a 2 and a half hour ride. I get back early evening. I got the same clothes on I left with Monday morning. I'm in good shape, though, reasonably sober. Who's standing on the gangway but Kunopke!

He says, "What are you doing back? You don't have to be back here until Monday."

I says, "To be honest with you, captain, I'm broke."

"Well, how much you need?"

"$125."

"Come on up to the room. Sign. Just be back Monday, Ron."

I says, "OK. Thanks, captain."

Now I'm gonna go back up to Thailand, I'm gonna go to Bangkok. But I says, you know what? Fuck that bus ride again. Everybody was hanging around the Swan Lake Hotel, nearby. Cuz the other guys told me, hey, everybody's over at the Swan Lake. The ones that didn't take the time off or just wanted to go over, like the steward department had to be there, guys in the engine room had to be there, they were going over to Swan Lake on their off time.

So I get the taxi and go over there. And for two dollars you got this big pile of fucking shrimp with some kind of sauce on it. It was fucking great. I end up with this big fucking Thai girl.

She says, "You want to get a room for the night, me and you?"

I says, "Yeah, OK." I had a couple of drinks in me by then.

We get to the hotel room, and she says, "You know, your friends are here."

I says, "My friends?"

She says, "Ship. Same ship."

I says, "What room?"

She gives me the room number, and I'm thinking it's gotta be one of the guys. So, just for the hell of it, you know, I still had my clothes on, I says, "I'll be back in a minute."

I walk over to the room and knock on the door, and I hear Jim Mock's voice.

He says, "Come in."

I open up the door. Here he is, she's naked on the bed, he's at the foot of the bed, kneeling down, sucking her toes. There's the bottle of whiskey. He's just, "Come in." He started sucking her toes again when I open the door.

I walk in and I says, "How's it going, Jim? You got back from Bangkok, too."

He stops sucking her toes. He says, "Yeah, I got back. I ran out of money, and I came back, and I just got here yesterday. You want a drink?"

I says, "OK."

He starts sucking her toes again.

I get a drink. "I'm down here in a room."

"OK, I'll see you later."

"OK, Jim."

Unreal.

So we basically spent a weekend there, and it was Sunday I got out of there because I wanted to get back to the ship so Monday morning I'd be functional. I stayed with that big screwball there, the fucking monster. I ended up in a fistfight with her.

"Oh, you no go, you no go!"

You know, more abuse, more stress.

Me: "I gotta go."

I get back. Sunday, I'm OK, I'm just taking it easy on the ship.

While we were gone, two of the young engineers had rented a motorcycle and ended up driving themselves off a cliff. One of them was in the hospital. He had sprained both ankles and both wrists. The other one was all skinned up. He came back to the ship, and here Kunopke was making a fucking case for this guy's guitar. It looked like a little coffin.

I says, "What are you doing, captain?"

He says, "I gotta make a case for this guitar! Fucking kids today! Goddamn it, run themselves off a cliff!"

Every day something was happening.

Monday morning we all turn to at eight o'clock. Everybody's back. Mock's back, Crummel's back all screaming and fucking beet red from his drinking and blood pressure. And the fucking bosun, that grumbling, miserable prick. So the next thing you know, I mean, this is eight o'clock we turn to. We're waiting to get our jobs. The chief mate comes on and says, "We're gonna be here 'til at least Wednesday. Captain wants to see you guys."

Go back up.

Captain says, "We came up short on the money to pay for this. Now this is a little different," he says, "but if any of you guys want— $12 a day, Monday, Tuesday, and Wednesday. We're not gonna leave here until Thursday morning at the earliest. Any of you want to go?"

Now everybody's still debating the $12!

I says, "Three days? Sign me up, captain, sign me up."

I think Mock went for it, too. He was making less as ordinary, obviously, but he didn't care, he was fucking out of his mind. I think he and I were about the only ones that really took him up on the offer.

The captain says, "Boy, Ron, I'm glad you're here."

I says, "Yeah, captain, I'm glad I'm here, too."

We went back over to Swan Lake with all that money.

He says, "Come back if you need a draw."

Well, we made it. We came back Wednesday night, left Thursday.

I thought we were going back to the States; they said we're going to Singapore. We're gonna load asphalt in drums for Da Nang in Singapore. This is fucking great. I don't give a fuck what we're loading, you know, I'm going to Singapore, right, first time I've ever been there. We're trying to recuperate on our way up.

Ty was really funny. He had a big scar on his side. I saw him one day, cuz when you go down the passageway to take a shower, you come back with just cutoffs.

I says, "Damn, where'd you get that scar?"

He says, "Oh. I young. I bad boy." He'd have like one drink and he's fucked up.

I says, "Where'd you get that?"

"Hong Kong." They were getting paid *nothing*, you know, I'm talking back in the '30s or '40s. He said they knew they were going to this next port, and they needed sugar. So they're stealing sugar off the ship, and they're gonna smuggle it ashore and sell it. He was walking with the sugar from the ship. A cop on a bicycle stopped him on the side of the road. He got into a fight with the guy, the guy cut him with a knife. But he said he hit him, and he knocked him down a ravine, and he took off running.

He was kind of funny cuz he had married a Chinese girl and hadn't seen her in 20 years. She was in China. The commies took over, and he was smuggling money to her. He finally smuggled her out and got her to the States. But in the meantime, when he was living in San Francisco, he'd taken up with a Mexican girl that he said was crazy. They had a daughter, half Mexican, half Chinese. Well, he finally got the wife out of Hong Kong. He never married that Mexican girl, but the daughter stayed with him. The daughter was 21 years old. When his wife came over, the wife, his daughter, they said, "OK, we're family."

The wife didn't know any English. The daughter did. So he'd get letters from the wife and the daughter, but he couldn't read English. So, on the way up to Singapore, I walked in the foc'sle after watch, and he's sitting at the little desk we had in there. I see he's reading something. I see it's Chinese and then I see English, as I walk by.

I says, "Oh, that's nice, you got some mail, huh, Ty?"

"Yeah, yeah," he says. "I get mail from my wife and my daughter. But my wife no write or speak English, and my daughter no speak or write Chinese."

So I says, "Well, I hope everything's alright."

He says, "You do me favor?"

I says, "Yeah, what do you need?"

He says, "I read Chinese, my wife. You read English, my daughter."

I says, "You want me to read your daughter's letter?"

He says, "Please?"

"If you don't mind, I don't mind." So I start. It says, "Hi, Dad." You know, this and that, "Mom's OK."

"Oh yeah, yeah, yeah. Wife say she OK, daughter OK. Yeah, yeah. You go on."

I'm getting down there. She's getting married to an American guy: "We're engaged and we're gonna get married and everything's going along pretty good and we're gonna make sure you're here for the wedding." There's a little girl from Hong Kong that they adopted, she's fine.

"Yeah, yeah, yeah. That's what my wife said. OK."

I says, "That's about it." I says, "You need any help writing your daughter a letter, in English, I'll try to help you." I says, "I'm not Shakespeare, but I'll try to give you a hand."

"Oh, thank you, thank you."

I had a single bunk, he had the double bunk, and Mock was up top. And he starts bitching about Jim drinking. About a day later, before we got into Singapore, he says, "You help me write letter to my daughter's fiancé?"

I says, "Your daughter's fiancé? The American guy?"

He says, "Yeah."

I says, "Well, yeah, don't you think you ought to write to your daughter, not to the fiancé?"

He says, "I want to write fiancé. I tell him she have flat feet, maybe he no want her."

I says, "Whatever you want, Ty." I helped with the letter. Did my good deed for the day.

We get to Singapore. Singapore Customs says, "We won't search the ship, captain, if you let the guys come on and sell watches and booze, and the girls come on and prostitute themselves. We won't search the ship."

"Fine," captain says. He's in a bad spot, you know, cuz they're gonna find something wrong. They can *always* find something wrong.

So there's hookers all over the place, guys selling watches and booze. Everybody's fucked up. I was on gangway. The girls were just wandering all over. One of them had wandered up the inside ladder way and got up to the captain's deck. He had the door open, so she's gonna stick her head in and look for some business, right.

He jumps on her, picks her up bodily, and throws her down the fucking steps. They had a Singapore security cop on there, and he brings her over to me on the gangway.

He says, "Look what happened to her."

She's holding her arm, she's fucked up.

I says, "Occupational hazard."

"Captain do! Captain do!"

I says, "Oh, fuck." You know. Why him? I says, "You wait here." I go up the ladder. The captain's door is open. I knock.

He says, "Yeah?"

I says, "Excuse me, captain, it's Ron."

He says, "Yeah, Ron, what do you need?"

I says, "Captain, I kind of hate to bring this up, but one of the girls is down by the gangway with the Singapore security cop. She's swearing to God that you threw her down the steps."

He says, "Yeah, that's right."

I says, "Well, you know, she's hurt, captain, she's holding her elbow and she's crying."

He says, "I told them hookers they can't come up here! They can go on the main deck! I told them not to come up here! I don't want those hookers running all over this goddamn ship!"

I says, "I'll see what I can do, captain."

I go back down. It's kind of funny when you deal with Orientals, you know. You run over there for awhile, you kind of get that it don't make a whole lot of sense, but they understand it. I told the guy, "She's not allowed to go up there."

He says, "She didn't know."

I says, "That doesn't make any difference. She's not allowed to go up there."

"Oh. OK. But she hurt."

I says, "Wait a minute." I went and got her some bars of soap, matches, cigarettes, shit like that. I says, "Here you go. But you can't go up there no more."

"Oh, OK."

She wandered off.

It was fine.

We had this guy, retired Army, drunk all the time. He was kind of useless. Little short guy with glasses, heavy drinker. They had a spare room up there that he had the key to. So he's drunk, and he takes one of the girls in there, and he locks the fucking door and passes out. Well, now *she* can't get out. So she's beating on the door, screaming and yelling. The mate had to go in there, let her out.

Turn around, we're at a launch cuz there's islands there. Singapore itself is a bunch of islands. So we're gonna take the launch in. So me and Mock, and Benny and Rudy, the two Filipinos on the 12 to 4, they're good dudes, we're the only ones really going ashore, but we're going. I mean, we're hitting it, you know, we're fucking hitting it. Singapore, '71.

Me and Mock end up at this 7th Story Hotel. We're gonna get rooms. The last launch was ten o'clock or eleven o'clock; it's cheaper to get the hotel room than to catch the seven o'clock or seven thirty launch in the morning and get to the ship at 8 and just go to work. So we get to the 7th Story Hotel, and the place to go then was Boogey Street. It was a couple hundred yards long. They had closed it off to traffic, and it only opened at night. There were merchant seamen, hookers, female impersonators, fags, drunks of all types . . . an idiot's delight to be there.

And here we are. You got this egg foo stuff, which was scrambled eggs, shrimp, for like three Singapore dollars, which was one American at the time.

I says, "This is great."

The female impersonators used to hang around the men's bathroom. Shame, too: they looked better than the hookers.

We got back that first night to the hotel. They had a doorman, an Indian Sikh with his eye cut out. It was a British possession at one time, so he ended up there. He was the doorman, he let us in; we go and crash. Get up in the morning, back to the ship. We're doing this every day, we're there for like 10 days. Weekends we had off. We just kept the rooms at that hotel. He had a room and I had a room.

We stopped one night at the Paradise Bar at the Singapore waterfront. Allegedly, the writer Jack London drank there, when he shipped. Jack London: patron saint of merchant seamen. What a nut he was: drunk, suicidal, socialist, out of his fucking mind. And we get in there. It was like British style, all the bars and hotels, you know, the decent ones, anyway. We're in there drinking, and they had a little Chinaman behind the bar, you could barely see his head and shoulders. There were some Norwegians there. I was talking to this Chinese girl, or Malaysian, or whatever she was, having a beer. Next thing I know, the Norwegians are really aggravated. So the fucking Chinaman figured he's got some nuts on his hands. He's speaking broken English, and the Norwegians, back and forth.

I think this is going to go sideways.

Next thing I know, this little Chinaman is coming over the fucking bar swinging a blackjack. He hit this Norsky right in the head. *Boom.* You could see the fucking blood fly. He must have smacked him in the eye. *He* goes falling back into a table. Some Oriental was sitting there; *he* punches *him* in the fucking head for falling into the table. The Chinaman hits another one. *That* one flies over by me. I pick up a chair and throw it.

Here we go—the whole fucking place.

That's where I got my scar, the only scar I got, in my shoulder, with the broken beer bottle I caught it in my shoulder that night. I got out of there before the police came, and I never went back, obviously. Went back to the hotel, and the next morning went back to the ship. Threw the shirt away and poured some peroxide on it.

Go in again. I don't know when we're sleeping, I mean, we're going on like 3, 4 hours sleep a day.

In the evening we went back to the hotel. We made a point, we're just staying at the hotel that night. Just stay there, not get in any fucking trouble, pick up a bimbo, freak out with her all night, and go to the ship.

I don't know how we acquired 'em, but we acquired two girls. I had a Malaysian, and he had a Chinese. And in the 7th Story Hotel, the seventh story was a restaurant. It was a real clean place. We're up there, and they had these large windows open, you know, for the Singapore harbor. It looked like a picture, really, with the ships there, the sailboats, all the lights at night. Looked like a real nice picture.

So we're drinking, we're eating. There's a real menagerie up there. They had a guy with a patch on his eye, another young guy with some

American girl. Oh, it was a real fucking zoo. Nice place. I mean, clean, but . . . Singapore, 1971.

Anyway, I'm wearing cowboy boots, had jeans on and another shirt. It must have been eight o'clock at night. We're having a late dinner, sitting at the table. All of a sudden, I don't know, it was just like I kept thinking: if they could only see me now. I put my feet up on the window ledge, and I got this Malaysian hooker hanging on me, and I got this big quart of beer—idiot's delight.

I look over at Mock, and I says, "Hey, Jim."

He says, "What?"

"I wonder what the poor people are doing today?" It's the only thing I could think of. You know. I mean, hey, stop the world, I want to get off, just leave me here. I could stay there forever.

We stayed in that night with the girls.

We got up again in the morning, and I think we had to be at the launch area at seven o'clock. Here comes Benny and Rudy, the two Filipinos. They'd been out. They get there the same time we get there. We're there about 15, 20 minutes early, waiting for the launch. Benny and Rudy had just come in, got a hotel room for the night, and they were going back. And we're waiting, and waiting, and waiting, no fucking launch, right. Eight o'clock comes, no fucking launch.

I says, "Maybe we oughta chip in here, get a launch and go back, and the company will pay."

From where we are, they want something like $100, some ridiculous amount of fucking money. So it must have been about eight thirty.

Jim says, "I'm going back to the hotel. They don't have the launch here."

Which, technically, it is their fault, it's not ours. We're *there*. There's no launch to take us *back*.

So Benny and Rudy says, "Yeah, we're gonna go back to our hotel."

I says, "OK, we're gonna go back to ours."

They get a taxi before we do. They get the first taxi, and they're gone. We get in a taxi, and we leave. Next launch isn't 'til four o'clock in the afternoon. So we come back to the hotel.

They says, "You're back again?"

"Yeah, don't worry about it. Wake me up at three o'clock." I go lay down, I was out like a fucking light.

Phone rings, three o'clock, I get up, throw some water on my face.

I go tell Jim, "I'm gonna catch that four o'clock launch."

He says, "I ain't going back for 1 hour."

I says, "OK." I go back. Here's the four o'clock launch.

Chief mate's down on the dock with the bosun.

I says, "Excuse me, mate, can I talk to you for a minute?"

He says, "Not now, Ron. I'll see you up in the office."

I says, "OK." So I go up there.

He comes up. "What happened?"

I says, "I was there this morning. Mock and I were there, and Rudy and Benny were there, too. We waited until eight thirty, there was no launch."

He says, "That can't be."

I says, "Jim and I left, and Benny and Rudy left."

He says, "That can't be."

I says, "Yes, it is, mate. That's what happened."

He says, "Benny and Rudy are here."

"Benny and Rudy *can't* be here."

"What do you mean they can't be here?"

"*They left before we did in a taxi.* They *can't* be here. We saw them leave. *I* saw them leave. There was no launch."

He says, "Well, they did get here late."

I says, "Mate, how? *How* did they get here? What 'late'? *Noon*? It's 45 minutes to get here!"

He says, "I'm gonna get them up here."

So Benny and Rudy come up.

He says, "What happened this morning?"

He never said anything to them cuz they got there late; as long as you got there, you were OK.

Benny and Rudy says, "We got to the pier. Jim and Ronnie were there before we got there. It was well before eight o'clock, it was 6:45, seven o'clock, something like that. We're waiting and waiting, eight o'clock, no launch. Eight thirty, no launch. So, you know, Jim and Ronnie said, 'We're going to the hotel.' We said, 'We're going to the hotel, too, there's no launch.'"

They get in the taxi, but they hadn't paid for their rooms for a week like we did. They paid overnight. They get in the taxi and leave, we get in our taxi and we leave.

But when they get in their taxi, Benny asks Rudy, "How much money you got?"

Rudy says, "I got nothing."

Benny says, "I got nothing, too."

They had no choice. They turned the taxi around.

They're sitting there about 15, 20 minutes, here comes a launch.

So the mate says, "Where's Mock?"

I says, "I don't know, mate, I don't know."

"What do you mean you don't know?"

I says, "I went back to the hotel. I didn't have any money, either," which was, you know, not quite the truth.

He says, "Well, OK this time. But that's close."

I says, "Yeah, I understand, mate, I understand." I don't think the old man would have done anything to me, anyway.

He says, "Go ahead and turn to."

The launch was leaving again at five thirty or something. We're supposed to work 'til 5. So I turn to for like a half hour or so.

Bosun says, "What are you even turning to for? I can't get any fucking work out of you now."

I says, "The mate told me to turn to, bos."

He was a miserable prick, anyway, that bosun says, "I don't need you for a half hour."

So I go back to the room, take a shower, change my clothes, and go down and wait for the launch, right?

Here's the mate coming by. "What the fuck you doing here *now*?"

It's not even five o'clock, you know.

And the only thing I could think of to say was, "I gotta go find Mock."

He thought about that for a second. "Oh, yeah, that's right, OK."

Who cared, you know?

So I shoot back in, go back to the hotel, and I see Jim's still there. I says, "We're covered, but," I explained what happened.

He says, "Benny and Rudy, they shoulda stayed gone!"

I says, "Well, it worked out."

That was a Friday night, and we had Saturday off. That was the night we're gonna go bounce around Singapore, because Saturday we want to go to this Raffles Hotel, a famous Sir Raffles, a British guy, had founded Singapore. So we're not gonna get all fucked up again, see, so we can go to Raffles Hotel, and all the dens of iniquity, of which there was tons.

Anyway, we're sitting in this one bar, and one of the girls says, "You wanna go see freaky show?"

I says, "How freaky?"

"All kind freaky."

I says, "Yeah, I'll go."

Mock says, "I guess I'll go, too."

We go there, and there's one guy and two broads, and they're blowing him, and he's jacking off, and they're freaking out with him and licking his asshole, and there's just all kinds of crazy shit, you could probably throw a German Shepherd in there, too. All of a sudden Mock gets up. The broad was laying on her back. He starts sucking the broad's toes and jacking off.

And I'm just thinking to myself: do I really need all this?

After that, we make a couple other bars, and we go back to the hotel. In the morning we get up, eat breakfast. We don't have to work Saturdays or Sundays. So we're gonna go to Raffles Hotel. We get to Raffles. We don't want rooms, we just want to go in to the bar and look at the souvenir stores.

We go in by the front desk, the bar's off to the left. There must have been 12 or 15 wicker tables with the big wicker chairs with the big wicker backs. Three of the walls were just one long cage with wild birds in there, parrots. It looked like someplace Sydney Greenstreet would meet Peter Lorre or Humphrey Bogart, you know what I mean?

We sat down and had a couple drinks. This is like noon.

There were shops in there. Jim was looking for these little snuff bottles, these old Chinese snuff bottles. In one store he found one he wanted, and he says, "Oh, these sell real good in the States."

I says, "Yeah, OK."

The guy had a jade turtle, he said it was from Red China, and it did look like it was. I'm not an expert on it, but I know that they got Indian jade, which is shiny and useless, but real jade looks like soap, you know, soapy green. I don't know what he wanted for it. I can't remember. But to this day, I regret not buying the thing, but . . . needed a drink and a bimbo.

We made the rounds that night, bouncing around. We gave up our rooms cuz we were supposed to leave that Monday. That big Indian Sikh would let us in. We'd give him some money cuz we'd wake him up, he's sleeping down there, "Uhhhhhhhhh." He'd come with the turban, knife in his belt, fucking eye slit open, you know. We'd give him some money, whatever we had. "Uhhhhhhhhh." He'd just grunt.

We said we gotta go now, the Singapore adventure's over. It was great, but it was a week of no sleep, or 3 or 4 hours a night. I don't care how young you are, it gets to you.

Now we're gonna take these barrels of asphalt to Da Nang. We get up there in about a week. Now we're all straightened out again, you know, put together. New adventure. Outside of Da Nang, you go through the gate. They were pretty lax by then, didn't bother you, you didn't have to go through security. They'd let you come back. Or they got tired of trying to stop us.

I had bought a bunch of these cheap, $5 watches. I bought them in the States, but it says some kind of brand name on there. I had four or five of them, and I figured if somebody stole it, I wasn't losing anything. If I had a bar bill, I could put it down for a $10 bar bill. Anyway, we're sitting there drinking outside the gate in Gonorrhea Gulch. At the time I had that Triumph. One of the Vietnamese kids says, "You want ride my bike?" He meant his motorcycle.

I says, "Yeah, sure." You know, give him a couple of bucks. We're riding along, somebody grabs my watch and takes off. It's 5 bucks. I don't care.

We get back, and mama-san says, "Oh, you lose watch, you lose watch! So sorry!"

Don't worry about it.

Next day I show up with another one.

"Oh!"

They couldn't believe it.

Anyway, they had an old teapot. The handle was fucked up, broken, wires holding it together, chipped and everything, little flower design, oriental.

Mock sees this. "Oh, man," he says, "antique!"

I says, "It's an old broken fucking teapot."

"Oh, no," he says, "it's an antique." Jim says to them, "How much you want for that?"

"Oh, no, no, no!"

"Come on, you gotta sell it to me!"

"Oh, no!"

"Yeah, you sell it to me!"

"No, no, no, another one, another one!"

"No, no, I want that one, I want that one!"

He thinks they're trying to keep him from getting it. They're beating him, right. This is a *valuable* antique. We're sitting there drinking and drinking. Finally, they agree to sell it to him, for whatever it was.

"Oh, I got a hell of a deal, man." He carries it back to the ship, drinking, right, we're both drinking. We get there, and he puts it on the table. He says, "Man, this thing's awful heavy."

He opens it up, they filled it with water, so he's carrying that water so it's even heavier.

Next day we're on day work. But he's looking at that thing.

"Oh, man, I got them. You know, this goes with my little snuff bottles. Oh, this is gonna be worth big money."

We go back that night. Here they got a brand new one. Same thing. You can go buy 'em down at the fucking store, they're mass produced. That was the end of that.

Then we started a riot. I think it was the night before we left. I can't remember who started it exactly, but Gonorrhea Gulch exploded.

It was one of those things that just starts pyramiding. And Jesus, I mean, we all took off, trying to get back across the railroad tracks. I guess somebody on the ship said we started it, or they started it, or who knows.

We got back to the ship at the dock, and you could look out there and see Gonorrhea Gulch, mass confusion, the Vietnamese police and MPs all over the place.

We got back, it was me and Mock and a couple of the other guys.

Here's Kunopke on the gangway. "This is no offense, but if the truth be known, I'm sure you guys had something to do with it."

I says, "I don't know, captain. Wasn't me."

Well, needless to say, we left there. Left the next day, stopped in Hawaii, picked up more fucking junk. There was even a fire truck on there that was smashed up some place. And now everybody's on each other's nerves, and T.T. and that Navy guy who's drunk all the time. Well, he turned around, and he was gassed up, and he was running around all day drinking. Finally, they got the best of him. Kunopke came down. I can't remember this guy's name.

Kunopke says, "Hey, Ronnie."

I says, "Yeah, captain."

He says, "Is so and so in there?" In my room, I was walking in my foc'sle.

I says, "No, captain. That's the 12 to 4."

He says, "I *know* it's the 12 to 4, but is he *in* there?"

I says, "No. He's 4 to 8, captain."

So they took all his booze away. Kunopke took his booze away.

After that, the captain pulled a raid looking for booze. I didn't have anything. Ty maybe had some of that Chinese whiskey. Mock always had a bottle. I mean, he fucking *always* had a bottle.

So Jim says, "Hey, Ron, the old man's liable to raid us."

I says, "Well, I ain't got anything, Jim."

He says, "Yeah, but I hid my bottle under Ty's bunk."

I says, "Alright." Cuz he figures he's not gonna look at Ty's, you know, he's gonna look at *mine, maybe* mine. *Maybe.* He knows he's gonna look in Jim's locker and bunk.

It must have been the next watch or something, Ty comes up to me and says, "I have to tell you something."

I says, "Yeah, Ty?"

He says, "Jim no fucking good."

I says, "What else is new?"

He says, "Look what I find." He found his bottle. "If captain find, he make me look bad. Captain fire me. He no fire Jim. He fire *me*."

I says, "Ty, I'll tell you what. You put the bottle in my bunk. Just hide it under my bunk."

"What?"

"Hide it under my bunk. Worse comes to worse, I'll take the blame."

"You sure? You sure?"

I says, "Yeah. Go ahead."

"OK. If you say OK, I do. But I don't want to get you in trouble. I like you. You and me watch partners."

I says, "That's good, Ty, but go ahead and put it there."

"OK, OK." He liked me, but he didn't like me *that* much. He was willing to do it.

The watch after that, now we're talking another 12 hours or so, Jim comes to me and says, "*Fuck!* Something's wrong!"

I says, "What's that?"

"That fucking bottle I hid in Ty's bunk! It's gone!"

I says, "Is that what I saw Ty throwing over the side?"

He went white, cuz that was his only bottle, you know, right. Just bug-eyed.

I says, "No, man. I got it."

He says, "What? You took it out from underneath that—"

I says, "No. *Ty* found it. He came to me and said look what the fuck you did to him. I told him to go hide it in my bunk. I said if anybody got caught, I'd take the blame for it."

"Oh, man," he says, "can I have the bottle back?"

I says, "Yeah, Jim, you can have the bottle back."

"Do you want a drink?"

I said no.

One of the guys, retired Army, he'd get all drunked up. A lot of people can drink and wander around, but they can't handle the booze, you know, they're fucked up—instead of just sitting and getting out of the way, they've got to walk around. So this guy used to do that, walk around and call people names, and everybody kind of just overlooked him. So one day he happened to be coming by. I was talking to the chief mate about something, and he didn't see the chief mate, he just came walking by and saw me. He'd go, "Yeah, Ronnie, you dumb son of a bitch, you asshole."

I just kind of shook my head.

Chief mate says, "Did you hear that?"

I says, "Yeah, mate. He's a little under the weather."

Next thing I know, chief mate goes and tells the old man.

And this is the way this guy, Kunopke, was. He comes down, *grabs* the guy, bodily, says, "*Excuse* me."

Now this guy's shaking.

The old man says, "I understand you're running around calling people dumb son of a bitches."

"I dunno!" The guy's *shaking*.

"Well if I ever hear it again, you're in big fucking trouble!"

This guy's, "I didn't know! I didn't know!"

Kunopke pushed him. That's the way he was.

From Da Nang we go to Hawaii. We went to Hotel Street, and it wasn't what it used to be. It was pretty well civilized. They had some bars there and some girls, but we made it back to the ship. Didn't even make a 90-day trip. This was all within 90 days. We went to San Francisco and paid off. And I quit. I'm getting off.

Captain Kunopke says, "I'm sorry to see you go, Ron."

I says, "Well, I'm sorry to leave, captain, but I gotta go."

We worked that day, and then at two o'clock we went up to get paid off. I'm in line getting ready to get paid off.

I says, "Excuse me, captain." And somewhere along the line he had paid me my transportation. But I says, "Could I have my shot book, captain?" See, you'd get your shots in the States, and the doctor would sign your book. When you went on board the ship to make the foreign voyage, the captain would ask that all the shot books be collected so he could keep them.

He says, "You know, Ron, I'm glad you brought that up. I forgot all about it. I'll go down and get it."

I says, "OK, thank you."

He comes back up.

I says, "Thank you, captain."

He says, "I'm sorry you're not making the trip. I gotta make one more."

I says, "Captain, I'd like to stay, but, you know . . . ."

He's practically paying me off in fucking coins here, I'm *broke* from all the fucking money he gave me, cuz he gave me more than enough.

Mock was staying. And that T.T. and that Ed, they were staying.

I'm at the airport in San Francisco waiting to get a flight. Who shows up but Crummel?

I says, "What the fuck are you doing here?"

He says, "I'm going back to Baltimore."

"Weren't you gonna stay and make the trip?"

"Yeah, I was," he says. "I went up there to get paid off, and that fucking T.T. got in my way and we got into a fight and the captain fired both of us."

Mock stayed on to make the trip, and I never saw him again. I heard about Kunopke later. Two or three years after that, he was on a North Atlantic run, and I heard stories about it. It was a hell of a storm, they were bringing vehicles back from Germany. It was just before Christmas, and they ran into a hell of a storm, and the Navy, MSC, everybody was saying, "Captain, don't bring that ship in!"

Kunopke's raging. "Don't tell me what the fuck to do! I'm gonna be home by Christmas!"

I think he was having a few drinks, or he just totally lost it. One of the two. Or both. He brought that ship in, and they said the first ones to come on board were the Coast Guard, the Navy, MSC, the company officials. They went right to his office, and they all sat down, and they says, "Captain, don't you think it's time you retired?"

He looks around at everybody, and he says, "Yeah, maybe I better."

They says, "Yeah, captain. We just think you ought to retire."

That just saved everything.

You know, he was a nice guy. I mean, I got along with him. He was good to me. But that was a trip and a half. Every day was drama on that one. Every day.

Rainbow

The *S.S. Rainbow*, better known as the *S.S. Rustbow*, 12/01/71 to 3/06/72. This was Oswego Steamship Company. I actually caught it 11/19/71. We went to Tampa, and they paid us off coastwise. They brought back some military cargo, and we're going to pick up a load of chemical fertilizer in Tampa to take to India. It was a wreck of a ship, but they were known for this. They would buy older ships, run them into the ground, and sell them. Two brothers owned this. The Burger brothers. They had an office in Lake Success, New York; one little office with a secretary and two phones on the desk. Guys were telling me if you ever tried to get your unemployment, one would swear to God you worked for the other one and you could never get it.

Had an old crazy black bosun on there. From Honduras.

It was a wreck, but I needed the money and never been to India, so I stayed on. We got to Tampa and we loaded and I says, "Well," it was gonna be winter anyway and I figured I'd go to India and kill most of the winter.

We turned around and went by way of South Africa. We stopped in Kingston, Jamaica first. We got to go ashore, and it was wild, you know, everybody's hanging around with the girls. Next morning, the bosun came back, and he had a bottle in his back pocket. Nobody could get him up. So we go to let go without him, and he finally gets up and then he swears to God nobody called him. You know, the booze couldn't have had anything to do with it. But what happened with him was they let him keep the bosun job because he would submit his overtime for the trip, and they'd cheat him out of it. This was before I got on there; he was steady on there. The chief mate on there

123

would say, "Oh, bosun, I lost your overtime sheet, but don't worry. I got it all written down." He'd beat him out of about 50 hours, you know. The guy wouldn't say anything. So he could still have the bosun job, steady.

He was an idiot.

Anyway, we're getting ready to leave, and when you bring the anchor home, you engage it. Over the years you had to engage it and disengage it by turning a wheel that was inside a big steel wheel, you put a metal bar in it, and you can engage it and disengage it by forcing it up and down. It was a wedge in there. Well, somebody had lost the wedge, and over the years, it had opened up. This ship was built in the '40s. Now they had just a piece of steel that was terribly thin, way too thin.

The AB climbed up on there when we were leaving Kingston, and he tried to disengage it, and he fell and broke his wrist, so we had to put him off there.

We get out of there, short an AB. We go to South Africa, and we're gonna have bunkers: they're gonna take on fuel. So we get about 4 hours, we manage to go ashore and just wander around. Didn't get in any trouble.

Now we find out we're going to this Kandla in the Gulf of Kutch, about 300 miles north of Bombay on the west coast near the Pakistani border. And trust me, if they were gonna give the world an enema, this is where they'd put the tube. We called it the Gulf of Crotch. We got there, and there was nothing. *Nothing!* It was desolate, and outside the gate there was just a few little stores and lepers and goats.

We had this crew messman we picked up in Charleston named John. At the time you had a messman that would come and take your orders, and then he'd take them back to the galley and get the orders and bring them out to you. This guy'd walk up to you and salute you. "Let me take your order." Old black guy. With him, it got to the point where they kind of got together and kind of worried if he was going crazy, right. So they went up to the captain, the three delegates—the engine, deck, and steward.

They says, "Captain, you oughta talk to this guy. There's something wrong."

So the captain says, "Alright, bring," you know, Gustav Swenson, right, Stud Swenson. "Vat? Bring him up. Vat?"

Yeah.

John goes up there and the captain goes to stand up, you know, he comes in the room. John goes to salute him. The captain thought he was gonna hit him. "Vat? Vat?"

"John reporting, sir." Old wiry black guy. He had this record player with him. He's playing all this religious music.

The captain says, "Move him. No more work. Put him in the hospital with his record player, he can play his religious songs in there."

Well, they kind of let him go ashore, out of the hospital. He takes the record player and the records and he's going there and all the little kids, the leper kids and stuff came out. He's playing the religious stuff, and they liked that. He turns his back and they steal his records and his record player. So now he's signed to take the record player ashore and the records. Now he don't have them coming back in. Now Customs wants to fine him for losing it. So the old man's gotta go get him. They go there and they fine him 50 bucks or something. The captain pays it out of his pay, and they call for an Indian psychiatrist to come and talk to him.

The psychiatrist says, "He's no crazier than anybody else. But you probably want to send him home."

Captain flies him home, and he gets paid. That was '71.

Now you gotta jump ahead to about 1976. I'm in Charleston, shipping out. I'm sitting in one of the little restaurants there. It was kind of a watering hole, they served beer and food for the seamen. It's a hot day in Charleston, had to have been 98 degrees. One of the girls that hung around there comes running in.

She says, "You gotta see this. Come outside."

I walk outside.

Here's John. He's walking down the street with a big overcoat on. He's got a mouth organ wired around to his mouth from the back of his head. He's blowing that, and he's got a drum rigged up in front of him, and he's got an accordion. He's just walking down the street like that.

I says, "Jesus. He was messman on the ship."

You know, he really was crazy.

And somebody else in there says, "Of course he's crazy. He's in and out of the nuthouse." They says, "You were on the ship with him that time in India?"

I says, "Yeah. They flew him home."

He had just gotten out of a nuthouse, right? Well, he had his seaman's card, they shipped him out. His family was suing the company for driving him crazy cuz they had a piece of paper saying he was sane. I don't know what they got out of that.

I mean, this was another crew of—you know—different personalities.

We had a guy, inbred, from Charleston. The family had money, and they were inbred in the Charleston dynasty for so long, he was just retarded. Born that way, stayed that way. He was a wiper, worked in the engine room. The best thing he had to his name was a pair of Florsheim shoes. He never took them off. Even to take a shower, you have to walk down the passageway. He'd walk in his Florsheim shoes, go take a shower, get back in his Florsheim shoes, and walk back to his room. The most he ever did was walk down the pier. That's the only thing he did in India. Once. A real goof. He used to complain about the food, and he'd order three full houses, you know, he's eating three meals a day, drank all the coffee in the morning, too. Useless.

Had an engine cadet on there. His name was Greg. This was 1971. Jump ahead to 2001, I'm on the *Harry L. Martin*, and we're in the Mediterranean, and we were bringing up some ship stores.

The chief engineer says to me, "Man, Ron, this ship is a wreck."

I says, "Yeah, chief. Pay's nothing on here, ship's a wreck."

"The food's bad, too."

"Yeah."

He says, "You know, I was on a ship in 1971, the *Rainbow*."

I says, "What?"

He says, "The one time we had any decent food, the third cook, we used to call him Cheesburg—"

I says, "*Cheeseburger*."

"How did you know?"

"I was on there!"

He says, "What were you doing?"

I says, "I was AB on there."

"I was engine cadet on there."

"Well, I'm glad one of us advanced."

He says, "You were on there?"

I says, "Yeah."

We started naming names. So, you know, it's a small world.

But anyway, we get to India, and I took a ride on a camel. We went into town, you could go outside the gate and go a little further into town, which was nothing. And nothing to do. No girls. I gave a guy a couple of rupees, and he let me get on his camel and ride it around. The place was the asshole of the world. I mean, even the Indians knew that. They had packs of dogs on the dock, and everybody adopted a dog, and we'd give them our scraps of food.

But the chief steward, the electrician, and the bosun were all gay or pedophiles. They were always trying to put makes on the Indian kids. They wanted to give them bars of soap and shit like that. Finally, the Indian police got the bosun, and he had to bribe them.

It was just a miserable trip. I mean, everybody was just down each other's throats, and nothing to do.

We called it the *Rustbow*. We put paint on something, you put the paint on the rust, and it would just absorb into the rust and then fall off from the weight of it. That ship was so rusty, they had us out on deck—this took a lot of nerve—they were giving us sledge hammers to knock this rust off the deck. We were actually putting holes in the deck with the sledgehammer. It took a lot of nerve. It was something. The Indians, it was a national Indian holiday, wanted us to dress the ship and put the flags up and everything. They came down and told us, "Don't even bother." You know: "Look at this thing."

We finally got outta there.

We says, "Yeah, it's the last trip, and it's scrapped." Yeah, right.

Stopped in Durban on the way back for bunkers, and the captain, Gustav Swenson, better known to the crew as Stud Svenson, Super Viking. "Vat? I have good crew. Good crew, no drinkers."

The chief mate told him, "Just give them a chance, captain. They haven't had the chance yet."

We get to Durban. We got the chance. We all took off. I mean, we *all* took off.

I took off with the second mate, we ended up in some fucking club down in Durban. We got separated, and we're both just fucked up. I end up walking back—it must have been about six o'clock in the morning.

Next thing I know this truck pulls up with a cage in back of it. These two white coppers, South African police, pull up, and it kind of shocked me. I remember that. That I remember.

They says, "Where you going?"

I says, "I'm going back to the ship."

"Where's your ship?"

"I don't know. It was right here a minute ago."

They says, "Where's your ship at, man?"

I tell them where it is. "Does that sound familiar?"

"Yeah, we know where it's at. Come on, we'll give you a ride." This is a truck with a cage in the back of it. I thought they were dog catchers or something. I go to get in the cage. They says, "No, you ride up front with us here."

I says, "What are you guys, dog catchers?"

They says, "No, we're South African police. But you're white, you ride up here with us. That's for the blacks and Indians."

I says, "OK."

We're going back, and I'm starting to sober up now. I go in my pockets, and I have five rand left, and I says, "Here, you guys need this?"

They says, "Naw, we don't want your money, man. We do this all the time. We find merchant seamen."

I says, "Look, I don't know when I'll be back, and you guys can have a drink on me."

They says, "If you want, put it back in your pocket, or just throw it in the hat. You know, one of our hats."

I throw it in the hat.

They get me back to the ship. It was cheaper than a taxi. The taxi would have probably charged me 20 rand.

I says, "Well, hey, thanks a lot, guys." I'm sobering up now.

They says, "Can you do us a favor?"

"Yeah, what do you need?"

"Do you have any magazines, like *Playboy* or anything like that, you know, men's magazines we could have?" You couldn't have pornography in the country. *Playboy* was considered pornography. The Dutch Reformed Church ran the country.

I says, "We got some. They're kind of raggedy and old."

"We don't care."

"I'll go get them for you." I go on board, get them four or five men's magazines, whatever we had. I mean, it was nothing really hardcore. We're not talking *Hustler* here. I don't think we're even talking *Playboy*. It was these cheap-ass men's magazines, not even full nude.

I go back down the gangway to give 'em to 'em, and I hear this guy say, "Customs here."

I turn around, it's a Customs agent.

He says, "What have you got there?"

I says, "Magazines."

"You can't land those here in South Africa."

"They're for these guys, the police."

He says, "Oh. The police."

Here come the two South African coppers. They says, "He's with us." And the one says, "We asked him to get those magazines for us."

Customs guy says, "If that's the case, I won't even look at them."

So, it's alright. I get back, go to sleep. Next thing I know, we're at sea. I wake up. I look out the porthole, and we're at sea.

I says, "What the fuck?" You know. "Well, I guess I'll make the log book for this one." Missed the watch, missed the undocking. It's four o'clock in the afternoon. I go up on the wheel for my watch.

The second mate looks at me and says, "You look as bad as I feel."

I says, "What the fuck happened?"

He says, "I have no fucking idea."

I says, "I remember we were at that club."

"And we were gonna go with these girls, weren't we?"

"I have no fucking idea. The next thing I know I was walking down the street. The South African cops picked me up."

"You were lucky. It cost me 25 rand to get a taxi back here. I was lucky to find one."

"Man, oh, man, how'd you guys undock?"

He says, "They had to get guys out of the engine room. The deck department was all gassed up. They had three people up with the chief mate, the bosun, and somebody out of the engine room, and they had three guys on the stern."

That was it! That's all they could get! The engineers were all fucked up, they couldn't get anybody up to go down in the engine room. I guess Greg, that cadet at the time, they had him undocking.

I says, "I guess I'm making the logbook for this one."

He says, "I don't know. They're gonna have to log *everybody*."

So that morning, nobody says anything, I just go back to sleep. The next morning I go stand watch and, eight o'clock, I'm getting off, the chief mate comes up at seven thirty. I had the last wheel, 6 to 8. Chief mate comes up, and he's kind of spitting bricks.

I says, "Morning, mate."

He says, "How are you, Ron?"

"I'm fine now, mate, but I guess I'm signing the book, huh?"

"Well, Ron, I'll tell you what. Remember when the bosun come back late and missed the undocking in Kingston, Jamaica?"

"Yeah."

He says, "I hate him. That pervert, him and that electrician and that steward. I told the captain I wanted to log him. And the captain said, 'No, no,' you can't log him." He says, "You know what, Ron? If I can't log that bosun, I ain't logging you, either."

"OK."

We had the little club going in the morning there. The engineer and mate that was going on watch at three thirty in the morning, we'd go and have coffee in the crew mess. And, technically, the officers got their coffee in the officer's mess. Well, they'd come down there and have coffee with us. We had a week to go, and they're saying, "No more Tuesdays." Then it's Wednesday, and "No more Wednesdays," everybody's counting down. Everybody was quitting. Then in the mornings we'd get off at 8, and we'd go up on the flying bridge, we had a little club up in the flying bridge. We'd go up and get sun, cuz it was a beautiful run, coming back.

We got to New Orleans, and Gustav Swenson says, "Why did everybody quit my ship? Vat? Vat?" To Gustav Swenson, the idea of a cold drink was a 7 Up.

We couldn't wait to get back. We went to New Orleans to load some kind of military cargo. And everybody just quit. I mean, the engineers were quitting—everybody—"Fuck this, we don't need it." It was like a suitcase parade. Guys are just piling off.

That was my first encounter with India and South Africa. South Africa, it wasn't that bad. It was white-ruled under the Dutch. The Dutch Reformed Church was running everything. You would assume—or from what you saw in the papers here in the States—that everybody else was suppressed, you know, they called it white supremacy. In reality, even the whites were suppressed, because you couldn't have any pornography. *Playboy* was considered pornography. But, at the same time, they had some kind of miracle cure down there. I never got any of it. It was very expensive, something like a vitamin pill, but it gave you energy and it was supposed to prolong your life. It was like a fountain of youth drug. It was barred in the States because it had just a little touch of opium or heroin in it. They wouldn't allow it into the States. But it was perfectly legal in South Africa. You couldn't have a *Playboy*, but you could have drugs. It was strange. It really was to that effect. But, I mean, they suppressed the whites as much as they did the blacks or the Indians. I mean, *everybody* lived under those rules. It wasn't the way that it was portrayed here in America. The whites got to vote and they didn't get to vote for a whole hell of a lot, cuz the Dutch Reformed Church ran the place. It was that simple. The British won the war, but the Dutch Afrikaans were the majority, and the majority ruled.

It wasn't that bad at all, really. It was very clean. I didn't have any problems with it. I liked it. You know, hey, if I ever see those cops again, I'll tell them thanks. Did me a favor.

Mormacglen

Back up to Sunny Point. Moore-McCormack Lines. First time I worked for them. Interesting trip. Summer of '72.

It was what they called an automated C3. The hatches were automated. You didn't have tarps to pull, but you had to wing the booms in and drop them down and bring them up. They were on their own winches. You didn't have to take them off and lead 'em to a hardhead. It was a winch. Used to be the niggerhead. Then they called it a gypsyhead. Or a Turkshead. Then everything got politically correct. Anyway, automated C3 is what they called them. McCormack had some of these, and they usually ran around to South America, but during the Vietnam War, as they ran these older ships all out, they couldn't run them anymore. They were falling apart. They would scrap them, and they would go to the companies that had been subsidized and say, "We need two of your ships." Moore-McCormack actually ran steady to South Africa and South America. They'd say, "Hey, we need your ships. We're subsidizing you. And we're gonna pay you x amount of dollars cuz you're under the subsidy program." They'd have to give 'em to 'em.

Captain on there was Joe Holland. He was an ex-stevedore, longshoreman, in New York, and he was an ex-prize fighter. He already had two or three lawsuits against the company for knocking out ABs. He hated able seamen. But the company always backed him up.

The watch partner I got was Jerry Tagger. He was 5 feet, laying or standing. I get him in my room, two guys in a room. Jerry was with his wife and his baby Jane in Savannah, and he had the only canary yellow mustang in Savannah. I understand his family had money, but it never rubbed off on him. You know, he just wasn't with the game.

Terry Crichton was another one. I don't know if he's dead or not. He probably should be. He gets on there as AB, another drinker.

We get loaded up with bombs, and we're gonna go to Vietnam, and we go through Panama. On the way over we stop in Subic Bay, Philippines. All the way over there, this Jerry Tagger's asking me, like Forrest Gump, "What do the girls charge for pussy in Subic Bay?" This is the guy who's married, you know, with his wife and his baby Jane. I understand she was 5 foot laying or standing, too.

We stop at Subic, not long. We went to Vung Tau at the mouth of the river going to Saigon to discharge. Vung Tau was almost like a resort area, in-country R & R for GIs, and it was probably the safest place in Vietnam.

We get there and take a launch in. I'm with Terry, used to call him Terrible Terry. Gassed up all the time, just every time you saw him he's drinking beer. I mean, he had a stock of beer, hidden, and when he would go up on the wheel, he would ask to go out for a cigarette out on the wing of the bridge. He had the beer cans hidden back there, but he wouldn't throw them over the side. So old man Holland found the empty beer cans up there. He comes in yelling, "That's it! Nobody's going out here anymore!"

Anyway, we go in there, and everybody acquires a girlfriend.

Terry says, "Oh, man, she's got a girlfriend for you."

Yeah, right.

We're gonna spend the night with the girls. We're drinking that rotten Vietnamese beer. These two girls are actually living together. We go over to their place. We turn around, and there's one room, one bunk's to the right, one bunk's to the left. There's a curtain in the middle, and then you got the mosquito netting, and then they got the fan there. But I got the fan on my side. And it's hot. Me and her are freaking out, and we pass out.

All of a sudden—you know how you think you gotta fart, and I thought I had to fart, the next thing I know—*plow!* A big, wet brown stain hits the bed, and I know what's coming next. All that beer.

I jump up, roll over top of her, I go into the mosquito netting, I hit this old fan, it's one of those old European-style fans with the metal blades, with the big openings. You could put your hand in the fucking thing. I knock the fan over, and I'm into that partition where Terry and his girlfriend are. I haven't pulled it down yet, but I'm stuck. I gotta find a bathroom.

And in the bathrooms over there, you stand up, you just try to aim for this hole.

She jumps up and starts screaming. She don't know what's going on. I had knocked the fan over. She jumps up, her big toe gets caught in the fan. *Bing!* There goes her nail, there's blood squirting.

"Bathroom! Bathroom!" She pulls me around the corner.

There's a square kind of concave in the deck, and you stand on these two foot rests and you squat and you gotta try to aim for the hole. I was trying to make a bouquet, you know, a figure eight out of it. You could forget that. It was just *shooting* out! And I'm looking . . . . No toilet paper! I'm squatting there yelling, "Paper! Paper!"

She comes back with cut up newspaper. You could sell a three-legged horse in Vietnam before you could give a roll of toilet paper away. They just didn't use it. I had this cut up paper. So I'm taking gobs of it. I'm trying to wipe and throw it, and I'm trying to aim for the hole. She's got a fucking stick, she's trying to take it with the stick and shove it into the hole.

And Terry, he don't know what's going on, he thought we got jumped or something. He's all fucked up. Another eventful night there. More stress. As I remember, we got back to the ship. Took the launch back in the morning.

We're going back and forth, and there was a helicopter repair ship there. It had helicopters on board getting repaired. Had an American crew. They're kind of running their mouths one night. One of the black guys had taken one of these little Vietnamese kids and was walking around with her, you know, holding her hand and begging. Terry's all fucked up. So Terry figures he's got a nut.

Terry says, "What are you, pimping for the kid? What are you, an asshole or something?"

The guy says, "She's an orphan. I'm just taking the kid around, trying to get her a couple of pennies."

Terry says, "Yeah, you're trying to pimp her or something."

The guy takes an attitude about it. Well, Terry gets an attitude. Terry figures this guy couldn't fight. This guy could fight. Terry's fist-fighting with the guy, and the guy's getting the best of him.

Here come the police. "You must stop fighting. You must honor South Vietnamese law. You must—"

I says, "Tell them, don't tell me!"

Terry's yelling at me, "What are you waiting for? Aren't you gonna stab him?"

I says, "If you got a knife, *you* stab him! I'm keeping my knife in case I gotta stab somebody trying to kill me!"

That finally got broken up.

On our way back Terry says, "Man, what happened?"

I says, "You got shitty with the guy, and the guy got shitty with you, and the guy fucked you up." I says, "You wanted me to stab him."

"Oh, man, did I say that?"

"Yeah."

"What'd you do?"

I says, "I told you, 'Get your own fucking knife. I need my knife in case I gotta stab somebody so I can save myself.'"

Get back to the ship, and Terry's still just nursing a beer. We're hanging around there and hanging around there and going in every night and coming back.

One night in there, too, the kids used to come by and sell everything. They had little trays of shit they would sell. They had these little nametags, and they would put anything on there you wanted. You know, you could pin 'em on your chest or whatever. One of them said, "Kiss my ass."

I'm half in the bag. I says, "How much is that?"

"Thirty cents."

"Let me have that one."

So the next day on the ship, it was hot, and we're on day work. I take this nametag and stick it on the back of my baseball cap. But I'm hung over, and I'm not really navigating correctly. I'm not thinking, just kind of reacting. *I'm* on autopilot. I know what to do as an able seaman, I know what they want done, but it's like an automated thing. And everybody, the bosun, starts laughing at my tag on my cap. "Kiss My Ass." The chief mate sees it, and he starts laughing.

Turn around, the bosun says, "Ron, go up there and wire brush the air-conditioning unit on the starboard side on the officer's deck on the outboard side there."

I go up there, wire brush it a little, get the rust off of it. I'm sweating, you know, the booze is coming out of me. I turn the hat around cuz my eyes are getting full of chips and sweat. I mean, it's fucking *pouring* out of me. I turn it around so now it says "Kiss My Ass" in front.

Old man Holland, miserable prick, he comes out there and says something to me about the work or something, and to this day I don't know what he said.

I says, "Yeah, I'm just doing what the bosun told me to do"—figuring that's what he's asking me about. I don't think too much about it.

It wasn't 15 minutes later, here comes the bosun. I can see he's enraged.

"*What are you doing?*"

I says, "I'm doing what you wanted done."

He says, "I don't care about that. Was the old man up here?"

I says, "Yeah. He asked me something about this. I told him we're cleaning up the grating."

"The old man went to the mate and said you're insulting him. It's that fucking tag you got that says 'Kiss My Ass' on the front of your hat."

I says, "It's a joke. Everybody thought it was funny."

"The old man didn't think it was funny! Take that fucking thing off before you get us all in trouble! The old man's already knocked out two ABs, got lawsuits against this company for fistfighting."

I says, "OK."

It kind of went on like that, you know, back and forth.

Every time I see Jerry it's, "How much the girls charge?" He went in one day, and I was going in every day, and it was kind of like cubicles they had there if you picked out one girl, you went in there like

I was saying about The Blue Goose in Panama. He was gonna go with this girl. I heard he died later on; he was so overweight. Anyway, he picks this girl out, so I get a girl, and I go into the cubicle next to his. So I turn around, and I can't help it. I gotta lean over the top of the railing to see what he's doing, you know? And some things are better left unknown, unseen. Really. I mean, it was just gross. He was having sex with her, just straight normal missionary style, and it was obnoxious. You couldn't even see her. I says, Oh, why did I even look? It was like a bad memory, or a bad trip. Anyway, he gets through, I get through, and I says, "How much she charge you, Jerry?"

Like Forrest Gump, "Charge me five dollars. Pussy's cheap over here."

"I'm glad you're happy, Jerry."

Then he gets a letter from his wife that he's not writing her. That was our first port. Her version of it was you could mail a letter every day, you know, from sea. Now, you figure, how the fuck . . . ?

So he had to send a message, "I'm writing you every day, honey."

And he had brought these old clothes over to sell.

I says, "What are you doing with that?"

He says, like Forrest Gump, "I'm gonna sell these over here. These are some old clothes I got, and I'm gonna sell them."

I think he ended up leaving them on the dock, nobody wanted to buy 'em, he's just in his own world.

On the way back up we came through Panama, and everybody went ashore for a few drinks and blow jobs or whatever. I had this old second mate. He was a professional second mate, nice guy. He'd been on and off with Moore-McCormack for 25 years. The second mate always did the navigation back then. I was on the wheel one morning. The second mate comes flying out of the chart room and says, "Put it on hand steering!" We were on automatic.

I should say: they had little ashtrays if you wanted to smoke in the wheelhouse. They had a little holder and the ashtray may have been a quarter of an inch deep, those little tin things you see. Those were the ashtrays, and this second mate smoked, too. I would clean 'em up before the end of the watch. Well, maybe the second mate had a smoke, maybe I had one or two, and there were three or four of 'em up in front of the wheel house, just under the windows, you could wind the windows down. And we had a couple of the windows down.

Make a long story short, the ship had sat to the right, ships will do that, no matter how you navigate it and you got it on automatic. Between the sea and the wind, it can push you over. They call it 'set.' We had set far to the right. I mean, we're talking about running into an island here, you know? I mean, the second mate was shitting himself. When he came out, he was scared, I could see. *"Put it on hand steering! Come left!"*

I says, "Wheel's coming left." I says, "How much left do you want?"

He says, "Twenty left. Twenty left."

"Twenty left."

"Just keep it on."

"Steady twenty left."

Now the wind's changing. The wind blows these cigarette butts out of the ashtray. I happen to see it, but I'm hand steering, I can't pick it up. You could feel it, you know, you can feel the turn of the ship and the wind's changing.

Here comes Holland. "What's wrong?"

Second mate says, "Captain, I have never seen a ship set that far to the right. *Never.* I've been doing this 25 years. I'm a professional second mate. I've *never* seen this happen."

Everybody's going in the chart room. We're sitting too close to these islands cuz we're coming up to go to Savannah, Georgia. I'm sure we'd have seen the island before we hit it. It was daylight, but you never know. You might have run up on a reef before you got there. We're drawing a 32-foot draft.

Anyway, second mate says, "I'll get your course, Ron, I'll get your course. Take the rudder off. Steady whatever course you're on. Steady whatever course."

I steady up the course, I'm still hand steering.

He says, "I'll get you a course here."

I says, "OK."

He goes back in the chart room.

Now this is like a major thing that's happened here. We're, oh, Jesus, 30, 40 degrees off course cuz of the set. So you'd think Holland'd be happy—"Hey, look, I'm glad you caught it, mate"—you know. Let's do a double check on this, make sure these problems don't happen again. You should be happy this got caught.

Holland looks down and sees the cigarette butts on the deck, and he points down and he says, "If I see any more of this, there won't be any smoking on the bridge."

Yeah, in the entire scheme of things . . . .

I says, "Excuse me, captain, that was in the ashtray when we changed course. The wind blew it out."

"Don't let it happen again."

"Alright, captain."

You oughta be happy we're here and fucking changed course, you know what I mean? He's worried about those fucking cigarette butts.

We get back up there, and we all quit.

Bosun, nice guy, says, "Ron, stick around. We'll be going down to South America."

I says, "Bos', I gotta go."

Holland, later on, ran one aground. He finally did. Years later, I was up in New York on a ship, and I went over to see somebody I knew on another one, another Moore-McCormack. I see Holland running around out on deck. You don't see the captain running around out on deck, you know? You see the *chief mate* running around on deck with the cargo, not the captain.

I told the guy that I knew, "Is that Holland?"

He says, "Yeah."

"What's he doing running around on deck?"

"He's chief mate."

"Chief mate? After all these fucking years?"

"Yeah, he finally ran one aground."

I mean, he was notorious for this.

I says, "Where at?"

"Down in South America." He said that he blacked out, and he woke up with two black eyes. His version of it was that he was up on the bridge, blacked out, fell down, hit his head, he got two black eyes. That was the second mate's story, and the AB said he didn't see what happened. He didn't know what happened. But I think the real story that came out was Holland came up there fucking with the second mate, cuz he was notorious for trying to knock people out. Well, the second mate was a fistfighter, too. I think the second mate got the best of him, and while they're fistfighting the ship ran aground.

Let's worry about that cigarette butt, you know.

Fucking amazes me. The whole fucking world amazes me.

Pioneer Moon

Ah, here's a good one. *Pioneer Moon*, Unites States Lines Company. They called it a Mariner Two, break-bulk freighter, another load of ammunition at Sunny Point. That's when I met Terry Turk. He was licensed electrician on there. This was 21st of December in 1972 all the way into '73. We got off March 29, San Francisco, 1973.

Yeah, me and Terry, still fast friends. He was licensed electrician on there. We had Whitey Johnson, old man Whitey Johnson, he's a good old man. He started sailing as a kid on sailing ships. Fucking sailing since Christ was ordinary seaman on the Red Sea. Chief mate was—well, if he liked you, he liked you, if he didn't like you, he didn't like you. Who cares? I was on watch with a little Mexican guy, a little third mate. He was a nice guy. And the bosun was a real fucking nut. Mills. A fucking idiot. The captain used to call him Clark Gable.

Well, Clark Gable made a movie right after World War II called *Adventure*. There were only probably two movies that were ever made that were any decent about the Merchant Marine. One was *Action in the North Atlantic* with Humphrey Bogart, and the other one was *Adventure* with Clark Gable. While Humphrey Bogart was like on the east coast, Clark Gable was on the west coast. I've seen both of them, and they are pretty realistic. Clark Gable was the bosun. It was realistic, but it wasn't—I mean, Clark Gable's the last one on board the ship, you know, and he comes in yelling, "Alright, let the lines go fore and aft." The *captain* tells you to do that, the fucking *bosun* don't tell you that. The bosun's up on the bow. But anyway, the old man used to call him Clark Gable. *Hated* him. Just fucking hated him.

So anyway, I'm just doing my watches. They had some kind of cement composite covering on the wings of the bridge, and it was cracking, so they wanted it cleaned out, squared up, put some more of this shit in there—cuz the water had gotten down under it.

I says, "Yeah, whatever you want."

So old man Johnson comes up. The mate had already come up there and told me what he wanted done.

Old man Johnson comes up and says, "You know where to get that stuff, Ron?"

I says, "No, I don't, captain."

He says, "Go tell Clark Gable to get you some of that."

"OK, captain." I says, "Clark Gable?"

"Yeah, the bosun. I call him Clark Gable."

"Yeah, OK, captain." This was after that movie, you know. The old man didn't know I knew that, but I'd seen that movie.

He says, "And you tell him I said for *him* to bring it up here, not you."

I says, "OK, captain, whatever you want."

So I leave the bridge, and, technically, you always should have two people on the bridge in case something happens to one of them. I go down and I find the bosun.

He says, "What are you doing down here?"

"The old man sent me down."

"What did he send *you* down for?"

"That composite for the wings of the bridge, that cement stuff."

"How much you need?"

I says, "Well, I don't know. I got a square cut out of it. Three feet by three feet."

He says, "Come on with me. I'll give you the stuff, and you can take it up there."

"That's not what the old man said."

He says, "What?"

I says, "The old man said for me to tell *you* to bring it up. He don't want me to bring it up."

He used to bullshit, but he loved the job. He ain't about to go against the old man, you know, right.

So I go back up there, and the old man says, "Did you see him?"

I says, "Yeah, captain, he's gonna bring it up."

"Did you tell him I said to bring it up here, *him* to bring it up?" *Hated* him—you know.

I says, "Yes, I did, captain."

He says, "OK." And he left.

So the bosun came up. I did the job. I took the stuff down with me when I got relieved just to get it out of there. You could feel the tension there. The bosun's attitude was always: "*I'm* bosun, *I* do what I want, *I'm* knocking people off, *I'm* giving them time, *I* run this ship."

Yeah, right, gimme a break. Who cares?

Well, me and Terry are drinking all the time. We finally figured out that we both like to drink. The old man liked both of us. The officers drinking was a little different than the crew drinking. This ship happened to carry an electrician that was an officer. And Terry would have to eat with the officers. The old man didn't really tolerate much from the officers. He'd put a foot in their ass if he had a chance. But he was a good guy.

We get through Panama, get to Subic. By now me and Terry are buddying up.

We get there, and we start drinking. I didn't know that Terry started at noon. I mean, he's gassed up at five o'clock when we're gonna go *in*. I didn't know that cuz I hadn't taken a drink all day. We're in there, and seven o'clock, I'm just even getting a buzz, he's fucked up.

I says, "Goddamn. Let's go back to the ship."

He's walking along. These Navy guys are walking along, some are in civvies, some are in uniform. Terry's walking along, saluting them, saying, "Fuck you, soldier boy, fuck you!" Then he falls through the bushes; I gotta get him up out of the bushes.

We get back to the ship, and I says, "You gonna be alright, man?"

He's all out of it, "Yeah, yeah, yeah."

Next day we're out on day work again.

I says, "Man, what'd you—"

He says, "You want a beer?" He had coveralls on cuz he's a licensed electrician. He was on day work, and I'm doing some chipping or something.

I shake him off. I says, "When did you start drinking?"

He says, "About 10 years ago."

"No! *Yesterday.*"

"I had a couple at noon. Was I really saluting everybody?"

I says, "Yeah. Surprised you didn't get us both killed."

"So you want a beer?"

"Well. Yeah. OK."

He's got cans of beer in his coveralls.

We were there about a week waiting for orders, and now they're gonna send us back to Vung Tau with the ammunition, and they're gonna unload from barges. So we get there. It was just towards the end of the war. The Americans were pulling out.

We went up the river first to Cat Lai where you tie up. There's jungle on both sides of you. We had Vietnamese security and Vietnamese cargo longshoremen. The Vietnamese were coming around, I was out on deck as usual, and one of the Vietnamese soldiers kept bugging me, "You have appo? You have appo?"

What he wanted was an apple.

So I says, "Alright, partner, I'll get you an apple. OK, friend, I'll get it for you."

Cuz they don't have apple trees. It's kind of a forbidden fruit there, they never see the apple. And the apples we have are the ones we take from the States with us, which are probably 6 months old to begin with. I mean, you ever see an apple that's like cardboard inside? Well, that's what we have. I tried to explain that to him. He doesn't care.

I get him the apple.

"Oh, you number one, you number one. Me and you," you know. To them, number one is the best, number 10 is the worst. Now he's, "Another appo? Another appo?"

I says, "I'll tell you what partner—" I was saluting him, you know, and he's saluting me. I says, "You want another apple?" I says, "You salute everybody, you'll get an apple."

"Oh, I salute, I get?"

I says, "You know, wait a minute, gimme your hand." So I took his right hand and I got a pen and I wrote on the side of his hand "Fuck you." I says, "Salute like that."

"Oh, salute." So he's saluting people, and the side of his hand is saying, "Fuck you."

I says, "You get an apple, partner."

He was just bugging me to the point where any man—you gotta get away from it, you know? Well, everybody thought it was hilarious. He's saluting every American he sees, "Number one, number one, salute, appo, appo." "Fuck you," right? Everybody thought it was hilarious, the chief mate was even laughing about it.

Anyway, I don't know this, but a South Vietnamese *major* comes on board to inspect the unloading. Now the South Vietnamese are all saluting him, and this guy salutes this *major*. The major knew English. The yelling and screaming that went on. I'm surprised this guy didn't shit all over himself. The major was screaming and yelling: *"What an asshole you are! You dumb shit! You goof! I'll have you up in the fucking front lines! You'll be parachuting into Hanoi, you idiot!"*

That guy—he chased me for 3 days. "You do me number 10! You do me number 10!" I had to hide for 3 days.

One day we're out there. Next thing I know I hear this fucking explosion. I look off to my right and here's a South Vietnamese Army truck being blown up. They had a little firefight going on over there. Somebody fired an RPG at the ship in front of us. It went through number one cargo area, the top tier, went in one side and went through. They had unloaded the ammo. Went through the other side and kept going. Never detonated. If there was ammo in there, it would have detonated, we all woulda been history, and the South Vietnamese were shooting it out with them over there.

I says, "Motherfuckers! Get me killed yet."

We turn around, they say go back down river. They wanted to get the ships out of there. We went back and now they're unloading there. Well, they had a big fucking rock sitting there. They'd tie two of the barges up. Years ago they had a GI sitting there. Now they had a South Vietnamese standing there. They gave them concussion grenades. They used to give them to us, too, to kill divers. Every ship I went over there, we had GI security and they had concussion grenades, and if they felt there was a problem, they take one and throw it over the side. *Boom*, kill divers. Or they throw them over the side just for fun.

So this Vietnamese, he turns around, and they used to tell them, hey, you better use up all your ammo, don't be scared. Well, instead of him taking his concussion grenade and throwing it further away, he drops it right between the two barges. Blew holes in 'em, sunk them both with the ammo, went right down.

It didn't bother me and Terry much. We didn't care. We're empty, right. Everyone ignored us, figured we're going back to the States.

We're awaiting orders at the mouth of the river there, and we're going ashore, me and Terry. And right outside the gate, you could go pretty much where you wanted to go, but you had to be back the next day to go to work. You could go in to Vung Tau, or you could go right outside the gate there, and they had a strip there, bunch of little bars, barber shop, things like that.

I go into one bar, and here's this young Vietnamese girl. I started talking to her. The other girls were hooking, she wasn't. She had a postcard from the States, with a winter scene on it, and she was pointing to the snow on the postcard saying, "Snow." That's her name. She's pointing to the snow on the Christmas card. We started hitting it off. She didn't hook there. She didn't have to. Her mother and father owned that bar, and two more bars in Saigon.

The only thing I could envision was marrying her, missing the ship—me and Terry—and we could just stay drunk. I'm sure the parents would've appreciated that.

"Oh, here's your son-in-law, and that's his friend Terry. And they're gonna stay drunk here for awhile, but we're married."

"Oh, you're married. Everything's OK."

I figured we coulda stayed drunk 'til the end of the war. The commies woulda wanted us to go to work. We woulda had to leave.

You gotta jump ahead to '75 when the war was coming to an end and everybody was trying to leave Saigon. I was in the States watching television, and I swear I saw her at the airport in Saigon with a bag going to France, where she had a brother going to school.

That was strange, like a lot of other things, where I'm watching something on television, and I've been there or seen it, or later on, I'll end up there seeing it. It's just strange how that works out.

Very pretty girl. I shoulda married her. Shoulda stayed drunk. I stay drunk anyway.

Well, back in Vietnam, like I said, we were awaiting orders. All of a sudden Terry comes running up. "Hey, we're going to Cambodia!"

I says, "*Cambodia?* Americans aren't supposed to be there."

He says, "I don't know about that, but we're going to Cambodia. Get ready, we're gonna have a good time here."

OK.

So I thought we were gonna keep going up the Saigon River and go to Phnom Penh. But instead, they only had one deep water port, Kampong Saom. That was the port where two guys mutinied a merchant ship and took it there with the ammunition. Clyde McKay was the one guy. This must have been '69 or '70. The Cambodians arrested them and took them to Phnom Penh, and the American government just gave the ammo to the Cambodian government for *their* Army. The other guy turned around and went over to the American Embassy and turned himself in. They flew him back to federal court in America, and he testified that he had taken LSD 1,000 times and he was having a homosexual affair with McKay.

They said, "That sounds real good. You're getting 10 years in the federal penitentiary."

The other one was being held in custody by the Cambodians in Phnom Penh. He, in turn, took off with some GI that was a U.S. Army deserter. They hit the jungle, and I don't think either one of them has ever been seen since.

Anyway, that's where they want us to go, this Kampong Saom, only deep water port they got. We get over there to pick up a portable Army bridge. That's what they wanted out of there.

We get there, we're docking, and it's a real small dock. As a matter of fact, there's what we call a coaster, a small ship that just runs the coast bringing cargo back and forth, with the old weighted booms on it. A big concrete pier, no overhead cranes. You always had to use the ship's booms to get the cargo. When we docked, it was close. I mean, it was fucking close. We had to have been 400 feet long, right, and you're talking another 100, 150 feet, for this coaster. We're bow to stern, we're almost touching.

We no sooner get tied up, here comes a big white Mack truck down the road onto the long, concrete pier. It's got these big teak wood trees on there, cut, three of them, monsters, chained on.

"Goddamn," I says. "What the fuck?" I mean, it just was strange to see it. Here you got the jungle, and then you got this truck and this old coaster, and here we are. Nothing on the dock, no way of getting cargo on board.

The Cambodians get on this truck and take the chains off, and the next thing you know, here comes this fucking guy riding an Indian elephant, just like you see in the fucking circuses or the movies. And I'm looking at this. We just got through tying up the ship. This elephant's coming down the fucking dock there and gonna push these logs off the truck and roll them over to the coaster, the other ship there.

I says, "I don't believe this."

You could smell the elephant. You can smell them, they got their own distinct smell, certain bouquet. It's a pukey smell.

I says, "I don't believe this."

I get on the ship phone back there. I'm thinking Terry's down in the engine room. He answers the phone.

I says, "Terry, what are you doing?"

He says, "Nothing. What's up?"

"Come on up here, man. You off or something?"

"Yeah, I can get up there."

I says, "Get up here. You gotta see this. You're not gonna believe this."

He comes up there, sees the elephant, says, "I don't fucking believe this. It's an elephant."

The elephant's knocking these logs off the truck, rolling them over to the side of the coaster, stopping them with his trunk. They're putting the fucking runners on 'im. The ship is *straining*, that's how big these things are! And they're just putting them down in the hatch. I couldn't believe it!

Not 20 minutes later here comes the U.S. Army, but they're all in civilian clothes, cuz they're not supposed to be in Cambodia.

They says, "We're here and we're telling you: don't get in any trouble, because you're not supposed to be here, *we're* not supposed to be here." They had a couple of women with them that I guess were liaison Army, hee-hawing. "Hee-hee." Fucking State Department puke, you know. "Don't get in any trouble, and don't drink the water, and don't bang any of the whores."

"Yeah, OK, sure."

So they give us the little pep talk.

And they put these Cambodian security on there. One of the guys is blind in one eye. His eye's all fucked up. One had a carbine, .30 caliber Army carbine. The other one had an AK-47, and one had an M16. None of the ammo matched.

The one with the bad eye, he's got a fragmentary grenade, and he's holding it. I got gangway security. I'm kind of looking at him, and the Orientals smile when they're embarrassed, you know. This guy's embarrassed. I'm trying to see if the pin's out of this fucking thing.

The chief mate happens to walk by and says, "What's going on, Ron?"

I says, "You know, mate, I hate to cause any problems or anything, but this guy's got a fragmentary grenade here."

He says, "Yeah, they use them like they do concussion grenades. They throw them over the side of the ship for divers."

"Yeah, mate, but that's a *fragmentary* grenade. I can't see if the pin's out of it. He's holding the arm, holding it tight. If he doesn't hold it too tight, he lets it go, and he tries to put it back together, it's gonna explode and kill all of us."

He says, "You sure?"

I says, "If that pin's out, mate, somebody oughta take that thing away from him."

Mate goes over and looks and says, "Oh no, no, it's OK, he's got the pin in it."

I says, "Would you tell him to put that fucking thing away? He's making me nervous."

So he goes over to him.

There was a Frenchman leftover from when the French were there. He comes over.

I says, "Could you tell him to put that away?"

"Yeah, these fucking Cambodians. They're useless. We should have killed more of them. They're no fucking good. I can't get them to work, lazy fucks."

I says, "OK, friend."

So me and Terry are gonna go ashore. But we knew we couldn't get in any trouble. If you did, they couldn't do anything for you, cuz you weren't supposed to be there.

There was plenty of transportation, so to speak. There were these motorbikes with a wagon attached to the back. You got in the wagon, and they took you to town for practically nothing. They wanted American money, cuz that Cambodian money was worthless. So we're gonna go in and have a couple of drinks, socialize.

Nice brick road, going into town. You get in there, and it's just a big central park type of area, kind of European style, with the houses, stores, and hotels, but kind of dilapidated. Been a long time since the French left.

We end up in the hotel, and the only thing they had was hunks of ice they put in the beer to keep it cold. It was kind of rotten fucking beer we were drinking, too. We're going from place to place, changing money, and they're just taking our American money and giving us that monopoly money. We didn't know what the fuck we were getting. We didn't care, either. We had something to drink, and we could see they had women around.

So we get to this one place that's actually a whorehouse, and the Cambodian Army's there. They're just beating these girls with sticks. One girl looked like she got hit with a fucking machete.

I says, "Man, these people are rough."

I think a short time was $3, pick whichever one you wanted.

It was fucking insane.

So we go in there, did that, came back.

Next day they bring part of the portable Army bridge. I think we're there about 4 or 5 days. We go in again.

They says, "Better be careful, the Khmer Rouge are supposed to be around. There's something coming."

We didn't care. We're still in there drinking, just having a good time. It was pretty calm. You see a lot of military. Hookers are all over the place. I assume the French tried to fix it up, but the Cambodians around there didn't do anything with it. The electricity would go off at certain times.

I was in a room on the ship with one other guy. He had bought a radio at the PX in Subic Bay. We didn't close our porthole, and somebody, one of the Cambodians, while they were working the cargo, somebody knocked the screen out, went in there, and took the radio. But he was pretty cool about it. You know, "Well, hey, shit happens."

But another guy we had on there, I'll never forget this guy's name: Isadore Eckerman. Izzy. Izzy could barely walk. Izzy had some kind of big, fucking, all-around-the-world radio. Well, somebody got his radio. He's demanding the American Consul come, and I mean just crazy shit, you know, we're not even supposed to *be* there. Isadore Eckerman, you can figure that out.

I was on gangway. I always seem to be on gangway when a drama is unfolding.

This Cambodian that spoke English comes running up to me and says, "I want to kill whoever stole radio. I want to kill."

I says, "Why's that?"

"America help Cambodia. You Americans, you go back, you tell Americans Cambodians steal, and you no want help Cambodia anymore."

"Well," I says, "I promise I won't tell anybody, but if you gotta kill somebody here, just kill anybody."

"What?"

"Just kill anybody. Anybody will do, and I'll go to America, and I won't say a word."

"Kill everybody?"

I says, "Yeah. Kill 'em all. Just shoot 'em all. You're bound to get the one who stole the radio."

He's kind of looking at me, staring, kind of wandered off.

We were gonna leave the next day. So me and Terry go in again. We're trying to spend this monopoly money, we're giving it away. We turn around, on the way back, we're fucked up, and we still got some left. We just gave it all to the little jitney driver. He's happy. He probably got killed the next day. Cambodians, Khmer Rouge, take everything he had. But he was happy then.

From Cambodia, we went to Okinawa to discharge that bridge and pick something up. And me and Terry are gonna go into town, gonna have a few drinks.

Of course Terry started early again.

We're walking through this part of town with the Okinawans. We got quarts of beer with us, we're not supposed to be drinking and walking. I look in a window and I see these *big fucking strawberries*. I'm serious, we're talking *baseball* size. Terry's more fucked up than I am.

I says, "Terry, when's the last time you had a strawberry?"

"I dunno."

"Wait here. Hold my beer."

"I'll go around the corner."

I says, "OK."

So I go in there and buy these strawberries. I go back out, and here's Terry sitting on a garbage can, drinking his beer. I go sit on another garbage can, and we're eating these strawberries and drinking beer.

Here comes this little Okinawan guy, smiling, they always smile when they're embarrassed. Smiling, with a cigarette. He's got this fucking suit, shirt, and pants that are three sizes too big, like a Barnum and Bailey-type thing, like a clown outfit, and he's smiling. Terry's eating his strawberries and drinking. We're down to our last strawberry. The guy's just standing there looking at us. So I go like this, like a hand motion, to jack off. And the guy makes the motion. So I point over to Terry.

The guy walks over to Terry, he's gonna try to jack Terry off.

Terry pushes his hand. "*What the fuck are you doing?*"

I says, "What's wrong, Ter'?"

He says, "*Goddammit, did you see that guy try to jack me off? These fucking queers. I'm sitting here minding my own business on this garbage can, having a drink. Fuck!*"

I says, "Yeah, we better get out of here, Ter."

He didn't know that I had done that for about 20 years, until I told him what happened. He said, "Remember the time that guy tried to jack me off?"

I said, "Well, Terry, I got something to tell you."

"*You fucking prick, you!*"

Terry was fun.

Anyway, now we walk into this bar, and they got Okinawan girls walking around, dancing. There's some American GIs in there. There's this one girl GI in there, Melissa or Melinda.

We're sitting at these booths. The dance floor's up there, and they're dancing down to their panties, they got a scarf or something around their tits.

So the girl comes by, the one that got through dancing, and all she's got on is that silk scarf around her crotch and around her tits. When she comes by, I try to lick her. She got away real quick.

Terry says, "Oh, don't worry, she'll be back, Ron."

I says, "Yeah, I'll get her next time."

She comes back around, right next to me, and was gonna let me try to take a lick again. I slide my hand around and put my finger out. As I go to lick, she jumps back and my finger goes right up her ass.

"*Ahhhhhhhhhh.*"

Yeah, well, they asked us to leave. I don't know why.

We had to take a piss, though. "We'll finish our beer, and then we'll go."

We go into the bathroom, urinals to the left. Cinder block with the pipes coming down into the urinals. Before you hit the overhead, the ceiling, you got about 2 feet.

Terry says, "Hey, Ron, that's where the girls change clothes! That's their dressing room!"

I says, "Gimme a hand, Terry."

So I'm trying to climb up on top of the urinal, and Terry's push-ing me. I get up, I get my arm over the top of the thing, and I get my head over there, and they can't see me. They're undressing. I try to reach down and grab one of them, and she fucking screams. If Terry'd a dropped me, to this day, I'd still be there hanging. With a broken neck.

So we're leaving. They want us out of there. This army girl, Me-linda, she follows us out, and she says, "Here's my phone number, call me later." Gives it to Terry.

Terry says, "OK."

We get back to the ship. Terry says, "I'm all fucked up here. Call this girl's number."

We go to the President Hotel. It was across from the ship. So we go in there to use the phone.

I says, "I'll go with you."

He says, "No, no, no. She's not like that."

I says, "Maybe she's got a sister."

"No, no."

"Maybe she's got a friend."

"No, no, no, no, no."

"OK." I call her up. I says, "Melinda?"

She says, "Yeah."

He grabs the phone, real pleasant: "Oh, hi, Melinda . . . ." He's got two different voices. Anyway, he's gonna go over there.

I says, "You sure you don't want me to go with you?"

"No. She just wants to see me."

I says, "Alright."

I go back to the ship, get some sleep. They call me at 7:20. I get up, throw some water on my face, get cleaned up, have something to eat, sparingly. At eight o'clock we usually meet out by the gangway, with the bosun, and he's gonna give us a job. So I go out there about 10 minutes to eight.

Here I look down the pier, here's Terry walking back. Comes up the gangway, just made it in time. Didn't even change clothes, eight o'clock, just goes down to the engine room.

Later on that day, I says, "Well, how was it?"

He says, "Man, you oughta be glad you didn't go." He had a mustache, right. He bathed two or three times, he said. He couldn't get the smell out. It was so fucking bad he had to shave off his mustache. To top it all off, she was going back to San Francisco and she says, "Here's my number. Come and see me."

I says, "That's up to you."

Then we went up to Yokohama.

Me and Terry are gonna go ashore again. Now we got the engine cadet with us. So we're bouncing from bar to bar, kind of taking care of the cadet cuz he didn't make any money. We get in a bar there, and we're all fucked up, and we're talking to some Norwegian seamen. They're going on about the Norwegian Air Force and their role in the war or some fucking thing—I don't know *what* they were arguing about. Anyway, this kid, this engine cadet, jumps up and says, "Well if you sons of bitches would pay your NATO bill, we wouldn't have that fucking problem."

Here we go.

They're arguing, and I'm saying, "We gotta get out of here."

Get back to the ship. Next night we're gonna go try it again, cuz we didn't have a good time, you know. Real smart.

We got in the subway, and they just literally packed people in, like sardines. Literally, if you die, you couldn't fall down. They didn't want to have colds, so they had these masks on. Well, me and Terry are both taller than the average Japanese, right. We're the first ones in, and we're trying to hold on. Some poor Japanese woman, small, she's got her nose right in my armpit. She's just looking up at me, and I'm like, What can I do for you?

We're doing the tourist thing. McDonald's was like a buck more then than it was in the States. We get to a bar. Always a bar. The hookers wanted a *fortune*. The dollar was devaluating at the time, and the Japanese yen was going up. We're saying, "Oh, no, we're not coming out of that kind of money." I mean, if you went ashore with $100

American, if you could get polluted and laid for the $100, you were doing something. You just about had to get married to get laid over there. It was tough, unless you wanted to spend maybe $400 or $500.

So we're gonna go back to the ship. We get in a taxi, and I step on something getting into the taxi. It's a fucking purse. Some broad must have left it in there. I go through it. A little bit of money in there, makeup, and all that shit. There's enough to pay the taxi driver to get us back to the ship. So, he's supposed to stop at the gate where the MPs are.

We says, "Fuck that." We go right through the gate, told the driver it was OK. He drops us off right at the gangway.

Here comes the fucking MPs. "*You can't do that!*"

Driver says, "They said it was OK."

"*You can't do that!*"

I says, "We won't do it anymore."

"You can't do that any time you want, you fucking guys, you know that! Jesus Christ!"

We're going up the gangway, and I got the purse.

I says, "Wait a minute, Terry, here's your share."

He says, "What?" He's fucked up.

I give him all the makeup and shit and all that, put it in his hand. Next morning he gets up, he's rolling over, he put the stuff on the bed and passed out. "Where the fuck did all this come from?"

I says, "It was your share."

Now we're gonna go to San Francisco, back to the States.

I says, "I'm getting off."

Terry says, "Don't. Make another trip."

I says, "Fuck no, I'm gettin' off."

"C'mon!"

"Naw, fuck it."

We get to Oakland, and I was gangway or day working and Terry comes by.

I says, "What's up, Terry?"

He says, "Hey, man. We gotta go ashore tonight. We gotta go over to Frisco."

"Why? What do we gotta go there for?"

He said the Academy Award of pornography's going on there: Linda Lovelace in *Deep Throat*.

I says, "Are you serious?"

He says, "Yeah, it's Academy Award material here, Ron."

"Alright then, we'll go."

But he starts at noon. And I haven't had a fucking drink, right. Five o'clock—you know—I've been here before. I know how to do this. He's fucked up already by six.

We take the bus over. It's cheap. Like we're not gonna spend everything we fucking got anyway. Well, now we gotta stop and have a drink. We walk into this joint.

Terry says, "I gotta use the bathroom. Get us a drink."

I says, "OK."

A girl comes up to me, and they got these girls walking around, dancers. "Hi! What can I do for you?"

I order us whatever we were drinking at the time.

The girl says, "I'm sorry, all we've got is champagne and beer."

I thought that was a little strange, but I know Terry wouldn't want the champagne. So I says, "Give us each a beer."

She says, "I gotta give you a pitcher." I think it was $25 for the pitcher. This is '72.

I'm thinking: what the fuck? I says, "Alright." He's still in the bathroom. So he comes back, I poured myself one.

He says, "What the fuck'd you do?"

I says, "What?"

"What'd you order beer for?"

"They got beer and champagne, Terry, I didn't think you wanted the champagne."

"Well, no. But that's all they got?"

"Yeah. And drink slow, too."

"Why is that?"

"That pitcher was $25."

He says, "*Goddamn, we should walk out of here! Motherfuckers, try to rob us!*"

I says, "Yeah, Ter."

We're done drinking a beer, and what it amounted to was the girls would get up and they'd dance three dances, one with like a bikini on, then without the top, then without the bottom. Then they try to hit you for drinks. If they looked a little better, we probably would have stuck around, but we had a mission here. We finished the beer and got the fuck outta there. Didn't wanna go back there.

Terry knows where this place is, this theater—*supposedly* he knows. We finally find the joint, get in there. Terry's sitting next to me, and the place is crowded. And it starts. And, I mean, it's terribly done, if you've ever seen it, it really is. It's like a home movie camera. The photography's terrible. We're about halfway through it, right, and there's like a calm part in there, it gets real quiet.

I says, "Quick, Terry, jack me off."

"*You rotten fucker you!*"

I wanna get outta there. He's drunk. I'm not, but getting there. Now we're stopping at every bar, but they're closing the places up. This is getting late, you know. I'm fucked up by now. Terry's fucked up; he was fucked up at seven o'clock.

Terry says, "Come on, I know a joint we can get a drink at."

I says, "OK, Terry."

We go into this horseshoe-shaped bar, and there's a little restaurant on the other side.

"What can I do for you guys?"

Whatever we were drinking.

This one guy down the bar says, "You guys don't come in here much, do you?"

Terry says, "No, we're off a ship."

"Oh, you're off a ship?"

I says, "Yeah, we better get back. We'll get fired."

"Well, I work for the *San Francisco Inquirer*. You guys need jobs, don't worry about it, I'll get you jobs."

I says, "Man, that's real nice of you." What the fuck? We just walk in here, this guy's gonna give us a job? We're not thinking *San Francisco*, they're all fags. Neither one of us were on that wavelength.

I says, "Man, this is . . . ," and I'm looking over, there's all guys at the bar and there's all girls in the restaurant. I says, "Man, look at all the hookers." And I'm looking. And I'm looking. Now it's starting to dawn on me. They're dykes and these are fags. Fuck, Terry, you got us into another one.

Just when I'm about ready to say that, Terry says, "Hey, Ron."

"Yeah, Terry."

"You see that guy at the end of the bar staring at me? He keeps smiling like that, I'm gonna knock him off the barstool."

"You might as well, Terry, because you got us into it again."

He says, "What happened?"

I says, "These are all fags, Terry, and those are all dykes."

"What?"

"Terry, it's a fag joint. This guy's not trying to give us *jobs*."

"Oh, fuck, I didn't know that!"

"You've been in here before!"

"I didn't know!"

We get out of there. We get back to the ship, and about then I was ready to get off anyway. I quit.

Terry made another trip, and we kept in touch all those years.

Mormacscan

The *S.S. Mormacscan*, Moore-McCormack lines, 7/02/73 to 9/28/73.

That's the first time I ran into that chief mate, Grayson Parker. Mr. Parker. He was something, that Mr. Parker. Good guy, but he was right by the book. I got along with him. I did.

We had this ordinary seaman, Chester Tanner. I know he's dead. Cancer. We got this AB, Anton Selma. I know he died, too. Drank himself to death. Called him Slick. Bald headed. Slick was kind of an interesting story because his father was pay master for Texaco or Gulf Oil down in Port Arthur, Texas. He had bought quite a bit of land with the money around the area there. Invested it. Slick ended up marrying a girl from Charleston. Why he wanted to ship when his dad had money is beyond me. Mitch was back on there, too. Mitch the Bitch. And this Ray Adams. Another drinker. Just your usual bag of mixed nuts.

Left from Sunny Point, North Carolina, through Panama, going to Guam to drop those 500-pound blockbusters off to bomb North Vietnam. We get to Guam, and it was pretty much a nothing to do, nowhere place.

We had that ordinary seaman, Chester Tanner, and Chester was always talking about all the women he was handling. He was from West Virginia, and Chester was useless.

Me and Slick and him were on watch together, and Chester would come up and mop the deck. The ship never really pounded, but it would come up and go down into the waves. Chester'd be mopping, and he'd say, "Oh, God, here comes one." You feel the ship going up, and it would slide back down rather than pound, you know, and

Chester would have one hand on the mop, one hand on the rail, "*Oh God! Oh God!*" He was useless. He's dead now, poor guy, but he was just useless.

On the 4 to 8 watch, they'd eat in the morning, one AB and the ordinary would be down there, and the rest of the crew, the day workers and that, would eat at 7:20. They get called at 7:20. Well, 8 to 12, you usually let them eat first, the three guys that were on watch. Boy, that fucking Chester, he couldn't stand it. You know, 20 'til, he'd jump in there so he could be off *exactly*, and he'd run out of that mess hall at 10 minutes to 8.

So, one day, I said I'm gonna get him, cuz we had a phone on the bridge we could call anywhere. I says, "You know what I'm gonna do?" I says, "At 20 'til, I'm gonna ring the phone in the mess hall, and Chester's gonna at least have to get up and go over and answer that phone, and there won't be anybody there."

Well, this wiper, this guy from New York, he takes it a step *further*. He's sitting over there by the phone. So about 20 'til, it's on automatic steering, and Parker's in the chart room, I ring it. The wiper takes it a step further. *He* answers the phone. He told me later, Chester had just gotten the food and was just getting ready to sit down to eat. The wiper picks up the phone and waves him off: "Don't worry, Chester, you don't have to get up, I'll get it." And he says, "Oh. 'Ordinary to the bridge.' Got it." See, he took it a step further.

So I'm up there, it's about quarter 'til. Here comes Chester.
"Did you call me? Do you want me up on the bridge?"
I says, "No."
He says, "You called."
I says, "I didn't call."
He says to Parker, "Did you call me?"
Parker says, "No, I didn't call you. Nobody called you."
Chester says, "Well, *somebody* called for me." Wandered off.
Parker looks at me and says, "You know, you and Selma are right, he really is fucking losing it." The only place you can call from is the bridge, and "I know *you* didn't call." Right? Yeah, we're just fucking with Chester.

When we were in Guam, there was something about when you were in American ports, you had to set the sea watches at noon. Well, Parker didn't set them 'til that night, at midnight. He says, "If I owe you guys 4 hours overtime, I'll pay you. Go see the patrolman at the end of the trip." It never did get straightened out here for that overtime, but it did later, another time I was with Parker. I'll get to that.

Mitch the Bitch is all fucking drunked up. They had sent him over to, of all places, some kind of Mormon or some non-drinking church, or some kind of hospital or recovery place, and they didn't even want to talk to him. They just sent him back, you know. They said, "This guy's an alcoholic, that's what's wrong with him."

And there was an oiler and a fireman together. The fireman was as nasty as the oiler. He had a heart attack later on, got paralyzed half of his face. I saw him years later. Couldn't happen to a nicer guy, you know, just a miserable fuck. He had two drinks, and he was just a miserable prick. This guy, he had had open heart surgery, and they were both drinking all the time, and just fucking miserable. Well, Mitch is down there, too, right, and he's never relieving Mitch on time.

We turn around, me and this old guy Slick, and we're out there drinking. Here we go into a bar, and the third mate's passed out on the couch. We're drunk, and this guy says he's supposed to go on watch. The more we drink, we're thinking we're gonna do him a favor.

Slick says, "Ronnie, pick him up, we'll carry him back to the ship."

We're thinking maybe we'll carry him out the back way.

"Naw," we says, "just carry him down the road."

So I pick him up and drop him a couple of times. As we're going down the hill, I'm dropping him, picking him up, dragging him. We finally get him back to the gates, and we're dragging him. I don't know what happened, but we leave him and go back to the ship. He misses the watch. Parker logs him.

We see him the next day. He says he woke up under a truck and he didn't have his shoes. He says, "You know what? I appreciate you guys trying to help me. I really do. But next time just leave me where you find me. You'll kill me if you try to help me anymore."

Slick goes back in, and I go out later and go back up to that bar, and I walk in, and Slick says, "Ronnie, come here."

I says, "Yeah, what's up?"

"You remember anything about yesterday?"

"I was trying to get the poor guy back. I was dropping him four or five times."

"You remember we were gonna take him out the back way?"

"I remember something about it, but we took him down the road."

He says, "Let me show you the back way."

We walk to the back door, Slick opens it, and here it's steps about a foot wide, about 100 of them going almost straight down the side of the hill. He says, "We'd a fucking killed him." Just dropped him and killed him.

On the way back, that same wiper who had answered the phone, we got to Panama and we brought up the mooring lines—you stow the lines when you leave your last foreign port 'til you get to the next port, you put 'em under the next deck down. So we bring up the mooring lines, and usually you don't use 'em in Panama, but you bring 'em up just in case. Well, we bring 'em up, we're going back to Sunny Point.

Well, it's 5 days, so you usually ask permission, you ask the bosun, bosun asks the mate, "Why stow 'em, we're just gonna have to take 'em up again in 5 days." Cuz it's some work, you know. Then he asks the captain, and the captain says, "OK. Yeah." Well, if you get bad weather, then you gotta run out there and stow 'em, but, anyway, unbeknownst to us in Panama, Parker's not letting anybody bring any booze on board. And this wiper, he drinks what he's got left, and he ain't got nothing left now, maybe a day out. Well, he goes back on the stern, instead of having them flaked out next to each other, we got them coiled in a circle on pallets. He's pissed off, and he unlashes it and lets the eye go over the side. The weight caught it and just pulled the whole line out.

Next fucking morning we hear: "Somebody threw one of the mooring lines over the side."

So now they're gonna make junior G-men out of us. They're gonna leave the lines up, we gotta check 'em every hour to make sure they're OK. Well, instead of sitting in the mess hall, you gotta go out and actually *do* something. That pisses Chester off, cuz Chester didn't want to do anything. Well, I should say something, too, about Chester.

When we got to the Philippine Islands, this is the beginning of the trip, Chester's always talking about women, this and that, how he's taking care of things.

We'd be like, "Hey, come on, Chester, if you ever got a hard on, you better take some of this Red Hand—" you know, the cement we got on the ship, you could take a toilet bowl with this stuff and seal it—"if you get a hard on, you better take some Red Hand and slap it on there and keep it for awhile."

Every bar he went to you'd see Chester out there talking to the girls, and as soon as he'd see a lot of crew members, he'd leave.

And the girls would say, "You know Chester? You know Chester?"

I'd say, "Yeah. I know Chester."

"That Chester, he's pussy. He's pussy."

Anyway, this wiper, he threw the lines over the side.

So now we gotta be junior G-men.

And Chester's bitching, "We gotta check the mooring lines every hour, and nobody in the deck department never even did it."

And we're not gonna snitch on this guy.

So Slick tells Chester, "Chester, you fucking cunt. If you keep bitching, me and Ronnie are gonna go up and see the captain and Mr. Parker, and we're gonna sign a statement saying we saw *you* do it."

He went screaming and ran off like an old whore.

Eventually, the wiper goes up to the old man and says, "Captain, I want to admit it. I did it. I threw the mooring line over the side."

Captain says, "Can I ask why you did it?"

He says, "I came back, and I had a few drinks, and I didn't have any more, and I was pissed off. I just went back there and did it."

Captain says, "I'll tell you what I'm gonna do." He says, "That was an old mooring line." He says, "I gotta report you. But I'm gonna put on here it was an old mooring line, you might not have to pay for it, or see the Coast Guard, or anything."

Parker kind of hemmed and hawed about that, but it was OK. He wasn't in charge.

We stopped somewhere on the east coast, and I took it up to New York. Now it's me and Slick and this Ray Adams. And Ray Adams, him and Mitch got a load of booze wherever we stopped, and they're both fucked up. We're in New York getting ready to pay off that day, and Ray Adams is so drunk he's going up to the officers asking them for their order, you know, what they'd like to eat, and he was sup-posed to go call it down to the galley. Then when they'd sent it up, he'd take it and give it to them. Well, Ray was so fucked up, he was just walking over, getting their orders, and he wouldn't even call them in. He's just all fucked up, and we're all getting off.

About 2 days before, Mitch the Bitch is all fucked up, and this one oiler is relieving Mitch. Mitch tells him in the mess hall, "Billy, 'bout time you fucking relieve me on time some time."

The guy says something like, "Fuck you, man. I don't know what you're talking about."

He walks out of the mess hall, and Mitch says, "Hey, Ronnie."

"Yeah, Mitch?"

"I'm gonna beat that motherfucker's ass before we get off here. He drank all my whiskey."

I says, "Yeah, whatever you gotta do, Mitch."

So this is the last day now. Ray Adams is all fucked up. Mitch is all fucked up. Everybody's getting off. But you gotta work 'til like two o'clock 'til you get the money. Eight o'clock in the morning, you know, we gotta turn to.

Well, the bosun, he's a nice guy, he says, "OK, gonna give you something to do here." He says to me, "Why you get off my ship?"

I says, "Oh, bos', I gotta go."

"Well, you get a chance, you come back."

"I will, Bos'. I promise I'll come back."

Five minutes after eight, the general fire alarm goes off down in the engine room.

I says, "What the fuck?"

We're all charging out, gonna go to our fire stations. We figured,

Jesus, last day and we got a problem. More fucking stress.

What had happened was this Billy was coming down late—again—to relieve Mitch. Well, Mitch just said, "Fuck it, I'm getting off anyway." They get into a fight in the passageway, up and down, fistfighting each other. Mitch fucks this guy up, but this guy pushes Mitch over, and he lands *again*, cuts his head up, *again*. The other guy's all fucked. Now ya gotta get the ambulance for both of 'em.

They're trying to get the shipping commissioners, the old man's going crazy.

What a fucking operation.

So then I'm going back to Cleveland. Now Slick, Ray Adams, and Mitch are gonna go down to Charleston, South Carolina. They're gonna fly back. Me and Slick are at the airport.

Here comes Mitch, same clothes he was wearing the day he got in the fight, stitches in his fucking head. Grumbling, "Fuck that motherfucker." Got a stitch where they shaved part of his head. "Fuck that motherfucker."

Ray Adams is just wandering around in a daze, walking into bulkheads and shit.

Slick says, "I'll take care of him." Slick tells them, "Give me your money, and I'll go up and get our tickets." You could do this then, you know. Slick says, "Yeah, I got three tickets for Charleston."

The girl says, "Is that for your two friends over there?"

I think I was holding Mitch up.

He says, "Yeah."

She says, "They're going to be alright, aren't they?"

He says, "Yeah, they'll be fine."

I saw Slick later on. He told me Mitch ordered a drink on the plane, and they wouldn't give it to him. He's yelling, *"Give me a parachute and I'll jump! I'll jump off this plane!"*

Austral Entente

Charleston, 12/26/73; New York, New York, 1/2/74. *Austral Entente*, Farrell Lines. Brand new container ship running to Australia. First time I was gonna get that run.

And when I got it in Charleston, the dispatcher Laddy Holstom says, "Say, Ronnie, you might like this one. Brand new ship, going to Australia."

I says, "Yeah, I'll try it for a trip, Laddy." You know. Why not?

I get on board, and it'd just come out of the shipyard, brand new. The whole crew is from Mobile, Alabama—Mobilians. They weren't Alabamians, they were *Mobilians*. What a fucking bunch.

We had a radio operator that was fucked up. The officers had a place to eat off to the side that were on watch so they didn't eat with the passengers. We had passengers on there, tourists who wanted to go to Australia. People that want to get off, just take a ride on a ship instead of fly. These were all subsidized ships. They had to be able to carry up to 12 passengers. After 12 they had to have a doctor. But it was a subsidy thing, so if you wanted to take a ship to South Africa or South America, they took this. The only runs we didn't have passengers is when we were going to Vietnam or something for the military. People would want to go for a sea voyage, you know, doctors would say it's healthy for you. Or they'd want to just go to Australia, get off, then fly back. People in Australia would want to take a ship to America rather than fly. I tried to avoid the passengers because they were nothing but fucking headaches. If I saw them ashore, they might ask me where to go, and I'd tell them where to go that was halfway normal, cuz I knew where I was going. But I tried to avoid them because they were nothing but trouble. Like women on these ships now.

There's enough fucking drama and stress here, I don't need it. That's why I go ashore alone, majority of the time.

Anyway, the radio operator, he would get to the point he wouldn't even put on his uniform, you know, he'd go to eat in the duty officer's mess. He wouldn't shave or anything, he'd just go in there all fucked up, drunk. We dropped anchor somewhere, and it was in the evening, so the captain put the anchor light on the bow.

Here the radio operator comes up and gives us a time check up on the bridge. "Here's the time check."

Well, you don't *need* a time check when we're at *anchor*. You know, we *know* where we're at.

"Time check! Time check!"

Captain says, "*We're at anchor! We don't need a time check!*"

Anchor light's *blinding* you. You know, he just came up and wandered around.

First time I saw Australia, and you would think—you know—it's Australia, New Zealand. I wasn't impressed with it.

We got back, and I got off. I just couldn't apply myself. I just didn't feel it was anything I needed. I'm not saying people don't like it there or it's not a nice place. I got no animosity against the Australians or New Zealanders. I went there later and did have a pretty good time. Would I want to go live there? No. But then again, I wouldn't want to live a lot of other places, too.

Mormaccape

A typical run down to South Africa, and back up to Mozambique, but this, in Mozambique, was like the turning point. Lourenzo Marques became Maputo, the southernmost port in Mozambique next to South Africa. The South Africans were pretty much still the same way. They were still under that Dutch rule. When I first went there, Mozambique was under Portuguese control.

The Portuguese were leaving, FRELIMO was taking over; black communists. It was an intermediary government, and people there were leaving in flocks and droves. The Portuguese were coming out, trying to get rid of their money. The establishment that was actually running the country was leaving. Everybody was going. And they were gonna have a brand new country and change the world and this and that and—you know—the usual commie thing, or you can reverse it, from communism to capitalism, the *new* world. Another "ism."

Like I said, it was interesting to the point where the Portuguese were just done with it. All construction was coming to a stop. And there was a very large Coca-Cola sign high up on a building in Maputo. I remember seeing it the first time I was there. It was almost like a landmark, like a lighthouse. When I first was there, you could get Coca-Cola. *Now* you couldn't get any Coca-Cola. They tried to keep a front up there to keep it going. You could still walk around. They still had girls. The Portuguese were very, very liberal on prostitution, alcohol, having a good time. They were more or less founded on that principle. Spain, Portugal, they were very Roman Catholic, they were very, very liberal.

We had these passengers on board. And the government was in

transition. We had 12 passengers, retired schoolteachers, stuff like that, people trying to get away. The Portuguese were still there, but the new government was taking over. What it amounted to was they changed these people's money on board. They had them scared about getting caught. Well, it was a big long pier, and you had to walk down to the gate to get out. They changed their money on board. Then they walk all the way down to the gate, and they had to go through the FRELIMO Customs.

And they says, "What jobs do you have?"

They says, "We're all retired."

"You can't go ashore here because Maputo is now for workers only." You know: "Oh, no, you're *capitalists*. We only let *workers* go ashore. You're retired."

They wouldn't change their money back. So they got stuck with this money that was no good anywhere else in the world. New government.

I go ashore, I run into a German, *Wolfgang*, of all people, at one of the bars there. He was on a West German ship, I think they were loading sulfur to take to Australia. He was night watchman for the gangway. It was kind of an interesting thing. The ship had been built in the Soviet Union, and they had Russian engineers on there. When the Soviet Union built a ship for you, even if it was in the West, like a West German ship, which was a "democracy," so to speak—the Russian engineers would stay on board and work there for 1 year. This Wolfgang was telling me that they had Russian engineers on board, and they wouldn't let them come ashore for some reason. He later invited me over cuz they got two cases of beer a week, and I went over that evening and stayed polluted.

Anyway, as I was stopping in the bars, there was a feeling of euphoria—I remember running into a black girl in a bar. She had just come from Rhodesia. It was an open border, and now she was free. She felt she was free, when in reality, there was nothing, the country was in collapse. The building had stopped completely. Portuguese ships were in the harbor loading cars, vehicles, everything you could think of. Portuguese people were leaving in droves. It was actually depressing to see a mass exodus of people. They were already starting to lay up the fishing boats because the Portuguese had the fishing boats. The intellectuals were leaving, and the communists were taking over. It was an even trade there, you know. You'd see one truck full of FRELIMO troops, the black troops, going one way, and you'd see Portuguese troops going the other way. I mean, the war was over. Portugal was leaving, but there was still animosity, and there was shooting at night. Somebody didn't like the idea of leaving, and somebody didn't like the idea of letting them go without killing them.

It was a terrible thing to see a happy, free, anything-goes society, change to communism . . . . I don't think it ever recovered.

On the way back we stopped in Cape Town, South Africa. This was when I met the Queen of Sheba. "Queenie" they called her. She was an old whore running an after-hours joint in Cape Town. I got a taxi after the bars were closing, they closed early there.

I asked the driver, "Can you get me to an after-hour joint where I can get a drink?"

The taxi driver, white guy, says, "Well, you're white, and if you don't mind, this is kind of a mixed Indian and black place, and white. If you don't mind."

I says, "I don't care as long as they'll give me a drink."

He takes me over to this dilapidated house, and he knocks on the door, comes back, and says, "Yeah, you can get in there and get a drink." He agreed to come back in about 3 hours and get me.

So I go in, and there's an Indian girl behind the bar. It's mixed in there, mulattos, Indians, blacks, whites, which you couldn't do at the time. No integration down there, it was all apartheid, everybody's equal but separate. And it was after hours.

I just want a couple of beers. I tell the girl, "I'd like to get a beer."

She says, "Yeah, that's fine, but I should tell you, if the police come, you're in bigger trouble than we are." She meant me being white.

I says, "How many ways are there outta here?"

"There's only the front door and the back door."

"Well, if they come in through the back door and the front door together," I says, "just follow me, I'll *make* a way outta here."

I'm sitting there bullshitting with everybody, and I turn around. Queenie, this old mulatto woman, starts bullshitting with me, and I'm gassed, and I'm just running my mouth, you know. I appeal to her.

Anyway, they're passing around this Durban Poison. And, I gotta say, I never smoked. I don't smoke grass, and I don't cut it, either. But I'm fucked up with the beer, getting worse.

They says, "This is stronger than anything you have in the States."

I says, "I don't smoke in the States, but," I says, "it can't be that strong."

One of the guys says, "Give me one of your Marlboros."

I give him a Marlboro. He opens it up, breaks it apart from the filter. He takes a pinch of this—Durban Poison they called it—and he puts it in there and he mixes it all together, works it and works it and works it with his fingers. Said he was getting the oil out of it, working it up, you know.

I says, "Yeah, I don't care what you do."

Then he puts it in a skin, a paper, they call it over there a skin. He skinned it up, and he says, "Here. You won't be able to smoke the whole thing."

"Whadya mean I can't smoke the whole thing?"

I took three drags off of it, deep ones, just to show him I could do it.

I fell off the stool.

They prop me against the wall, you know, sitting. I slide down. They prop me back up again. Jesus Christ, it was like pins and needles were all through my arms. I'm seeing, like, *flutes* flying around in the air. *Noise* is amplified.

I says, "Goddamn, I'm gonna die," I'm gonna die in a mulatto whorehouse here in Cape Town, South Africa. All of a sudden one of the girls walks by with a plate of prawns. This is a small joint, too, she's stepping over me. I see the food and turn green. I go to throw up and catch it.

They're yelling, "Queenie! He's gonna die!" They were afraid cuz I'm a white man. He's gonna die in *here*, you know. They're yelling, *"You alright? You alright?"*

I swallow and says, "Yeah. I do this all the time."

They get me up, I can walk, very weakly, and they take me to a back room, and they says, "Lay down. You're gonna be alright."

I says, "Yeah, I hope so." The sensation starts to fade. It was really quick. I don't think a half hour went by when all this occurred. I get up and says, "Jesus Christ."

I get out of the room. I don't know what time it is. They're still sitting in there drinking, fucked up, smoked up.

Queenie says, "You alright?"

I says, "Yeah, I'm fine now."

The guy that skinned it says, "You saw how much I put in there. You saw it. It wasn't us!"

I says, "I know, it wasn't you guys." I says, "Maybe I better leave."

"Oh, no, have a beer."

Beer was the furthest thing from my mind, I just wanted to get the fuck outta there. They gave me some water, and the taxi driver came back.

I says, "Thanks. Sorry about that little incident."

Queenie says, "Oh, no, no. I got another place." She says, "Come over there tomorrow night."

I says, "Yeah, OK." So she gave me the address, and I took it back to the ship.

I was just fucking sick the next day. I had to work 'til five o'clock, and I laid down 'til about 7, took a shower, got my head down, and I says, "You know what? I'm gonna go check this out." About eight o'clock, make a run again. Matter of fact, I think that's why I did it, cuz the weekend was coming and I didn't have to work. It was Friday.

I got the address she had given me, and it was to another, bigger place. This was more of a house than just a straight through shot thing with some rooms. Still in the ghetto area, I mean, still trashy, dilapidated.

The taxi driver says, "You *sure* you want to go there?" You know, cuz you had to get a white taxi driver. They had signs on the taxis: "colored only" or "white only."

I says, "Yeah, I'm sure."

"You want me to come back and get you?"

"Let's see if I can get in." I knock and she answers. I says, "I'm gonna get the taxi to come back."

She says, "We'll get you a taxi later, don't worry about it."

So I paid him off, and he was gone. Everybody is telling me they called her the Queen of Sheba. She'd been there working after-hour joints for years—Queenie. She had hangers-on and a bunch of crazies, you know. Anyway, they were talking about, "Queenie really likes you." She had to have been 60; I was in my 30s.

And I'm thinking: What the fuck? Do I need this? Did I sign up for this?

Well, after about 27 beers I end up with her for the night.

Next day is Saturday.

She says, "Do you have to go back to work today?"

I says, "No, I just need some coffee."

"We can spend the day together."

"Yeah, that's cool," not really thinking, you know…. She had the coffee and some bread and butter and jam and kind of like an English thing going on.

Anyway, there's this white guy, "Glen" I think it was. He was kind of a runner for her. And she's gonna go make a deal with somebody over her Arab-Indian partner in this.

Turn around, she says, "We gotta go see my friend here. We have a business together. Would you like to go?"

I says, "Yeah."

She says, "You have to ride in front."

So I'm riding in front with the white guy, Glen. She was in the back seat, and we're going all through Cape Town. Soon we go into these high-rise apartments, meet the half-Arab, half-Indian guy and his girlfriend, and it was some kind of a deal for running these after-hour joints. Some money changed hands there.

She says, "This is my friend, Ron. He's off the ship."

You know, hey, how are you?

Basically, did a little tour of Cape Town that day.

Now she's starting to hang on me again.

And I'm thinking: What the fuck am I doing with this old screwball, you know?

So we get back to her place.

She says, "Would you like a drink?"

I says, "Yeah, I still have a few bucks." We're sitting there drinking, and I'm thinking: I am getting the fuck out of this, you know, I don't need this old screwball. How the fuck did I get myself into this?

I excused myself—I didn't have to go back—but about ten o'clock, I says, "I gotta go."

"You can't stay tonight?" She's all whiney.

I says, "No. I'm sorry."

"Oh, well," you know, clinging, "can you come back?"

"I don't know if I have to work tomorrow." We were gonna leave Monday. So I says, "We're leaving Monday. I probably have to work." I'll be a son of a bitch: I get back and go to sleep, fuck all this, Sunday I'm kind of hanging around the ship, I didn't have to work, I didn't want to, I was trying to figure out how to maybe just go ashore and wander around, the guy on the gangway says, "You got a phone call."

I says, "Who the fuck knows—?" *She* had gotten the number somehow or another.

"Ron?"

"Yeah."

"This is Queenie."

I says, "Hey, how are you?"

"You coming out tonight?"

I says, "You know, I'm working right now and probably not, cuz we gotta leave tomorrow morning."

"Well, you know…I'd like…you know…if you could come back…."

And I'm thinking: I don't fucking need this old crazy woman. I'm sobering up here. *Fuck* this. I says, "We're leaving."

"Well, if you can, can you come over?"

"If I can, I will." I says, "Promise, I'll be there." Eww. Fuck that. I stayed in that night.

The next day, we're securing. We're probably gonna leave about six o'clock at night. The radio operator and the captain were feuding about something. The captain was always on this guy's ass. He turned around, and he went to the doctor that morning and, at the time, you couldn't sail without a radio operator. He came back with a "Not Fit for Duty." We couldn't sail! He was gonna get even with the old man because, you know, you're delayed sailing, and all that costs the company money. They had to fly a radio operator from New York to South Africa.

It was unreal.

I'm thinking: what if she calls again? The only thing I can say is, "We're restricted."

The old man had to tell them: "We don't have a radio operator, but we want to leave."

They says, "We can't let you leave without a radio operator. You're not seaworthy. We can't give you a pilot."

The old man says, "OK. I'll go out here to anchor."

They said no. Because they knew the old man, once he got out there at anchor, he's likely to just keep going, you know, right. He wanted to get away from the dock because they were charging for the dock space whether you were working or not. Maybe he wouldn't have taken off because that would have been a real violation to sail without a radio operator, but he was gonna try to save the company the money.

I'm there thinking: geez, let him go to anchor so we can just get *out*, so she don't call anymore.

Never did call again.

I was happy about that.

Must've said that we sailed or something.

The radio operator came the next day, and we were outta there. Never wanted to see her again.

But I couldn't help myself: on another run down there on one of those Moore-McCormack ships, I did ask. I was sitting in a bar, and I asked one of the girls, "Queen of Sheba still running an after-hours joint around here?"

She looked at me very strange, "You know about her?"

I said, "Yeah, Queen of Sheba, Queenie."

"She *died* about a year ago."

Anyway, back on this trip, we stopped in Walvis Bay, South-West Africa. It had been an old German protectorate. They lost it after World War I, it's Namibia now. It still was called German South-West Africa, and the South Africans were actually administrating the country. It was Dutch Reformed Church. This is where they had the diamond fields, where you could literally walk along out in the sticks and pick up a diamond. If you strayed too far from town, the police would come and pick you up one time and take you to town. If you did it again, you went to jail. Matter of fact, when we first dropped anchor there, we had to go to the dock to pick up our cargo. When you pick the anchor back up, you bring it back home, it acquires mud from being on the bottom. I had the hose there, and you wash the mud off to try to get as much mud off as you can, otherwise it goes down into the chain locker and dries up down there and turns into cement.

The bosun said, jokingly, "Don't wash too hard. There might be a diamond in this."

South Africa was really under control, it was a locked-in society. To me, too, that was a shame.

Matter of fact, I think that was the trip when they first were getting television down there. In South Africa, they had a TV in the window just to show people what a television looked like, and it was gonna come and there was gonna be cable from Pretoria, the capital. In other words, the media was gonna be controlled, too. One program would be in Afrikaans, and the next program would be in English. There were no commercials. I remember *Bonanza* in Afrikaans, it ran 46 minutes.

It was kind of strange, you know, when you get into it, to look at things like this. They showed you what they wanted to show you.

Meadowbrook

This was an inter-coastal tanker, ran from the east to the west coast. Money was very good. I was quartermaster AB. I believe I got about 50 or 60 days out of it as a medical relief. I didn't like it because there was no adventure. They called it a "drugstore ship." It carried numerous cargos, chemicals. It was a choice job, maybe one of the best jobs in the NMU, National Maritime Union, quartermaster AB on the bridge of the ship. That's all I had to do was steer. We'd go from the east coast to Philadelphia, Charleston, through Panama and to the west coast. I couldn't wait to get off.

Run by Keystone Corporation, Charles Kurz. He was an interesting story. He started during World War II, Keystone Tankers out of Philadelphia. He started on a shoestring. Sometimes he didn't have enough money to pay the crew. He could only get what they call 4Fs, the ones the military wouldn't take. No offense to the U.S. Merchant Marine, but that's where most of the merchant seamen came from during World War II. They were 4Fs. They couldn't go anywhere else, so the Merchant Marines would take them. That's 4F, mentally or physically.

Charlie turned around, and one chief engineer I guess was really to the point of quitting, and Charlie said, "If you stay with me, I'll take care of you." The guy actually went insane and had to be put in an institution. Charlie paid for the institution, and Charlie paid his wife chief engineer wages, every month. As they got raises, she got a raise, too. She went right along with it.

And this was about the only ship you didn't have to take physicals for. You took the job, you went to the ship. You didn't go to the doctor and take a physical. All the other ones you had to. Charlie was real good about that.

He later passed away. His brother took over. As usual with a regime change, it all changed, as I heard. I don't think I ever worked for them again, or if I did, it was a very short time. I was never into just making money. I mean, that wasn't the name of the game. The game was escape. You know, I'm escaping, I'm leaving. I'm leaving reality. Like I always said, where else do they call you a half hour before you go to work, and when you get there, you don't have to produce? And it was just acceptable. And if you got somebody that did produce a little, you wanted to keep them more than you did anyone else, because you had some real numnuts out there. I never worked overtime, or seldom did. But by the same token, when I did work, I *worked*.

And, you know, it behooved them to keep me around cuz I would keep the overtime rate down for the company. I actually was working on watch when it was my watch and actually getting something done, but I wasn't costing going into the overtime with them, so they got to keep their overtime down.

And, I never caused too many problems.

I kept under the radar. You know.

Ringbolted

I caught the ship in Charleston 12/12/74 and took it up to New York on a coastwise, ready to make the foreign voyage. We signed on to make the trip, and I was kind of hesitant about going, mainly because I didn't know the captain. He was notorious amongst Moore-McCormack captains, like the other one, Joe Holland. They were very, very . . . . I'll use the word "opinionated."

I could feel that the bosun, Dutch, he was just—it's strange, but you get a feeling in life when somebody's eyeballing you, somebody's staring at the back of your head—you know—you can *feel* it. It's almost like you can picture them doing it. Yeah.

He assured me that it'd be an easy gig, we're just gonna go and make some money, and we're gonna get out of here.

I said, "OK, I'll do it." I had money, I had just gotten off that tanker. I didn't have a chance to spend any, and I had the vacation pay coming from that, too. But anyway, I said, "Yeah, OK, sounds good to me." I think a few drinks were involved in that.

We went down to Cape Town, and it was kind of uneventful. Cape Town: everybody usually did the same thing, looked at Table Mountain, looked like somebody just cut the top off the fucking mountain with a sharp knife. They had these cape rollers down there, too, these waves, like these surfing waves, and it literally picked the ship up. It had something to do with the currents coming around South Africa into the Indian Ocean, and they called them cape rollers. And, literally, you'd start dragging your anchor because it's a sandy bottom there, and it'll move the ship around, but it just rolls you. So you'd anchor out. Cargo ships were anchoring out cuz this was being used as the main transit point. I should say this is the time when the Suez Canal was closed down, so this was a main transit point: South Africa. You couldn't use the Suez Canal because of the war between Israel and Egypt, they shut it down. So the cargo ships were anchoring out before they could go in.

So we got there, we had to stay out at anchor, and it was 1 day day work, 1 day gangway watch.

And Dutch was gonna make a new ship out of it. He says, "I'm gonna be here maybe two trips." Dutch wanted it done *this* way. We gotta get *that* done, we gotta get *this* done—we call it "make a new ship out of it." He's gonna make points, you know, show how good he was as a bosun.

So the friction started there.

We hit the usual ports: Cape Town, Port Elizabeth, East London, Durban.

I turn around, I was going ashore, I was off at five o'clock. And a couple of the other guys I was having a few drinks with, they says, "Go ahead, we'll meet you at the first bar outside the gate."

I says, "OK."

Unbeknownst to me at the time, one of the runners or something had parted, and it had to be changed. So those guys actually couldn't come ashore. They had to stay there and work on that. I had already left.

I walked outside the gate, went to the first bar, which was the Queen's Hotel Bar. I was sitting there waiting for the guys, and the bar was packed. It wasn't that big of a bar, but all the seats were taken. But there was one large table, empty. I got a beer, sat down there. It wasn't 20 minutes later, a group of about nine Englishmen came in. They wanted to drink, and they were looking around for somewhere to sit.

They look over at me and says, "Do you mind if we sit here?" They thought I was South African, but I opened my mouth, they knew I was an American.

I says, "Yeah, go ahead. Please."

They were on the *Port Saint Lawrence*, which is a Port Line ship, it's a subsidiary of Kennard, who ran the *Queen Mary*. It was a freighter division. I told them I was on the *Mormaccove*, Moore-Mc-

Cormack. We started talking, and I said I was waiting for the guys to come, and they were going back to the ship, they had had a half a day or something, they just went out to do a little shopping or something, they were going back, and that they had a bar on board. This is where I met Ken Bottoms, good guy, friend to this day. One of the guys they called Bubbles, too.

They says, "Would you like to come back to our ship? We have a bar on board, prices are right."

I says, "I better wait for the guys." Unbeknownst to me that they weren't coming.

I think I waited 'til about ten o'clock. Nobody showed up, so I just went back to the ship. I found out that they had that problem with the runner.

Next day was a Sunday. I wasn't working any overtime. Since they had invited me over to *Port Saint Lawrence* for a beer, I went over there. I said I'd been invited on board, and I think I mentioned Ken and Bubbles; there was a guy named Clem, and Ginger, and their deck boy was Split Pin, a cadet. I don't remember why they called him Split Pin. He was beginning going to sea. They called him a deck boy, or apprentice—Split Pin. He was their runner, used to go get the booze for them, did the dirty jobs.

I get on there, I get to their bar, none of them are there. The bartender happened to be married to an American girl. He had been in the British paratroopers, and they assumed that he had hit his head a few too many times. But anyway, I had a beer, and I met some of the guys, and I says, "I don't have any money. I can pay in South African or American, but I don't have any British money."

They says, "Don't worry about it, we'll get it later."

Later on, nobody showed up, so I said, well, gee, I wonder where those guys are at?

They had mentioned some bar, so I took a walk. I wanted to go into town anyway and look around. They happened to be there, so I met 'em in a bar, then we went back to their ship and had a couple more drinks.

And that's where this basically started.

Our ships were gonna be making the same run, same ports, and we kind of teamed up and, "Hey, you gonna stop over?" We liked the booze on their ship, and they liked the food on our ship. So we kind of traded back and forth. They'd come over for dinner, and we'd go over there and drink.

One time I was over on their ship, and Ginger was on security, AB gangway. Some black girl came up the gangway.

She says, "I'd like to come on board."

Ginger says, "I can't let you on board."

"I have friends on board."

It was an all white crew. They didn't integrate.

Ginger says, "You a working girl?"

She says, "Yeah."

"OK, you can come on board." She needed the business. What are you gonna do? They gotta make a living.

In Durban, Ginger got arrested for a dirty deck of playing cards. Oh, they were *filthy*. Customs had found them. He was going outside the gate. He had picked them up in England or something.

Anyway, he got busted, and he had to go to court. I went over to the ship the day he was going to court. He was out on bond, and the captain gave him a letter, said he was a "rare breed," you know, a good seaman. Ginger drank a lot, but we were calling him that after that: the "rare breed."

I came on board, and I had a *Playboy* on the American ship, and I stuck it in my back pocket. He was gonna go to court that day, and I says, "Here, Ginger, here's something to read while you're waiting."

Ginger takes it and looks. "*What are you doing?*" He starts laughing.

I says, "Just kidding."

He went to court. They fined him something like 50 rand, $50.

The judge said, "Even though the captain's saying rare breed—in this day and age, in some countries, this might be tolerated—here in South Africa, this is *filth*."

I think the judge looked at them four or five times, just to make sure.

There was some girl sitting there, too, where her father was accused of beating and molesting kids, and she was sitting there with Ginger, and Ginger's trying to put the make on her, and she's crying.

Oh, it was hilarious.

She says, "What are you here for?"

He says, "I'm here for pornography."

"Oh, really? My dad's in here for molesting kids and beating them with a stick."

"Oh, really?"

Yeah, a real nice "what's up?" kind of conversation.

God! What a world!

I turn around, and we were in Port Elizabeth, South Africa, and we were supposed to shift the ship. I had injured my hand, I went to a doctor, and I had 2 or 3 days "Not Fit for Duty."

A couple of the crew members and myself were sitting in a bar with them. They were off.

The other guys from my ship says, "We gotta go back and make the shift."

I says, "I don't have to go back, so I'll just sit here with this English guy."

Ken says, "You sure you don't have to go back, Ron?"

I says, "Oh, no, I don't have to go back because we're just shifting."

Well, we're sitting there drinking, Ken had to use the head or something, the bathroom there at the hotel bar, and he comes back and says, "Hey, Ron, the ship's leaving."

I says, "No, it's shifting."

Ken says, "No, Ron, it's going out! It's *leaving*!"

I says, "Well, I think I just blew it." You know, right. And: "I don't know, I'm not sure, I'm 'Not Fit for Duty,' I don't know how this is gonna work." Because now I failed to join, you know, right, I should have been on the ship. It's going to Durban, the next port. So we had to have a few more drinks, see, before we figured out what to do. Alcohol always helped. Alcohol was an inspiration, trust me, it still is. Always sit around and have a few drinks before you make a major decision in your life. It helps you along.

So Ginger says, "Don't worry, Ronnie. We'll just go ahead and we'll ringbolt you, cuz we're going to Durban, too." They called it "ringbolting" when they'd stow you away and take you to the next port. It sounded like a good idea to me, but I didn't have enough inspiration yet. In other words: I was still sober.

I says, "You think you guys can really get away with this?"

They says, "Hey, Ronnie, you're not gonna believe this, but listen to this."

They told me how they were in London, and most of them always worked for this Kennard Line, this Port Line company. They used to go to New Zealand, Australia, they liked those runs. It was really a party back in the '70s for them. These guys would usually ship together, too, they were Port Line stiffs, they always worked for the same company. They said that in London they were getting ready to make a trip, and one of the guys had met a girl from Australia who had an English girlfriend. They were hanging around the wharf area there.

At the time, they used to call girls wharf whores. Australia and New Zealand were famous for it. When a ship would pull in, the girls that were on the dock would go on board that ship and get made up with somebody. Well, when that ship would leave, they just get off the ship and go back on the dock, and the next ship that docked there, they'd go on *that* ship. And sometimes they would ringbolt them. If they fancied the girl, they would take her around with them, she'd be a stowaway, so they had companionship. Well, anyway, they were saying that they met these two girls, one was from Australia, the other was English. She wanted to go back to Australia, so she got made up with one of the guys, and the other girl got made up with one of the guys. So they ringbolted them. They stopped in Spain. They had snuck them ashore and were in a bar and were having a few drinks. The second mate on the ship happened to see the girl in Spain.

He came into the same bar that these guys were in. "Oh, you meet these girls?"

"Oh, yeah, we just met 'em here."

"Oh, OK."

They snuck 'em back on board. They go all the way down to South

Africa, go over to Australia, and they dropped the girls off in Brisbane. They were outside the bar, having a drink, saying goodbye to the girls.

Here comes the second mate walking in. "Boy, those two girls look familiar." He didn't know that they ringbolted them.

Then they went to New Zealand. Well, one of the guys got made up with one of the girls in New Zealand, one of the wharf whores, and she always wanted to go to London. So now they reverse the process. They took her all the way back and dropped her off in London.

They were telling me they had a girl, a New Zealand girl they called Port Line Sue. Port Line Sue had never paid passage on a Port Line ship, but she'd made every run that Port Line had, anywhere in the world. Port Line Sue had been everywhere. Yeah.

So they says, "We can do that for you. We can get you to Durban." It's the next port. Then I'd join my ship there.

We had more drinks first.

I says, "Yeah, sounds good to me."

I go on there, and they give me one of the spare rooms. They're feeding me, I'm getting three meals a day, cigarettes, booze, they're coming in to talk to me.

When the *Mormaccove* got to Durban, it anchored out, they couldn't get to the dock. There was a launch service. The *Port Saint Lawrence* gets there, and they get hung up, too. We get anchored out. So we're stuck there. Now instead of just an overnight thing—I turn myself in and say I hitchhiked up—now we're *stuck*. So I'm still on board . . . I'm still on board . . . I'm still on board.

Now my captain is calling their captain on the radio saying, "You got my man on there?"

"No, no, no, no. I don't have him here."

So the captain's gotta make a search of the ship. He calls the steward up there, the bosun, the mates. "Do we have any stowaways on board?"

From what I heard later, the chief mate looked at the second mate, "Do we have any stowaways on board?"

The second mate looked at the third mate, "Do we have any stowaways on board?"

The third mate looked at the chief steward, "Do we have any stow-aways on board?"

And he looked at the bosun, guy named Duncan, they called him Drunken Duncan cuz he's gassed up all the time. He says, "No."

The guys come and get me. "Oh, man, something's up, Ron."

I says, "Maybe I better turn myself in."

They says, "No! Don't turn yourself in! We got this! We got it! We'll take care of this!"

How are we gonna take care of this, right?

The old man pulled a surprise inspection.

More drama. More stress.

I can't remember exactly how I heard it was coming . . . .

Inside the room I was in, there was a small wooden locker for clothing. It was about 4 foot high, maybe 3 foot deep. It had a little metal latch. I don't know why, but I had tried already fitting in there, and I could. Maybe I thought they'd pull a surprise inspection on me. I could take my seaman's card—size of a driver's license—and I found that if I put that in it would stick to the latch that fell down into the groove that locked it. I found that if I could close the door slowly, I could put my card through there, a reverse of getting in, you know, I'd knock it down and it would look like it was locked from the outside. Then I could knock it out. Why I did this, I don't know. I really don't, because I kept that room clean so that, if they opened the door, it would look like nobody lived in there. I kept the bunk made up, too. I made it look like nobody was in there.

So all of a sudden they're gonna pull a surprise inspection. I can hear the commotion outside. I go into the closet and do that little trick with the latch.

You can imagine: I'm what? Six foot three? I'm wedged in there.

I hear the captain saying, "What's in here?" He's going into *all* the rooms, doing a search so he could say, "Yeah, I searched the ship and there's nobody here." And it was more or less a surprise inspection. More than less, trust me.

Now, there were three rooms in this area. One the steward had kept some extra stores. The other one was where they used to keep empty kegs.

The captain says, "What's in this one?"

"That's the empty kegs from the bar, captain."

"What's in here?"

"I got some storage in here."

"What's in this one right ahead here?"

I hear all this. So I go into the locker and latch myself in.

The steward says, "Oh, nothing, captain, that's just a spare room."

"Open it."

"Captain, there's nothing in there."

"Then open it up."

I hear later, they were standing behind him, Drunken Duncan and a couple of the ABs, you know: *we've all had it now!*

They open it up, and I'm not in there. They said all their jaws dropped. "What the fuck? Where did he go?" The porthole's locked from the inside, you know.

The captain walks in. I can hear the footsteps. I'm a foot away from him. He looks around. "Nobody in here. OK. By the way, open that other one with the kegs."

Opens it up.

"Yeah, OK, nobody in there." He says, "This one, you've got what in here?"

"I've got extra stores, cans and stuff."

"Open that up."

Opens it up.

"OK. We're done."

As soon as I hear them lock the door and walk away, I hit the latch with my card. Sweat's pouring off me.

It wasn't 10 minutes later I hear a knocking on the door. "Ron! Ron!" It was some of the guys, Ken, Bubbles, Split Pin. "You in there?"

I says, "Yeah."

They says, "Open up." Cuz they didn't have the key then at the time. They were stealing the keys to get in. They had later made some for everything, but I open up. "Where the fuck were you?"

I point. "In there."

"You fit in there?"

"Yeah."

"How the fuck did you do that?"

I show 'em how I got in.

They says, "How did you even think of that?"

I says, "Look, guys, I got a lot of time on my hands, I figured if I had to hide in a hurry, I couldn't go out the porthole." I guess that's what sold the captain. When he saw the latch down on it, he assumed that no one would be in there cuz it was locked from the outside.

They says, "Man, we can't keep pulling this. We're gonna have to find someplace else for you."

I says, "Yeah, OK."

We're stuck out there for 2 weeks. So, they're looking around, and they would come get me at night so I could take a shower. I'd sneak to use the head, but not the shower. They had a head the same as we did, down the passageway, with the showers. The passageway was going fore and aft, there's a forward ship passageway right there and to go across the ship to the other side, to the port side. Then in between was just a big area with heads and showers. So I would go in there. They'd sneak in and come get me at night. "OK, Ron, coast is clear." They'd stand guard. One day I was in there taking a shower. The chief mate walked right by me, didn't even look.

The kid, Split Pin, says, "My God, Ron!"

I says, "What's wrong, Split Pin?"

"That was the chief mate! Walked right by you!"

If he'd a looked to the left he woulda saw me. I couldn't believe it.

So they're getting nervous, saying, "We gotta find somewhere else for you."

Like I said, I was on the starboard side. If you opened up the door, there's a little passageway. Then there was the starboard passageway, and then it was a forward ship passageway, going back and forth. If you made a left, you were going towards the stern, there was a metal door on the right, and that was a little passageway, and then it was an escape trunk for the engine room. It was locked from the outside, but if you had to get out of the engine room in a hurry, you could come up through this. It was about an 8 foot drop, and there was a hatch there you could go in and climb up the ladder to the opening, walk about 4 or 5 feet, and open this door from the inside. It was an escape hatch for the engine room; in case you had a fire down there and you couldn't get out, you could get out this way.

So they says, "The only problem we got with you going in there is we gotta get a key for that to unlock it from here to get you in there, cuz we can't take you through the engine room."

I says, "Yeah, OK."

That's when they got keys. They says, "We got keys for everything now. We stole everything." Cuz they'd go through the cargo, you know: "You need any envelopes, Ron?"

I says, "Where'd they come from?"

"Oh, we got it out of the cargo. They got some lighters down there, too. You need any lighters, Ron?"

I ain't supposed to be there and now they're stealing cargo and giving it to me.

I says, "Yeah, OK, this'll work."

So they got a key for that lock, and they says, "We better try this out just in case we have to go in a hurry, and we're gonna give you the key." So they unlocked it one night, and I walked in about 4 feet, it's about 6 feet high. I mean, this was just a hole with a ladder, and you went down there, and you were standing on top of the escape hatch. You came up the ladder about 8 feet. Then you walked up there, and you opened up the door from the inside, and you could escape.

So they says, "This is where you'll be going every time there's any kind of a drill, any kind of a thing." They says, "If you hear the alarm, just go—there'll be confusion," which there is, cuz they would have surprise fire and life boat drills, inspections. They says, "If we can't get to you in time, just get down here yourself. That way if he searches the room again, you won't be in there."

I was calling it the Black Hole of Calcutta, after the old British thing where they all got killed, they stuck them all in there and they all died. So anyway, if I heard the alarm, or if they'd come and say,

"Hey, we're gonna have a fire boat drill. You go ahead and go," they'd lock the door behind me, and I'd put the key in there, I'd go in, I'd lock it behind me by hand, and then I would go down in case they did open it, they would have to walk all the way in and look down to see me. Out of about 16 days on the ship, I think I was in there four or five times.

But it was kind of interesting. Guys were good. They had bought parakeets, large parakeets. These are big birds, you know. They bought them in Cape Town, and they had them as pets. They were allowed to have pets, we weren't.

Even though they were all English, and they were all white—they didn't integrate crews—they all didn't get along, it's the same thing I assume you'd find in any office, some people you don't associate with. "This guy is goofy, we don't like him." Birds-of-a-different-feather thing.

But I got along with everybody. I mean, I had to. But I just did. Different people were coming, giving me food, it was the deck department taking care of me.

They'd bring me some food, and I'd say, "Thanks, guys, but I just ate. The steward was here."

They says, "The steward? *He* knows you're here?"

The guys in the engine room were coming: "Hey, Ron, you got enough to eat? You need some cigarettes?"

"Thanks."

The others guys would come back: "You need some smokes?"

I says, "Well, yeah, but a guy from the engine room was just here."

"*They* know, too?"

The whole *ship* knew I was there, you know? I just couldn't be *found* is what it amounted to.

But they had these parrots. Well, when you bought it, they gave you a shoe box to take the bird with you, with holes in it. You could buy a cage for like two bucks. This one poor guy in the steward department, he wasn't all there, you know. He'd come give me food, and he liked to talk. "How are you?" "Yeah, fine."

This poor guy—they would take the birds out on deck, but they'd take them out in the cages, you know, so they wouldn't fly away—decided his bird needed some air. So he walked out—he was too cheap to buy a cage—with the box. He just opened the box. The bird jumped out of the box, looked around, saw land, and took off. Last he seen of it. He came in, just stunned, and told me. "You know that bird actually jumped out of that box and took off and flew away?"

I thought: well, birds *do* that when they have the chance.

So this is going on and on and on, and my captain's swearing to God, "*You and I know he's on there! You've got him on there!*" I'm hearing this from the guys. Their captain knew I was there, but he didn't want to find me cuz it would have been a terrible fine, for smuggling me, ringbolting me.

The day finally comes when the guys came and told me, "The *Mormaccove* just went in. We're supposed to go in tomorrow morning at eight o'clock. Be ready to go," you know, "maybe we can get you off of here as soon as we dock."

If they catch me anywhere on the *pier*, then my story was gonna be that I hitchhiked up.

Meantime, my captain had already told South Africa Customs: "I want that ship searched. I want that ship searched because my man's on there, he's stowed away on there. If he's not on there, I'm going down to the American Consulate to declare him a deserter." You know, right, which he really couldn't have got away with cuz I left my clothes on the Moore-McCormack ship. I mean, the law is the law is the law. But when somebody took it to court and challenged it, they didn't bother changing the law, because years ago they had taken it to court, about desertion, and the court said, "As long as he's left his clothes on there, you can't charge him with desertion, just failing to join the ship." Plus, if they'd left me in port—I don't know how that would have worked out if they would have said I was "Not Fit for Duty" and I missed the ship. I could have said, "OK. I was 'Not Fit for Duty.' Why didn't you send me home?" So now there would have been a conflict. So I wasn't sure about that. That's why I—plus the booze—I agreed to the ringbolt. Sounded like a good idea. Like a lot of things in my life, it sounded like a good idea at the time.

Anyway, we came in, all of a sudden, instead of eight o'clock in the morning, they're gonna shift us in at five o'clock, which was God sent, or devil sent, anybody you happened to believe in, or both of 'em. Every once in awhile I look up, I say, "Enough is enough," and I look down and I say, "Enough is enough." You know, you gotta give 'em their due.

Five o'clock we shoot in, and we musta got to the dock like six thirty. It's just getting daylight.

The guys came by and says, "We're at the dock. Everybody's gone to eat now. There's nobody around. You got a South African security guard at the gangway. Now's your chance, Ron. Go for it."

I says, "See you guys. Thanks." Phew!

I shoot out. The guard had his back to me. I go down the gangway. I didn't even think he saw me. And Customs was waiting for eight o'clock to come to the ship. So I'm gone. I'm down, and I can see the *Mormaccove*, and I take off, I cut through the railroad yard. I get there, and I go up the gangway, and we have these South African older guys for security.

Didn't say anything. I mean, didn't even pay attention to me. I spoke English, that's all that counted. You're American. "OK, yeah. Go ahead."

I get in there, I see my watch partner, I go to my room cuz there's two in a room and I knock and he says, "What are you doing back?"

I says, "I just thought I'd stop back here. Heard the captain was putting the draw out, you know, I needed the money."

"*Where you been? The old man's getting ready to write you off! They got Customs coming down here! They're gonna hang you and crucify you and you better spread your arms out, get ready for that cross!*"

So we go wake up the bosun, Dutch. "*Where the fuck you been? They been looking all over for you. You were on that British ship, weren't you?*"

I says, "No."

"*The old man and the mate, they're going fucking crazy up there, and they're steaming, and the old man's cooking . . . .*" you know.

And I'm thinking: if you're gonna have a heart attack, have it over something else, don't have it over me.

Eight o'clock, I go up, go see the purser.

I says, "I want to turn myself in."

He says, "Well, you gotta go see the mate and captain."

"OK."

So I go up and see the mate, and the mate says, "Oh. You're back?"

I says, "Yeah."

He says, "What happened?"

"Well, I was 'Not Fit for Duty,' and I thought you guys were gonna just shift the ship from one port pier to the other, so I was ashore. And you guys left."

He says, "Yeah. Where you been for 2 *weeks*?"

"Well, I got made up with a girl down in Port Elizabeth. And I was gonna take the train up, you know, and she kept calling Durban, and you guys weren't coming to the dock yet. So I said, 'Well, what's the sense of going up here?'" I says, "I was down there with her, and then when I found out it was coming to the dock, I was out of money, and she didn't have any, so I just hitchhiked up here."

He looks at me and says, "That's one hell of a story, Ron."

I felt like saying, "Yeah, I like it, too." And I also felt like saying, "That's the only story you're gettin' outta me," yeah.

He says, "You gotta see the old man."

"OK."

We go up to see the old man, Williamson. He's just a miserable old prick. White hair, crew cut, just a miserable fuck. "Yeah, well, you're getting logged and this and that, 10 days logged—"

And I should add this. It was funny. I missed the ship in Port Elizabeth on 1/30/75. January 31. At the time, we didn't get paid for that day. We got paid for what amounted to 30 days a month, no matter how many days were really in that month. So, technically, there were 4 days a year we never got paid for. When he went to log me, he was gonna log me from the 31st to the 11th.

And the purser, who was a real cunt, he says, "Captain, you can't do that. He didn't get paid for the 31st."

The captain says, "What do you mean?"

At the time, that was true. In other words, if you worked February 1 to February 28, you were entitled to 1 month's pay, even though it was a 28-day month, you got paid for 30. But if you worked January 1 to January 31, you got 30 days' pay. You didn't get 31 days' pay. That *really* pissed him off!

I'm thinking, you know, in the entire scheme of things, ain't nobody gonna give a fuck about this anyway.

He's grumbling, "You're getting logged, and fined, and you're going to the Coast Guard!"

I says, "Yeah, OK." No comment. It was senseless to argue with him.

This other guy says, "Captain, what're we gonna do? He was 'Not Fit for Duty' anyways."

Captain says, "If you really were 'Not Fit for Duty,' they should have sent you home right away, and that doesn't excuse you from taking responsibility, you should have come up to Durban right away. You should have made the move with the ship."

I says, "Well, captain, I'll just talk to the Coast Guard about it. We'll see what they have to say." Final judge, you know. So that was that.

So I got logged, and I turned to.

Good old Dutch, the bosun, I just got back, right. He couldn't say, "Well, you know, wait 'til noon or something." No, it's "Yeah, I got a job for you. Paint these winches over here."

Unbelievable.

That same day Split Pin comes over to the *Mormaccove* to see me, and I catch him and I says, "What are you doing here?"

He says, "I wanted to see what happened to you."

I says, "Man, get the fuck outta here before you get grabbed." I says, "Split Pin, they grab you on here, they're calling Customs, Immigration, FBI, Interpol. This old man's out of his mind. Don't get caught on here, kid."

"Oh, I'm sorry, I'm sorry."

"Just go on get outta here."

He splits, and here comes Dutch. "Hey, I heard Split Pin was on board and he wanted to see me."

I says, "No, Dutch, he didn't want to see you, he came on board to see what happened to me."

"What'd you do with him?"

"I got him out of here."

"Well, yeah, but he wanted to see me and I—"

Typical, egotistical, you know.

I says, "You can go over tomorrow to *Port Saint Lawrence* to see him."

That day went pretty smooth, and we were supposed to leave the next day. So they said sea watch is at noon. I was off at noon, took off, went over to the British ship, telling them what happened. So I came back at four o'clock, and they'd delayed the sailing 'til the next day. Now I'm on board, and they had Durban Immigration come see me, up in the old man's office.

I come up there, and they says, "What happened here?"

I says, "I was injured. I didn't think I had to make the ship, you know, the ship was just gonna shift. It was gonna stay there in Port Elizabeth. I didn't have to work. So I just figured I didn't have to worry about it." I says, "You can check the ship's log book."

"Where were you for 2 weeks?"

That was always a sticking point for some reason.

I says, "I was in Port Elizabeth. I had a few dollars left." I says, "I had some South African money. I guess I should have turned myself in, but I met this girl at a bar there, and she agreed to let me stay with her, and she was calling. I told her I'd pay for my own train ride." I says, "She kept calling, and the ship wasn't in Durban, it was in anchor out there, nobody could get to it. There was no launch service."

They says, "Where were you earlier today when we were here?"

"I had time off. I was ashore."

They says, "You just wander off whenever you feel like it, don't you?"

I wanted to say, "Yeah, I'll do anything I feel like fucking doing here or anywhere else in this world." But, I says, "I was off, so I decided to take off." It was getting to the point where I was—you know how you're sitting there and you're talking to them and you're just completely looking the other way?

They says, "Your attitude's terrible."

I says, "Yeah." Now I'm thinking: why don't we just get in a fistfight and get this over with?

They says, "Your attitude's *terrible*."

I says, "You know, it's hard to believe, but I've had complaints about it before. But you know, it hasn't done a thing for it."

That was it.

"Why don't we get in the truck and go down to Immigration?"

I'm surprised they didn't handcuff me.

Now I'm going down the gangway, I'm in the back of the truck, I'm in the cage. Now we're going to Immigration. But I did have the papers that the old man had logged me, 13 days logs and fines—you know, Coast Guard, looked like some kind of fucking summary execution, the paper they hand you before they shoot you. "Do you want a blindfold? Read this before we blindfold you."

I turn around, and they get me down there, and they says, "You gotta go in the cell."

"Yeah, OK."

Well, at the time, it was segregated. But it wasn't segregated for Immigration. I wasn't there that long, 6, 8 hours. I guess they let me cool my heels. It was dark already by then. They came and got me out. I just went in a corner and sat down. They gave me some soup or something, a fucking pencil would have stood up straight in it. In the States you'd call that "soup from the bottom," you know, it's really thick.

They come and get me out and says, "You have to see the head of Immigration." Put the coup de grâce on me.

I'm sitting out there in the office, and he calls me in and says, "You can have a seat."

I says, "Yeah, thank you."

He says, "What's gonna happen out of all this? What do you feel should happen out of this?"

"Well, I don't know about here, but, the captain already logged and fined me."

He reads my papers. "Well," he says, "this almost is like double jeopardy to do anything else to you." He says, "How long were you in detention?"

"Eight or 10 hours." I think I was there 5 or 6.

"Well . . . you know . . . . Your ship's leaving when?"

"Any time now. It's supposed to leave today, but we're hung up. It'll be probably sometime early tomorrow morning."

He says, "Well, we wouldn't want you to miss your ship again, would we?"

I says, "No 'we' wouldn't."

He says, "Tell you what. We're gonna take you back to that ship. I'm gonna instruct the officers here to put you back in the cage, and you're going back to that ship. And that's the only ship you'll be going on. I do not want you to get off of that ship until it leaves. Do not come back into Durban. Do not walk down the pier to any other ships. Do not say goodbye to anyone. Just stay on there. And leave." He says, "Is that OK?"

I says, "That's fine."

"I'll call them now, and you can go."

"Yes, sir."

I got back to the ship.

I knew the South Africans weren't gonna do too much to me. They wanted me to roll over on the British, because they didn't get along: British called them yarpies and the South Africans called the British POMEs: prisoners of mother England. I knew if I kept my mouth shut, that—you know, nobody wanted trouble. South Africa didn't want any problems with America, because America was on them for being apartheid. I don't think anybody really understood apartheid, the way it was set up. From what I see on TV, the reporting, and the version people get of these countries, as I said, South Africa, apartheid, it was portrayed here as the blacks are oppressed. Well, the rules were for *everyone*. You couldn't walk down the street and just punch somebody black in the head cuz they were black. You couldn't do it. And I noticed over the years running down there, they were getting more and more freedom until they, mainly cuz of peer pressure from the other countries, changed it around and give them their way. You know, majority rule. Well, I think it's shown through history, majority rule doesn't necessarily make it right.

Anyway, we left and went up the next day to Maputo. Sure enough, the Coke sign was still there. Big sign, Coca-Cola, it's probably still there to this day. This was 1975. We get up there, and the communist government comes on board, and they're saying if you change any money, you have to change it with us, cuz they wanted the dollars. If you get caught changing money in the black market, you're in big trouble. Blah, blah, blah.

Well, we know better. A couple of us go ashore, and we're looking around at different things there, and we're changing our money illegally, getting more escudos, which is really now not any good anywhere else in the world. Not even Portugal wants it now. We're looking around in different souvenir stores that are still run by the hard-core Portuguese that may have communist leanings, that's why they can stay there. Now we're talking abandoned buildings, places just folding up, closing down, buildings half built. Progress is a thing of the past.

This one storekeeper says, "I'll take dollars. I'll give you a hell of a deal in dollars." Souvenirs were almost free.

I says, "Excuse me, but I have some South African rand, and I have dollars. Some English friends of mine will be coming up, and they have pounds. Will you be interested in changing their pounds?"

He says, "I'll take anything. *Anything*. I'll give you escudo. I'll take anything." Basically, what he was doing was, he didn't want to leave his inventory. I guess his life savings, so to speak, was in escudo. So he was willing to trade anything to get anything to get out of the country.

Well, a couple days later, the Englishmen show up, so I go over to the ship.

They says, "What's going on?"

I'm trying to explain to 'em about the guy who can change their money. So we're pretty much ashore. The captain on my ship hated it, he's waiting for me to fuck up again. And the Englishmen are just the Englishmen, you know, they're going out, getting all drunked up, pissing out in the street. I think it was Ginger was the one who walked outside and pissed in the flowerpot of one of the bars we were at. We're going along, having a pretty good time, and I'm on their ship going back and forth.

One day I was over there, and they weren't working, they were all in the bar, and Drunken Duncan was still their bosun, and I couldn't find the guys. They had gone already or they had left or were sleeping. They were gonna leave to go to Australia and Tasmania. We were gonna leave to go back to the States. Drunken Duncan, the bosun, was supposed to be there all the time.

Duncan says, "Come on in my room, have a beer."

I says, "OK, Duncan."

So I go and we're sitting there having a beer, and the tide's going out. The ship's going *down*, and the gangway's *up*, but now it's almost falling in.

The chief mate, he's in charge of the deck department and what goes on on deck, he sticks his head in and says, "Excuse me, Duncan, if you don't mind, we're getting ready to lose the gangway."

Duncan put his beer down.

I go, "Oh, hi, mate."

"Oh, hi, Ron."

I'm on a first name basis with everyone. This is after the stowaway incident.

Duncan goes out to help. Except there's nobody around. So I go out to help.

Duncan says, "I don't have any help!"

I says, "I'll give you a hand."

So I go out on the gangway. I get it rigged up. I says, "OK, take it up now. Move it in." I hold it back. It didn't slam. We got it.

The chief mate's just standing there looking at me and Duncan, and after we get this done he's still leaning on the rail, and he looks at me and says, "You fancy a trip to Australia?" Like, you know: "You're the only one I can get to do something around here, and you're not even signed on."

And I was thinking about it. Later on I told the guys, "The mate said I could go to Tasmania."

"Why didn't you say 'yeah'? He'd probably take you, if you want to go. It's not bad at all, Ron, Tasmania's nice. Australia, too."

Back then the story going around was there was 20 women for every one man in Australia. Well, that was true, but it was like the west coast of Australia where this was happening, not so much on the east coast. Basically, you had women all over the place, and when these ships would come in, these wharf whores, they would come and hope you would immigrate there, or stay there or take them with you or something. Let's face facts: everybody wants to dominate, we need a domination thing in our life. And we're there to fulfill that mission in life or something, I don't know. I was almost going along with the idea, but I figured I was in enough trouble.

Then they says, "We're going back to England then, Ron. You'd like England."

So what it was gonna amount to was: I was gonna go over, take the trip there, then I was gonna go back to England with them, and I could just turn myself in to the American Consul in London, after I ran out of money, and say, "I'm a destitute American seaman."

They'd say, "Oh, you missed your ship here in London?"

"No, actually I missed it in South Africa."

"When was that?"

"Five months ago."

"Where have you been for 5 . . . ?" you know.

It was hard enough explaining where I was for 2 *weeks*. I says, "No, but thank you," but I did toy with the idea. It would have been great fun, a great adventure.

Anyway, we're bouncing around there, and that last night, we were getting ready to leave. We were going back to the States, and they were gonna be there for a few more days and then they were going to Australia and then Tasmania. We had all this money left, all of us. Everybody had everything they wanted, all the souvenirs, and we had all this money left.

So we says, "We'll have one big blowout."

We went in this restaurant, and it was one of the few restaurants where the Portuguese were still going to. It had that feeling of: "Hey, I'm here, I'm gonna stay here, this is my place, I'm not going back to Portugal," whether they had communist leanings or not. You know: "One government's the same as another." We went in there and turned around, and we had all this money, and we said we'd like prawns, which are big shrimp, and I mean *big*. I mean, their versions of prawns were 5 inches long, or more. We even took some of the girls with us, some of the half-castes—half Portuguese, half black—we'd picked up along the way, acquired them in our travels, or they acquired us, as the case may be, who knows? Who cared?

We got fried prawns and beer. Some of the prawns were split in half. Some were boiled. We just said we want to spend this money. We want all the prawns and beer we can get. We literally gave everything we had. And they wanted it. They were still using it as currency. They were more than happy to have the money, and we were more than happy to give it to them.

The interesting thing about the girls that were there: you know how Westerners tear the head off the shrimp and just eat the body, you try to get rid of the vein back there, clean it up before you fry it or boil it and shell it. There, whether it's fried or boiled, they give it to you with the head. You tear the head off, then you skin it, then you eat it. Or, if it's fried and cut in half, you peel it out. But the head is still there. The head's fried, too. The girls are sucking the heads out of the prawn.

We're all kind of looking at them.

They says, "This is the best part."

In their society, I assume it was. To us, it really wasn't. But there was so much we couldn't eat it all. It was just one big party.

And we agreed to keep in touch with each other, and to this day, me and Ken Bottoms, we're still fast friends.

I went back to the ship, they went back to theirs. We left in the morning. They could barely get me up to secure. I was falling asleep on the wheel, hand steering.

This captain still used the bell system. On ships they didn't have clocks many, many years ago. And how they would know a 4-hour watch would be: eight bells signal the end of one 4-hour watch and the beginning of another. I'm just giving a for instance: twelve o'clock noon would be eight bells. Half hour after that, twelve thirty would be one bell, one o'clock would be two bells, one thirty would be three bells, two o'clock would be four bells, two thirty would be five bells, three o'clock would be six bells, three thirty would be seven bells, four o'clock, you start a new watch, would be eight bells. There was just a little line going up above the ship's wheel, the old wooden wheel like you see in the old movies, and it would lead out to the front of the bridge. Nobody could hear this fucking thing. But the old man wanted it. *Ding.* Cuz he could hear it in his deck down below. *Ding.* Fucking nut. I think it was the only thing kept me awake. Every half hour I'd hear it. *Ding.* You know, I'd be steering. *Ding.*

We got to New York and I quit five minutes before I was fired because they had a strange thing then. If you were logged like that, they couldn't punish you twice for the same crime. So basically, they couldn't fire me, for that offense, cuz they had logged me. They could say, "He fouled up, and we have the proof here, and we didn't log him, but he's fired." They could log me, but then they couldn't fire me. I saved them the trouble. I quit. Let's face facts: when you got 13 on you, the black spot, you're the black sheep, it's time to go. You don't want to stick around. I knew this, and I wanted to get off anyway. They couldn't believe I quit cuz I had already been logged, so why would I quit? But I says, "No, I'm going."

We're in the payoff line at two o'clock in the afternoon. I'm getting ready to go back to Cleveland. Like I said, at the time, we had shipping commissioners. Ronald Reagan did away with them later. Congress said there was no money for them. Back then, they made sure you got a fair break, made sure things were legal. They authorized your sea time, the discharges, they made sure that the company kept up to the agreements and everything. You had union officials there, but the shipping commissioners would take it if you had a grievance. Sometimes it worked, the majority of the time it didn't.

Anyway, everything was pretty much decided right on the ship. If you took your grievance ashore—say, "We'll take it ashore and settle it through the union"—maybe 3 or 4 months later you hear that you lost it. Most guys, if they really had a grievance, would go to small claims court in New York. That was the easiest way to do it.

Anyway, I'm there, and I see the shipping commissioner running around, bringing up the phone. Being paranoid, I was just: this has gotta be about me. I overheard a little of the conversation on the phone: he had a case of a seaman who had missed the ship and rejoined approximately 12 days later. According to the federal government and rules of the Merchant Marine, I couldn't have the sea time, because sea time counted for an advancement, and it also counted on your vacation pay, and this and that. He was calling to make sure that this is what the law said. If I wasn't on board, could I still be entitled to the sea time for those 12 days. Well, I would lose the 12 days towards vacation pay. I think then it was about 8 days for 30. But could I get this or not? And the answer was no, I couldn't. Then the Coast Guard was there, and the Coast Guard wanted to see me before the shipping commissioner could give me the money, cuz the shipping commissioner told me when he gave the discharges, "You gotta see the Coast Guard before I can pay you."

"OK."

I go over to the Coast Guard and they says, "You know, you've got a 'Failing to Join,'" and this and that.

I says, "Yes."

They says, "You'll have to make a hearing for this."

"OK."

"You want to come down tomorrow to New York to the Coast Guard for a hearing?"

I says, "As I remember it, I think I'm entitled to have the hearing anywhere I want."

They says, "Well, yeah, you are entitled to have that if you don't want to have it here."

"I'll be going to Cleveland tonight. I want to have my hearing at the Coast Guard station in Cleveland." Which at the time you could do. You were entitled to go anywhere you wanted to. You could have it in your home port.

Cleveland really wasn't big on hearings because they had only lake sailors coming out of there. And 1 out of 100 would there be somebody like me would say, "I want to enforce my rights, I want to have it in my home port." At the time I was living in Cleveland.

So they says, "You can have it anywhere you want." They says, "But you better be somewhere nine thirty tomorrow morning, you better be at a Coast Guard station, cuz that's when your hearing's scheduled. You can get a continuance, but you better be at a Coast Guard station. You understand that?"

I says, "I do." I turn around, I got a flight to Cleveland, and a friend picks me up. He says, "Hey, man, what'd you do this time?"

I says, "I got a slight problem. We gotta go down to the Coast Guard station tomorrow morning at nine thirty."

He says, "Whadya mean 'we'?"

"Well, I need somebody to, you know, tell them what a good, honest citizen I am, upright and all that, vouch for me."

He just looked at me like: What are you, out of your fucking mind? He says, "I think you're gonna have to get down there by yourself." He says, "Let me know what happens."

I was out drinking that night. I turn around, and I borrowed somebody's car. I dropped them off at their house like twelve o'clock at night, and I says, "Man, I better get some sleep."

I got up at seven o'clock in the morning, cleaned up, took a shower, got my paperwork together, had my coffee, and got down to the Coast Guard station on East Ninth Street in Cleveland at nine o'clock. I went in, and this is where I got my seaman's card, originally.

The secretary says, "Can I help you?"

I says, "Yeah, I'm here for a hearing."

She says, "I don't believe we have you on the schedule here for a hearing."

"This was supposed to take place in New York. But I'm entitled to have a hearing anywhere I choose."

"Well, I don't know about that."

"Well—I *do*."

She says, "Can I see some paperwork?"

I show her, did a brief explanation.

She says, "Will you have a seat here?"

"Sure."

There's two officers in back. She comes out with one of them.

He says, "You want to come in the back here and have a talk with us?"

Like I had a choice, you know. "Sure."

He says, "Can I see your seaman's card?"

I gave him my seaman's card.

He says, "Please understand, we're used to dealing with lake sailors here." He says, "How did all this come about?"

I says, "Well, I injured my hand on the ship. We were in Port Elizabeth, South Africa, I was 'Not Fit for Duty.'"

He says, "Why, cuz you were drunk?"

My eyes must have still been sunk in, you know. I says, "No, I injured my hand. Doctor gave me a 'Not Fit for Duty.' I had gone ashore because the ship was only supposed to shift to another berth. When I came back, they said the ship had left."

He says, "We got a discrepancy of 2 weeks here, from the difference in these discharges and what the captain logged you."

I says, "Yeah. I had a friend there that I stayed with that I had acquired in Port Elizabeth. If I turned myself in they were going to put me in jail." I says, "I was 'Not Fit for Duty.' I didn't know whether to go back to the doctor. I really didn't know what to do." I says, "She volunteered to let me stay there, and she would call the Port Authority in Durban, and when the ship came in the next day or so, I would just pay my own way up to the ship by train."

"What's this 2-week discrepancy?"

"The ship stayed out at anchor. There was no launch service. I couldn't get to it 'til it got to the dock, and as soon as it got to the dock, she called and they said, yeah, they were in. I basically hitch-hiked up there."

He says, "Let me call New York."

He calls New York marine inspection, and he says, "Yeah, I got a guy here," he says my name. "Yeah." He looks at me: "How did you get here so quick?"

"Airplane."

"This was yesterday."

"Yeah."

He says into the phone, "He flew here. He's here. This is his home, Cleveland, Ohio."

I imagine what was said was, "He expressed his right to have the hearing anywhere he wanted, and that is his right." Cuz he's talking to the guy in New York at marine inspection. Off the phone to me he says, "You were supposed to show up *there* at nine thirty."

I says, "Did he explain to you that I had the—"

"Yeah, he explained that, but you should have showed up *there* and then said you wanted to come *here.*"

I says, "I'm sorry. I just flew in. I didn't think there was gonna be any problem with it as long as I showed up at a marine inspection."

He gets back on the phone with the guy, and I guess showing up is showing up. Rather than make a hassle out of it, he says, "This is right off the bat *here,* how do you feel this should go?"

"I'm innocent."

He kind of looked at me like: you could be innocent of anything? He says, "Go over this one more time."

I did.

And he says, "Let's get a continuance on this. We'll get more information, and we'll start again." He says, "How about giving us a week or so?"

"Sure, fine."

I go back a week later.

He says, "You know, we contacted the captain on the ship, and he's got a different version of what happened."

I says, "Well, he can have his version, and I can have mine, and somewhere in between . . . ." I says, "But, as for proof of anything, I can't prove anything, and I don't think he can, either."

He says, "You know, that's pretty close . . . . That's pretty close." He says, "Would you like to get this over with right away?"

I says, "Yes, if I'm exonerated."

"Well, if you plead more or less guilty to this offense, 'Failing to Join': no suspension. And we'll just kind of write this off."

"I already paid for that, 13 days logged and fines. Now it's extra."

"You might have something there." He says, "You plead out to this, and we'll just forget the incident. It'll just go into your records."

I was just gonna say "yes" to that when the other Coast Guard guy says, "You can't do that." This guy says, "If he pleads, if he says he did this, he actually missed the ship and everything, if nothing else, he's got to get an official warning."

I look at this guy, and this guy was kind of straight-laced about everything. I look at this guy that I got for the hearing, and we're both looking at each other like, you know: why did *this* guy even have to be in the room with us? Now *this* guy don't want to offend *this* guy.

He says, "If you'll accept that you were wrong, a warning is all you'll get. Don't do it again, and we can just shut this thing off right now. You agree to that, no lawyers, no involvement, no hassle." He says, "If you *do* want an official hearing, we'll do it, but, you know, now it's getting to a trial."

I says, "Let's get this over with."

It was interesting that they wanted to get rid of me. It was like Pontius Pilate, you know: "I wash my hands of this." Let the Americans deal with you. And when the Americans were dealing with me it was: "Why don't you just go away?"

I've found that in my travels all over the world. I'm 61 years old. I've been doing this since I was 21. Look at the different places where I was bribing people, where it was easier for them to take a $20 bill than it was to go through the hassle. It just mirrors society, just keep passing the buck and hope it goes to someone else. And it goes away. It just goes away. "Why don't you just go away? Why don't you go somewhere else and foul up? Give somebody else the problem." And it just constantly goes and goes and goes like that.

They ask me if I'd ever been logged before.

I says, "Yeah, one time in Saigon in '71."

"What'd you get for that?"

"The Coast Guard didn't even bother with me for 1 day. I got fined a day's pay."

They says, "Alright. Get out of here."

And that's exactly what happened. I got an official warning. That was the end of that.

Justice triumphed, as usual.

I was exonerated.

I could use the money

The *S.S. American Ranger*, steamship, United States Lines Company. They had a steady charter from Wilmington, North Carolina, Sunny Point, ammunition dump, over to Zeebrugge, Belgium. Discharge ammo, backload ammo, take it back to Sunny Point. I think it was only a 30-day trip.

Nothing eventful. I did it because I wasn't under suspension, and I figured I could use the money. I was trying to make my pension quota for the year.

An interesting captain on there, McNamara. The United States Lines had three captains. Every company had their captains that were notorious, and U.S. Lines had McNamara. Later on, McNamara, he dies, and the Wilmington Union Hall for Masters, Mates and Pilots— cuz he was captain, he would come out of that hall—they had a party when he died. Baked a cake.

It wasn't every day you got to lose one like him.

Some people took this more seriously than others is the only way I can phrase this.

Container ship. Half-assed container ship, I should say. U.S. Lines was going into complete containerization, and they needed container ships. So they tried to convert some of their older boom ships into container ships. It worked for a little while.

I think we had one day in Le Havre, France. I went to all the old haunts. But the old whores were gone. They all died off. This was '75, and they moved on to greener pastures. Le Havre was beating itself out, you know, it'd seen its better days. Matter of fact, the Mexican Bar was closed in Le Havre, and I walked up to another bar, it was even a higher class place than when I started in '67. I walked in, and the place hadn't changed. France was getting expensive, but it was something to do. You might have to take a little taxi ride to get into town because the container facilities were always a little further out of town where they had built new harbors to specially take containers, while all the break-bulk ships still went into the same spots that were in town. I walked in, ordered a beer, paid in francs. And the girls spoke English.

I says, "What happened to all the girls?"

She says, "The girls are still around, but they only fuck rich Americans and rich Frenchman—you know—one of the two."

One of the stops was in Rotterdam, which had a Chinatown, the den of iniquity area. They had about three Chinese and about a thousand prostitutes. We never really got a lot of time in port on the quick turnaround container ships. But I was entitled to a day off if I made the next trip. Most guys took it to be home with their loved ones when we got into their port of call, what they called home. I took mine overseas to be with my loved ones, so I could get a drink and talk to the girls.

Anyway, I get my day off, and I'm wandering around Chinatown, and I'm pretty well-blitzed already. The place closed for 1 hour every day, where they would clean the place up, get the drunks off the street, the seamen back to their ships. I remember one time they came through with a police car with a van, just picking guys up and trying to find out which ship they were on. You know, just passed out in the streets. Very humane of the Dutch to do that.

Anyway, I'm wandering down the street looking for a drink. I ran into this other merchant seaman from who knows where. I was a lot younger then, but he was a little younger than I was. We couldn't communicate, but we both knew we were looking for a bar to get a drink. He's motioning and waving to me to come on, follow him. I don't know what he was to this day, we didn't speak to each other. There was no speaking going on here. It was a different kind of language. "I can find a drink for us." I could sense this.

We get to this bar, and it had a rail going through halfway along the front window. The curtains were pulled. Even though it was only halfway, you could see that the bar was closed and the door was locked and no lights were on. And he's beating on the door.

I'm saying, "No, partner. No, friend. Look. It's closed. *Closed.*" I'm thinking: this guy's really fucked up.

Next thing I know, you can see a light go on, a door opens in the back. I'm thinking maybe he knows something. Sure enough, a guy comes to the door and lets us in and escorts us to the back. Here's a small bar back there. I mean, very small, but very nice, very clean, well lit back there. Get a beer, you know, they knew what we wanted. They're all speaking Dutch or whatever. I'm trying to drink the beer. Now I gotta use the head. I got a bowel movement coming.

So I'm asking, "WC, WC," you know.

"Oh, right there, right there." They point to the door.

I go in there, and it's beautiful. So I have a movement. Now, I can't find any toilet paper. I'm fucked up. So there's a nice, big fluffy white towel there, all folded up. So I unfold it, use it, and I fold it back and put it there, and I go back out and finish my beer. And I thought I better leave.

They says, "No, no. You stay. Stay."

"No, no, no. Thank you."

Now, the funniest part about this is, there is some seaman, somewhere in the world right now, saying, "You know, I was in Rotterdam in 1975, and I went in this after-hours joint, had to use the bathroom, and I went to use the towel to wash my hands, and somebody had used it as toilet paper." That's the really funny part.

Yeah, that was the end of that. I made two trips. They were 30-day roundtrips. There was nothing really spectacular about it. Just a few easy bucks. I used it to work at my hobby, which was sailing, to keep up my real occupation, which was drinking.

Who do you think I met at Omar Sharif's Cafeteria?

Green Forest, Central Gulf. Older ship. The Vietnam War was over. Yeah, November of '75. I made the coastwise and the foreign. It'd come back in from a foreign voyage that was going to New Orleans to pay off. The Vietnam War was over. The South Vietnamese finally gave up. There were still some ships going over, taking back some of the cargo that was left in the other countries. Shipping had to readjust itself again. The older ships that they were getting the last legs out of, the last couple of clicks, like this Central Gulf ship, these were interesting. I think there were five or six of these; these had been old World War II troop transport ships. The government actually went to Central Gulf and cut everything away. All you had was a hull. They made freighters out of them, with the house aft, engine aft, the hatches forward. These ships were all patchwork. We called them stem-winders. The hatch is forward and, literally, you drop cargo in. There was no such thing as tiers. They literally converted these ships and gave them to Central Gulf and said just run these and they're yours at the end of the Vietnam War. This one happened to get a commercial run after the war. They were on their last legs to go with a load of chemical fertilizer, government cargo. This was a government giveaway to the Island of Ceylon. Raggedy ass ship.

I caught it in Wilmington, North Carolina, took it to New Orleans, we paid off the coastwise. We were in New Orleans loading the chemical fertilizer, and then we turned around and went to Mobile to load the Army trucks for the Jordanian Army and Yemen. This is the trip to Aqaba, Jordan. This is where I met Omar Sharif.

This was the trip with the guy coming down the pier in Mobile.

He had missed the ship. He said he got car trouble. The captain wouldn't pay him for when he took the job in New Orleans, but he did give him the job there in Mobile. He was on the 4 to 8 watch, I was on the 12 to 4. Puerto Rican guy, nice enough guy; he had a big tattoo of Puerto Rico on his back, we later found out, and he had married some woman with about eight kids. We figured he was in jail or something, so he got the tattoo. He tells the captain he's got eight dependents, or nine dependents, or something, so they're not gonna take all the tax out. OK, maximum draw, maximum allotment. We could make allotments, you know, half of your pay after taxes and social security, you could send that half home. But then you couldn't get much of a draw in these foreign ports.

We turn around, coming out of Mobile, I had the wheel with the pilot, and this guy's gonna come up and relieve me.

Third mate says, "Do you know this AB?"

I says, "No."

He says, "Do you think he can steer?"

I says, "I don't know."

"Well, look, when he relieves you, stand by." Because you got the captain up there, the pilot who's giving you directions, and you got the mate on watch. I'm steering the old wooden wheel, hydraulic system. You had to fight to the finish with this thing, you had a lot of play in it.

He comes up to relieve me, says, "OK, I got you, what are you doing?"

The pilot had just given me "midships," which is center, no rudder on the right, no rudder on the left. You're in the middle. Midships.

I says, "The rudder's midships."

"OK. I got it. Midships."

The third mate says, "Can you steer?"

"Yeah, yeah, I can steer, I can steer."

He says, "Ron, you stand over to the side here."

I says, "OK."

The pilot says, "Steady." That means, wherever you're at, that's the way the pilot wants to go. You go steady on a course or you go steady on an object out there. When the pilot said "Steady," this guy grabs the wheel with both arms and both legs and says, "It's steady! It's steady! I got it!"

Third mate yells, "Get him off the wheel! Ron, you steer!"

Fucking nut. We had to get him outta there. They brought up his watch partner, who could steer.

OK, we're underway now. We're gonna go around Florida, through the Atlantic, over through the Med, through the Suez Canal. So everybody's saying this guy's gotta be able to steer going through the Suez Canal. We can't expect to put it off on somebody else or pay them overtime to do this.

The second mate's saying, "He's on watch with me. He'll be able to steer. This ain't gonna be a problem."

Yeah, right.

We get to the Suez Canal. He got lucky and didn't have to steer. So we go through. He doesn't know much about seamanship or anything, but he's out there working, trying to make money for his loved ones, all 27 of 'em that he married into.

At the Suez Canal, the captain doesn't have to put out a draw, technically. I was deck delegate, mainly because I could read and write the English language, you know, den mother, father confessor to the insanity of it all. I told everybody, "Don't wake me up. Don't aggravate me about anything. You're not gonna get it settled here, wait'll we get back." I said, "Write it down. We'll get it settled when we get back."

Which, we never did.

Matter of fact, this asshole came in one morning. I'm on the 12 to 4, he's on the 4 to 8. I'm sleeping at 8 in the morning. Everyone would get up for breakfast, I'd sleep in. I'd get off at 4 and I'd sleep in. I might get up at 10, go get coffee, and there'd be some pastry left over or whatever was left, I'd eat. I'd get ready to go on watch, I'd eat lunch at eleven thirty and have a sandwich and go up on the wheel or on deck. He comes busting in the room at 0800 screaming about the chief mate. They would give me the overtime for the week, see, and I'd give it to the mate, and the mate would give it back to me and anything that was disputed would be red-lined.

I'm just waking up.

"*Look what the mate did! He disputed it! Now I ain't getting paid!*"

I got 4 hours sleep, and I says, "What?"

"*The mate! Look what he did!*"

I had my knife there. I says, "You see that knife?"

He calms down. "Yeah. I see that knife."

I says, "Well the next fucking time you come barging in here," I says, "and wake me up," I says, "I'm gonna stab you with it."

He looks. "What about my overtime?"

I says, "Wait until I'm on watch. We're gonna take care of things when we get back to the States, like I told you. We'll get it all taken care of. Do not wake me up. I told you that. I don't want any bullshit beefs."

He slams the door and leaves.

We get to the Suez Canal. At the time, the Egyptians would come on. You had a whole slew of 'em. You had to have a light on the bow of the ship. If the ship had a light, you could use that one. If not, you had to rent it from the Suez Canal Authority. Even if you did have one, they wanted to use their electrician. Plus, you put these two boats on board, these two small wooden boats with a bunch of Egyptians on there; in case you broke down, you'd put these boats over the side. They would take your mooring lines and tie you up to the side to get you out of the way because of the convoys going through. They would sell things, too, souvenirs and shit like that. I bought some myself. I had a few bucks.

Anyway, this Puerto Rican guy wants a draw. Like I said, the captain doesn't have to put a draw out.

I says, "I'll go up there and I'll ask the captain for a draw, but he doesn't have to give it to you." I says, "This is a transit port or a bunker port. You only gotta give them when we're gonna be in port. We're not gonna stay."

"*I need the money. I gotta buy souvenirs for my family*"—my loved ones, you know.

And I'm thinking: why don't I just punch him right in the fucking head and get this over with? I go up and see the old man. "Excuse me, captain, I hate to bother you."

He says, "Yeah, what's up, Ron?"

I says, "What do you say about a draw for the Suez Canal?"

He says, "Ron, I really don't have to give you guys a draw for the Suez Canal."

"Captain, I know that. Basically, there's only one person that wants it in the deck department. I hate to even bring this to your attention. But he needs the money. He wants to buy some souvenirs for his loved ones, and I don't think anybody wants to lend him any money."

He knew who I was talking about. He says, "Ron, I don't think he's got a dollar a day coming," you know, when you take out the taxes and what he's got going home.

"Well, captain, if you could see your way clear—if not, I'll tell him."

He says, "No, send him up, I'll give him something." He gave him 40 or 50 bucks, which he wasn't even entitled to, cuz they could take it out of your overtime, but they weren't supposed to. He says, "If something should happen, I'll take it out of his overtime." He says, "But please explain to him that he's really not entitled to anything."

"I will, captain." I go tell this guy, "The old man's gonna give you something, but, I told you, he's telling you, you're not entitled to anything anymore."

"OK, OK, OK, I'll never ask again."

"OK."

He buys a bunch of fucking junk, stuffed camels, straw doodads.

We go around, we get to Aqaba, Jordan. We're gonna discharge the trucks. So I turn around, just before we got in there, he says, "Are we gonna get a draw?"

I says, "We're gonna be here awhile, we're all entitled to one. But," I says, "you're on like 50 cents a day, man. The old man gave you 50 bucks."

"Yeah, but I spent that."

"Put down what you want." So I get a list up, and I take it up to the old man.

Captain says, "Ron, didn't I tell you?"

I says, "You told me, captain. I told him. I told him you told me." I says, "We all told him, and he's still putting it down."

"What's he want to do with this?"

I says, "Captain, he wants to buy some more souvenirs."

He says, "Alright, I'm gonna give him a little more, but not much."

"Alright, captain."

Come back, I tell him, "You're not gonna get as much as you want, but you're gonna get something."

"Yeah, yeah, yeah. OK, OK."

The fucking guy ends up buying a fishing rod, he's gonna do a lot of fishing, there in port. I saw him fishing one time off the ship. I don't know if he caught anything, I was going ashore. I could care less what he did.

This is Aqaba, Jordan. We turn around, I go ashore with the young ordinary, we get a taxi outside the gate, I'm gonna go look around. Basically, there's nothing really there, at the time, but desert. You come to a crossroads, and there'd be like four or five buildings. We pulled into one place, and it said, "Omar Sharif's Hyde Park Cafeteria." I said, "Oh, this looks like a good place." So we go in, and there's a long, glass counter, like you'd see in a delicatessen, you know, with all these fresh fruits. In the States you'd see meats. Here, you see all kinds of fruits, some vegetables. There were some tables there. And the guy behind the counter.

I'm looking at him.

He says, "Can I help you?"

I says, "Do you have any beer?"

He says, "No. I don't have it, and my license hasn't come through yet to sell beer. But what I can do," he says, "I can send my helper out to go get the beer. You can pay me for it then, and you can sit here and drink it. Would that be alright?"

I says, "Sure."

He says, "OK. I'll get the runner."

"I'll give you some money."

"No, no. We'll see how much this is." He says, "Would you be interested in a cup of coffee?"

I says, "Sure, that'd be good." You know: "I'll pay you for it."

"Oh, no, no. Please, have it."

I says, "Well, thank you."

I'm looking at this guy. We haven't sat down yet. He's making some coffee, and I'm looking at pictures behind him, on the bulkhead, the wall, and there's pictures of Anthony Quinn and Omar Sharif from *Lawrence of Arabia*, and Peter O'Toole and that. I'm looking at these pictures, and I'm looking at this guy. He comes back with the coffee to hand it to me over the top.

I says, "What do I owe you?"

He says, "Oh, no. Please."

"Well, thank you." And I says, "Excuse me, you look a lot like Omar Sharif."

He says, "I am."

I says, "Yeah, you look a lot like him."

He says, "I am. I'm Omar Sharif."

"You're Omar Sharif?"

"Yes, I am."

I says, "What are you doing *here*?"

He says, "Oh, this is my time. My mother still lives in Egypt. She comes over here, and I go over there. This gives me something to do."

He's giving the joint away, really.

So I says, "It's a pleasure to meet you."

He says, "Let me give you a card." Omar Sharif signed this card, with his picture and stuff. I gave it to a relative; she's still got it.

The beer hadn't come yet.

He says, "Try one of my special fruit drinks."

I says, "We'll have to pay you for this."

"*No*," he says. "I'm just making food."

So he made it, and it was good.

So, he says, "I'm trying to get a little business started up here. It's something to do."

And we're talking, and I says, "Yeah, we're off the ship here."

We're talking this and that, and he says, "By the way, if you can, come back. Give me the addresses of your friends and your loved ones in America, I'll give them to my agent, and I'll say that I met you."

I says, "Thank you. I really appreciate it."

He says, "Ah, it's nothing. I'm doing nothing here. It gives me something to do."

About that time some Arabs walk in, dressed in suits. They had apparently been drinking. He goes over to their table to take their order, and whatever it was they ordered, they asked how much it was, and they said, "Oh, that's too much."

He said, "How much you want to pay?"

That's the way he was, you know.

We sat there and drank beer and thanked him, and we went back, and I'm sorry to this day I never got back again. I can't remember what happened, why I could never get back. Something happened. I wanted to go back.

We left to go around to Colombo, Ceylon in the Indian Ocean. Sri Lanka now. We get over there, get in to Colombo, and we have to anchor out, it's New Year's Eve.

New Year's Eve, anchored out, Colombo, Ceylon. Right.

Well, the old man decided we could have shore leave. And we were gonna do him right. We all fucking take off. I mean: every, fucking, body, takes off. Everybody. We got to the first bar, that's as far as we got. And we're just getting fucked up. I mean, just sitting there *drinking*. Next day they try to turn us to, lift anchor, gonna get out of there.

Turn around, I was passed out on the stern. I just laid down there. I don't know whose wheel it was. So we send this Puerto Rican guy up cuz he'd been like hand steering in the ocean, which is nothing, you know, just trying to hold a course. We send him up there.

He goes up. And basically, when you start heaving up, you go slow ahead, because the anchor's gonna have a strain on it, you're gonna be out, the anchor's gonna be leaning forward. This makes it easier to pull it in, plus, as you're going forward, you're helping the anchor, there's a lot of strain on the winch. So it's half ahead, right now. We're getting there. OK, stop. We're still going ahead, you know, so this anchor's coming up. OK, anchor's home now.

So the pilot says, "Hard right."

The guy puts the rudder over hard right, we're starting to come in towards the harbor.

The pilot says, "Midships."

The guy brings it back. "Midships." But we're still going right.

So the pilot says, "Steady."

The guy does the same fucking thing he did before: he grabs the wheel with his arms and legs. "Steady!"

The old man's screaming, "*Get somebody up here who can fucking steer!*" We're coming around. "*Stop the engines! Get him off the wheel!*"

Surprised we didn't hit the other ships at anchor.

Somebody went up there to steer. Then we got to the dock, and it was a kind of a far out dock there, away from town. We tied up, it was gonna be awhile. We're on day work, and, technically, you could work Saturdays or Sundays if you wanted to, but I didn't. So I'm taking off, and we're doing the tourist thing, wandering around. It was a beautiful place. Like I said, they were communist orientated. The whole side of a wall of a building was a picture of Zhou Enlai, the premier of China. *Monstrous* fucking picture of him. Boy, were they sucking ass with that country.

I went over to the seamen's club, and everybody was real friendly. The country was still building up. You had British colonial rule there, then you had the communists. I went over to the seamen's club, wrote some postcards, had a couple drinks. Went into one souvenir store, which is kind of funny. Talking to the one girl in there, she was talking about America and Americans and this and that.

She says, "Do you have appo?" Appo. She wanted an apple.

I explain to her that the apples we have on the ship aren't really the best, they been there for awhile.

She says, "Could I have appo? I never have appo."

I says, "I'll do my best to get what I can for you, but I can't promise anything."

I think we ended up being there 2 weeks. We're doing some day work, and they're unloading the fertilizer, taking it off in scoops.

So I managed to get back, gave her an apple. She was very thankful. I assume I coulda got laid, but she didn't look that good. You get that way, you know. I mean, you're there, they want to meet strangers . . . . I had a tendency to pick the ones that appealed to me, rather than just hit on anyone.

So, we're going along the waterfront area, and you can just literally walk from hotel to hotel along the beach, and you just walk and get a drink. Or if you sat out there, they'd come out there and give you a drink, or you could go in the restaurant, have something to eat, they didn't care. Noticed a lot of people there that were kind of—other than Ceylon people, but it was like they were getting their first meal in a month, like, "Well, mom and dad, keep in touch, write often, even if it's only a couple of hundred bucks"—one of those deals, you know, where the family finally sent 'em some money and they were *eating* now. I seen quite a bit of that all over the world, people on the bum like that, still hitting up their parents. I mean, *older* people. I could see if you were living in paradise and you didn't want to leave and you couldn't make it there. But there were a lot of foreigners. Ships coming in and out, and guys I guess would take up with some girl, like they have since the beginning of time, and just stay there, hope for the best.

We found a house of ill repute. And there, if you wanted to, like a lot of places, you could get the taxi for the entire night. The taxi would stay with you. We were changing our money at the Intercontinental Hotel, which when you walked in, there was a desk, lobby, and then there was a big area on the ground floor. It was nothing but tables, and the waiters would come and bring you a drink, and you sat in the built-up area right in the middle of the hotel.

That's where we were changing our money, and they were giving us a good rate.

One night I had the taxi driver, and he says, "You pay me for the whole night."

I says, "Yeah, OK. I'll keep it for the night."

I was by myself. I turn around, and he takes me to the whorehouse, the girls of ill repute, my favorite kind of women. I'm half in the bag. I had been there before, and now I was running out of money, and I says, "Can you change some money?"

They wanted to give me a ridiculously low price.

I says, "No way!"

I turn around, and I tell the taxi driver, "Take me to the Intercontinental Hotel so I can change my money."

I would actually save money, even after I'd paid *him*! I felt like, look, you know, I'm spending the money *here*, why don't you give me *more* than the legal rate? They cut their own throats in a lot of ways. I get in the taxi, get back to the Intercontinental Hotel. I'm three sheets to the wind. I'm gonna walk in and change my money and get back in the taxi and go back to the whorehouse.

Here come three Americans walking out. They were off another ship, a different company. I was with Central Gulf, and I found out later they were with Export Lines. They were officers.

The one guy says, "Hey, what are you doing?"

I says, "I'm gonna have a good time," you know.

He's gassed. "I'm gonna have a good time, too!" I think his name was Smitty or something like that.

The one guy says, "Hey, wait a minute, we'll talk for him."

I says, "I hope somebody talks for him before I do."

The other guy jumps on *this* guy and says, "Hey, wait, he's been trying to cause trouble all night." You know: let's see what he can do for himself here.

This guy, this Smitty, he says to me, "You got a problem?" He says, "You know, I can—" Something to that effect.

I fired on him. Hit him as hard as I could, and he went down.

The other guy says, "Wait a minute, wait a minute—"

I says, "Yeah?" And I hit him.

The *third* guy, who had instigated it, who said, "This guy's been looking for trouble all night," I says to him, "Now it's your turn."

He says, "I didn't do anything."

I hit him, too.

Meantime, the first one I hit is getting up. I throw at him again. I miss. I go right over the top of him. He ducks, I flip over him. Get back up. He turns around. I hit him again. *Boom!* I hit him right in the nose this time. Blood splatters all over the fucking place. So now this other guy jumps on me. We're tussling and rolling around. I'm hitting him. The one guy that said, "Hey, let this other guy get whipped," he's not doing too much, he's already got one good shot, you know, I got him real good. *Boom*, hit him in the face. I punch this one a couple of times, I get up and I want to kick him, but I figure if I kick him in front of all these people and he dies, I got a big beef. About that time, here come the police. Now they're breaking it up. People from the hotel, they're coming out, the security and that, they're coming out, getting between us.

I says, "Alright, we're not fighting." OK. You know. I says, "They jumped on me." I don't know who saw it, but it sounded plausible. Would I attack three people?

I'm a little beat up, my hand's hurt, and I'm scuffed up from rolling around with this other guy, this Smitty, he's holding his fucking nose. There's blood all over the place. This guy's got a bad eye. The other one, the big one, I just caught him with a glancing blow.

They're separating us, and now the police are gonna get us out of there.

Well, here's the taxi driver. "You give me money, you give me money."

I thought he wanted his money, which is fair. I think I gave him 8 or 12 dollars. I says, "Is that enough?"

"Yeah, yeah, yeah, yeah. It's OK."

I get in the police car. Now they're taking us to the fucking jail. We're in there, you know, and the one cop that spoke decent English says, "Of all places to fight, you've got to do it in front of the Intercontinental Hotel?"

I says, "They jumped on me."

He says, "Are you all Americans?"

I says, "Yeah, American."

"Yeah, yeah, we're Americans, we're Americans, and we want the American Consul, we want the American Consul."

He says, "How about you?"

I says, "I don't want anybody. Just put me in my cell."

He says, "You're pretty easy to get along with, aren't you?"

I says, "Hey, I don't want any trouble."

Smitty says, "Yeah, we're trying to get you out of this, too."

I says, "Smitty, you don't want to get me out of this." I says, "As a matter of fact, you don't even want to get me in the same cell with you, cuz if you get me in the same cell with you," I says, "I'm gonna finish out what I started. Not only your nose," I says, "you're fucking ears are gonna get fucking smashed in."

Cops go, "Ohh, separate them, separate them."

I says, "I don't want to be around 'em." I says, "They attacked me."

"Yeah, yeah, yeah, I understand, I understand."

We're going down a long passageway. The cells are to the right, brick wall to the left, 6 feet, 8 feet, from the cell door to the wall. Gotta be 12 cells. Then there's a big steel door. So this big, heavyset old copper, old Ceylonese, Indian, whatever they trace their ancestry to, he takes me down there, he opens up the cell.

He says, "You."

"Yeah, yeah." So I go in there and lay down, you know, I figure I'll just lay here, what the fuck, they'll come and get me when they're ready.

I hear these guys yelling over there, "We want the American Consul! We want the American Consul!"

I'm thinking to myself: you know, you're only digging your hole deeper. Only digging your hole deeper.

So I'm laying there. I don't know how long I laid there. I don't think it was more than an hour. This big heavyset cop comes again, he comes to the cell door, unlocks it. I get up. I'm standing with my back to the cell wall. He swings the door wide open, and he's motioning for me to come out.

I says, "No."

He motions, like: come on!

I figured they're gonna get me out there and beat my fucking brains out. That's what I think is gonna happen. More abuse.

I says, "No." I'm thinking: if you're gonna beat my brains out, you guys are coming in here, where we're all close in, where I can grab hold of you guys, too. You know, right, not where you could get me out there and just swing me around and beat my fucking brains out. There's not a lot of room in the cell, I figure they can't get their clubs going real good. I says, "You're gonna have to come in here. All of you come on in." We'll see what happens.

He's motioning: come on! Not *saying* it, but now he's getting aggravated, now the hand's in it, he's motioning.

Now I'm thinking: what the fuck? Something else is going on here. I wasn't that drunk, you know. I walk out, and he's backing away to the wall as I'm walking towards him. I look to my left down the long hall, cuz there's only a big steel door on my right. There's nobody there, but I can hear those other Americans yelling down there.

So I says, "What the fuck is this?"

He's literally *pushing* me away from this cell door out in the passageway, cuz I'm out now. He locks the cell door back up. Puts the key in the big steel door.

I'm thinking: where the fuck am I going *now*? Now I'm going *down*, now they're *really* gonna fuck me up, you know? I'm going *down* somewhere in a dungeon.

He opens up the door.

I look.

Here's the taxi driver in the parking lot in the back of the jail, and he's standing there with the back door of the taxi open.

I'm like, What the—?

And this guy's, "Go, go. You go. You go."

So I says, "What the fuck's going on?" I walk down three steps. I'm in the parking lot. There's nothing out there, nothing but this taxi driver with his door open.

I'm thinking he wants his money. I walk up and I says, "I paid you already. I paid you for the night."

He says, "Naw. You don't pay me." He says, "Money you give me, I give them, let you out jail." He says, "Now you get in taxi, I take you back hotel, we get change, then I take you back whorehouse."

Un-fucking-real.

These guys are still yelling for the American Consul. I just gave 8 to 12 dollars, I'm free again. These guys are still yelling. To this day, I don't know what happened to them. Don't care.

I get in the taxi, and I thought about it, and I wasn't feeling too good. I hurt my wrist. I turn around and I says, "No." I says, "You know what? Just take me back to the ship, and I'll pay you."

So he took me back to the ship. Next day my wrist had swollen up, I couldn't use it.

I showed the bosun, and he says, "I can take it easy on you, but you might have really fucked it up, man. That's swollen."

So now I go see the medical officer, the chief mate.

He says, "Jesus Christ, that's swelled up. What'd you do?"

"Well," I says, "first, it didn't happen on board the ship. I'm gonna be honest about that. I'm not gonna sue or anything. It happened ashore. There was an altercation."

He says, "I hate to say this, but we better send you to the doctor. We could soak it in Epsom salt, but if something goes wrong later on, you'll be sorry. Let's send you to a doctor. I'll fill it out: 'altercation ashore.' We'll be truthful with this."

He was OK. He knew what he was doing. Cuz if we're on our way back to the States and the swelling shouldn't go down or something, then you're really in trouble. So they set it up to send me to a Ceylonese doctor. So I go to the doctor, and I got the paperwork with me. I'm sitting there, I go in.

Doctor says, "What happened?"

I says, "My wrist."

He looks at the paper. "Oh, you were in altercation? Fight?"

I says, "Yeah."

"Let me see wrist." So he's trying to bend it and this hurts, you know.

I says, "It hurts."

He's looking. "You were in altercation, huh?"

I says, "Yeah."

He says, "How heavy? Get on scale."

What's the fucking scale got to do with my hand, my arm, my wrist? I get on the scale. Whatever stones it was, 220 pounds. "You really hit him hard, huh?"

I says, "I didn't try to hit him light."

"Sit down, sit down."

So I think he's gonna look at my wrist, not how much I weigh. What's that got to do with anything? He says, "Were any bottles used? Did you use any bottles?"

I says, "No, just my hands."

"No clubs? No chairs? You didn't hit him with the chairs? Did you get hit with a chair?"

I'm thinking: what the fuck? Is this guy getting off on this? I says, "Look, partner, it's my wrist."

He feels it again. "Oh, yeah, yeah, yeah." He says, "Oh, it be OK, it be OK. Here's some lotion." He says, "How many you fight?"

I says, "Me against three guys."

"Three. Yeah, yeah."

It was actually like he was sorry he wasn't there to see it for himself. I thought he was gonna climax right there. So he gave me some salve, and he says, "Just go back to the ship." It's a fucking waste of time, you know. He gives me a 'Fit for Duty,' I get back to the ship, I go see the mate.

He says, "So what did the doctor say?"

I says, "He wanted to know how many people I was in the fight with, if I hit them with bottles or chairs. He wanted to know how much I—"

Mate says, "That's not got—what about your *wrist*?"

I says, "I think this guy was getting off on me telling him about the fight, you know, living vicariously through me."

"Well, tell the bosun to give you an easy job or something. Take care of it, soak it or something."

"Yeah, OK."

So I don't go ashore much anymore. I'm taking care of the wrist. I'm waiting for the police to come and arrest me again for beating these guys up. Nothing happens. We're still there, and I'm kind of recuperating. All of a sudden the mate comes and gets me and says, "Are you still deck delegate?"

I says, "Yeah, what's up?"

He says—the guy who needed the draws all the time—"We sent him to the doctor."

"Yeah, OK."

"He had a hernia. They operated on him. So he's calling, telling the agent he needs soap and matches and this and that, and he needs money." He says, "Look, we told the agent take care of him, but he said he wants to see somebody from the ship. You're delegate, you go. The agent's gonna take you over to the hospital."

I says, "Mate, I'll go. But can't the agent to get him soap?" We're talking he's in a hospital, he can't get soap?

He says, "Go see the steward, get him some soap, matches, get him anything you can get him. Put it in a pillowcase, and take it over to him."

"Yeah, alright, mate."

So I go see the steward, and the steward's whining, "This costs money. I gotta account for this." Like pulling teeth, right?

I says, "You got a problem with it, go see the mate, cuz he's the one that sent me down here." So I take some of my soap, I go around to some of the guys. "Just give me some soap and matches." Couple packs of cigarettes we threw in there, matches. We threw some money in there, too, you know, whatever we had, change and shit. Anything that was free we threw in there, plus the money.

There's the agent to take me over.

So the agent says, "I take you to the hospital, and then I come back and get you."

"Alright." But I got my own American money with me in case something goes wrong. I've been doing this for awhile.

We drive over and the taxi stops and the agent says, "Here. I come back and get you later."

I says, "This is a hospital?" I mean, you talk about—*this* is a *hospital*? This dilapidated fucking building?

He says, "Yeah. Just go in and ask for him."

"Alright."

I go in. I couldn't believe it. The British had left it, and the people there never did a thing with it, they just moved in. I mean, this is fucking incredible. And the guy just had a hernia operation.

So I walk in and say "hello" and mention his name.

They says, "Oh yeah, yeah. You want to see him, huh?"

"Yeah."

No escort, no nothing, just: he's all the way at the end room. It was like a recovery area. Straight shot down, old wooden doors with fucking big gaps in them where they're dried out and rotten. I walk down there, I'm looking to my right and my left, here the doors that are open, there's pregnant women in there. This is a maternity ward or some fucking thing they got. I think: what is this shit? I walk all the way down. His door is open. He's in the end room on the left, and he's looking out the window. There's a funky bed in there, old wooden bed, an old wood cabinet falling apart. This is like something out of the 1930s. There's a table and a chair. I wouldn't sit on the chair, it'd probably fall apart.

He says, "Oh, you're here, huh?"

I says, "Yeah, man." You know, I says, "OK, friend. What's up?"

"Oh, man, you gotta get me outta here."

I says, "I can't get you out of here. They told me you needed soap."

"I don't have any soap, I don't have any nothing, they ain't give me *nothing* in here."

"Well, look, friend, I got a bag here. There's some money in there. There's some Ceylon money." I says, "I don't think the old man's gonna give you any more money. You're overdrawn now." I says, "Your allotment's gonna keep going. That's never gonna stop until the end of the voyage. But, you know, trade the cigarettes for what you need. There's a little money here, too."

"You gotta get me outta here!"

I says, "Man, I can't get you outta here. You just had a hernia operation."

"I don't wanna get off the ship."

I says, "They're gonna fly you home. You're on the payroll. You were injured on board the ship. You're gonna get paid. They'll take care of you. You're gonna get $8 a day, and when you get back to the States, you can call the company. Not only will you get your pay, they'll give you something for having a hernia, for the injury."

"No, no, no, no."

I says, "Man, there ain't nothing I can do for you. That's the way this is."

"Oh, man, goddamn, nobody's doing nothing for me."

"Look," I says, "I gotta get out of here."

I needed a drink. Walk back through, now I notice all the doors are closed, they don't want me looking at the pregnant women, which is OK with me, too. I get out there, and I'm waiting out there, I'm waiting out there, I'm smoking cigarettes, I'm waiting. I must have waited a half hour, 45 minutes, no agent.

I says, "You know what? Bullshit." I start walking. I find a taxi. I says, "Take me to the seamen's club." I go over there, get a drink. I guess I got back about seven o'clock or so.

I see the mate on watch, and he says, "The mate was waiting for you. You're supposed to be back a while ago."

I says, "I got delayed." Another important decision had to be made: do I come back here, or do I get a drink? The drink won out. I go up and see him.

He says, "Where you been?"

I says, "I'll tell you the truth. The agent dropped me off. That wasn't a hospital. That's some kind of a maternity ward. They got women in there getting ready to birth. He's all the way down on the end. He says he has nothing. I didn't see anything in the room. I gave him the sack with the soap, the cigarettes, matches, some change we had. He wants to come back to the ship."

He says, "He can't come back here. He's 'Not Fit for Duty.'"

"I know that and you know that, but he don't know that. I gave him the stuff and told him to trade the stuff for whatever he can get." I says, "Best bet, call the agent and see if the agent can get him something."

"Well, I don't know about that. We're leaving in a day or two."

"OK, mate."

He says, "Don't get in any more trouble."

I says, "OK." I went back ashore, I'm getting another drink.

We're getting ready to leave the next day, but as the hatches are getting emptied, we're securing them, you had to pull tarps. There was no deal here where the hatch folds up like an accordion and closes hydraulically. These are the old ones, put the pontoons on top, put the tarps over, batten them down, top battens, side battens, put the wooden wedges in. We're doing this, right, and we're gonna leave next morning.

I happen to look down there on the dock. Here he is, walking down the dock. I tell the bosun, "Here he comes."

He says, "Ah, fuck!" You know, what does *he* want?

I says, "He probably wants to come back on board." I don't know what transpired. I didn't see him leave. I don't know what happened.

That night we stayed on. Next morning, turn us to at six o'clock to secure one more hatch. Here comes the mate out on deck. I thought he was gonna come out with something about the way he wanted it secured or something extra. He says, "As soon as we get the hatch secured, we're not leaving, we gotta search the ship."

I says, "For what?"

He says, "He never went back to the hospital yesterday. Did you see him?"

I says, "Yeah, he came down to the ship."

"We ran him off and told him to go back down to the hospital, the agent will take care of him and fly him home. He didn't want that. We ran him off. He left, but he never got back to the hospital. He's wandering somewhere around Ceylon."

We search the ship for an hour, he ain't there. Can't find him, OK, we're leaving.

To this day, I don't know what happened to him. He might be still wandering around Ceylon.

What a fucking nut.

It was kind of uneventful going back. We had to clean the hatches out, get the wood out that was securing the trucks. One thing they did have us do, they had us put the dunnage—the wood we used for shoring—all on the starboard side of the ship. I wondered what that was for, you know; they told us don't throw any of it over the side.

We turned around, we got back to the Suez Canal. Unbeknownst to me—well, you could sell anything in the Suez Canal. They can't get wood there, obviously. This dunnage is worth money to 'em. They had a guy there, they called him Mickey Mouse. He's dead now, I understand. They would call the ships: "You got anything for sale?" You could sell your mooring lines, food, lumber, anything. Well, the captain, chief mate, and bosun were making a deal to sell the dunnage, cuz technically the ship had to be clean when we got back to the States. They finally made a deal for $300 for the lumber. The captain got $100, the chief mate got $100, and the bosun got $100, and they never cut the deck department in. What we could have was overtime for cleaning out the hatches, which we should have got anyway, because we had to clean it out. They usually throw that dunnage over the side because it's scrap. So they picked up $100 apiece, in 1975. They didn't even buy us a bottle of whiskey, rotten fucks.

At the Suez Canal we had to take bunkers, fuel. And we're running out of fresh water. Well, water costs more than oil there. They had some problem down in the engine room, and they couldn't make enough fresh water, or something was wrong with the water, so they had to buy water. And this is a no-no with these companies. You don't buy water. You're expected to make the water that you have last. This is fresh water for showers, food, washing clothes. It's a big thing. You can actually refuse to sail if you don't have fresh water.

Somehow or another, when they were taking on the fuel and the fresh water at the same time, somebody fucked up and they switched the hoses or something with the valves down in the engine room. They got the oil in with the fresh water. We leave the Suez Canal. It was like taking a shower in Jell-O. Yeah. The chief engineer had enough nerve to say, "Wash your clothes together, we gotta conserve water."

What the fuck? Now we're gonna get even *more* screwed. Plus, we didn't get anything for the dunnage. So now we're gonna get together, the three delegates for the engine, myself, and the steward department. We're taking samples of the water. You took a shower, you were sticky. They're giving us canned milk to drink instead of water, cuz you couldn't drink it. They're telling us, "Oh, yeah, we'll take care of you guys." So we're putting down, every day, no fresh water, cuz you get paid extra for that. Right? That's a big thing, no fresh water. We come through the Med, they don't stop and try to fix this, no. We're going to *Mobile*. So we're taking samples of the water.

We get to Mobile on the weekend. Well, they never paid off on the weekend. If they paid you for Saturday, they'd have to pay you for Sunday, too. So they always paid off on Monday. We got all the paperwork ready, we're ready for our union official to come on board, and I think they had some kind of little deal. The engineers didn't get anything, and the mates didn't say anything, you know, they kind of calmed it down. They gave them overtime in lieu of the other deal. "Work this in here, but don't put in for the water," that type of thing.

They couldn't calm us down that much.

Monday morning, we're gonna pay off at two o'clock in the afternoon. The engine delegate and the steward department delegate kind of put it off on me to take care of it.

I says, "Well, alright."

Now the guy that got off, the one with the hernia, he's got all his souvenirs on board, right. Nobody wants them. So Customs is running around saying, "Whose is this stuff?"

I says, "He got off."

"Somebody claimed them. Somebody paid a duty on it."

I says, "You better see the captain."

Captain says, "I'm not paying for that stuff. I don't want that junk."

I says, "I'm not paying it."

They says, "Somebody's got to pay it, or we'll have to confiscate it."

Duh. Take it. We don't want it.

The whole thing's fucked. I'm trying to find our union official from Mobile. It's like *hours*, you know, nobody can find him. So I finally find him.

He says, "Yeah, yeah, what's up?"

I says, "We got a helluva beef here," I says, you know, "No fresh water."

"Oh, the only thing we can make them do is clean the tanks."

I says, "We're not talking about cleaning tanks. We're talking about *oil*, they take the bunkers in Suez there, and somebody screwed up in the engine room, and they mixed it. We had to stop in the Bahamas and get fresh water. They had to pump all that shit out and get fresh water." And it still wasn't right because they had pumped it into the tank, but it was better than nothing. Better than what we had. Chief engineer lost his job over it. They fired him. I says, "We're talking we had to stop to get fresh water. We had water, OK, but it was all contaminated with the oil. Somebody down there opened up the wrong valves and fucked it all up."

"All we can do is make them clean the tanks."

I says, "You mean, 3 weeks, approximately, we can't have water, we can't wash, we take a shower, it's like taking a shower in Jell-O, and we can't get—"

"No, no, no. We can make them clean the tanks. They'll do that when they're in the shipyard here when it's laying up for a couple of months before the next trip. We'll make sure that happens."

I says, "You know what? Fuck this." I'm thinking: I'll never be fucking delegate again. I told them that, the other delegates, after I talked with him.

They come sneaking around. "What happened?"

I says, "You guys take it." I says, "We're not getting anything."

"*What? What?*"

I says, "*You* go talk to him. Don't put it off on me." I says, "That's what he said. Here's all the fucking paperwork we did for all the days and all the samples of water we took, all signed and initialed and proper."

Fuck this.

I get my money. I get paid off.

Commissioner says, "You got any complaints?"

I says, "No way, get me out of here." I could have probably bitched to him, but I—you know, fuck it.

Turn around, I get my gear, I'm going down the gangway, and the third mate I had stood watch with, this guy Miller, real nice guy, matter of fact in Ceylon when I came back that night from the fight, I told him what had happened and he said, "If the police come, don't worry about it, I'll just tell them you're not on board. Go ahead and go to sleep." He was a nice guy.

Anyway, I'm going towards the gate with my bag, and here he is.

He says, "Hey, where you going?"

I says, "I'll be honest with you, Mr. Miller. I'm just going out to the airport, get a flight outta here."

He says, "Come on. I'll take you."

I says, "I appreciate that."

"Yeah. I stood watch with you." He was a nice guy. We're going out there, and he says, "By the way, can I ask you something?"

"Yeah, sure."

He says, "Whatever happened to that water beef you had?"

I says, "You know, you're not gonna believe this. All the work we did putting the paperwork together, and our own time finding out what days things happened, and how it happened, and taking all these samples of the water. I finally find the National Maritime Union patrolman and explained it all. He said we can't do anything but clean the tank. I said, 'Hey, we took fresh water in the Bahamas, just to take water, we didn't go ashore. They flushed all those tanks out, but they put the fresh water in on top of that again. We should even get it for that because the tanks weren't really clean.' He said, 'Oh, we'll clean them out here real good. Blah, blah, blah.' I should have called U.S. Public Health or something like that." I says, "Make a long story short, we can't get anything."

He says, "Well, I'm gonna tell you what happened, and if you ever repeat this story, I'll deny it." He says, "I was up in the old man's office waiting to get paid off. Your union patrolman came on board and said, 'Captain, I understand there's a helluva beef on here about the water.' The captain said, 'Yeah, but I kinda like to get that taken care of.' He had maybe four or five $100 bills. The union official took the money. He said, 'Don't worry, captain.'"

Can you imagine what that would have cost for all those days with no water for the entire crew to get paid?

So the company saved money, and they probably wrote it off on overtime, expenses, miscellaneous, or something over the trip or a gratuity, cuz the gratuities were real big and you weren't supposed to do them overseas, but you did 'em.

    I says, "Really?"

    He says, "Yeah, but I'll deny it if you ever tell anyone."

Austral Ensign

The name of the ship is the *Austral Ensign*. Another run to Australia by Farrell Lines. Container ship. I got on board April 13, 1976. I made two trips on there. Long sea voyages again. It was gonna be the same thing, these container ships usually keep the same runs, same ports. So I knew it was gonna be 2 weeks over from Panama to New Zealand. But now I had friends there. One of the Englishmen I had kept in touch with, Ginger, he had married an Australian girl, Betty, and they were living in Sydney. Ken Bottoms, at the time, was working for an Act Line company, a British outfit. The names of their ships were Act One, Two, Three, Four, Five, Six. That's just the way they named them. They were running to Australia. So now it was gonna be a little different. I might get to see Ken again. I knew I could see Ginger and Betty.

So we get to Panama, and you usually got that 12 hours or something in Panama, always go ashore and get a blow job and a beer. I wrote Ginger a letter and posted it through the Panamanian post to get it to Sydney. I knew it was gonna take at least 2 weeks to get to New Zealand. I figured he'd get it in time. I wrote him that I was coming over, approximate date we'd be in Sydney, the name of the ship, I believe I even got in the agent's name so he could contact them. And if we got a chance, hook up.

We go over, get to New Zealand, then we go over to Melbourne and Sydney. Here's Ginger, right at the dock. "Hey! What's going on?" It was nice seeing him again.

In the meantime, after I left them, they had a British double-decker bus, and they were gonna try to drive around the world in it. God bless them. They got as far as India, and they couldn't get any further because they wanted like millions of dollars to put the bus on a ship. So they drove the bus back to England, and that was the end of that. They wanted me to go with them, but I didn't go.

Anyway, Ginger says, "Ken's coming on the Act Line ship, but we don't know if he'll be here." Cuz we only had a couple of days. So he says, "We gotta take you to Montgomery's. Ken said to make sure to take you to Montgomery's in Sydney. It's a hotel bar."

I don't know anything about it, you know, cuz the other trip I didn't get into anything. So we're going to Sydney, right. I turn around, and it's kind of a mixed bar. It's a bunch of wharf whores that hang in there, and they'll go with anybody. I mean, they just like sex—black, white, orange, pink. It's a seamen's bar.

We're drinking, this and that, I'm checking the girls out, and: "Oh, this is my friend Ron, my mate from America." Betty's just telling me her stories. So I'm looking around, I'm checking this one girl out. I didn't know they had transvestites in there.

And Betty says, "What are you doing?"

I says, "Checking that one girl out."

She says, "Ron, that's a *guy*."

It was the best looking one in there. I keep forgetting, you know, women don't have Adam's apples. I says, "Forget it."

We couldn't get in too much trouble; Betty was with us all the time. She kept a close watch on Ginger.

But I turn around and says, "Hey, OK, thank you."

They says, "Hey, keep making the run, come on back."

"Sure. Fine."

We missed Ken. So I made one trip. Get back to the States, sign on to make another one. So again we go through Panama. And before I left Australia I says, "You want anything from the States?"

Ginger says, "Could you do me a favor?"

I says, "Yeah, what do you need?"

"Could you get me a watch, a decent watch. I'll pay you for it."

"You want any kind of watch or just . . . ."

"Just grab me a decent watch, cuz I really don't have one."

"Yeah, OK."

So on my way through, in Panama, you could get watches cheap in the duty-free zone. I picked him up a little Seiko. We make the crossing, go to Melbourne first, and who's gonna dock behind us but one of the Act Line ships. Ken was on it! I don't believe this. They're going to the dock. We're going in, they come in behind us. So I get off my ship.

They dock, and Ken's all, "Hey, Ron!"

I says, "Hey, Ken!"

Well, they gotta put out what we call an insurance wire, the captain wants an extra line out. So Ken's down on the dock, and they're gonna throw it out.

So I says, "I'll give you a hand."

The bosun's up there saying, "Oh great!" You know, it reminded me of Drunken Duncan, you gotta get somebody else to work. You know: "Ken's mate's gonna give us a hand."

OK, yeah. So we put the extra line out.

And Ken says, "Come on, have a beer." On the ship there.

I says, "Yeah, thank you, friend Ken, I appreciate that."

We get a beer, we go to his room, very big room. He's got it kind of decorated, they dress it up a lot better than we ever did on any American ship I've ever seen. We're just bullshitting.

I says, "You going up to see Ginger?"

He says, "I'm not sure, you know, if we get some time off or something." We're bullshitting, and he says, "Can you do me a favor?"

I says, "Yeah. Whadya need?"

"Those cowboy boots you wear. Can you get me a pair of those?"

"Yeah."

He says, "Well, you know, I hated to ask you cuz I didn't know if we'd ever see you again."

"Well, you're seeing me again." I says, "You'll probably never get rid of me." I says, "Your best bet is to draw an outline of your foot, mail it to me, and when I get off the ship I'll take it right to the store and I'll get you the boots."

He says, "I'll pay you for them."

I says, "We'll work it out somewhere along the line."

"OK." And he says, "Ron, let's go up to the bar and get a drink."

"You know, can I buy a case or two of beer?"

He says, "*Buy* a case? I'm gonna *give* you a case! You don't buy *nothing* here! Your money's no good here."

We go into the bar. They got all the wharf whores in there. So we're sitting there drinking. The girls are going by, this and that, and they had a cook on there, and Ken says, "Everybody hates this fucking guy."

So the cook says to me, "Oh, you're awful big for a fucking Aussie, aren't you?"

I says, "I'm sorry, I'm not Australian, I'm American."

"Oh, that's even worse!"

I says, "You know, you're older than I am, but if you really want to see about it, we can go down to the dock."

Ken jumps up. "Listen, he's a mate of mine. *I'll* fuck you up if you fuck with him."

So he stumbles off.

What it amounted to was he was trying to grab one of the wharf whores, and she was more or less pushing him off, and he was gonna pick an argument cuz I wasn't crew. He assumed I had just walked on there to get a drink; unless you're invited, you don't go in there. Right. Yeah. I was gonna pick up one of their women, you know, one of the loved ones there.

So Ken says, "You fancy any of these?"

I says, "Oh, she don't look too bad."

He grabs her and says, "Hey! Look here. This is a mate of mine, an American." He says, "He's gonna take you over to his ship, have a good time."

She's all giggly. "Oh, really! I've never met an American." In other words, "I never blew an American" is what she's saying.

But now I gotta sneak her on board, cuz you're not allowed to have women on our ships. So I get her over there, and I get her on board. I get her in the room. We're freaking out. Somebody found out I had her on board. So now they're all trying to knock on the door and peek, you know—fucking guys. Get your own.

So now, the next day, we're getting ready to leave. I still got her on board.

Oh, *fuck!* You know?

Ken's over beating on the fucking door. He just got on my ship. "Ron! Ron! Get up!"

I says, "Yeah, Ken."

"Goddamn, man." He says, "Jesus, where is she?"

"I got her."

"You gotta get her off here. You guys are leaving, and we're leaving. We gotta get her off here. We're running all of 'em off here."

"Yeah, OK, OK."

He says, "Get her back on my ship."

I says, "OK. Soon as I can."

I get her up. I says, "Come on, you gotta go."

I had a cover over my porthole, my window, just to keep it dark.

She says, "It's not even daylight yet."

I says, "I got a cover over it." Real fucking idiot. "I gotta get you outta here."

So, I leave the room and go down. I'm trying to see who's on the gangway so I can sneak her off, cuz I gotta get her back to Ken's ship.

So: fuck.

I go back. She ain't in the fucking room.

This. Fucking. Goof.

So now I gotta go look for her. I'm trying doors next to me. Here I knock on a door, a guy says, "Come in." I open the door. Here he is sitting there and she's jacking him off.

I says, "Hey, I'm sorry, but you gotta go."

"Does she have to go right *now*?"

I says, "Yeah."

"What about me?"

I says, "*Come on*. I gotta get her outta here!"

Get her outta there, run around to the other ship, run her up the gangway. "Here, Ken."

He says, "OK. Here's your case of beer. I'll send you the foot cut-outs to your home address for the boots."

"We got it. See you when I see you."

Like: No trouble, mate. Here we go. Here's your beer. Here she is. I'm outta here.

Fuck. More stress. You know, I'm not making this up, cuz it is just too fucking stupid. *Nobody* in their right mind would do this shit.

We went to Sydney, and for some reason Ken's ship didn't go there that time, they went up to Brisbane. But I got hold of Ginger. He came down to the ship, and we got stuck there for some reason. I think that's why Ken's ship bypassed us. There was some kind of strike going on. We were the last ship to get in there.

They'd strike over anything over there, the longshoremen, they were very militant. Years ago I was told that if you had too much grease on the runners—we didn't have that, runners, we had booms—but if there was too much grease on the runners, the longshoremen would knock off until you got the grease off there. I also found out later that the Australians would come on board—the Australian longshoremen, stevedores—and before they'd work the ship, they would compare the wages of that ship to the wages of Australian seamen. And if you paid less, the ship made up the difference and paid it into the longshoremen's pension fund. So I'm sure we were making as much as the Australian seamen were at the time. It was almost a blackmail. Like: "We won't work your ship because the third world ships, Panamanian, Liberian . . ."—I'm sure they weren't up to snuff. So this would have to go into the longshoremen's pension fund, the difference in a day's wage. They were very, very militant. Nice guys, but they had their way of doing something. I'm not saying it's right or wrong. I'm sure that the American longshoremen were pulling little performances, too, with the pension plans and whatever.

Anyway, we get up there and we get stuck, and so I had the weekend off. So they just said, "Why don't you come over and stay at the apartment?"

I says, "Sure, if it's OK with you guys."

I gave Ginger the watch. He was all happy. "Thank you, thank you, what do I owe you?"

"It's on me." You know, they got me staying here.

Betty had good sense. She had got up and gone to work. And the way the doors were set up, the locks and everything, you couldn't lock the door back unless you had a key. I was sleeping on the couch. I was wandering around the apartment trying to find coffee. Here Ginger comes out of the bedroom. We had a few drinks the night before. So we get coffee and something to eat.

He says, "You wanna go, Ron?"

I says, "Yeah. If you wanna do something."

So, he says, "Damn, Betty locked us in," as opposed to "Betty locked us out." In other words, we'd have to leave the door unlocked. He says, "That's OK. We can go out through the balcony."

So we hung-dropped about 10 feet down, coming out the balcony. Little did I figure: how we gonna get back in unless Betty comes home? We were out until she came back.

We just bounced around Sydney, stopped at a few places, shot some pool, did dumb things. Betty came back. I went back to the ship and stood the gangway watch. They came and picked me up again and went in, came back. That was about it, really, just said, "See you next trip." It was nice, though. It's really nice having somebody where you can go in port, where you can go and know somebody, you're not finding your way around on your own.

We went up to Brisbane. Then on the way back we stopped in Wellington. There's a mountain there with a cable car going up. They told me, "Stop at the Northern Light"—name of the hotel bar. And they're kind of laughing about it, when they told me, but I got the chance, so I go there. I don't know anything, but they told me: the Northern Light. What they didn't tell me was it was a fag bar. It's a joke, you know. I mean, just for a laugh. Or they figured I'd punch somebody out. We stayed in trouble constantly.

I took a taxi. I said, "I want to go to the Northern Light."

I'm in there, and there's no girls in there, there's all these guys. And I'm thinking, you *guys*. I know they're laughing, right, you know, "If Ron went there, wait 'til he sees *that*."

OK. I get outta there. I start wandering around. Of all things, I run into the second mate. He's wandering around having a few drinks.

So we kind of buddy up. It's early yet. We wander into this hotel bar. They had a thing there that if you were there drinking after, say, ten o'clock at night, the bar was only for people who had rooms, so I'm talking to this one girl, and she's from Canada, originally. I'm talking to her, and the second mate's talking to somebody.

Her name was Jean. Turns out she was from Vancouver, Canada, and on a whim, she had answered an ad years ago from New Zealand. She'd just gotten out of secretarial school in Vancouver and responded to an ad for a working vacation in New Zealand, and it had a whole list of occupations, receptionists, clerks, whatever job she went to in high school, graduating, got this degree, went to secretarial school for a year or two. So on a whim she called them up, and they sent her the paperwork, and she thought it'd be like a working vacation. Basically, it's: we'll fly you over; you pay your way to wherever the job is that we have for you; we find you an apartment; you go right to work; if you last a year, we reimburse you your airfare back to where you came from.

So she says, well, I'll pay my way to New Zealand. I'll get the job. I'll work for a year. That way, they'll reimburse me. I'll come back to Canada. Take a working vacation. See what it's like in New Zealand.

She flies over. She gets there. Her year's up. She gets made up with this New Zealand seaman, right? Well, he just happens to be on a ship sailing somewhere. She's in the bar having a good time. No children or anything. We're hitting it off pretty good. But now the second mate is getting into it with somebody, and I'm trying to get in between this, and about that time, they said ten o'clock, time's up, if you don't have a room, you have to leave or have somebody sponsoring you.

She says, "I'm sponsoring him," pointing at me.

I says, "Hey, thank you. I appreciate that. But I gotta get him outta here."

She says, "What ship you off?"

I says, "The *Austral Ensign*."

We go back to the ship. It's kinda like: I'd rather get him outta something than have to hear about it the next day, leaving him behind. Next day on the ship, gangway watchman is trying to find me. There's a phone call. It's Jean.

She says, "'Ron,' right?"

I says, "Yeah. Hello?"

"It's Jean."

"Jean? Well, hello."

She says, "You never came back."

I says, "Well, I got him back to the ship."

She says, "You off tonight?"

"Yeah, I can get off about 6 or 7."

"I'm in room so and so at the hotel."

I couldn't remember the hotel. Oh, Christ, you know, but I knew it was close to this Northern Light. I knew the area we walked because I knew it was the first place we hit after the Northern Light.

So I says, "Sure. OK."

She says, "Stop up."

"Alright, no problem."

I had to take the bus to get to town. Once I got downtown, then I could take a taxi. So I'm waiting in line for the taxi, queued up, and there's this girl behind me.

Taxi driver says, "Where you going?"

I didn't know what to tell him. I says, "Actually, I'm going to the Northern Light."

He looks at me a little strange, right?

The girl behind me says, "We're going the same way. You mind if I share your taxi?"

I says, "Well, no, of course not."

Get in there, and she's in the back seat; I'm in the front, and the taxi driver says, "Do you *really* wanna go to the Northern Light?"

I says, "Look, I'm gonna be perfectly honest with you. The last place I was in was the Northern Light. I saw what kind of place it was. I got outta there. I walked around the corner. There's a hotel there. I went up there to get a drink. But a friend of mine I'd met just walking in the street, another shipmate, we got up there, I was talking to this girl," and I says, "he had a problem. We decided to leave. I figured I'd better get him back to the ship. She called me and invited me back." I says, "I know her name. I know the room number. But I don't know the hotel name."

This girl in back cracks up.

Taxi driver says, "Right around the corner?" He mentions the name of the hotel.

I says, "I'll know it if I see it." So we go around the corner from the Northern Light.

I says, "That's it."

He says, "OK, fine."

So the girl says, "I wish you luck."

I says, "Thanks. I'll probably need it."

I go up there, and we get a drink, and I stayed the night with her. In the morning I says, "I gotta get back to the ship."

She says, "Well, OK." And she says, "Are you off again today?"

I says, "Well, I think I gotta work 'til noon." That was the setup at the time. I says, "I think I'll be working 'til noon, but I don't know for sure."

She says, "Well, alright. I'll probably still be here."

I says, "I'll get back to you at the hotel." I told her I'd buy her a cup of coffee or something.

So I turn around, and I go back. Sure enough, we only had to work 'til noon. At eleven thirty, the phone rings on the ship.

I says, "Jean?"

She says, "Yeah."

I says, "Hi." And it's raining. I says, "How's it going?"

She says, "When you working?"

"I'm off at noon."

"Good. Now you can buy me that cup of coffee you promised."

"Sure. Where you at, the hotel?"

"No, I'm not there. I'm downtown. I've been kind of wandering around here." She says, "Can I meet you downtown?" She named someplace.

"Sure."

We took off again, and this is when we took the cable up to the mountains, you couldn't see it in the rain, and we were doing the "loved one's" thing, quality time together.

Turn around, she says, "Look, I gotta go back." We were in Wellington, she was from Auckland. She says, "I gotta go back. Here's my number. Are you coming back?"

I says, "I don't know when I'll be back, or how I could come back."

"Is your ship still gonna be here?"

"Yeah."

"Can you call me tomorrow morning at this number?" She says, "I'm gonna take the train back today."

"Sure. I'll call you in the morning." I get up in the morning; before I call, she's calling. I says, "I was gonna give you a call. How's it going?"

She says, "Not really good. I slipped and fell on the train." She says, "I'm in the hospital here in Auckland."

I says, "Hey, I'm sorry."

"I was hoping you'd be there so maybe you could come down here. My husband's still gone and everything, he'll be gone for another week or two."

"Hey, I'd like to . . . ."

"Look, do me a favor." She says, "If you'd like to see me again, you've got that number I gave you . . . ."

"Yeah."

"Call the number, but call it at noon if the ship comes into Auckland."

"I'll keep the number, and I'll give you a call." I says, "Really nice meeting you."

We left; go back to the States; I quit; I didn't want that run anymore. Like I tell you, you get tired of staying on the same run if you don't have to. To this day, I don't know what happened to her. I hope she's alright. I hope she's still with her husband. I hope he didn't kill her. Her name is Jean. Other than that, I don't know.

Green Wave

The name of the ship was the *S.S. Green Wave*. November 23, 1976. I caught it coming back from a foreign voyage, took it to New Orleans to pay off. Got a couple of days' pay, went to New Orleans, and turned around and loaded vehicles to take to Hudaydah, Yemen for the Yemen Army.

We got there, loaded up. Had a captain, nice guy, but he never bathed or changed clothes, and we used to have bets on when he'd bathe or change clothes.

It's a pretty uneventful crossing. Go through the Suez Canal, go to Yemen, and on the dock they had tons of cargo. It was just open because it obviously never rains there, or it rains little. There was so much cargo there that people were building boxes and living there. There was soap from Russia, canned hams from Denmark for the Yemen people. They don't eat pork. Who does the thinking here? Stupid, dumb motherfuckers. One night, myself and the third mate, we decided to go through the cargo down there because there's nothing happening on the ship. We were going through the cargo, and finally a Yemen soldier caught us and took us back to the ship, told us we couldn't pilfer any cargo.

On the way back we stopped at Rota, Spain.

Captain says, "We're gonna get some time in Rota."

The third mate tells me, "I'll bet he changes clothes and bathes to go ashore in Rota."

I says, "I'll bet he changes clothes but *doesn't* bathe. You say he bathes and changes clothes. I say he just changes clothes."

I won.

He put on clothes we'd never seen before. I mean, it was like he had two sets. It looked like he combed his hair with his shoe. But he was a nice guy.

It was pretty much open in the Navy base there, and we took a taxi over to Cadiz, and the third mate and myself were wandering around, and we stopped in a little place, they had like three stools, which is kind of common in Spain, you see smaller places that you just go in for coffee or a beer, they don't even have tables. We stopped to get a beer, we were looking for women, and here comes this middle-aged woman. She was working in a whorehouse down the street, and they heard we were wandering around and came in and invited us over.

So we turned around and went over there, and we're discussing prices, and the third mate says, "Look, it's about seven o'clock at night. We can probably stay 'til 4 or 5 in the morning and get back to the ship." He told the madam running the place, "How much do you want to just lock the doors, and we just take care of the three or four girls that are here?"

I believe it was 50 bucks apiece, and they'd lock the doors. Just have a good time. So we did it. We just bought the whorehouse for the night. I think we got about 2 or 3 hours sleep, if that, and they got us up at 4 or 5 in the morning, and we left and went back to the ship, and they were already getting ready to leave. Here we come. You know.

Went back to the States.

Had a good time. Yeah. A good time had by one and all.

It's a long story, Mr. Parker

This is the *Mormacsaga*, 2/8/77. Foreign voyage over to South Africa and up to Mozambique. These Moore-McCormackers, they made the same stops. They didn't hold that missing a ship against me. Nice of 'em to do that. This is when I ran into Grayson Parker again. We had a bunch of fuckups on there. You could see it coming. You could just see it coming.

We took it up to New York. And it was me, the bosun, and this one ordinary seaman, Raymond. Well, this ordinary, Raymond, he needed help, you know, guidance in life. I mean, really.

We were going up to the bow, and as you walked up to the bow of the ship, underneath there were two big metal doors that opened up, and this was actually for tow motors. The bosun was using it as a storage area, and he had the day working AB in there. We take a ladder to go up to the forward part of the ship above this area, and there's four or five wooden pallets laying up there.

So the bosun tells Raymond, "Raymond, get these pallets and put them down by the front of that locker down there." He says, "Ron and I are gonna go up here and do something."

We're doing something with the anchor, and, oh, about 2 or 3 minutes later, Raymond comes walking up. And he's kinda cross-eyed and really didn't have a great handle on life itself. He's pushing his gloves together with his fingers, nervous-like.

Raymond says, "Bosun?"

The bosun says, "Yes, Raymond," gentle. Cuz that's how you had to talk to Raymond.

"Bosun, I think something's wrong with your day man."

Bosun says, "Well, Raymond, why do you think something's wrong with the day man?"

"He's laying on the deck, and there's blood coming out of his head."

The bosun looks at me, and I look at him like: *What the fuck?*

We go back down there. Here's the day man laying there. The pallet's laying there. The day man's looking up at the cut in his head.

"What the fuck happened?"

Raymond says, "I was doing what you told me to do. I was putting those pallets down in front there, and the day man yelled. I don't know what happened."

What he was doing was picking them up and throwing them down there without looking. Raymond did that the entire trip. Raymond kind of wandered, you know.

The day man went to the hospital, got some stitches in his head, came back. I think the company gave him two or three hundred dollars for the stitches.

This is at the beginning of the trip. So you could see how the rest of this was gonna go.

We had this ordinary seaman named Porter, who used to constantly take off, and was just fucked up. Try to put him to work, and he'd wander off, wouldn't do anything. Just a real asshole. Years later I saw him in Norfolk. He had half a lung taken out because of asbestos. They offered him $75,000, and he wouldn't take it. He'd rather wander around Norfolk and hold out to the very end. Well, he died before he got the money. Fucking idiot. Always was an idiot.

Anyway, we're in Durban, South Africa, and they had this white South African, Dusty Miller. And they had what was called the Dusty Miller gang. Dusty used go around outside Durban, and he'd pick up these black guys, these South Africans, and they'd sign a contract with him to work on these ships. They'd come and they'd do all these dirty jobs. They'd clean out the bottom of the hatches. *Anything.* At night he'd take them to this compound. I saw it. It looked like a POW camp. But he fed 'em, he took care of 'em, and when their contract was up, he'd take 'em back out and drop 'em back off where he found 'em. That's the way it worked. And they earned money. They were raggedy, dirty, coveralls. I mean, these guys were *filthy*. You didn't talk to 'em much. I talked a little bit to Dusty—"Hi, how are you?" kind of thing.

One day the bosun says to me, "Take Porter, get two 5-gallon paint buckets, hull grey, two man-helpers, two rollers, go down on the dock, and paint the side of the ship."

"OK, bosun." I says, "I gotta take Porter, huh?"

He says, "Yeah, it's your day with him."

"Thanks." I think I had a hangover.

And it's all Porter did was run his mouth. Just useless.

We get down there, we're each carrying the paint and rollers and everything, and now he wants to sit right next to me.

I says, "Porter, you go down on that end, and I'll go down on this end, and we'll work towards each other." So I don't have to listen to you, you know. I think I did have a hangover.

I'm rolling out. It was 15, 20 minutes later the bosun's down there on the dock.

He says, "Where's Porter?"

I says, "He was over there a minute ago."

He says, "Where is he?"

"Well, he ain't in my pocket, bos'. I don't know. Is it my day to watch him?"

"Yeah, it is, now that you bring it up."

"I sent him down there to paint. I don't know where the fuck he went."

We start looking around. Here's Porter bullshitting with some of the black South Africans. He's American, you know, and he's telling them how they're gonna be free one of these days.

We says, "Come on over here and start painting. Do that on your time, not company time."

Anyway, we finally start merging together, and here comes one of the Dusty Miller gang, carrying some trash, he's all dirty. Big black guy. And Porter's got this portable radio, he's listening to the radio. One arm he's rolling, the other he's got this radio.

Porter says to this guy, "Yeah, man, one of these days you're gonna be free. You're gonna have something. I'm American. You're gonna have something."

This black guy puts his stuff down, and he looks at Porter, up and down. Now I'm watching this, right, I figure he's gonna kill him.

He says, "What?" Very good English, this South African black guy. "I've got a wife, three children, a farm, 12 head of cattle. What do you have? A portable radio?" And picked his stuff up and walked away.

I crack up. Porter's gonna tell these blacks how good he's got it and how miserable they are. Yeah, right.

We stopped over at Madagascar, the island off Africa, went to a place called Hellville to get frozen fish. That was their main export, except that it was pretty much a tourist area. Real nice area. They had the old French Foreign Legion fort, cuz the country used to be French. First time I had been there. Very laid back. It was a resort area.

We go up to Mozambique again. Now this is Maputo, the old Lorenzo Marques. Now it's full commie. You talk about depression. Everything's shut down. *Everything.* The Coke sign's still there. Just everything is shut down—the place we had the party with the Englishmen, that big dinner with all the prawns and girls. That's closed up. The good times were gone. The bars, the restaurants, were closing up.

Anyway, Raymond wanted to go ashore.

I says, "Yeah, Raymond, we'll go and see what's what."

"I want to go in." You know. Cross-eyed.

So I says, "Yeah, Raymond, we'll go in."

Raymond just wanted to see Maputo. Some restaurants are open. You can go in there and eat and get a beer. Well, Raymond don't want any beer, but I do. So every time I order a beer and Raymond gets a soda, they give me a sandwich. I'm not eating that. The roll looked alright, but I'm not about to eat that meat.

I notice there's a little black kid standing there, a little ragamuffin. He's looking at the sandwich. So I give him the sandwich. I says, "Here." Then I get another beer. Kid's just sitting there. Kid's eating. I get another beer. It comes with another sandwich. I says, "Excuse me, I don't want this sandwich, I just want the beer."

They says, "Oh, no. New law, if you get a beer, you have to have food to go with it."

This is freedom, right. When the Portuguese were there, you could just order a beer or a sandwich, either one, now you *had* to have food with your beer.

So this kid's eating a lot of sandwiches. Every time I give it to the kid. Kid's got a big smile and eating. Now he tries to grab my beer. I says, "Gimme that." You know, right? It didn't dawn on me he didn't have anything to wash this down with. I had to buy him a soda.

We stopped in a couple of the stores on the way back, but they didn't want to sell us anything cuz you couldn't take anything out of the country. So that was the end of that.

We go up to Beira, that's about the furthest north I'd been in Mozambique, and if you thought Maputo had been shut down, Beira was, literally, doors wide open on homes, cars vandalized, left empty. *Nothing!* Buildings in town, doors wide open. People were going in there to sleep.

Communism had improved their lifestyle.

When we first got to Durban it was the weekend, so I took off. I'm all gassed up, and I go get a taxi, and there's this girl already in there, in the taxi.

She says, "Oh, hi, how are you?"

I says, "Fine." I'm gassed up.

She says, "Where are you going?"

I says, "I'm going back to the ship."

"You wanna stop somewhere for a drink?"

"Sure."

Make a long story short, I ended up at her apartment. She's at 10 Point Road. It was on the point where it led out to the harbor in Durban. Her name was Ann Brandyke.

I was really slopped up, you know, and in the morning I got up, and I'm looking over. I says, "Well, I guess I had a good time." Trying to not wake her, thinking I better get the fuck outta here. I don't even know where I'm at. I didn't even look to see if I had any money. I'd figure out my way back, one way or the other.

All of a sudden she says, "Wouldn't you like to take a shower before you leave?"

I says, "Well, yeah, OK."

Turn around, she was from West Germany, and her husband had taken a contract job in South Africa and brought her and the three daughters down there. Germany always did have an affiliation with South Africa—you know, South-West Africa, Namibia. America couldn't deal with them, but Germany—West Germany—could. He had gotten killed on the job. Well, she stayed there, and she was getting a pension from the West German government from the company he worked for, *and* from the South African government, *plus* they had the girls in a free West German boarding school in Africa. They only showed up on the weekends, and they were just like, "Well, this is Mom, and we gotta come here, and she's out of her fucking mind, and this is some guy she picked up." She was a prescription junkie.

We ended up being there 2 weeks. It got good to me.

So I was going over there every night, and the weekends I just stayed over there with her, and we're stopping in the bars and restaurants, and we're having a pretty good time.

But she kept talking about this church behind this big apartment building she lived in. It was all white at the time. She says, "There's this church back there." She says, "One day, I'll just get you drunk, and we'll go over there and get married."

I says, "I don't think I'm that denomination."

Just what I need. Every Zulu headhunter to the north of me, and then to the south of me I got the ocean with every shark. And I'm stuck in the middle. Sure thing, Ann.

Anyway, we turned around, and one morning I couldn't get up. I couldn't make it. We'd been out drinking, and I just could not get up. It's like nine o'clock, ten o'clock.

You know, just, "Aw, Christ." I says, "I wish you got me up."

"Well, I tried."

Yeah, I'm sure she did. Anyway, I still gotta get back to the ship. I says, "Parker will log me for this one. I'll make the book for this."

She says, "If you're gonna get logged, why even bother going back?"

"Well, it's," you know, "the *appearance* of *trying*." Make it *look* like

I care.

She says, "You give me the phone number, and I'll just call Mr. Parker, and I'll explain everything."

I says, "No. That's not gonna work. Don't help me out here."

Now, these two other guys are fouling up right and left. They're getting logged right and left, I mean for everything. They missed the ship, drunk, never turn to. Well, he logged them, and so I know I'm getting it, cuz you can't discriminate like that. So I turn around, and I get back to the ship about noon.

Here's the bosun. He says, "You know, I had you covered up until ten o'clock. Parker knew you were missing at eight thirty. 'Where's Ron?' I said, 'He ain't here, mate. But he's no fuck off. I got 'im 'til 10.' So Parker said, 'OK. He's not a fuck off. I agree with that. And OK, you got him to 10. So if he's not here by 10, *I* got 'im.'"

I get there at noon, right?

So, one o'clock, the bosun says, "Go up and see him."

I says, "Yeah." So I go up, one o'clock. I'm standing outside his door, and Parker comes out.

I says, "Hi, Mr. Parker."

He says, "Oh, Ron. Back?"

"Yeah." I says, "You like to hear what happened?"

He says, "No, no, no, Ron. When'd you get back?"

"About 11, eleven thirty."

"Well, you know, the bosun had you covered 'til 10."

"Yeah, I appreciate that. I do." I says, "It's a long story, Mr. Parker."

He says, "Yeah, and I don't want to hear it, Ron."

"I didn't figure you did." I says, "Well, if it's OK, I'll just go ahead and turn to now, one o'clock to 5."

He says, "No, Ron, let's just call it a day. Let's just call it a day."

I says, "OK, Mr. Parker."

"Have a good time, Ron."

"OK." So I figure I'm getting logged a day and a day's pay. I clean up, no sense staying here. I go back over to her place.

She says, "What happened?"

I told her. I says, "He told me to take the rest of the day off."

"Oh, that was really nice of him."

I says, "Yeah, he's a good guy." Which he is, you know, he's pretty good.

Anyway, I says, "Whatever we do, we do *now*, because I'm leaving here about ten o'clock at night. I'm being on board tomorrow morning."

Next morning I get up, eight o'clock, bosun says, "Go up and see the old man. The mate's up there, too. You and about three others he's logging for fucking up."

I'm last in line, waiting. So I hear, inside: "You're logged, fined a day's pay." And OK, he comes out. Then the other one comes out. Same thing. Then I go in.

Captain says, "Failed to turn to, such and such a day. You're logged for failing to turn to that day." No fine. You know, cuz they could take a day's pay. He says, "Do you agree with this?"

I says, "Yes," and no comment.

"OK. Sign."

I sign. I walk out, and Parker's behind me. I says, "No fine? I didn't lose a day's pay?"

He says, "You remember when we were on the *Mormacglen*, Ron, and we were in Guam? You guys had 4 hours coming to you, and I didn't pay it? And I said I'd pay it, you know, if it was straightened out. It never did get straightened out. But you know what, Ron?"

I says, "What's that, Mr. Parker?"

He says, "We're even now. I ain't taking your day's pay."

"Thank you, Mr. Parker."

He says, "It's alright, Ron. Go to work. It's OK."

I kept in touch with her. We came back down to Durban. Saw her again.

We're going to Cape Town, then we're going back to the States. In Cape Town, whatever rand I had left, paper money, I put in an envelope and posted it to her. I says, "I hope this does you some good. Keep in touch."

I get back to the States, and we're getting in, and these other guys, he logged them and fined them. Well, they put down they wanted to stay on. But, you know, you ain't staying on with Parker. So Parker has to give them dismissal slips, even though you weren't supposed to log them and fire them, Parker would do it. Nine times out of ten, it stood up with him.

Anyway, I'm on the bridge, and it's probably the day before we get in. I put down "quit."

Parker says, "I put something on your desk, Ron."

I says, "It isn't personal, is it, Mr. Parker?"

He says, "I fired them. Now I gotta fire you. But I'll tell you what," he says, "why don't you take your gear, put it in my room, and then go down to the union hall, and maybe you can get the job and come back."

I says, "Thanks, Mr. Parker, I appreciate that. But I think I'll be getting off."

He says, "You don't want to go back down to see your girlfriend?"

I says, "I don't think so, Mr. Parker."

I got off, and I got home. She'd asked me to get her two pairs of jeans and pantyhose. She couldn't get pantyhose for some reason, or she was too cheap. I got her the jeans, I got her the pantyhose. I packaged them up and sent it to her. I put my return address on there. I put a little letter in there: "Don't know when I'll be back, but here's your stuff, nice meeting you," and all that. "Hope everything works out for you." You know, "it's not you, it's me" stuff.

About 2 weeks later, I'm at home in Cleveland, the phone rings. I pick up the phone, and they says, "Is this—" and they use my full name, with my middle initial.

I hesitate when somebody says that.

I says, "Yes."

"We have a telegram for you." A voice telegram.

"OK."

The telegram says, "Thank you much. Received the package. Everything I asked for. Thank you again. Love, Finn. F-I-N-N." From Natal, South Africa.

The girl says, "Do you know anything about this?"

I says, "Finn?" It was *Ann*. But it looked like an "F" and an "I." It didn't connect. I says, "That was 'Ann.'"

The girl says, "You banging some black broad down there?"

I says, "Actually, that Natal, that's a province of South Africa, like, this would be a county, you know." I says, "It's Durban." I says, "She's a white German girl."

The girl says, "Oh. OK. We'll send you a copy of this."

"OK."

I can't remember what happened after that. Can't remember what happened to her. I hope she's alright. We had a good time. I just wasn't getting married with three kids. I can barely take care of myself.

Later on, on another trip down there, I looked her up in the phone book and couldn't find a phone number for her, so I turned around, and Point Road was kind of like hotel bars, and you went out to the point which led out to the harbor. I was with some cadet, we started walking, and sure enough, I found the apartment building where Ann lived and, at the time, apartment buildings were either all white or all black. It was government owned. I went in there, and I saw there were different names on there, and I saw a black couple come in, and they were looking strangely at me, you know. So that was the end of that.

Off to see the wizard

This is the *Export Bay*, American Export Lines, 7/12/77 to 10/10/77. First time I sailed with this company, American Export Lines. Break-bulk freighter, boom ship, had a hard time getting a crew for this. Matter of fact, they were calling all around, looking for ABs, cuz of this captain on there, Kaufmann. Miserable fucker. Notorious prick. All he needed was a rubber to make him a natural prick.

I'll give you a story here that I know is true, but I wasn't on board. It was before I started shipping. This Export Lines, years ago, had a captain named Davie Jones. He hated one of the ABs. They were in port in New York. He told the bosun, "I want the smoke stack painted."

Well, on the stack, you use the bosun chair, not a stage. It's a one-man deal, with a line. You slack yourself down. You're sitting in a chair, a bosun's chair: it's just a piece of wood with two lines coming up. It's a special hitch you put in, almost like a square knot hitch, and you slack yourself down as you're painting. Like I said, the outside's a dummy. You climb the inside of the stack. You got so much room, and then it's the inside that's the stack itself. Well, you can climb up there, and the ordinary would give you the paint. You'd pull it up, or he'd hand it to you, and you'd paint going down, or clean. Sometimes they wanted it cleaned.

Hated this AB. So, in port in New York, he turned around and told the bosun, "I want the stack painted." Said, "I want this AB to do it."

Like a flunky, you know, "Yeah, OK, captain, OK. Yeah, I like my job."

He sent the AB up there to do it. He waited 'til the AB was right by the ship's whistle—the whistle comes out of there on some ships—as soon as he got by the whistle, he blew it. I don't know how far he fell, but he got all fucked up.

Well, he sued the company, and he got so much fucking money it was unbelievable, right? And they could never really prove that he did it on purpose. But now when you go on the bridge of a ship, if there's anybody going aloft, there's signs on the radar, or anybody going on the flying bridge. "Turn the radar off." "Do not operate whistle." "Caution." All from that incident.

The insurance companies had a lot to do with it, like for safety, keep your insurance rates down. Stages and bosun chairs, same thing. Guys were falling. They were rigging themselves improperly. Lines were bad. Ropes would break. You could demand a new line anytime you wanted it. You'd say, "I'm not refusing to do this, but what I want is a new line." And you took care of that line because, you know, you put a nick in one of your lines, yeah, you drag it along the deck, you don't know if you're gonna get a good nick in it. If it's an old line: you don't know if you got some soot from the smokestack on it and that acid would eat into it. You used to have to break the line to see if there's any mold in it. You'd open it up like you were gonna splice it, look inside, and you could check it along to see if there's any mold in there. If there was mold, that means it was rotten and it would just part on you. So now, between the insurance company and the Coast Guard, you could be negligent. Years ago, you just went for the negligent part on the part of the company to sue them. It was very easy for a merchant seaman to sue under that '36 Seamen's Act. As time went by, it got to be "criminal negligence." It got to the point where it's gonna be criminal negligence on somebody's part where they can actually put you in jail for it. Everybody's real good about that now, you know. "Oh! Safety first!" They're not saying, but it's the insurance companies, and you could go to jail for it now.

Anyway, they flew us from Charleston to New York. I was shipping out of Charleston. Nobody wanted the job. I got on there. We went down to Beaumont, Texas to load for the Middle East. We're actually loading Pepsi-Cola for the Saudi Arabian Army. Not a whole ship, because we stopped in Egypt on the way back. This was what they called giveaway cargo. I think the Saudis paid for the Pepsi. They wouldn't take Coke because the Jews had something to do with Coca-Cola, so they'd only take Pepsi-Cola. Serious. That's for real.

I think we stopped somewhere else to load hogsheads of tobacco for Egypt. That was giveaway, too. I guess the Egyptians needed the nicotine and tar.

But we had a bosun on there, Henry Rider. Henry was about five foot six, glasses, just a nice guy. He knows it's all bullshit, he's just making a few more bucks sailing bosun than he did AB. He talked me into staying. "Come on," he says, "We're gonna have a good time." You know. "I need you."

I wanted to quit, Henry talked me into it. I says, "OK, Henry, I'll do it."

We leave, and I got this young third mate, Henshaw, very intelligent. As a matter of fact, I'm about halfway across, I says, "What the fuck are you doing sailing with this outfit?"

He said he felt it would be easier to get a captain's job going through the company rather than he would with the union starting out.

I says, "Yeah, OK." I got along good with him.

Well, this captain had to get some work out of you. He wasn't fucking happy unless he got some work out of you. He found all kinds of dumb shit for us to do. He used to get all fucked up on booze, and he stayed fucked up.

We had a chief mate on there, one of the first black chief mates I've ever been with. Just in over his head.

We had a second mate named McEvy. Chief mate used to call him McIvy.

Anyway, one day they needed something painted up on the bridge, and it was a certain color, almost like an ivory color, not white, but an ivory.

So the chief mate says to me, "I can't send you down to get it." What it really was was: they'd have to pay me what they call penalty overtime. I would actually leave the bridge and that would be a penalty hour, see. I was up on the wheel noon to two, and then I'd go out on deck for 2 hours during the day 'til four. At night I either had the wheel or lookout. You know, we'd reverse it. Anyway, he didn't want to pay the $3 or $4. You know, make himself look good. He says, "I'll have the bosun bring the paint up."

So Henry, the bosun, had to mix this paint. We're only talking about a gallon or maybe half a gallon was all I needed. These are stupid little fucking jobs. They weren't happy unless you were working. Henry comes all the way up to the bridge from the paint locker with this paint. So we're trying to match it. And it's not the right color. So Henry's gotta walk all the way back down. Twenty minutes later, he comes back up again. Look at it. Still don't match.

Henry says, "Ah, fuck it!" and he threw the paint over the side. "Fuck this!"

This is all in a matter of the 2 hours I'm up there. By the time we get the color right, I was gone already, my partner had come up for the other 2 hours.

The chief mate: nothing's right for him. "That ain't right!"

So, obviously, we can see where this is gonna be a fucking problem here.

Kaufmann, he'd come up there, always wore shorts and a khaki shirt. He wouldn't wear khaki shorts, he'd wear a different color, but he'd wear a khaki shirt with the shoulder boards, like, "I'm captain, master after God."

He'd go up to the flying bridge, which is the topmost part of the ship. I mean, the bridge of the ship has all the controls, but up on the flying bridge there's an extra wheel in case of an emergency. These were a holdover from World War II, in case something happened on the bridge, you could go up on top, the flying bridge, and still control the ship. It's the roof of the bridge, so it's completely open to the elements. Well, they had a dodger for the wind, almost concave, but, I mean, it was open. He would go up there and walk around naked to get a suntan, right. What a fucking goof. And drunk, he's fucking scotched up all the time. It got to the point even Henshaw couldn't stand him. "This fucking guy's an idiot."

He'd come up there, and anything you did was wrong.

The third mate happened to put a can of Coke on some papers up there, and it left a water ring. "Look at this! It put a water ring on there! Get a coaster for that!" He'd nitpick anything he could find.

So we're going across, and we're gonna go through the Suez Canal. We can see this is starting, where we're gonna fuck him up some way or the other. We go through the Suez Canal, get to Saudi Arabia. They'd want to see the log books for 2 years back, to see if you had dealt with Israel. If you had been in an Israeli port, they wouldn't let you unload the cargo.

We didn't go to the dock. They'd come out with the barges and unload us. They had West Germans doing the cargo operations. They were on a 90 days on/90 days off contract, I think. That's all they did was work for 90 days and then go back to West Germany. We could go into town if we wanted to, but there wasn't a launch service to go in. There was nothing there.

That moved along so-so, the chief mate used to try to do our work, which was against union policy, but he would try to do our work to keep from paying us overtime. He was a miserable prick. Fucking idiot.

Now we go back through the Suez Canal. We're going to Alexandria, Egypt. I'd been there before, and we dock right next to the passenger dock terminal to unload this cargo, and there's this girl, Farita. She worked at the passenger dock terminal, and everybody used to go see Farita.

Farita.

Everybody tried to put the make on her. You know, she's blowing off guys right and left, but everybody figured they'd try their luck. Who knows? Matter of fact, I don't think you ever wanted to marry her or live in Egypt, you just wanted to see if you could get lucky. Needless to say, I didn't.

Anyway, now we're gonna be stuck there for up to 3 weeks. That's what they're telling us. Three weeks to get the cargo off. That's what it took. I know this sounds strange. That's why they went to containers. The cargo goes in the containers, the containers come on, the containers come out. These old ships, you had to go through the top tier. You had to go along with what the longshoremen were doing, how lazy they were, how good they were, how slow they were. Did they work through Ramadan? Did they slow down? Did they take off on holidays? That's just the way this thing worked. I mean, we used to get 2 weeks down in South Africa sometimes. The cargo wouldn't be ready for us to take back if the longshoremen were slow getting it off. They didn't have anywhere to put the cargo. They couldn't deliver the cargo immediately. They didn't have trucks. This all comes into play. And Egyptians were never really swift in their later years. I don't know how they got those pyramids built; well, I do know how they got the pyramids built. I think they got a foot put in their ass is what happened.

Anyway, we're getting the weekends off. The old man, he put out one draw when we got there. We went through that the first weekend, wandering around, fucking up.

Me and two other guys, Henry was one, we're going around to the little café bars, we're getting fucked up. We come out of one, and we're lit, we're trying to get a taxi to go to another one.

Here this Egyptian kid's got this fucking baboon like you see at the zoo. The fucking thing's 3 foot high, you know, got a muzzle on. I'm looking at the kid, and the kid's smiling, and the baboon's looking at me. So the kid's like, I don't know how you sense these things, but you know: the kid wanted me to get a coin and give it to the baboon. That's what the kid wanted me to do.

So I got a coin, and I'm showing it, and the baboon sticks his hand out, and I drop the coin in the baboon's paw, and it closes it, and looks at it, and looks at the kid, looks at the coin, looks at me, looks at the coin, gives the kid the coin, and flips. Does a flip.

I says, "That's cool." You know. What will entertain people, especially when you're drinking.

So I get another coin out.

Now the guys are yelling, "Come on, Ronnie! Come on, we got the taxi!"

"Wait a minute! Wait a minute!"

Now in my mind, me and this baboon are becoming friends. I give it a coin. Takes the coin, looks at it, looks at the kid, looks at the coin, looks at me, the coin, the kid, gives the kid the coin, does a flip. Now me and this baboon are buddies. See. So in my mind, what I'm gonna do is, I'm gonna take the baboon back to the ship, see, cuz we got the taxi. And we all hated that chief mate, so what I was gonna do was, I was gonna take the baboon back to the ship because we're buddies. I was gonna tie his leash to the chief mate's doorknob, and I was gonna kick the baboon three or four times and pull his muzzle off and then knock on the chief mate's door. And when the chief mate opens his door, this thing is gonna attack him.

So that's all going through my mind, because Henshaw had told me the trip before, one of the ABs hated this chief mate. Well, everybody hated the guy. He was a real fucking idiot. But anyway, they had these pipes coming down the front of the house where we slept. This is separate houses. The crew slept aft, officers slept forward. We had these big breathers up on the flying bridge. They stuck up almost like mushrooms, and they actually came out on the front of the house. So you would see these square things along the front of the house. These were air vents going down.

Well, this able seaman climbed up there one night, and he lowered a line down from the flying bridge in front of the house where the chief mate's room was. He marked it, and then he pulled it back up, and he tied on a little chipping hammer, which has two points on either end, we use it when we're chipping rust. So he drops this down through the air vent so you couldn't see it and tied it off up there. So when the ship would roll, it would knock back and forth, try to drive the mate nuts. I think that's what gave me the idea of the baboon.

God bless Henshaw for telling me that.

Anyway, this is going through my mind. So now the baboon puts his paw up to get another coin. I grab the baboon's paw, and I'm trying to take it over to the taxi, cuz me and the baboon are buddies.

Well, the kid, he don't like this. I don't think the baboon liked it much, either, to be honest with you. Now the kid's pulling the baboon by the leash, by the collar on the neck.

So I got the arm, and I'm pulling the arm this way, and the baboon's trying to grab the leash, and the guys are yelling at me. "No! NO! *Don't take the baboon,*" cuz they're in the taxi already waiting for me. "No, Ron! NO! Don't bring the—God, no! Not in here with us! No baboon! *Jesus Christ!*"

So I finally gave up on the fucking thing. He didn't want to go, so I let his arm go, and I got in the taxi, and we left.

But now we're not getting any more money. The old man's screaming and yelling about we're not working hard enough, and he don't want to give us any money, see, a draw for the weekend. His version of it is that he only has to give us one draw every foreign port. But there is something in the federal laws that say, in essence, every 5 days when you're in a foreign port. Well, now this is going back and forth.

Henshaw says, "Don't worry. You need some money, Ron?"

I says, "Thank you. I appreciate that, mate, I do." I says, "But I'm just tired of him and his rule by decree shit, you know, master after God. Fuck him."

So he's not gonna give a draw.

In the meantime, we're having it out with the chief mate, too. The captain's telling him what to do, he's telling the bosun—Henry—what to do. Well, now, somewhere there's a failure in communication. So, Henry's telling the mate, "Mate, *that's* not what you told me to do. *This* is what you told me to do." And the captain's on the mate's ass saying, "Can't you do anything right, you dumb fuck?" He's saying the bosun's not doing what he's telling him. So now he's gonna write what he wants done every day and give it to the bosun. So he writes it down so they're both on the same page, see?

I can't remember any of them, but we used to look at those little jewels every day. Henry would come down: "Look what he fucking wrote here." He couldn't even spell.

We go ashore one night, we get all fucked up. We had left a messenger line, a coiled rope about 100 feet, on one of the hatches. Over the weekend, they didn't want any of us to work and pay us overtime, so they had Egyptian guards for security. They let them come on, and they were trying to steal everything they could. They got this line off the deck on a Saturday. But they didn't get it all, cuz somebody caught 'em, right, screamed or something. They let the line go. Now this line had been soaking Saturday night in this oily, salty water, the harbor water. Well, somebody pulled it up and coiled it back up on deck. Now the sun's beating down on it. Now we got, like, *wire* rope here.

On the same weekend, one of the ABs, Hucklesberry, he goes ashore and gets in an argument with the Egyptians, and they punch him in the fucking eye. He comes back with stitches, right? He's got about four or five stitches.

So Monday morning, he turns to, Henry sees the eye, says, "What happened?"

Hucklesberry's all mush-mouthed. It wasn't his fault. They attacked him, you know. Not that he was insulting *them*.

Henry says, "You know what?" He can still see that he's fucked up. Plus, he's got the cut and the stitches. Henry says, "Go on up to the bow. Go up on the foc'sle and go down in the line locker." We used to store our mooring lines down there. He says, "Go down there and count the mooring lines." In other words: "Go down there and get out of the fucking way." This is three tiers down.

So he opens up the hatch, leaves it open so you can tell somebody's in there, cuz you always closed it, last one out would close it. If it was left open, you know people were down there.

This is like 10 after 8 in the morning. He goes all the way down. I guess he went to sleep, or he was working, I don't know. Just before noon, we happen to be walking forward there, we're going by this rope that's like wire now.

Henry says, "We gotta kill some time before lunch." He tells this ordinary that was with us, "Grab that line, put it on your shoulder, we'll take it up and put it up in the bow cuz it's probably no good now."

It's heavy, this guy's pissed about carrying it cuz we've got to carry it from number three hatch all the way up. I don't have to carry it. I'm AB.

We go up. I'm standing there, the bosun's standing there, this ordinary, he's got the line over his right shoulder, he's standing next to the hatch. He can just shrug it off his shoulder and it will fall right in.

So Henry says, "OK, put it down in there."

I assume Henry thought he was gonna climb down there to the first tier and then throw it in.

Without looking or doing anything, this ordinary just kinda shifts his shoulder, and the line goes down, straight shot, three tiers down. *Poom.* Well, just about that time, Hucklesberry's decided to come up for lunch. I guess he got about two or three steps on the ladder, and the line hit him right in the face. *Boom.*

We hear: "Ohhhhh! Ahhhhhh!"

We look down. Here's Hucklesberry, lines all over him, stitches split open, blood coming out.

Bosun yells down, "Hucklesberry! Are you alright?"

We hear from down there: "Yeah. Next time drop a *mooring* line!" You know, a *bigger* line!

We get him up out of there. He's all fucked up. We go see the mate. "Yeah, we gotta send you back to the doctor." His stitches are all fucked up.

The ordinary says, "Why didn't you tell me he was down there?"

I says, "Why didn't you look or yell or something," you fucking idiot.

They sent him back to the doctor. He went and got stitches. He got back at three.

Bosun says, "Hucklesberry, take the rest of the fucking day off. Just go lay down."

Un-fucking-real.

Now they got it in their minds that we're gonna be there so long, they want some painting done. They wanted all the posts painted, the posts that hold the booms up in the air. You gotta climb up there to do it.

So the first day, Henry's gonna get this done, and we're gonna do it right. Henry's setting up the paint for us. Buff paint. So we go up there and we paint. The ABs are rigged up, getting paint all over ourselves. The one guy who was working with me, we set it up so we could paint as far as you could reach to either side, so we just had to make one drop doing the painting.

I'm not real happy doing this anyway. I'm not gonna get any money to go ashore so I can go get fucked up. I don't need much more encouragement.

Here I hear the old man's voice: "Hey. You missed a place."

I turn around in the chair and look, and here's the captain in the wheelhouse of the bridge looking out, inspecting the job. I look over and here's my partner, the guy to my left, he had moved over so we were leaving a streak there.

I says, "Yeah, OK." So I call down to Henry, "Tie me off a man-helper," a long wooden stick. I pull it up, kind of swing around a little bit, force myself around, and I says to my partner, "We gotta keep in sync on this."

He says, "Aw, fuck him, we don't have to do a good job."

"Yeah, we do, the old man can see us." I says, "So we better do a good job right *now*."

"OK, OK."

"Otherwise, we're gonna have to do this again."

"OK."

We get done for the day, we come down at four thirty, we're gonna knock off.

Henry says, "You know what? Take the rollers and just put them in the kerosene. Don't bother cleaning 'em. We'll clean 'em in the morning."

So we put all the rollers, paintbrushes, everything we were using, just put them in the kerosene. The ordinaries used the paintbrushes. They're cutting in as far as they can reach cuz they weren't allowed to climb up. We throw all this shit in there.

Well, we're still not getting a draw, and the old man was gonna save some money: see, at the time, you kept the trash in 55-gallon drums in the stern of the ship. It was a split house: like I said, we lived aft, there were cargo hatches in the middle, and then the bridge and about four decks where the officers lived. We're taking our galley trash and everything else and we're putting it in 55-gallon drums on the stern. We had 55-gallon drums hanging over the stern, too. This is how you dumped your trash at sea. When you got out to the 3-mile limit, 5-mile limit, you just dumped it over the side.

Well, we're there, and we're piling this up every day. This is no exaggeration, there had to have been at least 10 55-gallon drums filled with food waste. We're putting plastic over it to keep the flies and mosquitoes off of it. The Egyptians are stealing the plastic at night. And we're pissed off about that, too.

What the old man was gonna do was wait. Rather than call the Egyptian agent and have him send the garbage barge—which was nothing but a wooden barge with a couple Egyptians on it, probably cost practically nothing—and dump the trash in there, they're gonna charge for that, see, so he's gonna save some money, wait 'til we go to sea, then give the bosun and day man a couple of penalty hours for throwing all this garbage in the ocean.

So, we put the rollers in the kerosene to soak for the night so we can clean them in the morning and start working again. We got all the paint sitting in the locker there, we put it right by the houses where these posts were. We took it from the paint locker and start to work our way aft. The next morning, we're gonna turn to and do this shit, gonna get the rollers and clean 'em, get the kerosene off, roll 'em out, get them as clean as we can. And you can't mix kerosene and paint, obviously. It thins it out. Most people know that. I think Henry had a hangover that morning. He was doubly pissed, or triply pissed.

So Henry says, "You know," he just took the fucking rollers—I had my paint there, about a half of a 5-gallon can, to take with me. I had a board in there so you can roll the paint on the board and then roll it out so you don't have it dripping all over. So my board's in there. Henry's gonna clean the rollers. Usually he makes the AB do it, but Henry was that way. He'll clean it. Good guy.

Henry says, "You know what? *Fuck* this." Starts to clean it and just stuck it with kerosene, just stuck it right in my fucking paint. He says, "*Fuck* this."

I says, "Yeah, that's right Henry. *Fuck* this." You know.

He says, "Do you think that's enough kerosene in there, Ron?"

I says, "I don't think so, Henry." I says, "That still looks pretty thick to me."

So he just pours more kerosene in there. Everybody got the same thing. Henry went by fixing everybody. That paint went on like water, man. We were just putting it on, we didn't have to roll it twice.

And we were working. Well, Henshaw happened to have the deck that day, and he comes by and says, "Boy, Ron," he says, "you really got a compliment."

I says, "What's that, mate?"

He says, "The captain said he was looking at you working. He says, 'Boy, that Ron, he does good work, but he's so fucking slow.'" Henshaw said he looked at him and said, "Captain, you just paid him a compliment. His ambition is to be the laziest man in the world."

Now we decide we're all gonna start going to the doctor, see, so we don't have to do any more work. I got a stomach flu. But there were so many of us, they brought the doctor to the ship, and the doctor gave me 2 days "Not Fit for Duty" cuz I had a slight fever. Fucking Kaufmann was *pissed*. He had to pay me for 2 days, and I didn't have to work, and he had to pay the doctor, too. But we're all pulling it. Wrists, fingers, ears, runny nose, anything we could think of, right? He's fucking with us, we're gonna fuck with him back. So, turn around, now my filling falls out. I mean, this doctor might as well come on board the ship at eight o'clock in the morning and just stayed on board and paid him.

So now the doctor's gotta come back.

"Now what's wrong?"

I says, "I want to see a dentist. My filling's out."

So he says, "Yeah, you need a dentist. Go set up an appointment." He says, "It'll be for tomorrow."

I says, "No, it can't be for tomorrow. Tomorrow's the weekend. Make it for Monday." So I had Saturday, Sunday off; Monday I go to the dentist.

The Egyptian dentist says, "You don't want to come Saturday? It couldn't have been too bad."

I says, "No, I didn't have to work Saturday or Sunday."

"Oh, you get the day off?"

"Yeah."

So he says, "OK, I'll take my time with this." I think he charged me something like $15, but it was worth it. I had the whole day off. So I go stop to see Farita, bullshit with her.

She says, "Every time I see you, you never work. Don't you ever work?"

I says, "I don't work a lot, Farita."

We turn around and—this is all in a period of 3 weeks—we do manage to get the entire thing painted with all the kerosene in the paint except for the first two. Now he's got other jobs for us to do. Well, we're not getting any fucking money.

I get together with Henry and says, "You know what?" I says, "Fuck this. Twelve o'clock today, if he hasn't put out the draw, we're going to the American Consul."

So the deck department—it was always the deck department, cuz he couldn't fuck with the engine department much, and he couldn't say too much to the steward department, you know, the *food*, so it was pretty much us. The deck department were the only ones he could really aggravate. All captains could. So we're gonna go to the American Consul in Alexandria, Egypt.

So here we are . . . .

The American Consul overseas can take care of any American. If you're an American and you've got a complaint, you go to the American Consul. Passport problem, merchant seaman, there were special laws, '36 Seaman's Act, if you had a problem, you went to the American Consul and you got it taken care of. Alright, we load up. There's six or eight of us, all the drunks, you know, cuz we're all going to see the American Consul. We're off to see the wizard. And here we go, down the yellow brick road. Fucking screwballs. Matter of fact, I had the Harley at the time. I had a Harley Davidson T-shirt: "Ride your Harley." We're just off work. We get to the American Consul, and there's Egyptian guards there, and they see we're American so they're gonna let us through.

The Marine guards say, "What do you guys want?"

"We want to see the consul."

"Who are you?"

We show them our seamen's cards.

They says, "It's noon. It's supposed to be lunch."

I says, "It's the only time we get to come here."

"OK. I'll see."

So this guy comes out. "Come on in, gentleman. Sit down."

I says, "We're pretty dirty."

He says, "I don't care." He says, "It's your tax money, my tax money, who cares? Sit down. What's the problem?"

I says, "We're off the *Export Bay*." I says, "We're having problems with the captain." I says, "He won't give us a draw."

This guy looks in the book, and he says, "Well, it says draw in every foreign port, every 5 days." He says, "There's a lot of ways to interpret that."

I says, "Well, look, there's at least 10 55-gallon drums of garbage we're dealing with. We don't have any money to go ashore. Our rec room is on the stern of the ship." I says, "You open the door to the stern, there's at least 10 cans of garbage there just spilling over. The captain refuses to call and have this taken away. That's a health issue."

He says, "Yeah, that would be."

I says, "Look, we gotta have a draw." The other guys start chiming in, too.

He says, "Well, I understand you're here as a group."

I says, "We're not here as a *group*, we're here as *individuals*. We all have the same complaint, plus a few other individual complaints, but we're here as *individuals*, not a group." I says, "That's like 10 individual complaints you're getting, not one."

He kind of looks at me like: maybe this dumb fucker does know something.

So he says, "I'll tell you what—"

I says, "Look, we gotta get back to the ship, or he'll log us. We gotta be back by one o'clock."

He says, "I'll tell you what. I'm gonna come down to the ship. But let's face facts, guys, it's not like you're suffering any cruel or unjust punishment."

I looked at him, and I pointed to myself. "*I'm* suffering mental anguish over this."

He looks at me like: you could suffer mental anguish? You know, beard, cowboy boots, Harley t-shirt. Like: how could you suffer *anything*? He says, "I'll come to the ship."

I says, "I'll tell you what. I'm taking you at your word. But I'll be totally honest with you." I says, "If you're not on that ship by five o'clock today," I says, "I'm gonna be back down here at eight o'clock tomorrow morning, sitting in this chair."

He says, "If I'm not there, I want you to come back."

"OK. We'll all be here." I didn't mention we're all gonna get fucked up that night, you know, with the couple of bucks we had left, and we're *really* gonna storm the place the next day.

So we get back, and we're working, we're touching up everything with the kerosene paint.

About two thirty somebody comes and says, "Hey, Ron, the consul's here."

Well, I can't knock off 'til three o'clock, coffee time is three o'clock to three fifteen, no more, no less—15 minutes. So I wait 'til three o'clock, and we go to our crew mess, which is right near the stern, where this trash is. So we get in there, and the consul comes.

Oh, I should say, we did put in for a draw, the deck delegate took it to the captain, he didn't want to give us one. The captain threw the paper down and said, "I'm not giving those animals any more money!"

So the consul comes in. He says, "Sit down, gentlemen." He says, "I've talked to the captain. He denies calling you animals, so it's basically his word against yours."

Now it's a he said/we said, you know, blah, blah, blah. We figured we weren't gonna get anywhere with that, but he did call us "animals." He was drunk, we were drunk, you know, that's OK. It's OK for *him*, but not us. That's why he called us "animals."

He says, "About the draw: the captain did put out one draw. I'm sorry, but I'm going to have to go along with that. Even though it says 5 days, it's not really clear. And he did put one out."

I says, "What about the guys that didn't get a draw?"

He says, "You have people here that didn't get a draw?"

"They didn't put in for one."

He says, "Those guys are entitled to a draw."

So between the three guys that didn't get a draw, we got them each to get $500, so then we borrowed the money from them. The consul sees this: "Hey, lend me this." "Hey, yeah, I'll get $500." "I'll get $500." "I'll get $500 cuz I didn't get a draw." "How much you need? How much you need? How much you need?" Yeah, fifteen hundred bucks, it was good.

Consul says, "You guys want $500 apiece, huh?"

"Yeah."

"OK," he says, "you'll have it, and you'll have it by five o'clock this afternoon."

OK.

"Now is there anything else?"

I couldn't let it go. I says, "What about the trash? It's right out here."

He says, "Now wait a minute. I don't want to go out there and see one trash can filled with trash."

I says, "If there's not at least 10 cans of food waste and trash back there in 55-gallon drums," I says, "I'll fucking eat it."

He says, "Let's go."

I go out there with him.

There's at least 10, maybe even 15, cans by now. The Egyptians had stolen the plastic again. The food waste was just piled on top, spilling over onto the deck, and there's flies and mosquitoes. Fucking mess.

He looks at that and says, "That will be gone by five o'clock today."

I says, "If not, can I come back down to the American Consul and sit in your chair again?"

"If you guys don't get a draw by five o'clock and that trash isn't gone by five o'clock, you come back."

"OK."

He says, "We all set here now? We done with this? Cuz I'm going back up to see the old man."

I says, "Five o'clock?"

"Five o'clock, or *I'll* be back." He was *pissed*.

He goes back up and leaves.

Four o'clock: here's an old wooden Egyptian barge with a couple of raggedy Egyptians. They're pouring all this trash on. Quarter to five: the old man calls the three guys up, gives them their $500 apiece. They come back and give us the money. We're off that night.

Next day we're at work again, Henshaw comes by to see if we're doing something on deck, painting, I think we're still using the kerosene paint.

Henshaw says, "Don't fuck up, Ron."

I says, "Why is that, Mr. Henshaw?"

He says, "The old man knows you led the charge down to the consul." Henshaw explains the agent charged him $600 to get that trash off, and we're talking a wooden barge, two or three Egyptians, dumping the trash and taking it away, when if we'd of got to sea, he'd of paid the bosun and two deck maintenance ABs 2 hours apiece. We're talking 50 bucks, right? So now he's really *pissed* it cost the company. Cuz he's keeping the costs down for the company, see. He's *really* pissed at me. Henshaw says, "You fuck up, he's gonna get you. You know, I'm company, and me and you are OK." He says, "The old man really is stepping out of bounds."

I says, "OK. Thank you."

On the way back we stopped in Taranto, Italy. So now he's gotta give us another draw. We get the money. We're bouncing around Taranto for 2 or 3 days. So there, you walk into a wine store, and some of 'em didn't have bottles of wine, they had it on tap.

So Henry's gonna buy some wine. "Hey, guys, you wanna chip in and get some wine to take back with us?"

I'm thinking we're gonna buy bottles of this, right. I says, "Yeah, OK."

We had to decide what kind of wine we want. So they're giving you little glasses. You sit at the table and drink.

"Do you like that?"

"No, we'll try this tap."

So we're sitting there getting all fucked up. So we finally decide on something cheap, the cheapest they had. But now Henry ain't gonna get a bottle. He's gonna get a big fucking vat, this glass thing with the wicker. This thing's a fucking *monster. The glass vat cost more than the wine.* It was 3 feet tall! But we're chipping in, right? We couldn't carry it. This is the one we want, right?

Henry says, "We'll chip in."

They fill this fucking thing up. I mean, a half hour to fill this thing!

Now how we gonna get it back? We're fucked up, see. So we try carrying it. We're taking turns carrying this thing down the street. Like idiots. It's fucking *heavy*, and there's only two handles, two guys would carry it at a time, 10, 15 feet, we had to put this fucker down. People are looking at us. We don't care. We're half fucked up from sampling all the wine. We're gonna get this back no matter what.

Finally it dawned on somebody, "Why don't we get a taxi?"

It's night already. So we get this thing back to the ship. We put it in Henry's room. Whoever happened to be on watch just let us through; he knew he was gonna get some later.

Henry says, "We got booze all the rest of the way back. We got something to drink."

I mean, guys were coming in with mayonnaise jars, Henry's tipping the fucking thing over. It was like a bottomless pit. We were sitting there one day, we spilled some of it on Henry's desk. We were fucked up. We couldn't even get the stain outta the desk, that's how cheap this shit was.

On our way back, I would have lookout, either midnight to one in the morning, or I would have it from 3 to 4. I'd have first lookout, or last lookout. And when I had first lookout, I'd have a small radio with me, and I'd go up on the bow of the ship to relieve the other AB, and I'd put the radio on. I'm supposed to be looking for ships, and I had a phone to call up. But I turn the radio on, and I was getting Radio Luxembourg, the largest independent radio station in the world, in English.

I put it on one night, and all of a sudden I hear this song "Telephone Man." I think it was banned in the States. Very suggestive lyrics. It sounded too sexy.

I see this light, a ship, it's a long way off when you see a light.

I says, "Fuck." I'm listening to this song on the radio. Cuz then I should turn the radio off, get on the phone, call Henshaw, and tell him: "Light, two points off starboard."

But I could see it's no danger, it's a long way off.

I says, "Fuck it," I'm listening to this song, you gotta have some enjoyment in life. And then, I'm just getting ready to turn the radio off at the end of the song and phone Henshaw, then they come on and say they're gonna play "Love is Blue." That was another song I think they banned in the States.

So now I gotta listen to *this*, you know. Another 3 minutes go by. I see the light's still there. Now we're talking 6 minutes. I'm getting ready to turn the radio off and call Henshaw, tell him there's a light.

Now what do they put on now? Some other song, something sexy by this English girl. You know, these things they did in England you couldn't do in the States, this Radio Luxembourg. I hear this. Well, now, the light's gotta wait again, see. I gotta listen to this. So, it's 10, 12 minutes have gone by since I saw the light.

The next song I didn't care for. I turn the radio off so he doesn't hear it in the background when I call him. It's just a kindness you do. Cuz you're not supposed to be listening to the radio, so you don't flaunt something like that. Henshaw's a good dude. I didn't want to flaunt it. I turn the radio off, I get on the phone to call the bridge, and he answers.

"Bridge."

I says, "Mr. Henshaw, this is Ron, I got a light here, two points on starboard."

He says, "What the fuck you been doing up there? I saw that fucking light 15 minutes ago!"

But you could talk to him, you know. I says, "Well, Mr. Henshaw, I was gonna call it in, but, first of all, the 'Telephone Man' song came up on Radio Luxembourg, then 'Love is Blue,' and then another one." Cuz you could talk to him. "Those came on, so I had to hear those songs before I reported the light."

He says, "Oh, OK, Ron, I understand. Thank you." He hung up.

Another night I go up there and turn the radio on, and there's an

Elvis Presley song going. That's cool. Now there's another one. These are all in a row. There ain't no lights out there to report this time. I woulda turned it off if there were. Now there's another Elvis Presley song. I'm thinking: what the fuck is this? All of a sudden they break in, "We have a caller from Denmark." This is Radio Luxembourg, you know. "What are you doing, sir?" "Just sitting around listening to his records." Who's this fucking goof? He's got nothing better to do than sit around listening to Elvis Presley records? Then they break in: "Elvis Presley has died. We're devoting our entire time to Elvis Presley songs. Elvis Presley has died." I was like: Aw, fuck. Not that I didn't like him or anything. I mean, we all gotta go. I just turned the radio off.

This happened on the way back, too: the officers were gonna have a cookout. They bought food, but we couldn't have any of it because that was *their* food that they bought. So we said, "Hey, we don't care." The engineers and the officers, they were their own union, you know, they bought this stuff and you can't say anything.

I'm on the stern, sitting there one evening, and you could hear them up there, having their party with their steaks and hot dogs that they bought.

All of a sudden Henshaw comes down and says, "What do you want, Ron, a steak or something?"

I says, "Ah, don't get in any trouble, mate. You know you're gonna get in trouble with him."

He says, "Fuck him. I'm tired of him anyway. What do you want?"

"A steak."

"How?"

"Well done."

"I'll get you some hot dogs, too." He says, "This is good stuff we bought in Italy."

I says, "Thank you. I appreciate that. I do."

He says, "Don't worry, Ron."

Just a nice guy. He came down and gave us all some of the food, you know, the old man wouldn't. "Damn *them*, this is *ours*. This is for the *officers*."

On the way back the chief mate says, "I'm getting off, bos." He says, "But we gotta have an inventory. We've gotta see what's missing and what we need for the next trip."

So Henry says, "Yeah, OK, mate, I'll take care of it."

So the next day the mate says, "OK, bos', I'll go around and—"

"Oh, you got everything, mate."

"We got everything?

"Yeah, you got everything."

We *didn't*, but Henry wrote down that he *did*. Henry wrote it all down, right?

Then when you go through the Suez Canal, at the time, coming or going, you either supplied the light to go through on the bow of the ship, or you rented one from the Egyptians. They come on board from their boats. I should say, too, that the Export Lines was the only company that didn't have credit to go through the Suez Canal. They had to pay. You got to the Suez Canal, the company had to send the money to the agent, and the agent gave it to the Suez Canal Authority cuz they had fucked them so many times, you know, they wouldn't let 'em use it unless they paid ahead of time. No credit. Anyway, they had their own light because that way they didn't have to rent one. You bought it and you had it down there when you needed it. Henry said he broke that light, too.

Now you can imagine, the chief mate's telling the new chief mate, "Yeah, you got everything. Here it is. I checked."

Henry just filled in what he was supposed to have, no matter how short they were.

Henry says, "Yeah, you got this much."

They didn't have anything.

One time on the way back, too, Henry says to me, "Get a chipping hammer, scraper, and a wire brush." He says, "Go back on the stern, and all along the cap rail on the stern," he says, "all the small pieces of rust, hit them with the wire brush, scrape 'em down, square 'em up. Wire brush it, get it ready to prime." He says, "Tomorrow we'll go around. Between four and five I'll have the other AB that relieves you cover it over with some primer."

"OK."

So I go back and I'm fucking around doing it, I'm doing a halfway decent job just to kill time. So now I've got a wire brush, scraper, and a chipping hammer, total cost at the time for this, maybe $12 brand new. So I got this stuff, and the paint locker's all the way to the bow. I'm all the way to the stern, 300-foot walk anyway.

About quarter to four Henry comes back and says, "You know, fuck it, we'll worry about priming it tomorrow. I'll wire brush it again and have somebody primer it. Don't worry about it." He says, "Go ahead and knock off."

So I got this stuff in my hand. My room is 15 feet away, the bow is 300 feet away. I says, "What do you want me to do with this? You want this stuff back in the paint locker?" That's where that stuff stayed, in the paint locker.

Henry says, "Well, your room is 15 feet away." He says, "The paint locker is 300 feet away." Up on the bow. "We could put it in there. Or," he says, "you can just put it in the big locker." The ocean—used to call it the big locker. He says, "We'll never fill it up."

So I just threw it over the side and went to my room.

We came in, and that kerosene-paint was drying the whole time. It was summer when we got back. All the paint was just fucking cracking and peeling. Everywhere we'd painted with the kerosene was just dried up and flaking off and cracking. It looked like a mosaic. About 3 days before we got in that sun was *baking* it, and it was just drying that paint out.

We get to New York to pay off, and, oh, fuck, what a zoo. What a fucking trip.

The captain called Customs on us—you know—we're all a bunch of drunks and druggies. It was unreal; they're searching us. We get in like eight o'clock at night. We're gonna pay off the next day. So we tie up, we clear, and we're gonna do Customs the next day. Technically, we can't take anything off the ship. We got in about six o'clock, and it was like eight o'clock when we cleared Immigration. About four or five of us are going to go get a drink. We walk outside the gate, here's these guys in plain clothes.

"U.S. Customs! Up against the fence. You crew members off the *Export Bay*?"

We says, "Yeah, we are. We're just going out to get a drink. We cleared Immigration."

He says, "You didn't clear Customs yet. We're Customs."

They're showing their badges. So he's got us lined up against the fence.

He says, "We got a report," obviously from the captain, "that there's drug use amongst you and there'd be attempted smuggling." He didn't say the captain, but we knew it was him.

So I'm standing against the fence. I turned around to face the fence, and I hook my hands on top of my head like I was a POW. You know, Gestapo motherfuckers. I says, "Go ahead and search."

He says, "Well, you don't have to go through all that."

I says, "You don't have to go through all this, either."

They frisked us all down. "OK, you guys can go."

And, you know, I was so—you guys are just fucking lackeys for assholes.

Went and stopped at the bar, had a couple of beers, came back. Next day we got the fuck outta there, gone in the wind.

And that wine—that fucking wine lasted all the way back. I mean, guys are just coming in with mason jars, filling them up. That wine lasted all the way from Italy 'til we got back. Just as we're finishing up, Henry says, "Aw, fuck it. There's no more." He threw the bottle over the side.

I says, "You oughta take that home with you, Henry."

"I don't want that fucking bottle."

You know, the bottle cost more than the wine did. Yeah.

Then we bailed off.

That was a fun trip. That was a fun trip.

Green Lake

The *Green Lake*, 11/29/77 to 12/4/77. They flew me in. I took it back down to Charleston, and I quit after 5 days. Ship was a wreck, and it was going to northern Europe in the winter. I refused to make the trip.

Matter of fact, the captain even told me: "You stay, Ron, I'll take care of you."

I always was a rehire. I always was; 19 out of 20 times. You know, when they could get me to do something, I did it. They always wanted to keep me, because I excelled at what I did. They thought I was there for a steady job, and, "Oh, Ron, we'll take care of you." In reality, I'm thinking: "I'm doing this so you leave me alone, so I can stay here and do this 90 days, have a good fucking time, and get the fuck off of here and go spend this money." But in their minds, it was: "Oh, we gotta keep this guy. What do we have to give him to keep him here? Do we throw him overtime? Do we give him time off?" They never really understood that they couldn't buy me. It would blow their minds.

Like that one bosun told the mate, "He don't work any overtime, but he fucking works."

You know, I'm not blowing my own horn, leave me alone, just give me a job, and I did it.

On my fitness report he says, "You're a rehire, Ron." Even though I quit without completing the trip. He put down on there, "Competent able seaman who needs no supervision for standing watch."

I said, "Captain, I'm not taking this across the North Atlantic." I basically told him: "If you got any sense, captain, you'll look for another captain's job."

The pièce de résistance

This is gonna be a long one. This is the pièce de résistance. The *S.S. American Reliance*. I got off of that *Green Lake*, 12/4, and I caught this 12/5, the very next day in Charleston. I had just gotten off. I walked back in the union hall. This U.S. Lines ship, *American Reliance*, was what they call the racer types. Automated booms, automated hatches, like an accordion. Very nice ship, very fast, and they couldn't make any money. This is another one they put under charter to MSC, Military Sealift Command, and it was gonna take ammunition to the Far East. My kind of run.

The war was over, but they still used ammunition to replenish what they used in exercises. You had to use so much ammunition for war games, so they needed fresh ammo.

Any run around Christmastime, I used to call it the Christmas crews. Not the "cruise" that we would cruise on a ship, but the crew itself. These were Christmas crews. These were guys that didn't worry about their loved ones, didn't have any loved ones, or didn't want to be home for Christmas or New Years *with* the loved ones—you know—couldn't stand it. Most of the guys wanted to ship to get enough money built up so they could be *home* for Christmas. *These* guys, like me, we *wanted* to get away for Christmas, and we wanted to go somewhere warm. You had the real round of drinkers—I mean, there were a lot of drinkers out there, then, from the old man down.

This is the one when I came on board, I asked who the captain was, and they said it was Cavendish.

I said, "Oh, gee, I always wondered whatever happened to Captain Albright?"

This is the one where they said, "*Albright*? He was on here 6 months ago. They took him off on a stretcher. He *drank* himself off."

Anyway, I get on there, and they're gonna load the bombs, it's Sunny Point, North Carolina. We take half a load there, and then take half a load in Port Chicago, San Francisco to take across to the Far East. We're supposed to make the Philippines, Nationalist China, Okinawa, and then we're coming back to the States. We're gonna come back empty.

We go through the Panama Canal, and a day or so later they went down to check the cargo again, just to make sure everything's OK, cuz every hatch was halfway filled. The mate and the bosun went down there to check the ammo, make sure it was still shored up, cuz then you shored it up. It was in boxes or it was loose, and the longshoremen built around it to shore it up. It wasn't in containers. They found two holes in the side of the ship above the water line. The only thing they could think of was a tug at the Panama Canal must have hit us above the water line and knocked two holes in us, and nobody noticed it, and I guess the tug that did it wasn't gonna say anything. So we went down there, and we filled it up with cement and put boards against the cement, wedged it. It was maybe 3 or 4 feet above the waterline, but, you know, you could sink. I mean, you get that much water, you could, even though you had pumps.

We get to Port Chicago, and they said, "You gotta get that taken care of." So they're gonna take all the ammo out of the one hatch. Then somebody said, "Wait a minute. If you're welding, the spark could jump to the other hatches, and you'll detonate." And, during World War II, they did have a terrible explosion there, fucking took out *miles*. Killed hundreds, and had some kind of mutiny about it afterwards. So they were *really* hyper. They said, "Unload the entire ship, weld it, and then we'll backload you with a full load."

Well, we're gonna be there awhile, right? We go into San Francisco, everybody's getting fucked up, back and forth, and we get this new bosun. The chief mate was Reed. I got along with him, but I didn't have to work for him, either. I was AB, took orders off the bosun, and stood gangway watch. And for some reason, he just hated bosuns. He'd come by and tell me, "Oh, that fucking bosun, this or that."

What? Who cares? You know.

"*I care!*" You know, "Jesus Christ, *I'm* paying that guy—"

I'm paying that guy. Like it's coming out of his pocket. That's his attitude. He's a company representative, *I'm* paying that guy.

I says, "Mate, we're all making a few bucks, and we're gonna go home."

"*I don't care. I don't want*—You want the bosun job?"

I says, "No."

"*Well, I'm firing him. Fuck him.*"

You know, OK. Reed drank a little bit.

We're going through these bosuns fucking right and left down there. We get this one, looked like Alley Oop out of the comic strip. He shaved his head bald. You talk about a fucking nut. He had as much sea time as I did. He was West Coast; white hat, Frisco shirt, white shirt with black stripes going up and down, Frisco jeans. This guy was West Coast all the way. He comes on there, real deep voice, "Yeah, it's gonna be pretty easy." He thinks he's taking it easy on us, knocking us off at four o'clock if we're day work. This fucker's setting us up for something. This is too fucking good.

We're going to Hawaii first. Well, on the way to Hawaii, the day working first assistant engineer, he's working on one of the hatch covers, something pops, and it breaks his little finger. We get to Hawaii, they fly him home, and we get another engineer right out of the Hawaii hall. So that's the first one we lost on a medical.

The guys are fucking up in Hawaii. They're gonna rent a car. I won't go with 'em. I got better sense. The bosun and the goofy ordinary seaman and one of the goofy ABs and a halfway-intelligent AB, I don't know why he went. They're gonna rent a car, and they're gonna drive around for the weekend in Hawaii. They're drinking and they're driving. Well, now they're gonna fistfight, or at least gonna try, cuz they don't want the drunk to drive. The more they drink, you know, they're just gonna fistfight as to who was gonna drive.

It's a sign of things to come.

Next stop, Subic Bay, Philippine Islands. We get there on a week-end, and it's gonna be a 3-day weekend, with a holiday, and for some reason they said, "If you come back and stand your gangway watch, you'll be paid for it. If you don't come back, you don't get paid for it, but you don't get the problems, either." This is gonna be a choice. So, I'm gonna take 3 days off.

I take off Friday at five o'clock. I'm fucking gone. About four or five of us go out, and we go over this bridge in Subic. It was notorious. This is after the war. You go over the bridge, and they call it Shit River there. It smells, and the Filipinos are there in their little bumboats. They stand there and you throw 'em coins. Well, if you miss the basket that the girl's trying to catch the coin in, the little kid dives in the river to get the coin. So we used to miss the basket, on purpose, just to see the kid dive in. I mean, it was *filthy*. You know, you fall in you'd fucking *die* if you were an American.

That was Magsaysay Drive. Named after the president there. It was just a den of iniquity. Make a seaman blush. I mean, it was just fucking unreal. Anything you could think of, just every massage parlor was blow jobs, the girls were just blowing you and spitting cum in the corners. Mom's apple pie, that's why we fight these wars. So they're gonna go in the nearest bar, and they're gonna get a drink.

Then it was myself and a couple of the ABs, the day man, Steve. He was born in the States, but his father and mother immigrated right after the war. The dad had been stationed in Australia during the war, and he came back to the States and always wanted to immigrate back. He never bothered getting Australian citizenship. I guess he assumed he didn't have to. Well, I don't know what the fuck he did, but they threw him out of the country cuz he wasn't a citizen. So he's living in San Francisco. And there were a couple others, a crazy guy named Jegel from Toledo, Ohio. He always wanted to buddy up with me. I'm thinking: I ain't buddying up with you. You're out of your fucking mind, Jegel.

Anyway, they're gonna go in this bar, I'm gonna keep going, making the rounds, getting blow jobs and drinking. I go up to the 007 club, or the 7-11, I can't remember. One was above the other. I knew the owner there, Joe. I was sitting there, having a couple of beers, and these Navy guys came in, and they ordered a pitcher of this fucking

Sam Miguel rum. Fucking go blind. You mix it and make a punch out of it, and the fucking pitcher was about 2 feet high. This is behind the bar, you know, they're sitting at the table. Joe didn't have anything to stir it up with, so he just sticks his arm in there up to his armpit and stirs it up. Goes out there, give it to 'em. Oh, *God*, I could see it was gonna be a good fucking day, you know, I could see this coming. I'm talking this is *noon*.

And, Joe says, "Don't get all fucked up, Ron." He says, "Take a girl, get a hotel room, get laid, get a blow job. Come back later."

I says, "Naw, I'm gonna wait awhile."

At the time, you had to get a hotel room cuz they had a midnight curfew, the Navy shore patrol and the Filipino police would go around, getting people, just literally locking them up cuz of the curfew. So about three or four o'clock I picked one of the girls.

I says, "Here, go get the room and then come back." I gave her money to get the room.

She comes back, and I says, "Alright, I'm gonna go get some sleep, and I'll be back later on." Right?

Now I'm fucked up. We go to the hotel room, and we're freaking out. I pass out, really. About eight o'clock, there's a beating on the door.

Here's Joe with a tray of beer. "You never came back! *Here*. Stop by tomorrow."

I says, "OK. Thank you, Joe."

Me and the girl, we're smoking cigarettes. I'm putting mine in empty beer bottles. She's flipping them in the fucking sink.

I says, "Don't do that."

She's talking in that high-pitch whine they got. "*Yi ni ni!*"

I says, "Put it out. It's a lit cigarette."

"*Yi ni ni!*"

These are all wooden buildings. All fucking wooden buildings.

I says, "Don't fucking do that."

"*Yi ni ni!*"

Fuck you. OK, I told you. You're not gonna listen. Pass out again. Go to sleep. A couple more beers will do that to you.

When the fuck it was, I don't know, it must have been two or three o'clock in the morning. All of a sudden people are screaming and yelling, I hear this American voice: "U.S. Navy! This is U.S. Navy! There's a fire! Get out of your rooms!" They're beating on the doors.

I hear this, and the only thing I can think of is this fucking screwball flipped a cigarette out and started a fire. I'm thinking: you ignorant, fucking . . . setting a fire on me.

Put my pants on, I got all my stuff in my cowboy boots, you know, right? I pour that into my hand, shove it in my pockets, put my boots on, got my socks hanging in my pockets. I put my t-shirt on. Got my glasses. I'm fucking outta there. To hell with her.

She's yelling, whiny, "Come here, come here."

I says, "*You* come *here*." I'm at the door.

They're yelling out in the hall, "Fire! Fire! Everybody get out!"

Here, it's a fire across the street, in a wooden building. They're *all* fucking wood. So I stop and I look. It's like pyromaniacs. People are drawn to this, looking at the fire. Me *too*, right? We're all like moths. Sparks are jumping everywhere. The whole building's *engulfed*. The next buildings are catching fire. The fire department's coming.

The Navy guys: "Get out of this one! This one will go, too!"

Nobody's moving. Nobody's moving.

I went back to sleep. Fuck it. Next morning I get up, and I'm fucked up.

I says, "Oh, Jesus Christ, I've gotta go back to the ship and get straightened up here."

So, she's with me, we get back, stop in a bar, get a beer, breakfast of champions.

I says, "You want something?"

"Oh, I want—" She's pointing. Looked like pickled eggs in the jar. They were the things you see in Vietnam all the time: they would take the egg just before it hatches, and they would take it and they would put it up on top of a shelf in a bowl, and they'd wait 4 or 5 months, and then they'd break it open and eat the dead chick. This is a delicacy. They called it balut in the Philippines, but I never saw 'em pickled, and I thought she wanted a pickled egg.

You can imagine—my stomach. I'm drinking a beer, and she cracks the egg. I thought it's a hard-boiled egg she wanted to eat. She's eating a balut. I didn't know they pickled them, too.

I says, "I gotta go."

"You come back. You come back."

"Yeah, yeah, yeah, yeah."

I'm drinking a beer, going across Shit River, sweaty, dried out, hung over, fucked up, hot weather. I take the bottle, throw it in Shit River. Get there.

Marines let me in, they says, "Man, you look bad."

I says, "*Look* bad? You don't know how I *feel*."

Go back out to the ship, up to the room, take a shower, and I lay down, one man in a room on these ships. We shared a shower and a head though. I shared it with that screwball bosun. Fucking goof. He's out somewhere, too, you know, he's gone, he's out of his mind. I says, "Fuck it." I get up about eight o'clock or something, take another shower. And I says, "You know what? I'm gonna get something to eat here, and I'm gonna go back in." Back in and get all fucked up again and see Joe, right? Girl gets the room. Here we go again.

Next morning, get up, that was Sunday, so I said, well, we're gonna leave Monday, I figured I'm not coming back out, I'm gonna get a decent night's rest, cuz Monday morning we're getting ready to go. I get back to the ship again to change clothes and shower.

They says, "Oh, we're not leaving 'til Monday about four or five o'clock in the afternoon. It's a holiday, you don't have to be here."

I says, "I'm gonna take it easy." But then I thought: why the fuck am I taking it easy? When I'm old I'll be able to take it easy, and I won't be able to do this. Back in again, all fucked up again, with Joe.

In the morning tell the broad, "OK, I'll see you."

"You come back."

"Yeah, yeah, yeah, I'll be back. Keep a light in the window for me."

Head back to the ship, drinking the beer, throw the bottle in Shit River again on the way over. I get back about noon.

Now one of the ABs has gone nuts—Jegel from Toledo. He used to be a football player for Toledo High or some fucking thing. He's just a goofball. And we had this other ordinary seaman, too, Roberts. He was a pretty good guy, an old black guy. He'd done some time in Oklahoma when he was a kid. But he knew what was going on, a good dude.

Anyway, Jegel's running up and down the passageway calling ass on everybody. So I go to my foc'sle, and he's standing out there with pants and shoes, no t-shirt, and a bottle of beer, out of his mind.

I've got my free world clothes on, a shirt, jeans, and my cowboy boots. I'm trying to get my key in my door. I'm getting ready to go out and secure the ship, we have to leave.

So I says, "What's going on, Greg?"

He looks at me and says, "Ahh, what the fuck you want?"

I says, "Leave it alone, Greg." I open the door and I close the door, lock it behind me.

I hear, "Come on out, you punk motherfucker. Come on outta there."

I yell, "Leave it alone, Greg!" I'm changing clothes to get in some work clothes.

"Come on outta there. I'll whip your ass, you punk motherfucker."

I says, "You're working on it, Greg." I'm changing clothes. All of a sudden, I hear the beer bottle hit my door.

"Come on outta there!"

I says, "I'm coming, Greg! Just wait! Just stand there! I'm coming!" I finish getting in my work clothes. Unlock the door, go out. Glass is broken. You can see where the beer hit the door. I run into Roberts and I says, "Where's that fucking Jegel?"

He says, "Man, *nobody* wants to see him. But I heard him yelling at you."

I says, "*I* want to see him."

He says, "I think he went down by the gangway."

They had a gangway watch now, and the third mate is there. We picked this guy up in Hawaii, or the other one got off on a medical. We were losing people everywhere. I turn around and get down there, and I see Greg standing there with just his pants and his shoes on, no shirt. His back's to me, and he's aggravating the third mate, this older guy from Hawaii. He was ex-Navy and he's married a Korean girl and they were living in Hawaii. He wasn't a hell of a third mate, but he was a nice guy.

Anyway, he sees me. Jegel don't see me. I go by and slap Jegel in the head with just the back of my hand—*poom*—as I go by, and I go by behind the third mate, and I go down the gangway.

I says, "Come on down on the dock, you punk motherfucker. We'll see who's who."

Now he don't wanna fight, see. Now reality set in. He finally found somebody that's willing to fight him.

I'm like: *I'll* fight; if you wanna fight, *I'll* give you a fight; I'll give you the fight of your life.

Now he's trying to get a knife off the third mate. "*Give me your knife. Give me your knife.*"

Third mate says, "I'm not giving you *my* knife. You think you're bad? Go down and fight *him*."

He came down on the fucking dock, and my back's to him, and as soon as I heard his steps I turn around and hit him right in the face. *Boom!*

He tried to rush me.

I sidestepped him, but he did catch me, but I caught him to the side of the face, and he stumbled down. You know, I got out of the way, but he did hit me. He's not really coordinated, and I threw a left, and he pushed both hands, and when he did that, I hit him with a right. And I'm hitting him. He's going back, but he's not falling down.

I'm saying, "Fall down, you motherfucker you!"

Finally I knock him down, and I ain't letting this fucker back up. I jump on him, and he's strong as a fucking bear. Now we're rolling around, right? He's got no shirt on, my shirt's getting torn. I hit him in the fucking ear. He's trying to bite me. I elbow him up. Oh, this is a good one. We're going at it. I finally get back on my feet, and I'm firing at him, *rights* and *lefts*. I don't know how long this went on.

Next thing I hear is, "You gotta break this up! You gotta break this up!"

I'm on top of him, and I'm firing on him. I turn around and look.

Here I see the Marine security guard from the gate, and I saw the rifle is what I saw, you know, and I says, "OK. Sorry. I'm breaking it up." You know, I see the rifle. Get up, right. I says, "OK, I'm not fighting. Alright."

He says, "Government property here. I can't allow this on my watch."

I says, "OK, OK." I turn around to go back to the ship.

Jegel gets up and jumps on my back! Here we go again! *Boom, bang, boom,* we're fighting, and the Marine's saying, "Break it up! Break it up!"

I says, "You break it up!" *Boom, boom.* "He jumped on me!"

He radios, like, "Marine in trouble!" They send the *riot squad*: a Marine captain and a whole fucking truckload of Marines come down in a truck. They get in between us! The whole bunch!

And I'm: "Whoa, OK. OK."

The Marine captain says, "*What in the fuck is going on here?*"

In the meantime, they're trying to secure the ship. Now, the bosun is drunk, trying to get to the ship. You just gotta swing the booms in and drop 'em. Roberts and the fucking day man, Steve, he's all drunked up. He and Roberts get into a fight into who's gonna do what. He tries to hit Roberts. Roberts picks up a board and hits him in the face with it while me and Jegel are down on the dock. This third mate from Hawaii, he just wants to get his relief for the next watch turn. "You gotta come out! Ron and Jegel are down on the dock trying to kill each other! Roberts just hit Steve with a board!" That third mate, poor guy, he's just, "I don't know, I'm here just making a few dollars and going home." First trip on his license.

I didn't know that was going on.

Anyway, this Marine captain says, "*What the fuck is going on here?*"

The Marine private says, "Captain, we were told there was a fight here. We arrived, told them to break it up. This man broke it up. He went to walk back to the ship. This one got up and jumped on him again."

I says, "That's the way it happened, captain." I says, "He attacked me on board, too." I says, "We got down here on the dock." I says, "I don't want any problems. You say stop, I stop."

About that time, fucking Jegel's just wandering, cuz they don't have us in physical custody like handcuffed or anything, we technically are civilians, and the military can't literally beat us up. Jegel wanders off. One of the guys got a football down on the dock, they're playing catch, and Jegel wants to go play catch. This Marine captain's looking. This guy off our ship—he didn't like Jegel, he liked me—he says, "Hey, Jegel. Go out for a pass." He throws the pass, and the ball, he didn't care about the football, it went by the water, by the edge of the pier. Jegel went right after it and fell in the fucking water.

This Marine captain's: "*What the fuck is this!?*"

Our captain and the chief mate's up there, and our captain's trying to get everybody together to leave, secure the ship. The chief mate runs up there to the captain and says, "We can't leave yet, captain."

Captain says, "Why can't we leave?"

"They're down there trying to kill each other, Roberts hit Steve in the face with a board, and Jegel just fell in the water."

The old man hit the overhead. "*What the fuck's going on!?*"

I says, "Look, alls I wanna do is get back on board."

The one Marine says, "Yeah, he didn't have nothing to do with it, captain, the other guy started it."

About that time they get Jegel out of the water, and the captain says, "Bring him over here. Get that one over here."

He comes over there, and he tells the Marine captain, something to the effect of, "Fuck you," or "Who the fuck do you think you are?" or "I'll whip you, too," or something like that.

This Marine captain stared at him. Then he says to me, "You. Go back on the ship. You," he points at Jegel, "get in that truck. You're going to the brig. You're gone." So they grab him, put him in the truck.

I start walking.

The Marine captain says, "Wait a minute! I'm going up there with you." He says, "Who do I have to see on here to tell them that that man's under arrest?"

I says, "You gotta see the captain of the ship. He's up on the bridge."

"Can you show me the way?"

"Sure." I says, "Would you put a vouch in for me? You know, it ain't me?"

He says, "I'll do that for you."

We get up to the bridge. Here's the chief mate and the captain.

I says, "Excuse me, captain, this is the captain: do what you gotta do."

The Marine captain says, "I'm sorry, captain, but that gentleman I put in the truck is under arrest. He's going to the brig for fighting on government property. He refused to stop. He assaulted this gentleman. Refused to stop fighting. Insulted me. He's going to the brig. Do what you want. He's going to the brig. He's not getting out of that brig 'til I think he should, and that's it. Write him off, he's gone." He says, "This gentleman," nodding to me, "I don't think it was his fault."

Our captain says, "What am I gonna—"

"Captain, I don't know what you need to do. I'm just explaining to you what *I'm* doing here. This is government property. He broke the law, he's going to the brig."

They didn't mention about Roberts hitting Steve in the face with the board. Here's Steve now, purser's packing his nose and shit.

Anyway, there's Jegel. He's standing up in the truck, and it goes to pull out, and he falls down in the truck. They hit the brakes, he falls forward. It's a flatbed, right, just a pickup truck. So the Marine in the truck says, "Man, sit the fuck down in there, you fucking idiot!" They take him away.

Captain says, "Are we ready to leave now? Can we go?"

So we get the ship secured. Now everybody's friends again, right, except Jegel's gone.

And the other guys are saying, "Yeah, we're glad you got rid of him. We didn't like him anyway."

I says, "Why didn't one of you guys fight him, then?" You know, "I'm down there on the dock like a fucking idiot."

They fired Jegel. They packed all of his shit up and sent it back to the agent. They kind of overlooked me.

We get to Nationalist China. Discharge this ammo. They had a place called Helen's Bookstore right outside the gate. There was no copyrights in Nationalist China. Matter of fact, there was a notice that it was illegal to buy books in Nationalist China and bring them back to the States with no copyright. Helen had numerous books there, but it was also a little bar and whorehouse and gift shop. You'd tell Helen what age, what size girl you wanted, and Helen would get on the phone for you. I turned around, had a few drinks. It was a place to go. You know, you get a girl, bounce around. We were only there a couple of days.

The only real incident was—one night I got drunk, which is nothing new, and the ordinary seaman, this guy Smitty, useless, he was a lover not a fighter—we both had been getting fucked up at Helen's. Now we're pushing a bicycle around, we're taking turns pushing each other around the dock all fucked up. We try to get on the ship to leave, and I was all gassed up. I got out there and missed the undocking. But they got me up to stand the watch.

Bosun says, "Get up. I gotta stand watch. I'm not gonna stand watch. Get up there."

I went up there, blown out. I mean, I was *blown out*. I hand-steered that ship for 2 hours. The captain was just *staring* at me, sweat's *pouring* outta me, you know, and he wanted to say something, but I was handling it, I could steer. I was a good steerer. Got the 2 hours in and the next day I got the watch in.

The next day the mate gets me and says, "You know, Ron, we gotta put you in the book, for the failure to turn to for the undocking. I gotta put you in there," he says. "But what we're gonna do, we're gonna put you in that you failed to stand the watch, not the undocking. So that way, the Coast Guard will have to throw it out. It'll be our mistake."

I says, "Well, OK. Thanks, mate."

He says, "Nah. I feel some people out here deserve breaks. You got your downfalls," he says, "but you're a good AB."

I says, "Thank you."

Brings me up to the old man, and the old man says, "Mate explain everything to you?"

"Yeah."

He says, "You're logged for failing to stand the watch," which I had done, although I was sweating bullets.

Anyway, I sign.

The bosun says, "What did they log you for?"

"Failing to stand the watch."

"You stood the watch! You didn't undock!"

I says, "I don't know. I'm not gonna argue with it." I didn't tell him that it was already set up.

"They'll have to throw that out!"

I says, "Yeah, OK."

Smitty didn't like it, either. "Oh, man, you get all the breaks!" He later cried his way home.

We had one old man, Thompson, an AB, an old miserable prick, used to take pictures of the Filipino girls, naked. They'd all take their clothes off, and he'd take nudes of them. Nobody actually got along with him, we kind of tolerated him. And this Scray, a wiry, drunk older guy. Gassed up all the time.

They're down the passageway from us, right? Scray's got a bottle, and Thompson had snitched on him or something.

This Scray—fucking Scray—he's standing outside his room. You gotta picture this. Little skinny guy. He's going over to Thompson's door. "Come on out, Thompson! Come on out! We're gonna fistfight!" That was the whole thing back then, going back in the stern and punching each other out.

Then he'd go to his room, where he'd have another drink or two, get some courage going, and come out again, beating on the door.

"Come on, Thompson! Come on out here!" He's gonna have a heart attack right there.

Can you imagine these two old skinny guys trying to hit each other?

"Come on out, Thompson! Come out!" Scray's voice was just trembling. "It's me and you back on number twelve hatch!"

Scray was out of his mind. We only had five hatches. There ain't no twelve hatch.

It was hilariously funny, Scray trying to get old man Thompson to come out of the room to fistfight with him. Just fucking screwy.

We go up to Jinhae, Korea, and that's gonna be the end of the load, we're gonna go back empty. Korea was a pretty good place, still cheap. If you went outside the gate, there was a whorehouse to the left. Otherwise, you could go into town to the Navy base. The enlisted men's club was actually half on South Korean property and half on U.S. government Navy property. That way, if any of the girls got hurt from the fights in the joint, they couldn't sue. So we go up there. I stopped in the whorehouse a couple of times, you know, they had rooms in the back.

But the interesting thing was, there was a U.S. Navy submarine that pulled in there. The Korean girls were charging $5 for a blow job, or $10 for all night. You know, I mean, to each their own. I seldom, if ever, pass judgment, cuz, obviously, from all this, I'm not perfect. The only man who was got crucified for being that way. But, I go to use the bathroom—the head—in the enlisted men's club there, and now a Navy sub had pulled in, and these guys are in there. I go to use the bathroom, and the Navy guys were kind of lined up. I thought they were using the bathroom, and they says, "No, no. You want to use the bathroom, the head? Go ahead, on the other side."

I says, "Yeah, OK."

I go in, and there's a U.S. Navy sailor there giving other U.S. Navy sailors blow jobs for $5 a throw. The only thing I could think was: these broads are charging five and ten bucks, and this guy's blowing them for five?

I don't know.

Anyway, I got outta there. Didn't bother going back.

We get through discharging all the ammunition, and we're getting ready to secure to go back to the States. Guys are getting off, medicals and this and that, along the way. New guys are coming on. Matter of fact, the second engineer went home on a medical. Now this is the good part. They tell us we're not going back to the States, we're going back to Okinawa. We're gonna take four loads of ammunition from Okinawa to Jinhae, Korea. Only a day and a half, 2-day run. But it's

3 weeks to load in Okinawa and 2 weeks to discharge in Korea. God-damn, everybody kind of thought about going home, you know, this has been a wild trip.

Turn around, and the day working third engineer goes home. He says, "Fuck this, I'm going home." He goes and has the Red Cross send a message his parents are sick, so he pays his own way home. So we're still in Jinhae.

They fly out this third engineer—day work and third—here comes this old black guy, all fucked up drunk. "Day work and third? I thought I was a watch stander! I don't want any fucking day work." Right, here's another one, you know.

Anyway, we leave. On the way down we run into this bad weather. The ship's rolling. The second engineer is on the way down to relieve in the engine room, he trips and falls all the way down the ladder. He's all busted up and fucked up, right. We get to Okinawa, he goes to the doctor. He goes home. So now they make this day working third, he's got a second's license. Now he gets to stand watch. You know, right, all gassed up.

We get back to Okinawa. We're gonna be there 3 weeks. Now we're all going on day work, no gangway watches.

Now the bosun's: "Boy, we're gonna renew this ship." Now he's really getting into a swing. Like a pirate: "*Argh!* Work, you motherfuckers, yeah, *work!*"

He's got us out there painting. He's going out at like 15 minutes to 8 in the morning and setting the jobs, so as soon as we go out at eight o'clock he can fucking go ahead and get us going right to work, we're not *wasting* any *time*.

Fucking cunt.

I come out there one morning, and he was setting up a stage, rigging it, so we could paint over the side of the ship. A stage is just a board about 6 feet long, 2 feet wide. On either end, through the top, is a bolt about 2 feet from the end of it, through the center, that goes on what we call the horn, which is just another board, but going fore and aft. You have one of these on each side. Able seamen always did their own rigging, then. Now, they don't even want you to do it anymore, it's a thing of the past.

But what you would do: you'd get a block and tackle or just an eye to rig this up. You'd pass the rope through the block and come back, and you would take turns around the end, the outside part from that stage. You would take turns at it, then you'd put three turns around the front of the stage, and the line would hang down over the side. This is for working over the side or in front of the bridge of the ship, to paint or clean the windows or something. You had to have one line on the outside. The other line, the other guy had on the inside. It had to counterbalance.

He put the two on the outside of the stage. I usually put three or four, and I would put three turns around the outside of the stage. He put two turns. What you would do is slack the turns off the horn, and it was just gravity. You would have to take the line and pull it up and just slack it. It would bite, and as soon as you would get it some slack, the weight, and it would bite again. The three or four turns would hold. I always used four. When we were going down, you and your partner would get together and say, "OK, we're gonna come down." You'd reach down about a foot and start giving it slack so you come down together, so you're not at an angle.

He's rigging this fucking thing.

I says, "You want that rigged, bos'?"

"*I got it, I got it! I'm doing it!*"

"Yeah, OK."

Now he rigs it, he gets it on the cap rail, and he puts it over the side. You got a solid rail, to hold the sea back, but there was from the main deck up, oh, say, 2 or 3 inches, we called it a fishplate. Then the steel plate started. There was an opening there, maybe 3 or 4 inches. It was open to go out in the sea. In other words, you had the deck, the fishplate, the opening, then the steel plate, and you had the cap rail on top of that. So you had this opening all the way along there. He puts it over the side, and it catches, cuz there's no weight on it.

I says, "Hey, bos'," I says, "I'm not saying too much here," I says, "but isn't it supposed to be three or four turns?" He had two turns. I says, "Isn't it supposed to be three or four turns, and then a couple of turns around the horn?"

I thought he was gonna explode.

"What, are you, telling me, how to—"

I says, "You know, bos'—"

He jumps. Before I can say anything, he puts his hands on the cap rail and *jumps* over the side onto the stage. Now, it's about 3 inches below that fish plate. That's all. And he's standing in the middle of it. He went right over in the middle and *landed* on it. *Boom!* He's got his hands on the cap rail and he's over the side of the ship, standing on it.

It held!

He says, *"See? This'll hold!"*

He goes to jump up and down, and he jumped once and came down—it gave way. I mean, he was *gone.* I'm looking at him, and then I don't see him! To this day, I don't know how he did it—his reflexes were so quick, he grabbed that fishplate. He *grabbed* it! I look over the side of the ship, and here he is hanging onto the fishplate, and he's got his feet against the side of the ship.

I says, "You want a hand, bos'?"

"NO!" He walked, you know, with his *hands,* actually pulled his way over—that's how strong he was—to the pilot ladder we had hanging, grabbed the pilot ladder, and climbed back up.

And I'm still standing there.

He comes over, says, "Maybe you were right."

I says, "I'll rig it, bos'. Don't worry. I'll take care of it."

Anyway, this is going on, and we're going to the base and getting fucked up. Well, we're not working weekends, we refuse, because, you know, we're not working for this asshole. The entire deck department said, "We're not doing this. We're not doing it."

So Steve, the day man, the one who got hit in the face with the board by Roberts, he gets all fucked up one Saturday. He comes stumbling into my room, and he had a habit of taking his shoes and socks off when he was drunk and walk around the ship barefoot. It was linoleum, it wasn't like he was out on deck.

He comes in my room with these two jugs of whiskey. *"Yeah, that bosun's trying to kill us, that no-good motherfucker*—you want a drink?"

Both bottles are sealed.

I says, "Ah, Steve, put them down." I get up out of my chair, and I sit on the desk. "Have a seat, Steve."

"That fucking guy's trying to kill us. That no-good motherfucker."

I says, "Yeah, Steve. OK." I'm sober, just sitting there. I'm getting ready to go ashore. I says, "Steve, why don't you go lay down there for awhile?"

He just falls in my bunk. I take the two jugs of booze, I put 'em in my locker, and I lock it and I lock my door, but he can unlock it from the inside. I don't have anything in there to steal. I could care less. You need it? Take it, please.

There was another guy, Jim Krogstead, I was running around with, too. Jim was a pretty good dude. I was running around with him and Scray.

Scray comes in: "What the fuck?"

I says, "Let him sleep."

"He's sleeping in your bunk."

"What do I care? He's probably better there than he is out wandering around."

So we take off. We're gonna go to Naha gate number two at the air base. It was expensive. We weren't getting a lot of money. I think I had like $50. Scray might have had $50. That's not a lot of money in Okinawa, even in 1977, cuz Japan had taken over, they were using Japanese money. They had taken it over, I believe in '71 or '72. Nixon gave it to 'em, and the money went to the yen.

We hit gate number two at the air base there, and we're looking for a drink, right. We get out and see this strip, looked like some kind of fucking honky-tonks. We're walking down the street. All the bars are closed, it's like ten o'clock in the morning. We pass this place, the Sapphire Bar, it's the only one we hear any noise coming out of. So we try the door, and it's open. There's an American Marine behind the bar. There's a bunch of American Marines, and some Okinawans, in there.

They says, "Can we help you?"

I says, "Yeah. We'd like to get a drink. Would that be possible?"

He says, "Well, we're not supposed to be open, but . . . . Mama-san, is it OK to have a drink?"

"Yeah, yeah. Go ahead."

We're sitting there talking to them. They're a bunch of recon Marines from Onna Point. This is where the recon Marines stay, and this was their bar. They came every weekend or every night. This was their bar, and they would keep it open all weekend. They weren't supposed to, but they could stay in there, sleep in there. We start bullshitting with them. We like to drink, they like to drink, you know.

They says, "Come on back later tonight, when we open. You guys are OK."

So we're making a habit of going there, evenings, weekends. We were there for 3 weeks.

There's other crazy shit going on. We're going up to the base at night, too. Smitty's going to the doctor. He hurt his back. Ordinary seaman, Jeff, he's another cunt. He hurt his finger; he's going to the doctor. The bosun's screaming and yelling we're not working hard enough. Everybody's hoping he just has a heart attack and fucking dies.

The electrician, who's an old fag, I'd been on a trip with him before, he was the electrician that was on the *Rainbow* that I mentioned earlier, in '71—Staunton Rosborough. He had some kind of real bad skin thing going on, peeling. He said it was cuz he'd been dehydrated as a kid, and his skin color never came back, and it looked like the skin was peeling. Now that I'm thinking about it, it was probably an early form of AIDS. Liked little kids. Just a fag.

He's running to the captain all the time. "Captain, captain, they're drunk and they're waking me up at night."

So the captain says, "Calm it down, guys." He's gotta do something to ease this old queer. He's snitching on us all the time.

We had this young wiper, screwy black kid. I come back one night, polluted, and the kid's there. "Ron, you want some saké?"

Oh, this shit was terrible. I went to his room. We're walking down the passageway. We're gonna go get another drink.

He says, "Wait a minute! That fucking electrician's gonna be snitching on us."

This kid took a fire ax off the wall. We had fire axes in case you had to knock a door open or something, fire in a room you couldn't get in. They didn't have a real sharp edge, but it had a point, like a fireman's fire ax. He takes the fire ax, and all our doors open *in*. Well, he takes the ax and leans it so it's between the door panel and the doorknob.

I says, "Oh, fuck, I ain't getting involved in this."

Next morning Rosborough opens up his door, the ax falls right between his feet, takes a chunk of linoleum up. "Captain! Captain! They're trying to kill me! They're trying to kill me!"

Now the old man's gonna have an investigation, right? "Who the fuck?" You know. "For Christ's sake! You fucking drunks!"

He took all the fire axes away. Took 'em all, had 'em all confiscated. Told the chief mate, "Get every fire ax out of that fucking house." They confiscated 'em and put a notice to the mates. "If any disturbance by the crew, do not attempt to intervene. Either call the Japanese police or the Marine base. Get the Marines here." It was just insane. Every fucking weekend everybody's half fucked up.

They had another guy, Bill Moody, drunk all the fucking time. He was another one you didn't know he drank until you saw him sober, and you'd go down there in that engine room, a beer in his fucking hand, you know, Moody, all fucked up. He was kind of hanging around with the engine cadet, and the engine cadet was pissed off because his girlfriend sent him a letter cuz he didn't want to get married, and she said, "What do you think I am, some kind of harlot?"

I says, "Harlot? What are you, 200 years ago? *'Harlot'?*"

He was crying to go home. "Oh, she's gonna leave me." Whiney, "Ohhh . . . ."

I says, "You're better off." You know, a lot of sympathy for the loved ones.

We had another D-mac, old black guy. He was gassed up, too, drunk all the time. He had later lost a finger when a door slammed on it and actually cut his finger off when we had the ship going through some rough weather. Just fucked up, he didn't even notice, he's trying to hang on to the door, the door slammed shut, cut his finger off.

There's another D-mac, Jimmy. Well, this fucking Rosborough, he had married some woman and adopted her daughter who was 14 or 15. I guess trying to make himself look good, you know, they lived in some shack there outside Charleston, South Carolina. She had divorced him as soon as he had adopted the girl. So, even though they're divorced, he's got to pay child support for the daughter. Well, they were living there, and he's sending money home. He had to pay child support and alimony.

And I don't know whether he was queer or not. You get to the point in life where it's kind of like, well, I don't want him molesting any of my family, but if he's molesting somebody else's family, then fuck it, you know? As long as he leaves my blood relations alone.

I says, "Why do you get used like that?"

He says, "She put me in jail last time!" She had actually called up that he wasn't supporting her and got him locked up. He's sending allotments home. Then he gets a letter from her, said that they need new tires on the car. She needs $400 immediately.

He goes to the old man. You're entitled to have so much money.

The old man says, "Well, you're not going ashore. I'll give you the $400. You do need the money."

He wires her the $400. But now every time he tries to call her, there's no answer. He's calling from Okinawa, trying to see what's going on.

So somehow or another, Rosborough got Jimmy's phone number in Charleston. So he calls Jimmy's wife, without Jimmy knowing—I don't know how the hell he got the phone number—but anyway, he calls her and says, "Can you check and see what's going on at the house?" At *his* house. She *assumes* that Jimmy said this was OK. *She's* calling the house, and every time she calls there, there's a big party going on. They're having big parties, the daughter's having friends over. Well, Jimmy calls her and she says, "Oh, by the way, tell Rosborough that I've been calling, and every time I call there's a big party going on."

He says, "What do you mean?"

She says, "Rosborough called me from the ship and said that he's a shipmate of yours and that you wanted me to call to check on it because he just doesn't know what's going on. She keeps saying she needs more money, and every time I call, there's a big party going on there."

He comes back there, *pissed*. We're in the mess, sitting there eating. Jimmy grabs Rosborough by the shirt, shaking him and choking him, "Don't *ever* fucking use my wife to do your dirty work, you faggot!"

I got up and walked out. I figured I didn't need it. Every day was like that. I mean, it was always a drama every fucking day.

Anyway, I'm going back over to the Sapphire, and one Friday night I walk in, and I got $50.

"Hey, Ron, what's going on?" You know, "How's it going?" and this and that. "Bring the rest of the guys. You guys can come in here, just stay all night."

I says, "Hey, thank you. I appreciate that. I do."

Four people are in there playing blackjack. Mama-san, her younger sister, who was in her 40s, a hooker, but she was choosy about who she fucked, some old Okinawan guy, and one of the Marines. As one Marine loses his money, another one would get in on it. Four people playing blackjack. The Marines are taking their turns losing their money. I'm not playing because this was their bar, and it was illegal to do it, but nobody's gonna come in. So I sit down.

And I'm drinking. It's a dollar for a big quart of beer. It's the cheapest place, too, cuz it was their bar. I got a couple of beers in me, I'm sitting there.

Then as a Marine left the game I says, "I got $50." So we start playing. We're playing, we're playing. I'm getting blackjack. You win double plus the deal. I'm fucking winning everything, and I'm drinking, too. To this day, I don't know how much I won. I cleaned out mama-san, her sister, and the old Okinawan guy. I cleaned them out. So I have this big pile of money in front of me.

I says, "You know what? Give everybody a drink."

Mama-san says, "What?"

I says, "Give everybody a drink."

Must have been 15 of those recon Marines in there, and they're out of their fucking minds. I'm just spending money. So now we had to leave or do something, and mama-san says, "Oh, you good guy, you good guy."

I says, "Yeah," fuck it, you know.

Now they're gonna take me back to the base at Onna Point. They're gonna sneak me on there so I can go to sleep, cuz I'm all fucked up. Nice of 'em to do that. Turn around, we get out to Onna Point, they throw me into a bunk. They had lockers, and in the back of a locker there were two bunks, and there was a curtain in front.

I'm laying there passed out, just laying there in my shorts.

Here comes the sergeant in the morning to get them guys up to go do some work, right? *"Get up! Come on! You've got to get out there and do some fucking work, fucking goldbricking in here."* The sergeant sees me and yells, *"What the fuck is he doing here?"*

"Wait, wait, sarge, he's a friend of ours. He's a Merchant Marine. We're taking care of him."

This guy's losing it. *"Get him off this fucking base!"*

Jesus Christ Almighty, I says, "I'm going, I'm going."

They says, "Man, can we do anything for you?"

I says, "Yeah, gimme a cup of coffee, and how the fuck do I get outta here?"

They says, "We'll get you outta here. But we gotta sneak you out the gate."

The sergeant's coming back, yelling, *"Did you get him out of here yet? Goddamn it, you'll get me busted!"*

Get me some coffee. They talked somebody into letting me sit in the back seat of their car. He drops me off out there where I could make it back to the ship.

They says, "You come back again, Ron. We like you. You come back. You get in any trouble, you let us know."

So I go back, and I'm remembering something that happened when we were in Sasebo, Japan again. Some of the Navy guys were coming on board because they were a part of the operations there, supervising the ammunition. We mentioned that we were in Okinawa before.

This one Navy guy said, "Okinawa? Oh, man. We had them fucking recon Marines up here." He said, "And up here, we have an officers and enlisted club. Everybody mixes." He said, "They came in here and fucking wrecked the joint."

Now I'm thinking about that when I'm over here, you know. I says, "Well, if nothing else, I'll see you guys next weekend." So during the week we're working, and this is gonna be the last weekend before we go up to Jinhae. That weekend I go back, and that's when I remembered about that Navy guy saying some recon Marines wrecked the joint. I says, "Were you guys up in Japan about a month or so ago?"

"Yeah, yeah, we were up there."

I says, "You guys wrecked that fucking club up there?"

"Yeah."

I says, "Well, obviously, it wasn't your guys' fault, right?"

"No, it wasn't. We went in there to get a drink, and we had our fatigues on, and the bartender served us a drink, and then some Navy officer came over and said, 'You can't serve them drinks. They're out of uniform.'" So the bartender's taking the drink away. They said, "Well, OK, give us our money back." "Oh, you don't get your money back, you don't get the drink, either."

The one guy says, "You shoulda been there, Ron. You'd a loved it." He says, "I broke the leg off a chair and smacked that officer."

I says, "Ohh."

He says, "We wrecked that joint."

Then they were telling me, "You should come onto the base." They said *MacArthur*, the movie, was playing, at the base there. So they went to see it, and one of the officers, like a colonel or something, was going in there, too. And one of 'em had a red smoke grenade, so he pulled the pin on the smoke grenade and rolled it down there and yelled, "Fire." So that colonel said if you ever find out who fucking did it, they're going to the brig. Everybody's piling out of there. They were fuckups.

Anyway, I says, "We're going up to Korea, so I'll be gone for a couple of weeks."

"You coming back, Ron?"

I says, "Yeah." Cuz I'd gone around with them at night, get in fistfights. One of the guys threw a bottle, hit some guy in the head with it. Yeah. They were out of their minds. Anytime we left the Sapphire there was a fucking problem.

I says, "It's a couple of days up to Jinhae, and then about 2 weeks to discharge, and then 2 days we'll be back."

They says, "We'll all probably be here, Ron. But you know what? You see that wall over here?" There was just booths and then the wall. I noticed the names up there. "We got a thing here. Anybody who puts their name on that wall, they're all recon Marines. Anytime you come back, you're more than welcome to come in here and have a drink. We'll take care of you. This is like a brotherhood here. We take care of you." They says, "You put your name on there, and you put the name of the ship on there, and put Merchant Marine on there. Anytime you come here, you'll get in. You're more than welcome here. If some of us aren't here, you just point to your name in case you go back to the States and come back some other time, you do that."

They're all, "Yeah, yeah, put Ron's name up, put your name up there. Yeah, yeah."

I never did get back, after this was all over. I always meant to go back to the Sapphire Bar to see if it's still there and see if my name was up there. Never did get back. And I never knew how much money I won that night. I started with $50 going in, I cleaned everybody out, bought them all drinks, and woke up the next morning with $50 in my pocket.

We went to Korea, and then I got made up with this girl, Minh. Went to a whorehouse. I didn't even bother going to that club anymore after that incident with those sailors.

I says, "Fuck that, you know." This is closer; booze, women.

I'd go up there every night, give mama-san the money, and I'd stay with her, this Minh. Didn't speak any English: we got along fine. I always got along with the ones that couldn't speak English and I couldn't speak their language. No communication problem there. We used fingers, sign language, we figured out what to do.

Anyway, I'm going there and I'm coming back to the ship. It's actually a pretty good little deal, we're still getting a little bit of problems here and there on the ship. In Korea you could kind of vent yourself without booze; Okinawa, nobody really acquired a girlfriend. So then we're leaving there. We're gonna go back to Okinawa.

Now the bosun, he's really fucking steamed. He's getting worse by the fucking minute. All of this is progressing—6 months the officers could go home, the crew was a year unless you went on a medical. Well, we're going back to Okinawa. Now the same fucking performance. Everybody on weekends is going getting all fucked up, trouble, aggravation. Everybody's slow belling it, you know, just moving slow, guys are fucking up right and left. Oh, and we did get the ammo inspector in Korea, a guy named Jerry. I kind of buddied up with him.

We had this useless steward. Little fat Polack, rotten little motherfucker, wanted to beat him up.

Jerry came in late one day. Says, "Can I get something to eat, a sandwich or something?"

So I ask the chief cook, "Can you make this guy a sandwich?"

He's all whiney. "Well, he ain't part of the crew."

Roberts would say, "Chief, guys are asking if we can have fried chicken."

"You can get that ashore."

They didn't have anything to fry with. He was fucking useless.

Third mate asked him about getting some yogurt.

"You don't get yogurt on a ship."

Little miserable, fat fuck.

Anyway, Jerry says he couldn't get any whiskey. So he kind of buddied up with me and that Jim Krogstead. Jim and me could get whiskey in Okinawa, cheap; Jerry couldn't cuz he wasn't entitled to PX privileges.

So we got him the whiskey the first time, and Jerry says, "Is there anything I can do for you guys?"

I says, "Well, I hate the bosun. He's got us doing all this painting shit. We don't do that in the States."

"What?"

I says, "Yeah, that's unsafe."

So Jerry went and told the chief mate, "You can't do all that painting. I'm the ammo inspector. That's unsafe."

The bosun went crazy. "*You fucking guys are setting me up! I know you two had something to do with it!*"

I says, "I didn't have anything to do with it. What are you accusing me for?"

Oh, he's just fucking mad. Now they're head to head, fist to fist. Jerry's running around, anything they did wrong, any kind of safety thing. They couldn't paint anymore, couldn't do this, couldn't do that. Then the bosun put us *inside* to paint, and he says, "Well, that's inside, that's not outside."

Jerry says, "I'm calling up about this."

Then we said we couldn't breathe because of the paint. He had to put a blower down there. So now we're really knocking heads. We get back to Okinawa. Now this is going on again, and I'm trying to get the recon Marines.

They says, "Bring him over here, we'll fuck him up for you." They says, "We'll beat his fucking brains out."

I says, "I don't know if I can get him out. He won't come out with me."

It got to the point nobody would talk to him. Nobody would have a drink with him. Nobody socialized with him. You think he would take the hint.

Anyway, me and Jim are outside the base, and we're sitting at one of the little restaurants having a hamburger and a beer. Here comes the bosun, all fucked up. Just sits down with us, and Jim looks at me and I look at him.

Unbelievable.

I found out later he had been married and some broad fucked his mind up. He never really recovered. He was from a wealthy family, old money, in San Francisco, and one of his sisters had married a guy from West Virginia, and she moved there with him. Now the bosun's telling this story.

He says, "Yeah, my sister married that guy in West Virginia, and I went to visit them, and I really didn't like it there, and I came back, and then he drove my sister crazy, and she committed suicide." He says, "One day, I'm gonna go back there and kill him."

I says to Jim, "Wait a minute. We better get this guy's name," I says, "in case we know he's home, we can call up and tell him he's coming."

Jim says, "Yeah."

We're trying to get the name of the guy. We're gonna call him and tell him, "Hey, be careful, man. He's talking about coming out there to kill you." Hey, what else could we do?

We get outta there, go back up to Korea. We're gonna do three or four of those trips. I'm hanging with that Minh up there in Korea. Now she's outta the whorehouse. She got a place with her sister, so I'm just gonna stay there. Giving her some money, you know, and up and out.

She says, "Oh, I wanna get married, I wanna get married."

I says, "I don't wanna get married," you know, "I wanna have a good time here. Take some more money."

I bought her a watch and she says, "Ohhh, engagement ring! Engagement ring!"

I says, "I bought a *watch*, I didn't buy an *engagement ring*."

Anyway, we're having a pretty good time. We're bouncing around, back and forth. Every time we get back to Okinawa, it'd always be a fucking siege of sorts. There'd always be fucking headaches, or even in Korea with the bosun.

What I would do on deck would be: I'd turn to at eight o'clock in the morning. I would work 'til nine, and I would go to my room, and I would sit there for 20 minutes. Just sit there. Yeah, because you couldn't get any breaks. I'd take my own breaks, hoping the bosun would say something to me.

And then it was Scray, and this big, stupid fucking Costa Rican AB, and the ordinary were working together.

This ordinary didn't wanna work with these guys. He says, "That's Larry, Curly, and I'm Moe here," you know, with these assholes.

I says, "Just do what the bosun tells you."

The bosun got a real fucking attitude, and me and Roberts were doing something, and he tells me, "You're fucking everything up out here, it's all you."

I says, "It ain't me, bos'. You oughta look a little more closer to home."

He says, "You're telling these people what to do!"

I says, "I'm not telling anybody what to do. You got that all wrong."

He storms off, "Yeah, well . . . .," gritting his teeth and shit.

I'm digging for my knife.

Roberts says, "You know, he knows you're crazy. He knows you'd go down on that dock with him, cuz he knows you went down on that dock with Jegel in the Philippines. But I don't think you can whip him. He's a little too much for you."

I says, "Yeah, Robbie, that's why I got a sharp knife in my pocket. That way I can stab him."

This is *constant*. Every fucking day was friction, stress, drama. Every day was some kind of abuse going on.

Anyway, the chief mate's getting ready to go home at 6 months, they could do that. The third mate, too. I heard he died, later. I was on a tanker a few years after this, we had the cadets on board from Kings Point, and we were out on deck doing something. Two or three of them were talking and mentioned Phil's name, his last name.

I said, "Phil—" whatever his last name was.

They said, "No. His younger brother's going to school." At Kings Point. "Phil's dead."

I said, "Dead? I was on a ship with him, a foreign voyage. He got stuck over there. He wanted to do the 6 months, but he wanted to get off cuz he wanted to get his Corvette. He had to pay for it, and he had to get the money. And he was moving to North Carolina cuz the cost of living was cheaper down there, and he had his Corvette."

They said, "Yeah, they found him dead in the Corvette along the side of the road down there in North Carolina."

I said, "Jesus Christ. He was so young!"

They said he had gotten a job on a tanker, and these things were dangerous, they used to call some of them "drugstore ships." You're always working around some kind of petroleum product. They finally figured out that benzene kills people. From what they had heard, Phil had gotten off the tanker, he got sick on the tanker and just quit without going to the doctor. In other words: "I just wanna get off here."

So, I don't know if he got mixed up with the petroleum product, or it spilled on him, or anything else. He didn't go to the doctor. He got off the ship. They found him on the side of the road, dead, in the Corvette, sitting there.

Nice guy. It's a shame. Those tankers were notorious for killing people, breathing in the gas fumes, oil fumes. It's a shame.

Anyway, Reed says, "Well, Ron, I'm going."

I says, "I'm gonna miss you, mate."

He says, "Yeah, I'm gonna kind of miss you, too, Ron." He says, "You got your hang-ups and shit, but you're a pretty good AB. I wouldn't mind sailing with you again."

I says, "You're alright. We got along."

He says, "Yeah, can't get along with that fucking bosun though, can we?" Then Reed tells me: "You know, I'm not trying to make any points, but he's got you guys out here eight to five every fucking day, bell to bell." We called it bell to bell, no coffee breaks, no lunch breaks, nothing, no: "Hey, knock off at four thirty, four o'clock." He says, "I don't think any of you guys know about this. But I went to the bosun and I said, 'Hey, bos', why don't you knock these guys off a little early or something, give 'em a break here, you know, it's eight to five, and they're not working overtime on the weekends, you can't expect them—'"

And guys are going home right and left. We're running out of replacements. Steve went home. Jim Krogstead went home. That first engineer in Okinawa went to the hospital. Nobody knew where he was! He went down to the engine room and got in an argument with Jim Krogstead. Jim says, "Don't fuck with me!" He ran out of the engine room, about ten thirty, the chief comes, "Anybody seen the first? Anybody seen the first?" Now we're looking for him. We don't know what happened to him. About two o'clock in the afternoon, the base calls up. This guy just walked off the ship, went over to the base, turned himself into the sick bay, and they called and said, "You better get another first engineer. We're keeping him. He hasn't had a heart attack, but he's got all the signs." Guys are going home right and left.

Anyway, Reed says, "I went to the bosun and told him, 'Why

stress?'"

The bosun said, "*I* run the deck department, not you. *I* work these guys. *I'm* in charge."

Reed said, "Yeah, you are, but I'm still the officer in charge. I'm chief mate. I'm next to the captain. I'm responsible for the deck department."

"You don't tell me what the fuck to do."

He said, "You and me are going up to the captain right now."

Go up there, told the captain, captain said, "Well, wait a minute, you know . . . ."

Reed said, "You're not backing me up, captain."

Captain said, "Well, hey, you know . . . ."

And Reed is getting off in a couple of days.

I says, "Yeah, mate, that's the way he is."

Reed says, "I'm leaving tomorrow. If I don't see you, Ronnie, you take care of yourself."

I says, "Yeah, you too, mate."

He says, "Can I do anything for you before I leave?"

"You know what, mate? Can we have our fire axes back?"

"I'll see what I can do about it, Ron."

I said it kiddingly.

Next day the mate's gone, here the fire axes are back, you know, ready to go again in case we needed 'em.

Oh, the reason Steve got off: he had come back drunk one night, and he was in Jim Krogstead's room, they were in there drinking. It was right next to the purser. The purser gets up, this old fag, he was in his 60s then. He comes, beats on Jim's door, and says, "Hey! Can you guys keep it down! You woke me up!"

Jim says, "Yeah, I'm sorry, we'll shut it down. OK, you gotta go."

Well, Steve goes to his room, thinks about it, comes back, knocks on the purser's door. Purser gets it, Steve punches him in the face.

Purser screams, "Ahhhh!" Running down the passageway.

They fired Steve over that. "You gotta go, Steve," you know.

Guys are coming and going, getting off. Smitty had cried his way off, just basically cried, he had to go see his loved one. Guys are coming and going. They were actually running out of room on the ship's articles that the shipping commissioner had. Guys that were getting off, being replaced, *those* guys were getting off. You have to write on top. They're writing on the *sides* now. I can't remember who walked by and said, "Hey, it's nice to see a familiar face on here."

We're on Okinawa. More and more is happening. I gotta tell you about the fire in number two hatch.

You can imagine now we're on this long stretch of ammo pier. We're pretty far out at the end. There's an Okinawan fire truck. We always point bow out so in case something happens, we get the plant going, move out. It takes 12 hours to get the plant going on a steamship. Once you shut it down, you run on generator. Anyway, there's this fire truck, always stayed down there near the beginning of the pier. We're further out at the end of it. It's a long-ass pier, trust me.

And the bosun's going through some utterly dumb—trying to fix things that are unfixable, you know, shipyard work, not crew work. The next thing I know, they had just finished loading number two hatch and had sealed it. In other words, the accordion-type thing had folded down. We had this cargo net there between the pier and the ship, in case any of the bombs dropped or anything, they would fall in this net, not in the water. We always put that there for safety. And me and the bosun are on the stern.

All of a sudden someone comes running back: "There's smoke coming out of number two hatch!"

We take off running to number two hatch. The Okinawa longshoremen, they're jumping onto the cargo net to get outta there. Others are running to the gangway, knocking people over trying to get up there.

We get up there, and we had just got this new chief mate, heavy drinker, kind of egotistical, always hemming and hawing about everything: "Well, you know, I don't know about this." Completely different from Reed. Anyway, I go up on top of the mast house, which has all the electrical equipment for the booms, and I get the fire hose, and I'm standing directly to stern of number two hatch. The bosun's up there on number one.

The mate comes up there, walking: "Well . . . ."

I says, "Open the fucking hatch! It's the only chance we got! If there's a fire down there, we gotta put it out!"

He's all, "Well, I don't know . . . ."

I says, "Some*body* do some*thing* here!" You know, we gotta do *something*. We're gonna fucking detonate here.

In the meantime, the Okinawans in the fire truck that were sitting there all the time, they try to drive the fire truck up, give us help. Their hoses won't reach. Yeah. The fire truck can only go so far. They tried to stretch their hoses out, they can't help us. Duh! Didn't anybody think of this beforehand? You know, if there is a fire, they can't get that far up to give us a hand.

He opens up the hatch. We start calling for water on deck. We're flooding this hatch. But there's no smoke now. And I mean, we're *pouring* water in there, just pouring it in. Just on top of the cargo, these rockets that were in boxes, bombs. We're pouring water, just literally pouring water, down in there. I don't know how long this went on, but finally, we figure, nothing's gonna happen here, right. So they're gonna shut the water off.

Now, I don't know how long we put that water in there, but we put so much water in that hatch that the bow of the ship actually came down 2 feet. When we knocked off the water it was about 10 minutes to 3 in the afternoon.

The bosun says, "OK, let's go get coffee," which, kind of, you know, maybe we should stand around, maybe we shouldn't. I didn't have to worry, because 15 minutes after 3: "OK, let's go back and stand up there now. Go back to work." You know.

Un-fucking real.

The engineers had to pump the water out. Now we got everybody there. We got Marines there, we got the Okinawan fire department, we got the Navy fire department. We got everybody trying to figure out what the fuck happened. They're there all night.

They finally figured out there was dampness in there, and when they closed the hatch, some steam had come up. Or there was some kind of a hydraulic spray, and it looked like smoke. That's what they finally figured.

They wanted one of the crew to stay there and watch that hatch all night. We had this ordinary, Douglas. Useless. He was one of the new ones that had come on. He said he was in Norway back in the '40s. You gotta remember, this is the '70s. He was a heavy equipment operator there. He says, "I'm black, and I was an oddity there." I think he was gay, you know, but he says, "I was black, and I was an oddity there."

I says, "You're black, and you're an oddity on *here*." You know, you don't have to be *black*. *Nobody* liked him.

So I'm standing around there, and the second mate that was on watch says, "What's going on, Ron?"

I says, "Oh, nothing, mate. I'm going in tonight."

He says, "Stick around, there's gonna be some fun here."

I says, "There is every night on here." You know, *something's* gonna happen.

He says, "No. I just gave Douglas some ex-lax. And I told him, whatever he does, don't leave that hatch."

I says, "How'd you give him the ex-lax?"

"I put it in the candy and gave him some."

"You don't like him either, huh?"

"No."

About a half hour later, Douglas took off running trying to get outta there.

So, we're still making those trips up to Korea. Still got the girl-friend there, Minh. Still living with her sister. So when we'd get up there, I'd go there and stay. Come back down, back and forth. Guys are going right and left. I still gotta finish my year, but I'm getting fed up with this. It's getting to the point where I wanted to get off of there. Now it's getting to be May. I know we're gonna make one more trip up to Korea, come back down to Okinawa, load, and then it's gonna go two trips to Japan. I'm not that interested.

So my back never was completely right. So I turn around. The old fag purser's still there, right. I go see him. He sends me over to the doctor. "Just go ahead and go."

This Navy doctor takes an X-ray of my back, and he says, "Well, let me tell you. You don't have the best back in the world. I'm really doubtful, though, about problems you're having on the ship, cuz you guys are going right and left to the doctor over here for everything." That big guy from Costa Rica, he kept going, he wanted to get off on a medical. He must have went five, six times for physicals, and they said he was a fine physical specimen. Nothing wrong with him. This Navy doctor says, "What's wrong with that ship? Everybody's here!"

I says, "Well, doctor, there's a lot of problems there, you know, these guys got problems."

He says, "I thought the Navy had an alcohol problem, but three-fourths of the guys that are showing up here look like they're hung over."

I says, "Well, there ain't a whole lot to do here, doctor."

We had this one very old man, Tony. It was supposed to be a short trip for him. Why this guy was even working, I have no idea, unless he wanted to give it to his grandkids. He wanted to go home. He was crying all the time; he wanted to go home. So they basically told him, "Look. Go to the doctor, say something's wrong with you."

"Well, my grandkids..."

"Go to the doctor."

The doctor happened to mention this, not because he's speaking out of turn about a patient, but he says, "Geez, that old guy came here, Tony." He says, "You know him?"

I says, "He cleans up the rooms."

He says, "I sent him home. He was here crying. It was an emotional thing. There's nothing physically wrong with him, it was emotional."

I says, "Yeah, doctor."

He says, "But I'm having a problem." He says, "Your captain doesn't want to send people home. He always wants 'Light Duties.'" He says, "I don't believe in 'Light Duties'; you're either 'Fit for Duty' or you're not." He says, "What do you think?"

I says, "You know, doctor, I appreciate it, but give me another month. I gotta make the pension, and I need one more month."

He says, "You think you could do it?"

I says, "Doctor, if I can't, if I don't feel any better, I'll be back here."

So I go, and we make the last trip up to Korea, and I figure it would be just about a month when we got back. Then it was going to Japan. I didn't feel like going. It was June. It was gonna be warm in the States. So I says, "OK."

And he says, "OK."

So I go on one last trip to see Minh up there in Korea, give her whatever money I had left. I bought her a radio in Okinawa, gave it to her. "You come back. You come back."

I says, "Don't worry about it. Do what you gotta do for yourself. Don't wait for me."

So we come back to Okinawa, and I was waiting for exactly the thirtieth day of June. I wanted to get the weekend in because I was off those 2 days anyway. So I worked Monday, and Tuesday morning I just got up and I said, "You know, I'm not even gonna tell anybody anything." I just walked down the gangway at 5 minutes after eight o'clock in the morning.

Everybody's looking at me like, "Hey, you're supposed to be working."

I go over to the Navy doctor. He says, "You're back."

"Yeah."

He says, "I should have sent you home last month. What do I have to put on this 'Not Fit for Duty' here to make sure the captain lets you off that ship? I don't want you on there."

I says, "Well, I can probably dictate something to you."

He says, "Go ahead."

"This man's 'Not Fit for Duty,' to be flown home, to report to the nearest U.S. Public Health hospital for treatment." And there was a little more I put in. I says, "Can I have a copy of that?"

"Sure. Two copies. I'll give you all you want."

"Thank you, doctor."

He says, "You take care of your back. You watch yourself."

So I come back to the ship. The guys are: "Where you been? You're gonna get logged for this! You can't take off any time you want!"

I says, "I'm 'Not Fit for Duty.'"

The chief mate, this new guy, the drinker: "'Not Fit for Duty'? You didn't even see the purser!"

I says, "I had it set up with the doctor. I told the purser." I'm "Not Fit for Duty" now, and they can't do anything to me.

Now the whining starts: "I don't know about this . . . . We'll have to see what the captain says . . . ."

I says, "I'm leaving. I'll see you." I'm gone. I'm in the wind.

So I turn around, and the captain calls me up there.

I says, "I'm 'Not Fit for Duty.'"

He says, "Alright. Go pack your stuff." He says, "I don't want you carrying anything. Find somebody to carry your bag."

I says, "Oh, that's great." So I get Scray. This guy's got a beer in his hand from eight o'clock in the morning. I says, "Hey, Scray, you wanna do me a favor?"

He says, "What's that?"

"You wanna carry my bag for me? The captain says I shouldn't carry anything."

"Yeah, I'll do it for you."

I says, "Yeah, put down an hour overtime."

One of the D-macs says, "You're leaving, Ron?"

I says, "Yeah, time for me to go."

"Is that the 'Not Fit for Duty'?"

"This is a photostatic copy."

"Can I see it?"

"Sure."

He looks at it. "Goddamn, Ron, you couldn't have got this written any better than if you'd written it yourself."

"I dictated it."

He says, "Well, I'll see you."

"Yeah, you take care of yourself."

Said "so long" to a couple of the guys that were left that I drank with or talked to.

Captain says, "Be ready at eleven o'clock at the end of the pier." He says, "I'll be there, and the agent's gonna come and get us, and we'll take you over to the shipping commissioner and sign you off."

So Scray carried my bag. And—I'm serious—this is a long way to carry something from the ship. So Scray took a dolly. We're walking along, and Scray says, "Goddamn, if I'd a known this was gonna be this long, I'd a brought a beer with me."

I says, "Well, when you walk me to the end here, just keep going. Don't even stop."

So I'm standing at the end of the pier, and here comes the old man *and* the purser. They're both going in. They gotta give you your money in front of the shipping commissioner.

He says, "The only thing I can give you is a check."

I says, "Captain, we didn't talk about this before, and I realize we're a long way from the ship, but I'd like cash."

"I can't give it to you, Ron. I gotta give you a check. I didn't know this was coming up. I don't have the money."

Cuz they had to give me all the pay from the beginning of the trip that I hadn't sent home or spent. We were always entitled to cash. That was the '36 Seamen's Act. That's when the government finally took over and when the subsidies started, too. The U.S. Merchant Marine was in such bad shape, the guys weren't getting paid, there were no unions. That's when the shipping commissioners were authorized to make sure you got your pay. So, he's got a check.

I says, "Well, alright, captain."

He says, "You can go to the agent and get all the money you want against this."

They take me over to the shipping commissioner, and I tell the captain, "You've got a steady seat here, don't you, captain? You must own a seat."

He starts laughing.

I'm serious, the original articles were like 3 feet long, they had to find places to write all the names of the guys who were coming on. Guy's names were crossed out, and the new guy's name would be put on top of it. One would leave, they'd cross him out, they had to start writing on the side. It was all written over and written on angles.

He says, "Alright, Ron, I'm gonna get going. You take care of yourself."

I says, "Yeah, I will, captain."

He says, "I'm gonna leave the purser here. The purser's gonna take you over to the agent, and they're gonna take you over and put you in a hotel until they can fly you out of here."

Unbeknownst to me, Northwest Airlines was on strike, and they, in turn, had to put me in a hotel and feed me and keep me until they could get me on a plane back to the States.

So the purser says, "I don't wanna know anything about this. You're signed off now." He just turned me over to the agent.

They put me in the President Hotel.

The agent says, "You're entitled to three meals a day. No booze."

I says, "OK. What about money?"

He says, "Anytime you need cash, I can give you a draw against your check here."

I could get anything I wanted, and I would sign an I.O.U., and it would be deducted from the check when I got back to the States.

So I turn around, and there's really not a whole lot of people in the hotel. I was gonna go back and see those guys out at Onna Point, but it was a long way out there to say "so long." I says, "Ah, you know what? I'm just gonna go to the seamen's club." So I went to the seamen's club and got half in the bag. I got back to the hotel so late the front doors were open and my key was just sitting on the desk.

I get up in the morning, go down to the restaurant, and they says, "You can have all you want, just sign." They wanted to give me like one cup of coffee, two eggs. I says, "I gotta have more than this." I was entitled to eat all I wanted. I says, "I don't want a *cup*. I want a *pot*." A pot of coffee, at this time, '77, was something like $15. I'm serious. The cost over there was phenomenal. Americans living in Okinawa that married Okinawan girls were actually thinking of leaving and coming back to the States cuz the Japanese had raised everything so high.

Basically, I'm just bouncing around, and then I go eat lunch. A salad was 200 yen, which was the same price as a beer. It was ridiculous. The seamen's club was the best place to go. They charged decent prices, but the hotel bars, you know . . . .

But I told the girl, I would give 'em a tip, and over there, at the time, how it is now in a lot of countries, the tip is included in the bill. So I would tip the girl two or three bucks, and a beer cost the same as a salad. Well, I was eating filet mignon for lunch, filet mignon for dinner. And for dinner I would have three "salads." They would write "salads" and give me the beer. Cuz I couldn't get the booze, right? Nice of them to do that. In the evening I'd go to the seamen's club.

And I'm calling the agent: "Is anything gonna happen?"

He says, "We're backed up. I can't get you out of here. There's no coach seats, and I'm gonna have to put you on a coach flight and blah, blah, blah, blah, blah. Just stay there. I'll get you."

"OK."

Next morning I get up again, hangover, have breakfast, go out, bounce around some more, have lunch. I'm sitting there. Who's walking through the door? It's the second mate! *He* went to the doctor, high blood pressure, they got him off.

Here he comes in. *"Hey, I'm getting off, too!"* All gassed up, hung over, yeah. He says, "Wanna get a drink?"

I says, "Wait a minute. You're entitled to lunch." I says, "When you order lunch, give the girl maybe 100 yen, you know, two, three bucks. Salad costs as much—"

He says, "No, the tip's included!"

I says, "Wait a minute. Trust me. Give her that," I says, "and tell her you want the 'special salad.' That's booze: you get the beer, and she'll give you two or three beers and mark down two or three salads."

"Really? Hey, that's great!"

I knew he'd like that.

So now he wants to go out that night, so we're gonna make the rounds. It was so expensive, we just said, "This is ridiculous." He wanted to get a blow job. We went to a massage parlor. Those broads had to be in their 50s and 60s, and they were charging like 50 bucks. We says, "Who needs this?" So we just went back to the seamen's club. We stayed there. I had one or two days on him. We were there at least a week. We had filet mignon for lunch, filet mignon for dinner, three salads, right? We're running up these bills. We were coming back so late that both our keys were sitting out there. They didn't even have a deskman. Just: take your keys.

Next thing you know, here comes the agent. He comes over to the hotel, cuz they're sending him these bills. "Jesus Christ! It's bad enough with one of you here!" He says, "Boy, I'm gonna put you guys on first class just to get you out of here! You're breaking us!" He says, "You guys are eating all this?" You know, Okinawan guy, he spoke very good English, he's looking at the bills.

"Yeah, we're eating all that."

"I'm gonna see if I can fly you home first class, just to get you outta here. I'll never get you on coach."

They had to fly us back first class, Okinawa, Guam, Hawaii, San Francisco. Now they got me going to where I engaged the ship. Second mate's getting off in San Francisco. We're in the airport there. He's drunk. I'm sober.

My ticket was to Charleston, South Carolina. I says, "There's a mistake." There really wasn't a mistake. I said it was, it wasn't. They fly you to the port you come on at no matter where you lived. I came on at Charleston, South Carolina. So I says, "There's been some mistake here." This was in San Francisco. I says, "I want to go to Cleveland."

They says, "We can change that for you. You paid for this ticket, full price." But now it's coach, in the States. They says, "There's a $12 difference in the price."

I says, "I'll pay that."

They says, "No, the difference is in your favor, but we can't give you the money because this is on a card. Give us your home address, and we'll send you the check."

I says, "Yeah, sure."

Now I'm walking the second mate all over the place. He finally gets a discount for a car. He's gonna drive to Vegas. That's where he lived. He's gonna drive, right? Last I saw him he was going to get the car. I hope he made it.

They fly me back to Cleveland. So I go to U.S. Public Health, and the doctor says, "I don't think you need an operation, but you do need to take some time off. That's too long for you to keep going like that every day." It was my back.

I says, "OK."

So they had to pay me unearned wages. Then I sued them, and they were like a patsy, U.S. Lines, they just gave me $7,000. Well, I got five, the lawyer got two. I got unearned wages cuz I was "Not Fit for Duty." That ship stayed there, out in the Far East, for another 3 months.

So, I got like 3 month's pay, unearned wages, plus I took it to the union when I got "Fit for Duty," gave them that, plus the discharges. I got vacation pay for that. A lot of people didn't know you got vacation pay on unearned wages. So in the end I got more than if I would have stayed there and worked for that psycho case, right?

To really kick it off, about 6 weeks after I'm home, there's a letter from United Airlines. I says, "What the fuck do they want?" I open it up. Here's a check for $12. I took it right to the bar.

Thompson Lykes

Thompson Lykes, 12/27/78 to 2/26/79. A Lykes Brothers ship. I caught it as a commercial run up at Sunny Point. It was loading some ammo to go to Israel. The captain was a good guy. He was an old AB that got a license and went up to captain with the Lykes. He kind of liked my last name, cuz his was basically something like mine, you know, an odd name. No Anglo-Saxon here, right? I got along with him pretty good. He was being sued by somebody. He liked to punch people out, too. Well, he didn't want any trouble after that, so he wouldn't let the chief mate log anybody. Guys were taking off for an afternoon.

"Hey! Log these guys."

"Mate, I told you, nobody here gets logged."

He just kind of walked circles around that poor mate. When they were up on the bridge, we're at sea, and the captain came up there every day, that's where he liked to be. He was a hands-on type, he just liked being on the bridge.

The poor third mate, young guy, MacDonald, he had a hearing problem, this is his first trip on his license. He asked me if I can give him a hand. He says, "You got about 10 years in now, don't you, Ron?"

I says, "Yeah, sure, mate, if I can, I will."

Well, the old man would sit on the port side of the bridge, and MacDonald, I don't know why, he would always go to the starboard side, and I'm in the middle by the wheel. The old man would say something to him—the kid couldn't hear him. The old man thought the kid was *ignoring* him.

One day the chief mate came up there bitching about something. He says, "I need some coffee."

Captain says, "Mate, have some coffee." Cuz we always had coffee on the bridge, still do.

Mate says, "This coffee tastes like shit."

Captain says, "Well, mate, I couldn't tell you, cuz I never tasted shit."

I cracked up laughing. I couldn't stop. And the captain's laughing, and the mate's holding the cup of coffee. Finally, I calm down, and the mate walks up to me and says, "You know, it wasn't that funny." I crack up again. The old man started laughing again, too. He was alright.

These trips could carry passengers, like I said before. There was one on here: she had been married four or five times, and the last husband was Jewish, and he died and left her a ton a money, and she was gonna go and live in Israel. She used to keep taking pictures of me. The captain used to say, "Here, I'll make him pose for you. I'll make him pose for you."

She used to come up to the bridge, and I often thought about hitting on the old broad, you know, and I says, "You know what? I don't fucking need it."

We had an ordinary seaman on there. He was on watch with me. He was retarded. The ordinary had to do sanitary 8 to 10, and then he'd go out on deck and work 'til 12, call the watch at 11:20, for the next watch. It was a pretty easy job. He'd do his sanitary, and then you didn't work, but you were on standby in case something happened, they'd call you for whatever they needed you for.

Well, I had first wheel. I used to come down and just sit in the crew mess, and the ordinary would sit in there, too. Well, I'm sitting in there, here comes the chief mate, and the ordinary's sitting there. And some people are their own worst enemy, you know? There was a head up on the bridge, not *on* the bridge, it was after you walked out of the bridge to go down the ladder. There's a big sign on there: it's been agreed between the union and the company that the deck department will clean this head. So the ordinary seaman was supposed to clean it. Now here the ordinary seaman's sitting there, and the chief mate says, "You know you're supposed to clean that head."

He says, "Mate, I do enough work around here. I got all these rooms to clean. I just can't find time."

Just unbelievable.

He was a real fucking idiot.

They used to put cans of juice on the table. One morning, he's sitting there, and I'm sitting at the other table. He had two cans of juice on his table. I didn't have any on mine.

I says, "Do me a favor: hand me one of those cans of juice."

So he hands me a can of juice. I go pick it up. It's fucking empty.

I says, "This can of juice is empty."

He says, "Well, I knew one was empty and the other one was full, but I didn't know which one was which."

A wet, short-time towel for a brain.

So one day, I'm gonna try to do him a favor and give him a break. They wanted us to spray-paint something. It was a real small job in this confined space. You had to kind of climb over everything to pour the paint in, and the hose was let out. Instead of having him run and get the paint, I was gonna go ahead and let him do the painting, and I was gonna run and get the paint and pour it in, and when it went out, just yell at me, and I'll go get some more paint and pour it in.

He says, "I don't know how to do that." He says, "You know how to do it."

I says, "Yeah, I know how to do it. I'll show *you* how to do it." So I show him how. I says, "OK, *I'll* go spray and *you* pour the paint." You know, it's this simple. I says, "You sure you don't want to spray and I'll put the paint in?"

"No, no, no. You're the AB. You spray, I'll pour."

I don't think he still got it fucking right. Oh, he was retarded. Matter of fact, one of the other ABs says, "His brother sails."

I says, "You mean they got more like him at home?"

He was useless.

We stopped in Israel, dropped off the ammo. When you get to the dock, you let the gangway down, from a winch. A wire runs to the chain fall and lowers it down. Once you get it down on the dock, sometimes you have to pull it to get it into position away from the pier, cuz sometimes you're not alongside, you're further away. When you pull it you slack it as it goes down so the other guys can get it into position. Then, once it's in position, you give it some more slack. You unscrew the outboard side, the shackle, the chain fall. You bring it around and you shackle it into the other side so it doesn't block anybody coming up or down, and you're still hooked up.

Anyway, we get it down on the dock. They want it further out. So we both go down there.

How the fuck he did this is still totally beyond me. Instead of standing to the side, he's standing in *front* of the gangway, and it's got a roller on it, so it *rolls*. He's standing there as it surges forward and rolls right up on his foot. I don't know how fucking dumb he could be.

They lifted it up and he's yelling, "My foot! My foot!"

That's like standing on top of an open hatch on the main deck and jumping into the bottom of the hatch, you know. I mean, this is the same principle. They took him to the doctor, and then he came back, and nothing was wrong with him.

He says, "That man there," pointing to me, "saved my life."

I was thinking: How do you do it without me being here?

Then I met that Moroccan Jew girl. Israel takes in all Jews, but if you're an Arab Jew, you get the dirtiest fucking jobs going. There is really no work for you. They sweep the streets. Anyway, she's working in one of the bars. And, I should say, Israel is the hand job capital of the world, too. That's their thing, you know. The girls were for hand jobs. That's all they'd do. Yeah. It's a real trip. Anyway, I met her, and we were having kind of a good time, we were freaking out for a little while.

Then she got serious about it, and she was like, "You take a picture of me?"

I says, "Well, sure."

Here she's giving me passport photos.

I says, "What?"

"Well," she says, "I might come over to America and see you."

That killed that. That was the end of that performance. Yeah.

Turned out to be a wrong number.

This is when we started drinking at the London Pride in Haifa, Israel. A British Jew owned it. That's usually where everybody was, and there were a bunch of UN troops there coming in from the Irish Brigade. They were all gassed up. They were gonna defend Israel, or Egypt, I don't know, they couldn't even defend themselves.

We had one poor kid, died later on, Rod something or other, I saw his name later on. He was kind of out of it, always running around trying to bum one shekel, which was about 50 cents. He was something else. I don't know why he died, but I saw his name 2 or 3 years later in the "Final Voyages."

Shirley Lykes

Shirley Lykes, 2/28/79. I took the Lykes Brothers ship back to Houston, and I got off. Matter of fact, it laid up there. And I, in turn, I says, well, I'll go to the Houston union hall, I won't even go to Charleston, and I'll file for vacation pay. I walked in, and the union official who happened to come to the ship, while we were paying off in Houston, he sees me and he says, "You're an AB, right?"

I says, "Yeah, I'm able seaman."

He says, "Take the *Shirley Lykes*."

I says, "I don't want to work anymore."

This is the same type of ship; they had lengthened them. The house was in front, then you had hatches, and then you had the crew's quarters aft. They had split it open and put another hatch in. So they carried more cargo, make more money, or they would try to.

He says, "It's going to New Orleans. If you don't like it, get off."

I says, "Alright, at least I'll take the transportation." Cuz they gave me transportation back to Charleston. So I put that in my pocket. It was cash. I says, "Alright, if nothing else I can pick up a couple more days' pay, and I'll go to New Orleans and get off, and I'll go back to Charleston from there." We get to New Orleans, and I says, "Ah, I'll make the trip." It was going back to the Med.

So I turn around, and some of the crew's getting off. They don't want to make the trip, or they lived in New Orleans. Whatever. I see this guy on the dock and he's shaking, he's just quivering, he's got a little ditty bag.

I says, "God, I know he's the new ordinary seaman."

Sure enough, he comes up. Shaky, we used to call him. You talk about a tourist. We used to call them that when they didn't do anything, you know, they couldn't even function. We used to call them tourists. This guy's a tourist. Worse than useless, a tourist. Yeah, tell 'em to assist the AB, the AB's up there climbing, haul the tools up so the AB can paint. You look down, he's standing over there, looking over the side, "Oh, there's really something going on there?" He's supposed to be helping you . . . . A tourist.

So anyway, I get this Joe Price, and Joe's an ex-alky, and we're in a room together.

Joe says, "Come on. Make the trip."

I says, "Yeah, OK, I'll make it."

We see Shaky come on board. The bosun we had was drunk all the fucking time, couldn't hear. The chief mate, I think he was an ex-paratrooper, used to wear a beret and blouse his boots.

This oughta be a real trip.

The bosun's just all fucked up. He'd be sitting outside his room on a chair, passed out. I'd wake him up and say, "Bos', I think they need you."

"Oh. Thanks, Ron, thanks."

He comes out there one day and says, "Yeah, you know, I don't fuck with anybody."

I says, "Yeah, bos', you don't do *anything*." He was something else. The mate and him were always at odds with each other.

Well, now we're getting to Alexandria, and we've got a load of giveaway cargo—flour, grain—and the chief mate decided he wants to paint the bridge of the ship. It was kind of a pain in the ass, but it was good thinking, because that way you stayed away from the cargo operation unless you were needed. It was almost like a safety issue. Keep away from the deck cuz these Egyptians are coming and going, I mean, there's shit flying all over the place, it was all manual labor. They're carrying it out on their *backs*.

They had two smokestacks on there. The company emblem was a blue diamond with an "L" in it, for Lykes. They had it on the side of the wing of the bridge. The mate wanted these painted, so we gotta rig a stage.

So me and Joe gotta do it. Well, we fucking do it, and we're up high, maybe close to 200 feet. You're looking down, and if this line breaks or Joe makes a mistake, cuz we both gotta slack the line at the same time, if you fall, you're in big trouble. We're gonna drop into the fucking water here, you know? All of a sudden they move some barges over there. Now we're *not* gonna hit the water. We didn't have life jackets on. The mate told the bosun: make sure they got life jackets. The bosun, he's fucking wandering off. So we're painting this, we're passing it back and forth. Now we're maybe dropped down about 10 feet. We couldn't reach up and touch the top of the wing of the bridge. All of a sudden they move a barge down there under us to load some of this cargo off onto the port side. I'm looking down there, and here's the chief mate.

"Oh, man!" He's looking over the side of this to see how we're doing, he's worried about this, the fucking dumb shit paint, but it looks nice for the company. He says, "Oh, Jesus, they got a barge down there. If I'd a known that, I'd a never had you guys painting like this."

I says, "Mate, what is the *difference* if we fall 200 feet onto a steel barge or we fall 200 feet and hit that water? We're gonna be just as dead, mate."

"Yeah, Ron, I guess, huh?"

I'm thinking: you fucking goof.

Well, now he decides we did such a good job that we're gonna paint the front of the house from the bridge down.

I says, "Oh, fuck."

But OK, we're gonna do it. Well, we've got loose bags of flour, loose bags of corn, 50-pound bags breaking all over the place. It looked like we were in a Pillsbury bake-off.

He wanted it painted. We painted it. We painted over the flour, we painted over every, fucking, thing. We painted just like we painted the *Export Bay*. We *painted it all*. That's what he wanted, that's what he got.

We stopped in Israel again. I didn't check out that broad. I didn't need it. We came back into the lakes, and I paid off in Chicago, and they gave me transportation back to Houston, cuz that's where I'd signed on, so I just took the cash. As we were coming in, there was another Lykes ship coming in, too; somebody was telling me that captain had been on the *Badger State.*

The *Badger State* was going over to Vietnam with a load of ammo, and north of Hawaii they hit real bad weather. They lost the plant. When you lose your engine, you have no control. The ship just got beat up. The cargo, shored up with the lumber, started breaking loose. Bombs and rockets rolling around, one blew up, tore a hole in the ship. They sunk. I think damn near everybody got killed. That was the *Badger State,* 1969. This captain had been chief mate on there.

But we got back, and I bailed out. Took my money and ran.

Pioneer Moon again

I'm back on the *Pioneer Moon*. They called for an AB job in Sunny Point. It was gonna go to Lisbon, Portugal, and I'd never been there, and then it was gonna go up to Bremerhaven, Germany to pick up military cargo. You got 10% extra for hauling ammo, but the jobs were easy to catch cuz they were older ships. You made more if you were on a tanker or a container ship, but I walked into the hall, and I was looking for a job. I was gonna make the pension credit. I needed the money to keep drinking. One of those deals.

Anyway, run into an old friend—electrician Rosborough, the old queer guy, old scabby face. I got on and here's fucking Rosborough. Ray Adams is ordinary seaman, he was messman on that Moore-McCormack ship where he's all drunked up, taking people's orders, wouldn't call them down. He's on there. Oh, boy, we're gonna have a good time this time.

I knew the bosun on there, too, Bob Elsey, from one of the Moore-McCormack ships. I get on there, and it's gonna be an easy trip. This Captain Murphy, what a fucking screwball he was, too. He was ex-NMU, ex-able seaman, worked his way up to third mate, worked his way up to captain. One of those who's just pissed off about *everything*. Just, fucking, miserable.

Anyway, we leave, we're going across, we're getting ready to come into Lisbon to drop off the ammo. Lisbon, Portugal has the same thing that Sugarloaf Mountain has in Rio de Janeiro in Brazil: Christ with His arms stretched out. So if you see a picture of that, you're either seeing Brazil or Portugal, one of the two.

Well, it's night. I got the midnight to four, and we're gonna get in at something like six in the morning. So the old man's up all night, he wants to make sure everything goes alright.

We're coming into Lisbon, and here's a fucking ship. I got the wheel, but it's on automatic, and I'm standing there, and the third mate is there, and the captain's sitting in the captain's chair. The ship's coming down the port side. I guess he's going to go into the Med. Well, he's the burdened vessel. He's gotta move for us. It's just like the rules of the road. If the ship is on your port side, he's burdened. They have to go around the stern. All ships know it. Well, this guy ain't moving. He ain't coming around our stern.

So Murphy starts yelling to 'em, on channel 16, ship to ship: "You're the burdened vessel. You're the burdened vessel. Move."

Here comes this broken English: "You burdened vessel! You burdened vessel!"

Murphy says, "OK, cowboy." He tells me: "Put it on hand."

"It's hand steering, captain."

"Come hard right."

What he was doing was—this ship was supposed to go around our stern. *They* were supposed to come to *their* right and come around *our* stern. What he did was come completely right, make a 360 degrees, to get behind *his* stern. Not a bad maneuver. Theoretically, if you had two ships coming head to head, bow to bow from, say, one's going south, one's going north, going right at each other, and you had two coming east and west, you're all gonna meet, all four of you, bow to bow. If everybody went right, you wouldn't have a collision. So that's the theory on that. It's rules of the road. Every captain, *everybody*, should know that out there. Even sailboats should know it.

Anyway, we get into Lisbon, and everybody's gonna have a good time, but we're way out at this ammo pier. So we're trying to find our way in and trying to find ways to get out of work and trying to do this and trying to do that, and Captain Murphy, instead of just sitting in the office being captain, you know, he's gonna be a chief mate, second mate, chief engineer.

Chief engineer was pretty much of a prick, too. He wouldn't give the engine cadet any overtime on weekends. They were trying to keep the costs down all the time.

The name of the place to go was the Texas Bar. So that's where we went: the Texas Bar. There was a couple of them there. Lisbon, Portugal, it was still there about 10 years ago. That whole street's just a den of iniquity. We're up there drinking, talking to the girls, going back and forth, and it's kind of miserable on the ship. Food's not really good. It was the same *Pioneer Moon* I was on before.

One of the guys comes back and says, "Hey, I met a Portuguese guy, and he knows all the cheap places to go."

Up in the mountains outside of Lisbon, you go up there in your car or motorcycle, you stop, you pull over to the side of the road, and you got these scrub brushes about 3 foot high, and you turn around and these girls come out of the bush, and for like $3 or $4 they'll take you in there and blow you. Then they'd wipe you off with a napkin. That's all you see are fucking napkins for miles around, right?

I think that was the highlight of the trip for me. I mean, Lisbon looks like Spain, Spain looks like Portugal, they tend to run together.

Now we're gonna go up to Germany. Well, Bremerhaven, Germany wasn't much. But they got the seamen's club there, and they got girls sitting in the windows; you knock on the window and ask the price. They got the places to go—well, they're gone now.

We had this officer's messman, looked like a Japanese infantryman from World War II. He was Puerto Rican, but he had buck teeth. And Rosborough, right, Rosborough just had to get into something again. He was in something on that *Rainbow*. He was in something on that fucking *Reliance*. You know, he's always whining about something. Well, he couldn't pass it up here, either.

The engine cadet wasn't getting any overtime, right?

So he tells the engine cadet: "Look, I'm gay, and don't tell anybody, but if you let me blow you, I'll give you $20 the first time and $10 every other time, cuz you're not making any overtime."

The kid wanted to kill 'im. Goes up to the captain and tells Murphy this. Rosborough denies it, right?

Captain says, "I better not hear any more stories."

What's the next thing that happens? This officer's messman goes out one night, he don't come back. Here come the West German police about ten o'clock in the morning. Well, guess where he's at. Don't take no rocket scientist to figure this thing out. About an hour later, Murphy leaves with the coppers.

Third mate comes by and says, "Man, don't say nothing, but the officer's messman was in a park last night, and he was giving candy to the kids, and they got him for attempted child molesting."

Murphy had to go get him out, and they told him, "Just don't let him off the ship anymore. We'll forget this incident."

There was a young black kid, on our way back, I came up to relieve him on lookout at like three o'clock in the morning to do my three to four on lookout.

He says, "Oh, man, I'm glad you're here."

I says, "Yeah? Why is that?"

He says, "Oh, man, these lights in the sky. I saw them, these lights." He says, "My radio went dead."

I says, "Really?"

"Yeah. Yeah." He says, "Oh, man, I'm glad you're here." He says, "I think they were flying saucers."

"Well, I'll tell you what," I says, "if they come down and get you," I says, "ask them to wait a minute, come back to get me, and I'll go with you."

Next day, I get up to the bridge, and the young third mate we had up there says, "That ordinary, does he seem OK to you?"

"He's alright. No better, no worse than anybody else on here."

"Well," he says, "did you see any flying saucers last night?"

I started laughing. I says, "No."

I was glad it was a short trip. We came back with the cargo to New Orleans, and I quit. I don't know what happened to Rosborough or the other guy. And I didn't want to know. I didn't want to know.

Mormaclynx

Here we go. December 18, 1979, Moore-McCormack, *Mormaclynx*. This was a very nice ship running to South America. I caught this in Jacksonville—I had just moved there—and took it up to New York. It had come back from a foreign voyage from South America. The first port was Jacksonville. One of the guys got off, and I got on. We went up to New York.

That's the trip I was injured.

We're securing in New York, and a steel wheel snapped off on one of the booms. We're getting ready to leave to make the foreign voyage down to South America. We're winging the boom in to bring it in. They brought the boom back too quick, the wedge fell into place, it snapped off and hit me in my left knee. Knee's all swelled up. Well, we're leaving. Instead of taking me ashore, they throw me in my room. We leave. I'm limping around.

They're gonna take me to the doctor in South America. First port was Rio. The agent takes me over to him, and this guy looks like a Nazi war criminal. He had a big scar on the side of his face. I think he interned at Auschwitz. He was speaking Portuguese, and I didn't understand a lot of what he said, but I did understand when he took the big needle out and he said, "Cortisone."

He shot it into my knee. I wanted to kill him it hurt so fucking bad. It hurt worse than the knee. He wrapped a big fucking bandage around it, sent me back to the ship, "Fit for Duty."

So the entire trip, I'm going to the doctor every port with the medical papers.

Nobody went ashore in Buenos Aries, Argentina. You go up the Plata River to get up into Buenos Aries, and it's wider in some spots than it is deeper. You can actually feel the ship planing through the mud. We're drawing 32 feet. You can actually feel it. It's a strange experience. You're trying to steer, and you feel it planing, and all of a sudden you'll get out of the mud and come back in the water again. Plata River, yeah.

Anyway, we get there, and nobody wanted to go ashore because it was a dictatorship down there, and I thought: I never been here, I could care less. The streets are deserted. The rest of South America, the east coast of South America, it's just one big party. But Argentina was deserted. There's nobody out. I'm very serious. It was strange. Went to the Seaman's Institute there. There was a priest from New York, and he actually used to let the girls come in there, business girls, hookers, you know, or girls who were just looking for guys. His attitude was: "Well, they gotta have somewhere to go." He was just like, hey, you gotta let people live, they gotta eat, which was kind of him in a roundabout way. I mean, you would think that he'd be hell and brimstone, Roman Catholic priest, he'd be throwing 'em out: "You're hookers! Get outta here! I only want nuns in here," or some fucking thing like that.

Now we're gonna go back. That's as far south as we went. We're gonna go back up the coast, and I'm still going to the doctors. My knee's fucked up, right?

I turn around, it was Brazil, and we went to one of the local bars. There was a girl, and they kind of just grabbed right onto us. It was myself and the second mate, a guy from Jacksonville. I'd run into him back and forth before.

There's this girl leaving and going upstairs every once in awhile, then she'd come back, and then every 15, 20 minutes, she'd run upstairs again. I didn't think too much about it. But then I ended up going up there with her, freak out with her for a little bit. Get upstairs, here's a baby there that she was going upstairs to check on.

Like a dummy I says, "Who's the father?"

She looked at me like: what are you, an *idiot*? I don't know. *Somebody*. I'm a hooker!

Dumb.

Anyway, we kept going, and the next day I had to go to the doctor. It was the last time in South America. So I had all my paperwork.

One of the guys on the ship told me, "You better get photostatic copies of that so you've got copies, cuz you're injured."

I really didn't think about it. But I says, you know, I better get it done, so when the agent was taking me over, I told him, "I'm gonna need photostatic copies of all these papers."

He says, "Oh, I can't do that. The company, the company."

What it was was: The company wanted to keep the papers. Your medical records aren't yours. If the company's paying, they're the company's papers.

I'm thinking: well, it's either punch him out and take this shit, or piece him off with a twenty. So, he wouldn't do it 'til I showed him the twenty dollar bill. I got three copies of everything, and he paid for it out of that twenty. He wanted to take me home and meet his daughter. I never saw a twenty dollar bill go so far in my life.

We got back up to Jacksonville, and I went to U.S. Public Health, and as soon as I got there, they saw the medical records and said, "You're not going anywhere." Make a long story short, I ended up having to have knee surgery. Eventually, I got sent to U.S. Public Health Hospital in New Orleans, had knee surgery, and ended up suing the company.

I quit drinking for a year

 My knee was still bothering me, but I was gonna try to go to work, so I got a "Fit for Duty," and I got on a ship in Sunny Point again. They flew me up from Jacksonville. I lasted 3 days, and the knee swelled up so bad I couldn't work and got off again. Then I went back to Jax, and I was gonna have to have knee surgery. That was June of 1980. I couldn't work again until March of '81. That's how long I was off with that knee surgery. I mean I was *off*.

I got down to Florida with the girlfriend when I moved down there, I quit drinking. I quit drinking for a year. I shocked everyone. From the time I got off that ship and I hurt my knee, I was very apprehensive, very worried about the knee. I'd never had surgery before. The money really wasn't there, although I was borrowing money from people, and I was getting the $8 a day, maintenance and cure, and we were living on what she was making. I told her, "When this comes through, it'll be nice, and I'll cut you in." I told her that, and I did when I got the settlement money, but it was that long to get the operation and the settlement money.

I didn't drink, though. I just didn't drink. I was worried about the knee. They sent me to New Orleans, U.S. Public Health, to have the operation.

When I got there the doctor said, "If you have an alcohol problem—alcoholism is a disease—we treat it here."

I said I don't have an alcohol problem. I don't have any problem with drinking. I can drink a quart, a case, a gallon, two fifths. I don't have any problem drinking. I just don't feel like it now. And I didn't drink for that entire time. I started again after I started shipping again.

They had to open the knee up, fillet it, clean the damage out. The doctor said you could have driven a truck through the tear I had in it. Recuperation was a long time. And it was all that time, and he finally gave me a "Fit for Duty." I was flying back and forth from Jacksonville to New Orleans, he'd examine it, and then I'd fly back again.

I don't know if I was scared to drink or what. Like I said, I was very apprehensive about the knee. I'd never been operated on before, and the doctor actually tried to explain it. I told him I was apprehensive.

He said, "This operation is done thousands of times a day all over the world."

I said, "Yeah, but it's not being done to *me*."

I was miserable. This was the first time that I was actually laid up, where I was actually dependent upon someone else. And I really didn't like that. I didn't like the idea of not being able to move. I just felt totally . . . trapped. You know? At the mercy of who? Her? The insurance company? I just felt trapped. I was being told what to do constantly. I didn't like it any. And I was scared if I drank and fell down, that'd be more complications. I just felt that I didn't need it. I just didn't need the grief. The abuse was coming hot and heavy, and I felt I was getting all the abuse I could handle at the time.

When the abuse becomes too heavy—and I can handle abuse, you know, more abuse, heap it on me, I love it—I look up and say, "Enough is enough," and I look down and say, "Enough is enough." You gotta give him his due down there, you know what I mean? Hey, come on. Do it to somebody else. Pass the buck around here, give it to somebody else. I'm sure there's other deserving people in this world.

I even watched my weight, watched what I ate, because I wasn't active at all, I was on crutches. In other words, I was gonna get healthy as fast as I could.

Within reason. I wasn't going to keep getting a "Not Fit for Duty" to make it look better for the lawsuit or anything else.

About this time, too, I got a letter from Ken Bottoms' parents that he'd been arrested in Saudi Arabia. He'd smuggled the letter out to them. He was in jail in Saudi Arabia, and they didn't really know anything else. I called his parents.

They said, "Oh, that's nice of you to call, but there's nothing you can do, Ron. We'll keep in touch. We'll let you know what's going on."

I said, "OK. If you need anything, let me know. Ken did me a favor down in South Africa. The least I could do is try to repay it."

I find out later what had happened: he was smuggling booze. He was paying $10 a bottle for it in the UK. I'm talking *cases*. He got it on board the ship, and then he smuggled it ashore in Saudi Arabia. I'm talking *pallets* of booze. He and about three or four other guys, and they were getting $100 a bottle—$100 a *bottle*, not a *case*. This is, say, '77, '78. They had done it the first time and gotten away with it. And Ken stayed on. It got good to him, so he's gonna make a few more bucks. So Ken and the same guys were gonna do this all over again.

Meantime, other guys had gotten wind of this. Well, they had their booze hidden away.

They get back, Ken makes the same contacts: come on, pay him, they put it over the side on their own.

Now, the guys who were smuggling their booze, those three other guys, they couldn't make a contact to get rid of their whiskey. So they go to Ken: "Can we use your people?"

Ken said, "Well, yeah, OK." Ken got back hold of 'em and said, "Hey, we got another load."

They said, "Yeah, sure, we'll take it."

Somebody ashore got caught with a bottle of whiskey from that load.

They said, "Where did you get it?"

He said, "From three Englishmen on that ship."

Saudi justice being what it is, the Saudi police came on board and grabbed the first three Englishmen they found and took 'em off.

So Ken said, "Hey, wait a minute, that's not the way this works." So Ken went to his friends and said, "Look, that ain't the way this works. We can't let those guys go to jail."

They said, "They're gonna let 'em go. They didn't do anything."

He said, "They're not gonna let them go. That's the way Saudi Arabia is. If they can't put you in jail, they'll put your grandfather in jail. That's the way that works."

So Ken and these other guys turn themselves in. The Saudis didn't care. They just needed bodies. They put them in jail, they fined the ship I don't know how much. Then they put them in the compound. Ken said it was just one big massive area with four bathrooms. He said there had to be like 100 guys in there. It was just a big mess.

The British Consul came to see him and said, "You got 4 months to 4 years."

Ken said, "We didn't even go to court."

They said, "You don't have to here. If you want to appeal, you can, but they may give you *more* time." It's not like here where they give you *less* time. There they give you *more* time.

So Ken was just kind of resolved to it. He said guys were escaping. But you had to have a ride out of the country. And what one guy did was: they handcuffed people when they would take you around, but they only had so many handcuffs. So this one guy managed to get at the end, but he was handcuffed. He managed to pick the lock. But he had a ride to get out of the country. That's the only way you could get out. There's no way out of that place, you're surrounded by desert and ocean. When they found out that this guy was missing, the guy that was in charge of these people, they put him in jail with them. Yeah. I mean, that's the way that works.

Anyway, Ken was there, and Queen Elizabeth made a goodwill tour to the Middle East. So she visited Saudi Arabia, and on a whim the king of Saudi Arabia freed all British subjects in Saudi jails. Ken didn't know anything about this. The next thing they know, they take them to the British Consul there. He's in shorts and flip-flops and a T-shirt. That's all they had. They got a shower once a week. You got two boiled eggs for breakfast, boiled chicken and rice for lunch, and boiled beef and rice for dinner. Seven days a week. Somebody snapped a picture of them in there. I had never seen him that skinny in my life. Four months in there, right? But they took them to the

British Consul, and he called his parents.

They said, "Will you reimburse the flight home if we fly him home?"

The parents said, "Sure."

They put all these freed British subjects on a plane in what they were wearing in the jails. That's all they had. They took his passport and his seamen's passport. Both of those were gone.

He calls me. "I'm out."

I says, "When?"

"Just got out." Yeah, and he's explaining everything to me.

I says, "What are you gonna do now?"

Because his name went to Interpol for being a smuggler, he couldn't be a British seaman anymore. He couldn't work on the ships, but he could work on the dredges, so he got a job on a dredge. Local work.

I was living in Florida, and he calls and says, "Can I come over and see you?" He says, "I gotta get away. Can I come over?"

I says, "Yeah, you can come over. Glad to see you."

He says, "What about your girlfriend?"

I says, "I like you more than I do her. We'll just throw her out."

"How about the people at the apartment complex?"

"Ah, they don't know much. Don't worry about them."

We were broke at the time. I was still waiting for the money for my knee. And he had to apply for a passport again. Then he had to give *my* name. Then *I* had to vouch for *him*. *I'm* vouching for *him*. They got a sense of humor, don't they? Yeah, and this is at the same time, too, that the Cubans were just pouring into the country in *rafts*. Yeah. I'm vouching for *him*. That'd be like he vouches for me when I go to England, right?

He came over, and we just bounced around. We were drinking by then, but he said, you know, they had stories about hanging prisoners from their thumbs and shit like that. He said nobody did anything to anyone. He said it was just total boredom. They did the old thing of trying to make a chess and checkers set out of whatever they could. But he said it was just a big compound. You slept wherever you could. Four bathrooms. If you had to go in a hurry, he says, you were in trouble. He said the boredom was the biggest thing. He said he saw the British Consul once or twice. That was it until the British Consul came and got him out. He spent 4 months there. He was supposed to get 4 months to 4 years, and he was just over the 4-month time when Queen Elizabeth made the goodwill tour, and they let him out.

Exasperating, huh? More fucking drama and abuse. Unreal.

The next few ships I just wanted to see what would happen to my knee. And it worked fine, as best as I could expect. I didn't have any qualms about shipping after that. I got one that went down to the Virgin Islands to pick up oil. I went ashore. I knew the knee was alright. I got a little time off. I went to the local bar/house of ill repute rolled into one.

You'd be surprised at the number of American girls that were down there hustling. I don't know whether it was narcotics or their boyfriends or what. Can't think of the name of the place, but it was notorious down there.

One girl was saying, "Yeah, my boyfriend's got me in here hustling while he's out with other women."

Right. Top of her class in high school.

Getting hurt and getting lazy

The *Mormactide* was a South American run, and things were getting old. I mean, it all got to be the same. By now, '81, I'd been doing this 15 years. I knew where to go, what to do, get in, get out. I wasn't trying to acquire any girlfriends. I just did what had to be done.

South America's one big party anywhere you go. The places all run in together. It was pretty much the same in '81 as it had always been. It's kind of like sex, you know. It doesn't get better, it gets to be the same. That's the only way I can describe it.

I could pick and choose, I just had to make enough money to make ends meet. I wasn't that concerned with any adventure. I'd go and do the same thing I did ashore. I mean, I'd catch the hookers down in South America and get back to the ship. That was it.

But this is when I got hit with the mooring line down in Rio. I caught it in Jacksonville, took it up to New York and took the run, 12/18/81 to 2/16/82.

I turned around, we were getting ready to undock in Rio. We're trying to pull our line free, I'm trying to take the strain, and it parts and hits me in both legs. Sounded like a rifle shot going off. One leg turned yellow, the other leg turned black and blue. I'm laying there in the dirt on the stern.

Third mate says, "We got an injury back here."

I hear the old man say, "What?"

"That big AB, Ron."

He says, "What's wrong?"

"The line parted. I think it broke his legs."

This captain's name was Dobson. He was a reformed alcoholic, and he was miserable. He just didn't like any thing or any body. Nothing worse than a reformed alky, or somebody that gets religion. They call for the ambulance, and the ambulance takes me to the hospital.

We get to the hospital in Rio, and I says, "Crutches. I need crutches."

They says, "We don't have any."

I says, "This is a hospital and you don't have crutches?"

They says, "The guy that has the keys for the locker where we keep them went home, and he doesn't come into work until 10."

I says, "Why doesn't he leave the key here? Why would you only have one key?" I'm trying to figure this out cuz I need crutches to walk.

Anyway, I'm staying there, and the nurses are coming around. I was starting to get around after 3 or 4 days. I requested to be flown back to the ship, so they flew me over to Recife.

Boy, the captain was happy to see me! The *blot* on his record was off, you know, that I had been injured. Oh, yeah. So he was pretty miserable, but he didn't say too much to me.

This Dobson was another one. He would go up on the flying bridge. He'd come up, and he'd tell the mate on watch, "I don't want to be disturbed." He'd go up and do his calisthenics up there, like that other one that used to walk around naked.

Chief mate come up and says, "The captain up here?"

I says, "Yeah, but he's up there, and he doesn't want to be disturbed."

Mate says, "Jesus, I don't believe this guy." You know? "Don't disturb me, I'm doing my calisthenics." It's like, "I'm up there walking around naked, don't disturb me."

It was cold coming back into New York. That would've been in February. I went up on the bow for lookout, and I says, "Fuck *this*. This is *cold*." We're getting back into New York, this is *February*.

And on the way back the old man was, "How are you, Ron? You OK?"

I says, "Well, yeah, captain, I'm feeling pretty good."

"Well, good, Ron."

Other than that, he wouldn't talk to me.

So I'm up on the bow, and it's *cold*. And there's an old thing: If you took any spray over the bow, you'd call the bridge, and they would bring you up on the wing. The lookout at the time was supposed to be on the bow, until somebody finally figured out that they lost so many of the lookouts up there that, hey, it's a lot easier to put them up on the wing. Insurance companies again.

So I go up there, and it's fucking *cold*. I says, "Fuck this." I call up to the bridge, "I just took some spray up here." I didn't, but the mate says, "Come on up to the wing."

So I come up there, standing out on the wing, which is a lot warmer, out of the weather. Here comes Dobson.

Captain says, "Lookout reporting anything?"

"No. He's out on the wing."

"Out on the wing? Why isn't he up on the bow?" He didn't know it was me on watch.

"He was sprayed, captain."

Dobson says, "Fuck that. Have him go back." He walks over to tell me to go back up on the bow, sees it's me, turns around, and walks back in. He didn't want to say too much to me, cuz I had a good lawsuit.

So I got off in New York. I went to a doctor in Jacksonville where I lived, and I had knee sprains and calf contusions. I called the attorney in New York, and about a month later, he got me a real nice settlement. He got $30,000. I got 20, he got 10.

He said, "It's lucky you didn't lose your legs."

I said, "Would I have got more money?"

That was about all for that one. And like I say, at this point, I was living with a girlfriend in Florida, so—you know—you get laid steady, you get lazy.

Next ship after that was the *Amoco Delaware*, another wreck. Amoco had two ships, and they were both wrecks.

They did have a chief mate they used to call Crazy Horse Collins. The only time you needed him is when you were unloading cargo, and that's when he was drunk. He was going crazy one day, drunk, aggravating the guy down on the dock handling the valves, trying to tell him how to do his job. He came back up steaming by me.

The guy in the shack came up, and he had a wheel wrench in his hand, and he says, "Who was that guy?"

I says, "That's the chief mate."

"When does he go ashore?"

"Loading or unloading, he doesn't really go ashore. He stays onboard, that's when we need him."

"You see this wheel wrench?"

"Yeah."

He says, "If that motherfucker comes ashore, I'm wrapping this around his head."

Crazy Horse Collins. He was in love with himself. He was fucking nuts is what he was.

I didn't last long there. That was 4/27/83 to 5/28/83. I didn't last long at all, did I?

Export Champion

Export Lines had gone broke, and Farrell Lines had bought them. Farrell Lines was the company that was running to Australia. They had a big thing about: "Oh, yeah, we're going to Africa now, and we're going to Australia." And they're buying ships up. Make a long story short, they ended up losing all their new container ships. They almost went broke and ended up operating Export Lines ships, all the junk. I often wonder who bought who?

Anyway, this was a West African run. I always said if they're gonna give the world an enema, they'd put the tube in Kandla, India. Well, West Africa's the armpit of the world. I didn't want to make the trip, but I says, "Oh, I might as well," it was winter. I was hoping to kill most of the winter.

I had never lost so much weight in my life. We were starving on there. The food was just terrible. I mean, you'd ask for a sandwich for lunch. The steward would be there with a ham and a razor shaving off a piece. Two pieces of bread, a little slice of ham, and they'd give you like a slice of pickle, he shaved the pickle and give it to you. It was terrible. It was so bad, we're going ashore buying pineapples and coconuts and eating them.

I did have a good second and third mate, though. The third mate I stood watch with was real good. They had what I call a Night of the Long Knives again. It was Sealand and Moore-McCormack Line. Moore-McCormack had been sold to U.S. Lines, too, somewhere around here. Night of the Long Knives: a purge. They were laying their ships up and shifting around and getting rid of their captains and chief mates. Guys were going crazy, looking for jobs, and they were back working out of the union hall instead of out of the company like a chief mate or a captain would go through the company even though he was union. Second and third mate jobs always came out of the union hall. Now the *chief* mate jobs are coming out of the union hall. "Reorganization" I guess they call it in the free world. Real good guys, both of them, the second mate and third mate I stood watch with. Very easy to get along with. The system had beat them, and they weren't gonna push.

But this ship was a wreck. I mean, it was a *wreck*. You know, if they were wrecks with Export Lines, Farrell Lines got them now, and they weren't putting any money into them. Everything's falling apart.

So, they had some brass left up there on the bridge of the ship. Most of the time you painted over the brass rather than try to keep it clean. Well, this had some brass. I'm not into cleaning things, I'm into fixing things. You want me down on deck, fix a runner, a wedge, a block, change a runner, grease, slush, working gear, I'm all for it. Splice lines, I'm all for that. Being up on the bridge of the ship shining brass doesn't do much for me when I'm supposed to be on wheel watch. See, there always was a fight there, when they put it on automatic, they wanted you to work on the bridge and clean it. There was just so much you could do. I mean, it's repetitive. It's useless.

Anyway, hit New York, and it was just cold and miserable, and we get out there, and the third mate's a good guy anyway. You didn't work on the weekends up on the bridge, but the next day, we hit some warm weather. We hit the Gulf Stream pretty quick that time, and we're going to West Africa. It was gonna be a warm-weather run. It's around the equator there. So I come up there. It's the third or fourth day out.

Third mate says, "The old man—" you know, the captain, and this takes a lot of balls, trust me, I've been doing this a long time— "says he wants the brass up here shined."

I says, "You're kidding."

He says, "No, I'm serious, Ron."

"Alright, mate, captain wants it shined, I'll shine it for him."

So he gives me this big can of Brasso. It's a liquid cleaner, and it's white and creamy and it sticks to your fingers and it's nasty. So I'm trying to clean the radiator, and I'm getting the little brass pieces on the clock and everything, and I'm shining. You know, put it on, you almost have to chip it off with a chipping hammer it gets so thick. And I'm thinking: This ain't gonna fucking work. But I shine it anyway.

He made the mistake of telling me—or he did me a favor, I still to this day do not know which, cuz I never asked—"Be careful with that, Ron, that's the only can of brass polish we got on board."

Well, we didn't have *food* on board—what the fuck do I care about brass polish?

So that night when we were up there—and I saw where he put it—he goes into the chart room for something. I go over to where he put it, got it, walk over to the wing of the bridge, and drop it over the side. Needless to say, we never had to shine brass on there again, cuz they were too cheap to buy any more of it.

Yeah. The big locker. We'll never fill it up. It went in the big locker. Yeah. Stowed it. Stowed it for good. Used that big locker a lot....

We stopped at the Azores on the way over, the Air Force base there. We dropped off food for them. That was what made the money for the run, cuz these West African ports, the only thing Farrell Lines was picking up was empty containers. All the other companies were bribing the officials. They were getting all the cocoa, the coffee. They're getting it all cuz they're kicking back, and American companies can't do that. They're not legally allowed. It's more empty containers for Farrell Lines, which you have to do if you're in the container trade, but it was just the idea.... You know, you get paid for *cargo*, not *containers*.

We get there, and you just talk about an armpit. The first port we went to had been a French possession. There's some French expatriates left there.

A couple of the guys were going ashore, and I was scared to death cuz VD was terrible over there.

One of the ABs, John, was constantly out there banging anything he could bang.

I says, "Man, me and you are OK, but I—"

He says, "Come on!"

I says, "I am *not* fucking with this." I'm not doing it. I says, "I'm not even gonna try a rubber." Vietnam was one thing, and I was a lot younger, but now I'm getting older. And it's catching up with me, you know, I'm starting to worry now. I never really got it bad, and I didn't want it, knock on wood—the nearest thing being my head.

He ended up getting a girlfriend that was working at the Liberian Maritime Consul, and these Liberian licenses almost anybody could get. That was a big thing going on for many, many years: you registered the ship in Liberia, and you sent your officers there, and if you held like an able seaman ticket in America, they'd give you a third mate license or a captain's license in Liberia. You could go on a Liberian ship as a captain.

So he had this girlfriend, mulatto girl, and she was following him up and down the coast. She was in love. I met her a couple of times, and we were actually gonna try to talk her into getting us all phony licenses, with our name on it without even paying. Why we didn't, I don't know. We were drinking too much.

But as we're doing this, as we're going up and down there, I'd ask the third mate every time we dock at another port: "Where are we now?"

He'd say, "Goddamn, Ron, I just told you."

I says, "Gee, I'm sorry, mate. All these ports look the same to me."

They all looked the same, whether it was an ex-French or ex-British port, it all looked the same.

John and one of the other guys had rented a hotel room, and, turn around, John says, "Hey, man, you gotta come up to the hotel room tonight."

I says, "Why is that?"

He says, "We got this Italian doctor off a Greek ship. He's staying up there drinking with us."

"An Italian doctor off a Greek ship?"

"Yeah. Some old guy."

And, I mean, this guy was old. He signed on to go on this Greek passenger ship as the doctor for the passengers.

He says, "My room is full of water. They expected me to stay there, so I quit. I got off. Now they don't want to fly me home."

So he's up there drinking with us, right? I go up there, we're all drinking. And I had dropped something on my toe.

I says, "Hey, doc, can you take a look at this?"

"Oh, yeah." He says, "Well, you're not gonna lose the nail, but maybe you will."

I says, "You think you could get me a 'Not Fit for Duty'?"

He says, "Sure." He just got some paper and wrote on it. He was giving us "Not Fit for Duties."

I says, "I want some prescriptions."

He's filling out prescriptions.

"Anything else I can do for you guys?"

Oh, God, that was just one big joke.

This one guy thought himself a lover, and he was gonna take every girl he met back to America with him. They were chasing him all over, everywhere we went.

But it was a dump, Liberia. Just falling apart. When the British and the French left, it just fell apart.

Years later, Bill Clinton went to one of these ports in Africa, where the slaves left from, and there was a worn stone by the pier. Well, what he *wasn't* saying—I was there. I saw it. I was actually *there*. But what actually happened was, they would take the slaves to an island that was nearby. *Then* they would take them to America or Bahamas or wherever they were gonna take them. They didn't take them *right from that step*. You know, Bill Clinton: "This is history." Right.

On the way back we stopped in the Azores, and we all went ashore and got fucked up drunk there again with the Portuguese. Next morning we're all drunk. We're supposed to undock. We were at what was called a tanker dock. There was a short pier we were up against, so only, say, maybe a third of the ship was actually touching something. The mooring lines for the bow and the stern were actually out on these dolphins, just pilings that are out away with nothing around them. We used to have to take a bolt and put them on them, and then we'd pull ourselves tight there. It's not really good. It's for a tanker, more or less. It's not for a freighter.

Then comes a storm the next fucking morning, and I'm laying there passed out, right?

The mate comes running through: "Turn to! We gotta turn to! We're losing the gangway! We gotta let go and get out of here! We're gonna lose the lines in the storm."

I says, "Yeah, mate, and I'm losing my mind."

We go out on the bow. Here the gangway's twisting up. We're trying to get to the lines to let them go. We're just all fucked up. We get out there, the ships rolling all over. Turn around, we got caught in a trough. You know, you just get caught, you're always in this trough. It's always pushing you. You can't get out of it.

I was up on the bridge, and I'm steering.

This good third mate I had with me, he says, "Gee, captain, this trough's something."

The captain says—he didn't like me, I didn't like him either, he took a dislike to me, I don't know why, maybe he found out I threw that Brasso over the side—the captain says, "Yeah, I think we're gonna be in this trough all day."

I says—and remember, the *food* is just *terrible* on this ship—"Yeah, captain, that's like that hamburger I ate. I think it's gonna stay with me all day."

The captain turned around and looked at me, and the third mate looked up and started laughing. The old man just walked off the bridge. You know, I mean, "captain" is one thing, but you gotta ask yourself: I'm gonna be captain of *this*? this *wreck*? But, poor guy, I guess that's all he could do.

Anyway, after a day or two of that, and as soon as it calmed down, I went up to the chief mate's room.

I says, "Excuse me, could I talk to you a minute?"

He says, "Sure, Ron."

I says, "You know about the 24-hour notice before we get in to quit?"

He says, "Yeah."

"I'm giving you 12 days notice. I quit."

"Ron, why don't you close the door and sit down there. Let me talk to you for a minute."

"Mate, I'll close the door, and I'll sit down, and you can talk to me for an hour, but I still quit."

"Ron, why don't you stay on here for awhile? It's not gonna be that bad." All this and that.

I says, "Mate, I appreciate that. I do. But I'm outta here." I go up to the bridge and tell the third mate I quit.

He says, "You quit? You're leaving me here?" He says, "I gotta make another trip on this fucking wreck."

It was hilarious. We got back to the States, and I quit.

Now shipping had gotten very bad. This is '84. They were laying up the older ships. Ronald Reagan was in. He had done away with the subsidies for the ships. There was a complete change of command. Reagan told the companies, "No more blanket subsidies for building and operating these ships. You're complaining you don't have the ships to make money with." Because some ships do use too much fuel. This is when they were going to diesel. They had started diesels a few years before that. All these ships were steam. They couldn't make any money with them cuz the price of fuel had gone so high. Only the independent companies that went under a subsidy could have their own ships built. Well, what he did was, he let the companies pick the ships they wanted, the rest of the ships went into the Ready Reserve Fleet, 30 on the east coast, 30 in the gulf, 30 west coast, in case of a war or a national emergency. So, basically, what the companies did was, they turned in the ships they didn't want, took the ones that were gonna be profitable, and the government got the junk. Some of these ships were 20-something years old already. Well, when Gulf War One started in '91, these ships had literally been just sitting there. Somebody might go down every 6 months and say, "Oh, yeah, the ship's wheel's still here. Engine room still there? Check. Engine there?

Check." Well, now Gulf War One starts. "We need ships! We got all these laid up. Go start 'em up." This is like parking a car from 1984 to 1991, out in the open in the street, and just leaving it sit, and you're gonna go there 5 years later and start it up? Duh. It don't work.

Anyway, that's basically what happened. That was the Reagan plan.

Shipping really got tight. Companies were going bankrupt. U.S. Lines went bankrupt. They bought Moore-McCormack, and then they went bankrupt, and they only had three tankers left that they were operating. Their freighter division was gone. Farrell Lines, they lost all their container ships. They were operating the ships that they had bought from Export Lines. It was getting bad. Like I said, the second and third mate had been chief mates with the Sealand, and Sealand was laying their ships up and giving them to the government. They were cutting back. For us it meant pay cuts and fewer opportunities to ship.

First trip around the world

I got extremely lucky, and I mean *extremely*. I turned around, and I caught the *Potomac Trader* on 7/30/84. It was a tanker, diesel. One year old. Each tank had its own pump, so they could do away with the pump men. They already had a cut-down crew on this, but this ship was actually meant to operate and had the automation to it to make up for everything. The only thing we had to worry about was tying up and letting go. That they hadn't automated.

I was lucky to catch this, and I was gonna stay there. I made a point of it. The pay was still very, very good. I was there for about four and a half years. It was running coastwise when I got it, and as shipping had tightened up, it was a very good paying job at the time, all things considered. I finally got off in '88. This is where I met Captain Dwyer. He was chief mate then. We're still fast friends. He still calls me for jobs.

This was a coastwise run. No adventure on coastwise. But it had its moments. We were doing coastwises, carrying oil products to the Gulf, to the east coast, back and forth. Coming around Miami, you get a lot of traffic, a lot of sail boats, pleasure boats, passenger ships. It gets kind of hectic there. We monitor channel 16 on the VHF all the time, it's the hailing and distress channel.

Well, one night we're up there between 0400 and 0800. Coming around the Keys up to Miami. We hear this voice come on at 16.

American voice, male, saying, "Coast Guard Miami Group, Coast Guard Miami Group, this is sailboat so-and-so. Come back."

And this is the Coast Guard monitoring: "This is Coast Guard Miami Group back to the vessel calling. What's the problem?"

He calls back: "Coast Guard Miami Group, this is the sailboat," I can't remember the name. I really can't. He says, "I need assistance. I'm sinking. I'm sinking. I am standing in 2 feet of water. I need assistance. Come back."

"This is Coast Guard Miami Group to the vessel sinking. Give us your position."

"Well, it's not actually a position. It's a location."

And you could hear a long pause, like—what the *fuck*? *Location?* So they says, "Sailboat calling Coast Guard Miami Group, what is your location?" Like: "What the fuck are you up to?"

"I'm at Del Ray Marina, and I'm tied up alongside the pier, but my sailboat's sinking, and I was wondering if you could come out and bring me some pumps to pump it out."

Now there's another fucking long pause.

"This is Coast Guard Miami Group back to the sailboat. Can't you contact the watchman at the marina? Come back."

"No, there's no watchman here. There's nobody here but me. I really could use some pumps. Miami Coast Guard Group come back."

Now it's the Coast Guard's turn, you know, there's probably three or four of them at the station, sitting there all fucking night listening to dumb shit. Like: "*Now* what do we tell this guy?" You know? Get off the fucking boat, you asshole? So they says, "This is Coast Guard Miami Group back to the vessel sinking. You'll have to call the fire department or something to bring you some pumps. You're not at sea. We can't do anything for you."

"This is sailboat back to Miami Coast Guard Group. I'm calling you on 16, distress channel."

"Call the fire department. Call the fire department. This is Coast Guard Miami Group out."

Just dumb. Just fucking dumb.

About this time, too, the 80s, Filipino nationals actually took over shipping. It was cheaper to hire them, and a lot of companies, even though they were American owned, were going to foreign flag and hiring Filipinos. They would be like 49% owned American and 51% owned foreign flag, and they could do this. It was profitable. Anyway, they're taking our jobs away from us. So you'd be out at sea anywhere, and all of a sudden on 16, cuz you have to listen to it all the time when you're at sea or at anchor, for hailing and distress, you would start hearing, "Filipino monkey, where'd you hide the banana?"

And then you'd hear, in like a Filipino voice, broken English, all agitated, "*Filipino no monkey! Filipino no monkey!*"

This would go on all watch, and it's driving you nuts up there cuz you gotta listen to this dumb shit.

One particular night that I remember distinctly, someone with a British accent got on there. Now, when you get into any port, you called for a pilot. You told the pilot what time you're gonna arrive, and if you'd like the pilot to board immediately, and this and that.

Now this Englishman had it down to a science. I mean, this was *good*. It would be like: "This is the *S.S. Banana* to harbor port control. We're requesting a banana pilot on board on arrival. Have the banana ladder—" instead of the pilot ladder "—banana ladder 2 meters from the water's edge, and have a load of bananas ready for payment."

Oh, this was good. I mean, he went through all kinds of extremes with it, just like we would be calling for an actual pilot, but he just inserted "banana" everywhere he could on that. It was terribly funny. We should have tape recorded it.

This goes on constantly. It's harassment more than anything. I mean, you're getting this constantly, and they've got it down pretty good. You don't hear it in the States much, along the coast, but when you get out overseas, you hear it constantly, the Filipino monkey.

But the living conditions on here were great, food was great, pay was great, and I says, "You know what?" I quit drinking again.

I had kind of a deal with Dave. I would do 120 days on, 60 days off. After 60 days on board, if it was permissible or possible, I would stand my four to eight in the evening watch in port. I would turn around and pay somebody to stand my four in the morning to eight, and I would go out and drink, every 60 days. That was kind of an unwritten law with Dave and me when I stood watch with him.

He says, "I gotta have you. Is that what it takes?"

"That's what it takes."

I used to go ashore and get him *Playboy* and *Hustler*.

He says, "Start with the smut and work your way down."

I still get along good with him. I still work for him.

Anyway, this is the first time I made a trip around the world.

The crew was pretty much the same crew that had stayed on for the coastwise runs and, like I said, I just needed the money. Good food. Good paying ship. They called me back. I was doing 120 days on, 60 days off, 120 days on.

They called me. It was my time to go back, and they says, "You mind going foreign?"

I says, "No, I usually sail foreign, anyway."

They says, "Good. We got a load of grain from Norfolk, Virginia to Karachi, Pakistan. Are you sure you want to go back?"

I says, "Yes, I do."

I joined the ship in Norfolk, Virginia. We had the usual crew. Captain Strom was there; he must have passed away by now. He was a great captain. He'd been sailing since World War II. Good guy. Dave Dwyer was steady chief mate on there, now Captain Dwyer.

Anyway, we load at Norfolk, a load of grain to cross the Atlantic into the Mediterranean through the Suez Canal and around to Karachi, Pakistan. Two weeks in Karachi. It was a trip.

We get to Karachi, Pakistan. We were too deep to go in. They had a small coaster, this old beat-out freighter. We had to discharge into them to lighten our load so we could get into the harbor. Greek captain, Egyptian officers and crew. They had rats running aboard. We had to tie up to it out at anchor, and they came out, and they put an evacuator on us. This thing looked like a cross between a cement mixer and a Model A Ford. You put one hose down into the grain through an opening in the deck, and the other one across to the other ship into their cargo hold. This thing would suck the grain out into their ship, and when they had so much of a load, they would take it in. I would say we were 3 miles, maybe less, to Karachi. You could see it from where we were.

This ship was paid by how much they carried, for the job of lightening us. Well, we finally got to the point where our draft is up that we didn't have to give them any more.

The Greek captain said that he was worried about stability, because he says he didn't have enough grain on board to get into Karachi. We're not talking a sea voyage here, we're talking 3 miles, *maybe*.

Captain Strom says, "Look, you're only trying to get more money, cuz you're getting paid by how much you carry." Right? "We're at our draft that we want to be to get in. That's it, we're not giving you any more. I'll have my crew cut your lines, and you're *gone*. That's it."

So now we go to the dock in Karachi, and it was just . . . just a shame. It really was. Another armpit of the world . . . . Terrible. Really nothing to do there but go to the international hotels and get newspapers.

It took 2 weeks for these evacuators on board to blow the grain onto the dock. You had *piles* of grain. I mean, it looked like a *mountain* of grain, so much so that they were actually building *scaffolds* ashore, and the pipes from our ship that were down into the grain would go up the evacuator that was on deck, and then they had to build the scaffolding because the grain kept piling up, they wanted to keep throwing it on top. So they built the scaffolding and moved the pipe up so it would keep going on top.

Their mode of transportation there was flatbed trucks that were decorated in different colors, supposed to ward off evil spirits, I believe it was. They would back up to this pile, and the Pakistanis would be down there on the dock by the truck, and they would load the bags. One would shovel into these grain bags. They would sew it up right there, after it was loaded, and they'd put it on a Pakistani's back, and he would run up these planks onto the flatbed truck and throw it on the bed of the truck and jump off and get in line and go around again. Back in the Stone Age again, you know? This was how they did things. But because they had more people than they needed, at least it kept them working. They had cranes in the yard, but they were all rusted out and done away with. A crane would probably have replaced 30 or 40 people. It was cheaper to pay the people than it was to keep that crane going. We were there for 2 weeks, and nothing really too much interesting happened. It was an everyday affair. We were basically looking forward to 2 weeks there, come back empty.

If you wanted a drink, you had to rent a hotel room, and they would bring the booze up to you, and you could drink in a hotel room. Women were a little different thing. Being a Muslim country, the taxi drivers would take you around to women who were willing to have sex for money. None of us really wanted to go along with that. We didn't like that little theory. It was dangerous: you're at the mercy of the taxi driver. You're out. They might go anywhere to a woman they knew that was willing to bang you. And they'd go there, and they wouldn't even be in a home. They'd go out, and the taxi driver would put her in the car with you, and they'd take you out to some field and just throw a blanket down and say, "OK, go at it. And then after you're done, I'll pick you up and take you back." Nobody was comfortable with that, except one of the ABs, Raymond.

He gets a taxi, wants a woman, everything's set, whatever price they were charging him.

It was a setup.

Turn around, go to the woman's house, Raymond goes in. The police show up. "This is illegal here. Where's your identification?"

Raymond shows them he's an American, shows his passport. They take his passport.

They says, "We're fining you,"—right there and then, no judge, no jury, nothing—"100 American dollars."

Raymond says, "I don't have 100 American."

They says, "Alright, let's go back to the ship."

They take him back to the ship. "We're gonna hold your passport here. You go see the captain. Get $100, and we'll give you your passport back."

Raymond goes up to the captain, explains what's going on, the captain gives him $100 advance draw against his pay. Raymond goes down, gives it to the police, he gets his passport, comes back on board.

That's how they do business there.

But this company, like I say, wasn't subsidized. The company had built these ships with their money, making their payments to the bank for the bank loan. They can do pretty much what they wanted to do. They didn't have to answer too many questions. American flag, though, American crew. Anyway, a day or two before we leave, they says, "We got a charter for you. When you're done there, go to Bombay, India, get a load of naphtha gas, and take it around to Japan."

So I'm gonna get a little more sea time out of this, which is OK, I wanted to get 120 days minimum out of this.

We go over to Bombay, about a day's run. It was actually an island off the coast of Bombay, India. They came on board to inspect the tanks to make sure there was nothing in them. We clean out the hatches, get the grain out, the little bit that was left over. We were supposed to be in Bombay 1 day. We were there 3 days.

Naphtha gas is a cleaning agent, but very volatile. It's just liquid coming into the tanks. That's all it is, pumped from ashore. We have pumps on board to pump it out for the six tanks. I think the longest they could pump was 8 hours; then they found water in the cargo. It was contaminated.

So we tell them, call the dock: "You gotta shut it down. You got water in there."

"OK. OK. We shut down. We shut down."

This went on for 3 days. Water and then shut down. Water and then shut down. The captain gave us all an afternoon off cuz it was slow loading like that.

So I go into town. You had to take the launch in, and when you got off the launch in Bombay at the pier area, there was a sign there—you know, you see signs in different ports, "Watch your step," "Observe your head," or something—there was a sign: "Beware of cobras."

It was me and somebody else. We got a taxi, did a little tour of Bombay. It was kind of interesting because you saw the big, nice hotels, very clean. You go three streets in off the main drag, absolute poverty, rotten streets. It was one extreme to the other three blocks away.

They have a place there, Faulkner Road. It's called The Street Where the Girls Live in Cages. This is like three or four blocks off the main drag. A dirt road. What it amounts to is: these are all prostitutes, and they live—well, they'll live in a storm pipe if they can, I mean, if you put the pipes there for a storm ditch and you don't put them in the ground quick enough, people move in—these girls are in a cubicle that they had built. Two rooms. One room is where they sat there, and they had a cloth hanging in front. They would close that to keep the sun or wind out. That's where they would sit during the day to prostitute themselves, and then the other room is where they slept or where you got laid, conducted business. That was it. The girls in cages. It wasn't actually a cage, but it looked like a door to a prison cell.

We got out and saw some Pakistani walking a donkey cart and then a Mercedes Benz going the other way. It was that way probably in 1920, and it hasn't changed. If we went back there today, it'd be the same thing.

Nothing on Faulkner Road, girls in cages, nothing appealed to us. Nothing looked that interesting. Turned around, we got back to the taxi.

He says, "Look, I'll tell you what. I'll take you up to this place that's real nice."

So we go up there, and there's quite a few girls sitting around. I really wasn't too interested in any of 'em until one of them said she was from Tibet. These girls actually had come from Tibet because there was nothing to do in Tibet. They had actually come down into India to become prostitutes. To me, it's like coming from America, where there's, you know, like land of opportunity. You don't have to prostitute yourself, you can go to work and earn a decent living, a good moral Christian thing, to a country like Tibet where there's no way of making a living except, I mean, we're talking like 300 years ago in America. You can be a farmer if you can farm mountains. But prostitution was perfectly acceptable, like it is in a lot of South American countries. And I'm talking about countries that are capitalist, Roman Catholic. And it's acceptable. There's no stigma on the girl or anything else. That's just the way they make their living.

Anyway, I says, "Gee"—not that I was that interested because none of the girls really there interested me—but I says, "Gee, getting oral sex from a girl from Tibet." I says, "I wonder how many people have done that?" I says, "OK." Sounded good to me. It was 15 or 20 dollars. The taxi driver usually got a little cut, too, cuz we paid him for taking us around. And that was about it, a blow job is a blow job is a blow job. After you get so many . . . . It's like one girlfriend said to me, "Oh, doesn't this just get better?" "No, it kind of gets to be the *same*." Like one girl told me, too, many, many years ago, I said, "Yeah, we're getting along pretty good." She said, "Well, it's really not the size of the penis, it's more like the ass behind it." It's all in how you look at it. What's good for one isn't good for the other. Not so much was it good: it was a girl from Tibet. I mean, I'm not egotistical or a collector by any stretch of the imagination, but here I am in Bombay, India, got a chance to get a blow job off a girl from Tibet, now who's gonna pass on that? I mean, *come on*. Right? I may never be here again. I might get killed on the way back to the ship. The ship might sink. But I got a blow job from a girl from Tibet while I was in Bombay, India. Oh. That impresses people. Doesn't impress me cuz I do it for a living.

But like I said, water was coming in constantly with this naphtha gas. Which is very flammable. I think all the water in it helped calm it down a little bit. We're carrying thousands of barrels of it. If you detonate, you're gone. You wouldn't even know it. Ammo, they figure 12 to 15 miles. Tanker, about the same thing. If you detonate with a volatile load, you're history. I mean, they won't even find your shoelaces. And the funny thing about that, we never got paid extra for that kind of cargo. You got paid extra for hauling ammunition, but you never got paid extra for hauling any kind of volatile, liquid cargo.

Anyway, we come back, and on the launch—we had this guy on the ship who was gay, and he happened to be on the launch—he says, "What did you do?"

I says, "I went ashore and got a blow job."

This guy looked at me and says, "You coulda got that on the ship."

This other guy, young third mate, happens to be with us in the launch, too. He just looked at him like—he wasn't wise to the ways of the world, I guess—he just looked at this *other* guy like: "What the fuck is this?"

We leave Bombay, and we're going around South of India up into the South China Sea. We're going down through the Straits of Malacca between Singapore and Indonesia. We got the pirate watch, cuz if you go slow enough and you're a small enough ship, and it's night, they probably will try to raid you. During the day they're fisherman, at night they're pirates. It's acceptable in that part of the world.

We go around. Now we hit a typhoon, coming up through the South China Sea. We get up on the Philippines. We're making like a mile a day. The captain headed us into it so the bow of the ship was going completely underwater and coming up again, like you see in the movies. The sea's washing back along the well deck, cascading off. It's hitting the house. Basically, instead of having the house in the middle, you've got the house on the stern of the ship, straight up. The wind hitting it is pushing us back, plus the sea's pushing us back. I've been in others, just as bad. To people out here in the free world, it would be like driving in a bad storm. You're scared, but you're driving in it. We don't have the luxury of pulling over. There's no pulling over to the Howard Johnson's and get a room or a cup of coffee and wait the storm out. I'll tell you, the North Atlantic was miserable. I mean, I've seen sheets of paint come off the side of the ship when we'd hit. The sea would catch a crack in the paint, and it would just sheer it right off, and you'd see sheets of black paint flying off. We found flying fish up on the bridge of the ship. Yeah. After a storm you'll go up and see if there's any damage or you'll go up there to clean up, see what's going on. We found fish up there. That's a hard hit. Scared? No more scared than driving through a monsoon rainstorm at night, no more scared than that. It's just that you can't pull over. You can't say, "This is bad, and I don't wanna drive in this. It's dark. It's pouring heavy rain. As soon as I see a rest stop, I'm gonna pull in and wait this out." But it's no more scary than that. Believe me, it isn't. I mean, you still sleep, you still eat. It's ridiculous to do anything else. You can't worry about the inevitable.

And the bell of the ship is up on the bow. It's strictly ornamental. I mean, they do use it, supposedly, with the anchor. Every time a shot goes out, you hit that many times with the bell. So about 100 foot per shot of anchor chain. When they had phones up on the bow, you'd use the bell. If you saw a light, you'd go one bell for starboard, two for port, and three bells were dead ahead. You'd ring it one, two, or three times. But they're pretty much ornamental now. Anyway, the ship's bell, *after* that storm, we found it back by the house. It had knocked the bell off and washed it all the way aft to the house.

But the one funny incident was when I came up on the bridge that day. Captain Strom wanted to always keep us going into the storm so we wouldn't roll. You're not making any time, but you're not *rolling*. It's the duty of the master to keep the ship on an even keel at all times. And Strom was good. Strom was very, very good, and Dave Dwyer learned from him. What was interesting was: I came up when Dave was chief mate with the four to eight watch. I came up at four in the afternoon, and Dave was putting down in the chart how far we'd gone.

Dave says, "Hey, Ron, look at this."

I came back into the chart room, cuz it was on automatic. In a matter of 24 hours, we'd gone 3.8 miles. I mean, we're almost stationary cuz we're getting hit and the wind's pushing us. We didn't feel it much cuz we were going into it. We weren't coming up and actually slamming. We're coming in and diving in and coming up and just getting pushed back. The spray was hitting the wheelhouse. Yeah. I mean, you could see it coming over the bow. We were low in the water. We're drawing a 32-foot draft. Maximum load. We're talking waves 50, 60 feet. You could see it coming.

But it's a small diesel engine on there. We could roughly do fourteen knots. That was our top speed. I'm getting a little ahead of myself, but at the end of the trip, they finally figured we went around the world, I think, at thirteen and a half knots. That was our average speed for the trip. But in the storm, we had the engine full ahead, and we had a digital indicator on the bridge to show our speed, and I was looking at it, and when we hit a wave, it showed we were going 1.7 knots astern, *backwards*. And then it's funny. You either laugh or you cry, you know.

Anyway, we get through that, and there was a little storm damage. It tore a few things off, knocked the bell back.

We get to Japan, and Japan was so expensive at the time, nobody even bothered going ashore. The agent came on for the company, and we're doing this and doing that, and we're asking about going somewhere.

He says, "You know, it's so expensive, forget it." He says, "If your pumps can do it, you'll be outta here in maybe 24 hours."

As I remember it, you had to walk along the sides of the pipeline, and there wasn't even a pier. The pipes were out there, and there was a little walkway on either side. When you got to the land, he said you could walk outside the gate. Said they were very lax there. Said he believed there was a bar out there, a little restaurant, and that was basically for the people that were on the pipeline. So we decided we didn't need it that much. So I didn't go ashore that time.

And Japan did get very, very expensive. It was ridiculous. Like I said, even back in the '70s after the Vietnam War, you could go ashore with $100, you were lucky if you could get half drunk, much less get laid, too. Forget it.

So we really didn't know what we were gonna do after that. We didn't know if we were gonna come back empty or what we were gonna do.

We got there, and the company had called and said that when we were done there, go across to Valdez, Alaska and pick up a load of crude oil and take it around to Beaumont, Texas, all the way down the Pacific west coast. That's when I said: Jesus Christ, that's what I've always want to do: go completely around the world on the same ship. Cuz when I started in '67 they were canceling those runs cuz it just wasn't profitable enough. I said, hey, this is cool.

So we leave.

The old man takes us along the Aleutian Islands. That was interesting. Whales are jumping out of the water. It was kind of a trip. We got up into Valdez and got the load. Dave Dwyer had gotten off. We got another chief mate, Dave's time was up. So we turned around, and we got into Valdez, and we got the oil. Went into town.

Valdez: very small place. There was one bar, the Pipeline Bar. There were some Inuits there. They can't do firewater, they were in there fucked up, and the girls got the kids with them, and I says, "I don't need this." You ever go to Alaska and you feel like living up there, bring your woman with you. That was a typical case of people just living together for companionship or somebody to bitch at, you know? Just a real small town. Not much there. But going up into Valdez through Cook Inlet, it did look like someplace a prehistoric monster could come out at you. That's the way it looked. The *town* looked prehistoric. The *area* looked prehistoric. You could see the aurora borealis, the Northern Lights. You like the outdoors, you like cold weather, you're an outdoorsman, you like squaw-type women? Hey, you got it. Go to Alaska, friend. That's where it's at. Me, I prefer an air-conditioned bar.

So we load there, and we had a spill. When you're loading cargo, even able seamen know it, you have to pay attention. When you're getting close to topping off, you tell them to slow it down because you have air bubbles coming in, and if you keep it going too fast, we have breathers that come out of the tanks, you can actually see the gas fumes coming out. If you get one of these bubbles in there, and it happens to go up there and burst, it'll spread oil out. If you have a spill on deck, that's not bad, you can clean that up. But if you get a spill over the side, you've got to notify the Coast Guard. They or the Valdez authority comes, and the port authority, they come and clean the oil up, and they fine you.

We basically told the chief mate, "Slow it down." Everybody's telling him, you know, but *he's* chief mate; this new guy, not Dave. *He* was in charge of the cargo. Second mate told him, third mate told him. *We* told him: "Slow it down."

"No, no, I wanna hurry up and get outta here." You know, brand new command: *I'm chief mate.* Nice guy, as I remember, but, anyway, he says, "It's OK, it's OK."

Sure enough, we get a bubble. It comes through, goes up through the breather, *pops* out of there, and goes over the side. It was on the starboard side. We're portside. So you gotta call, right? We call them up, and they come out, and they clean this little area. Oh, it must have been 2 or 3 months later, I'm back on the ship after the trip. And everybody agreed that that was a *pint* of oil. A *pint* of oil that hit the water. Five thousand dollar fine. Can you imagine what the *Exxon Valdez* was?

I'll say something here, too, about that *Exxon Valdez* incident. When I was on this tanker earlier, and this was before the incident with the *Exxon Valdez*, Captain Strom called everybody in the deck department up to his office and said, "I got a notice here from the United States Coast Guard. If we have an oil spill, it's on us to report it. Any oil goes into the water, we have to call the United States Coast Guard and say that we've spilled oil."

I said, "Excuse me, captain. This is an American-flag vessel, and it's still the United States of America." I said, "Aren't there laws against self-incrimination?"

He said, "We're not here to discuss that. This is a directive from the Coast Guard."

I said that then, and most people didn't care, but I did, because it's like rule by decree again. You know, in other words, let's pass a law, and fuck everybody else. And we'll catch 'em, and then we'll let 'em debate it in court, and it'll cost them money. Yeah. *We* the *people.*

You want the real *Exxon Valdez* story? I made a trip later on with the third mate, Greg Cousins, who was on watch when it happened. When Greg called the captain, Joe Hazelwood, up there, "We've run aground and we've got a spill," Hazelwood came up on the bridge, he called the Coast Guard and said, "I have a spill." After *everything* was done, all the *lawsuits*, the *trials*, the name calling, all the stupid shit, he's convicted, blah, blah, blah, he appealed it. The appeals court said, "Yeah, no criminal liability here because he informed on himself, and there's laws against self-incrimination." It was all that "for the people." So all you environmentalists and all you fucking assholes that wouldn't buy any Exxon products to protest that, what they do with the Alyeska Pipeline is, all these oil companies have so much of the Alyeska Pipeline, they're entitled to so much of the oil. Well, that's all Exxon did—cuz you didn't want to buy *their* products—is sell *their* oil to the other ones, so they *still* made fucking money. So when you were buying Texaco, or Mobil, or Gulf, or Shell, you know, that BP company, British Petroleum, you're putting the money in the queen's pocket. You know what? You were buying *Exxon* oil, *assholes.* Go and listen to the fucking news media, you poofs.

Anyway, we're up there loading, we get outta there, kind of un- eventful going down, just a nice run really, down to Panama. Didn't get a chance to go ashore and visit The Blue Goose. Piss me off.

Well, one thing was funny. We had that new chief mate. When you get to Panama you convoy through, but first you anchor out, wait in line. So I had the first wheel, six o'clock in the morning, we're gonna get the anchor up. We got the pilot on board. My watch partner's up on the bow. We got that new chief mate, and the captain sends the mate to go up on the bow and get the anchor up. He's standing by with the AB up there, to get the anchor up. The pilot, the captain, and myself are on the bridge.

So the pilot says, "OK, captain, tell your mate, get the anchor up, we're gonna get ready to get underway here."

We're sixth in line. And you've got to keep going. If something happens, you just fall out, you don't make the transit. It's that simple. They won't take you through if you have any problems.

Well, the poor guy goes up there, and they go to pull the anchor up, and one of the couplings for the hydraulic line, the pressure on it, it gave way. But now it's six o'clock in the morning. It's dark. When they try and put it on, it blows, diesel fuel is going all over the place, and it looks like steam.

The chief mate yells on the radio, "Anchor won't come up! It's spraying everywhere! It's just spraying! Something's going wrong here! Something's spraying! Spraying!"

This is on the radio. We can hear this.

The pilot says, "Captain, if we can't get the anchor up, we'll miss our turn. It will be tomorrow morning before we can try this again. We'll lose our turn."

The captain looked at him straight and says—this is how cool the captain was—"Lose our turn? I think I'm losing the chief mate up on the bow." He says back on the radio, "Hang in there, mate! I'm calling the engine room! The engineers are coming up!"

It took five minutes. They had to tighten it up. Everything's fine again. We go through, it's a pretty easy transit going through there. It's nice to do it once, hand steer it.

We get through, and we go up to Beaumont, Texas. When we found out in Alaska we were going around to Texas, Captain Strom said, "I'll have you guys home for Thanksgiving dinner."

We kind of looked at him like, "You know, captain, how can you guarantee that?"

But you know what? Got off the ship. He paid us off. They had our flights for us. I flew back to Jacksonville. Next day, I was eating Thanksgiving dinner at home.

With the loved ones. The ones who are dependent upon me.

Yes.

I was so terribly happy.

The only thing I remember hearing was: "I thought you were gonna make another trip on there?"

Yeah, that was fun. That was fun.

Remind me to tell you about the *Exxon Valdez*, the true story.

Towards the end there, after that trip around the world, we started running down to Periquitos, Mexico, the oil terminal there for the national oil company. We were actually chartered to the American government to take Mexican crude oil up the river at New Orleans and put it in the tanks in the ground for the oil reserves. Monstrous tanks underground. That's the oil for the country. It was that cheap fucking Mexico oil, that high sulfur stuff. We had vents to vent off the tanks, so you wouldn't get pressure in there from the oil movement. And if the wind was right, you'd get blowback into our air-conditioning units, you couldn't breathe in your room.

Periquitos wasn't bad. We could go right ashore, take the launch in. There was a little town, it was nice, a little Mexican happy deal. I nearly went to jail there.

I went ashore one night with my watch partner, a Puerto Rican

AB. He's a relief. My steady watch partner had gotten off. He wanted to go in after we got off at eight o'clock at night. We didn't have to turn to 'til four o'clock in the morning.

So I says, "Yeah, I'll go in with you. We'll get a couple of drinks, check the ladies out."

So we take the launch at eight o'clock. It was a little festive Mexican town, just like you see in the movies. They're playing some music. They have nothing, but they don't care, drinking, carrying on. A dirty little town, but the people were very clean. The girls were clean. I mean, they made a point of it. There was the occasional hooker running around here and there, but anyway, it was about 2 hours, and we really weren't drunk, and we figured we'd catch the eleven o'clock, the last launch back to the ship.

I ask at the bar, "Would it be possible to get a bottle of tequila?"

The lady says, "Si, si, get you tequila. Good tequila."

So I paid for it. I think I was just walking down the street with it, and I had to take a piss. So I walk around the corner, and I take a piss on a building, and we start walking back to the launch. Next thing I know, there's the police.

He's speaking Spanish, this other AB's telling me what he's saying: "What're we doing? It's against the law to urinate in the streets. You've gotta go to jail."

Come on. You know? I had twenty dollars in Mexican money, and I had a twenty dollar bill, American. Now the Puerto Rican guy's gonna go with me, see, to translate. We get to the jail. We just go in, and there's a wooden desk, and there's a guy with a suit on there as well, and five or six Mexicans in uniforms.

The coppers are saying, "We caught him urinating in the street."

So the Puerto Rican guy says, "What's the problem? He had to take a piss. He went around the corner."

"You can't do that here in Mexico. You can't urinate in the streets."

I says, "Look, partner, I'm not trying to offend anybody."

He says, "You gotta get a fine for that."

I says, "Gee, that wouldn't be exactly what I've got in my pocket, would it?"

He says, "It's probably gonna be close."

I pull out the twenty dollars worth of Mexican money.

He says, "You know, that'll probably cover the fine."

I reach in my other pocket and pull out the twenty and says, "I bet that twenty will cover the fine, and this will just probably be something extra I'm gonna leave here."

He grabs it, puts it in his pocket, and he tells the Puerto Rican AB in Spanish, "You tell him, he's a nice guy. We like him. He can go home now, but he don't get his tequila."

We walk out, no tequila, go back to the ship.

There's a moral there somewhere. Don't urinate in the street in Mexico, especially Periquitos, Mexico, and if you do, have at least $40 with you. And a bottle of tequila.

That was around the world, first time I did it. It took like 116 days, counting the stops and different ports and that, because I didn't get 120 days and they wouldn't give me transportation back to Jacksonville. I had to go 120 days, and I said I really didn't care, I'd pay my own way home. I just wanted to get off cuz the ship was scheduled to go back on the Valdez run, back and forth, and I didn't want to do it.

I wanted to take vacation and come back. I stayed on there until we started getting massive pay cuts, and they changed the work rules, and I said, "Well, I have to go now."

Plus the union kind of shafted us, too. At the time, the unions weren't what they used to be. With the subsidy program gone, everything got really competitive. They had cut our pay, officers and crew, and then they changed the work rules: the union, in its wisdom, made me Group 1 status, because of my high seniority. I could go into the Union Hall and get a job, even though shipping was tight, because I was Group 1.

The way they constructed it, they said now there was gonna be special contracts, rather than a standard contract, and if you were working for a company that had a special contract, it counted towards the pension, it counted towards your medical, but it didn't count to maintain your Group 1 status. You had to sail so many days a year to keep your Group 1 status.

So if I'd a stayed there on a special contract, I would have lost my Group 1, and if the company went bankrupt or I got fired, I would go back into the union as a Group 2, lower seniority. Shipping would have been a little harder then.

I asked Captain Strom about that. He said he'd ask personnel. We were doing coastwise. He explained to personnel that he had an able seaman thinking of quitting because he was gonna lose his Group 1 status with the union. I was doing 120 days on, 60 days off, 120 days on, 60 days off. If you worked that out, that'd be a calendar year. I was getting my pension credit and my medical time in, and I was getting 4 months off, 60 and 60.

And this was the answer that personnel gave me. Stop and think about this. He told me they said, "You could, on your vacation, go to the union hall and ship out on a standard contract ship for 60 days and then come back to the ship, to us. And you would get 120 days a year, and that would qualify you to stay 100 days a year on a standard contract ship, and you keep your Group 1 status."

I couldn't believe he even told me that. In other words, I was supposed to work 365 days a year. And I should be happy cuz I had a job. No weekends off, no holidays off, just get right off the ship—don't go home to my loved ones—just file for my vacation pay at the union hall and have a seat in the union hall and hope to get a job. Then I would have to get off after 60 days or within, you know, whenever I got the job, and then I could have maybe a few days with my loved ones or something and then I could go back to work again.

I might as well be in a penitentiary.

But why would I want weekends off when I could work? That four letter word. Everybody thought that four letter word was "fuck." I never thought that way. I thought that four letter word was "work."

Lord knows I tried, and He knows I tried, too. If it was work, I avoided it. I saw what work did to good people who came over to this country. They could have a job and own their own home. It's like a death sentence. They got sentenced to *life*. I saw it firsthand. I got to see everybody go to work, get the weekends off. But if they got a chance, they worked on weekends or they fixed up their house.

I knew better. Took one good look around, girls across the street didn't look that good, and I had no intention of feeding children. I had a hard enough time feeding myself. I said, "Nope, nope, can't do that."

I quit the ship. I quit in good graces, though. Matter of fact, when I went to quit, Captain Strom says, "You sure you don't want a vacation?"

I says, "No, captain. Thanks. It's time for me to go. I want to quit."

He says, "Well, OK." He says, "Next port."

I go up to see the captain in Texas there at the port.

He says, "It's nice having you, Ron."

I says, "Yeah, captain."

He says, "Sorry to see that you quit."

"Quit?" I'm kidding around. I says, "Captain, I thought I got fired."

He kind of looked me up and down and says, "Fired?" He says, "If the chief mate brought you in here to fire you, I'd fire the chief mate." He says, "Cuz it's easier to get a chief mate than it is a good AB."

I says, "Thanks, captain."

He says, "Oh, by the way, personnel wants to talk to you. Maybe we can work something out on this."

"Sure, captain. Not a problem." I says, "I just have to go now."

About 3 or 4 days after I was off the ship, I was back in Jax and the phone rang. It was the girl from personnel.

She says, "What happened?"

I says, "You know, anything I say will be construed as sour grapes. It was just time for me to go."

She says, "You still want to work for us?"

"Yeah, but I can't work steady." I says, "If you have a relief job that's 30 days or something, I'll be more than happy to take it for you."

"Alright. Thanks, Ron. I'll keep you on the list."

"Sure. No problem."

And what I did was: I was parting company with the girlfriend. It was a real drama. It was something about my work and my work record and bringing money in and her not working and her telling me how to spend my money and what *we* needed to do. For some reason, I didn't recognize her way of thinking. I don't know why. I mean, I'm *sure* she knew better than I did how to live my life.

I'm gonna get to one more story, what I know about the *Exxon Valdez*, as I made a trip with Greg Cousins, and he was on the *Exxon Valdez* when it happened.

You know, it's almost kind of like: what do you want him to do, join the Audubon Society? This guy was still shipping after the incident.

But Exxon did have what they called a golden handshake before these three ships came out, the *Exxon Valdez* and the two other new ones. They basically gave everybody their pension money in a lump sum. Well, some of them who knew weren't gonna get a job anywhere else, they agreed to stay with the company, cuz they were a company union. Rather than change unions or go away, they wanted to stay with Exxon. Exxon, in turn, gave them pay cuts for these new ships. I mean, they really walked on them. They were actually hiring third mates as able-bodied seamen, saying, "Oh, you'll get the next third mate job." Well, whose third mate job are they gonna get, you know, but somebody who had been with Exxon for years, who passed on the pension, the golden handshake, and was still trying to make a living, cuz for one reason or another they weren't old enough or didn't have enough money or weren't settled in life to really get out, didn't want to go to another union. There was a terrible conflict of interest there.

The captain took the heat for it because it's always the master. The master's damned if he does or damned if he doesn't. I don't know how much of this story I can tell, but there was more to meets the eye than just the idea of what the media said, you know, drunken sailor runs the ship aground. There was well more to it than that, and it was never made known until years later.

One article I read was saying they couldn't get a ship through an opening 10 miles wide. Well, it may have been 10 miles wide, but there's different shoals and reefs in there. And you've gotta stay clear of them. So your 10 miles is cut down considerably, especially when you've been up 16, 18 hours a day, trying to get that ship loaded at Valdez.

And when a ship leaves harbor, the Coast Guard, the pilots, only had to take the ship out so far. They said that was safe. The Coast Guard had a radar station monitoring the ship to say whether it was in the safe lanes. They had a 12 mile range on, not 24.

And the amount of paperwork for the captain is unbelievable. Even after they leave, and it has to be done in a certain amount of time.

I mean, this was a combination of things that led to this disaster. To put it off on just one person is just—the government or the Coast Guard or anybody that was in charge of that, just that way of, "Why open up a real can of worms?" "Why not just persecute one person?" Or "prosecute"? Persecute. I prefer "persecute."

Nobody really looked into it.

They came up with all kinds of stories about how a 10-year-old could take a ship through there. Well, that was the U.S. Coast Guard admiral that said that at the time on the news. I'd like to see him fucking take a ship through there. You know, he's been sailing that fucking desk for so fucking long, he outta get out there and pitch. To have somebody like that say something about somebody who's working under heavy conditions where you're working 12, 16 hours a day, trying to load without a spill. You've got all these restrictions on you that you have to have done, that you have to get completed before you can leave. I don't think he has that type of responsibility. Later, if I remember correctly, he took that statement back, that a 10-year-old could do it. But to even say something like that, that's pathetic.

So we're going through the Mediterranean, and at this time, the war in Bosnia was going on. The United Nations had put a restriction on all vessels going into the Adriatic, any arms that they were carrying to facilitate the war in Croatia or Bosnia. We constantly would hear on channel 16 as we're going through the Med where they would say, "This is aircraft such and such operating under United Nations mandate such and such to the vessel that's such and such position. What is your name, cargo, and destination?"

The main result of this—I'm gonna jump back again—was that the *Exxon Valdez*, the tanker itself, got banned. In other words, you're banning an inanimate object. That's like saying any time you buy a steak knife to cut your steak with, you can kill your spouse. I mean, come on. That was to appease the American public.

Anyway, we hear this girl's voice come on and say, "This is the *Exxon Mediterranean*." They changed the name. "This is the *Exxon Mediterranean*, oil, Trieste." Name, cargo, destination. We all just looked at each other.

One of the major players in that incident, that caused the accident, ends up getting a job, while the others got hung. Is it fair? I don't think it is. They all should have gone. If they're gonna get rid of one, get rid of everyone. But, you know, that's the way that works.

And, once again, the American public could care less. If you asked someone about it today, they probably wouldn't even know what you were talking about.

Stella Lykes

I caught the *Stella Lykes*, an older freighter, in Charleston. The Lykes Brothers had got a run to the west coast of South America that I heard about. These were still subsidized, so they had good wages. They had the same work rules, nobody on day work except that this was like the old style yet, where the subsidies and the government contract made 'em stay to this level.

I got on in Charleston, and we went up to New Jersey and then down to Miami. Then we stopped in Cartagena, Colombia. Laid back town. Nice. We caught it during the day. It was a big tourist thing from Miami to fly down there since they couldn't go to Cuba anymore. But no action cuz it was during the day and we had to go back.

We went through the canal, stopped at Rodman Naval Base, and I got a chance to go up to The Blue Goose. Made the run up there, saw all the girls, said hello. Beers and blow jobs. But the place had changed over the years. It was like history going down the tube. They had actually taken off the swinging doors and put on these big wooden doors, and they put air-conditioning units in the big, Roman arch-type windows. They had actually put air conditioners in there and cleaned the place up. I was shocked. History down the tubes. I mean, doesn't anybody care? Geez. The girls were still nice, though. Every manner of undress you can imagine.

Then we went to Buenaventura, Colombia, the other side of the canal. Dirty little town near Cali. I believe it was actually the port city for Cali. Down to Guayaquil, Ecuador. There was an island there we went to that was the discharging spot. It was the port city for Guayaquil. Didn't really bother going ashore. It was kind of dirty. We had numerous security guards because of their stowaway problem. Trying to get out of the country.

Then down to Lima, Peru, Callao, actually, the port city for Lima. Lima was a little inland. Very wide open, again, daytime, and we left and went down to Valparaiso, Chile, furthest south I had been at the time. Very nice place. A lot of retired Germans. I think they were war criminals. They were running the fish factories down there, the restaurants. Acquired a girlfriend at the seamen's club. We spent 4 or 5 days there.

When you were out walking, they had a thing there: the kids would stay up on the rooftops and they'd throw bags of dirt down on you, or whatever they could find. They'd try to hit you in the shoulder. And as you were trying to clean yourself up, the other part of the crew of the kids would run up like they were trying to clean it off, and they'd pick your pockets. Nice of them. Yeah.

But I acquired a girlfriend, and what was kind of funny about it was we were just going all over Valparaiso, and it was on the side of a hill, and they were actually going to build another city there because it was getting ready to slide off into the ocean. One night, I was half in the bag, and she always wanted to take busses, cuz it was cheaper. That made more money for her, right? The more she saved *your* money, the more *she* could get of it. Yeah, they were like that. They were always looking out for you. Kind of like in America. The more money they save *you*, the more money for *them*. But they're looking out for *your* best interests, of course. They always are, the loved ones. There's always a moral issue there.

Anyway, what was funny was the bus driver. We're waiting for the bus. So you know how busses kind of go slow and with the traffic, and this was at night. We get on this bus. I think there's three or four people on the bus, and this young kid's driving. Almost like he stole it, you know? He starts driving, and I mean he's *flying*. He's going around cars, driving anywhere he feels like. I mean, this is a *bus* he's maneuvering, right? The kid's just *flying*.

I says, "Give this kid some more money. Let's do this again sometime."

We had an obnoxious young chief mate on there. I believe it was in

Callao, Peru or Lima, Peru. The hookers would sneak on board. Nobody was supposed to let them, but it was almost impossible to stop them. The tide was low and the cap rail of the ship itself was almost at the level of the pier. So they would just run down the dock and jump on board. Guys are taking 'em to their rooms, having a little bit of time.

Anyway, this chief mate would sneak around and peek at you, see what you were doing.

This AB turns around, and he gets one girl in the room, and he tells her, "This guy wants you. Here's the money."

So he takes her up to the chief mate's room, and he opens up the door, and lets her go in. Doesn't turn the light on, though. It's just: "Wait here." He closes the door. Well, sooner or later, the girl turns the light on, feeling her way around in the dark. She wakes up the mate, and he starts screaming.

"*What the hell!?*" He comes running out in his shorts. "*Who did that?*"

She says, "They told me I was supposed to come in here and blow you."

"I'm not like that!"

Just to get even with him, you know, a little fun and games. Yeah, we took that up to Baltimore, and I got off. I only had one trip on there, but it was very enjoyable. Very, very enjoyable trip.

Rover

I got off the *Stella* and registered back in Charleston to keep going on these cuz these were nice little runs here. Of all things, American Trading called me up to go on the *Pennsylvania Trader*, which was just carrying gasoline along the coast for 30 days. The ship was falling apart. It was kind of ridiculous. I did it just for the money. Then I got off and went back up to Charleston. And what happens but the *Rover*. This is hilarious.

The *Rover*. This was Central Gulf Lines, used to be U.S. Lines. When U.S. Lines went bankrupt, it was overnight. I mean, I happened to see it on TV. You know, the economy's going down, and they showed a picture of New York from a helicopter, these U.S. Lines ships. They went broke overnight. As soon as they went broke, it was a charter with ammunition to go to Europe. It used to be the *American Rover*, an old break-bulk freighter with booms. As soon as they went broke, Central Gulf took them over.

This is when they really busted up the captains, or you really just kind of got put in your place. I see it on television. The captain that's on vacation from this ship sees it, too, the U.S. Lines captain, that U.S. Lines is broke, right? Guys are telling me this story when I get on board the *Rover*, now it had changed hands already. It had been awhile. They'd made a few trips as the *Rover*, 30-, 45-day round trips.

So this captain—he's living in upstate New York—sees this on the six o'clock news, he calls the company the next day and says, "This is captain so and so."

"Yeah, captain, well, look, we're just cleaning up around here. We're getting everything taken care of. Everything's going to the insurance companies and the bankruptcy court. What can we do for you?"

He says, "Well, I'm captain. I've been with the United States Lines 30 years, 20-some of it as captain. I just happened to hear about this on the news."

You know, "captain" is a big thing, right?

They says, "Look, captain, if we owe you money, talk to the bankruptcy court. We're cleaning up the offices here."

"What about the ship? Do I still have my job? Is the—"

"Captain, we gotta go."

We don't give a fuck about you, right?

But: "I'm captain!"

You know, don't overestimate your importance in this world. There's another lesson. You can be replaced. You're only penciled in. They got a big eraser. The big eraser. "We don't need you anymore." That's why God put erasers on pencils. "It's time for you to go."

He calls the agent for U.S. Lines: "I still got my gear on board that ship! I left it there cuz I didn't know this was gonna happen!"

They says, "Captain, we're sorry, but U.S. Lines owes us money, too. We can't represent you anymore. You're not the captain now."

He says, "What about my gear? What about—" You know: "I'm *captain*."

"Captain, what don't you understand about this? *You* didn't pay us. *U.S. Lines* paid us, and they're *not* paying us now. We don't care."

He calls the union, Masters, Mates and Pilots, in Wilmington, and he says, "Well, what about my—"

"Well, captain," they says, "this company's going over to Central Gulf Lines now. They're putting their own captains on. We've got word here."

"So what about my—"

"Captain, we don't know anything about that. We just know about the jobs. You don't have one anymore. You're gonna have to talk to—" So now it starts going in circles, talk to him about that, talk to them about the other.

He finally gets hold of the ship itself, the captain there, and says, "Some of my gear's on board there, captain."

He says, "Well, I just got on here." This was a couple of trips before I caught it. "Yeah, I just got on here, what do you want me to do with it?"

He says, "Can you send it up to me?"

"If you send me the money."

"What do you mean, send you the money?" You know, and: "What is all this?"

This captain actually flew down on his own to Wilmington to get his personal things off that ship. I think the union did help him out, getting on board and getting his personal stuff. What I'm getting at is: this is how you're repaid for 30 years of your life. You know. It's the big eraser. Yeah, the big eraser. "Well, you're gonna get your pension from the union. Talk to them. Well, talk to the agent. Well, U.S. Lines didn't pay us, we're not responsible. Talk to the company. We're bankrupt. Talk to the union."

Anyway, I catch this, and it's going over to Germany. It's just a trip. Matter of fact, the pay was low. I had this little watch partner, Pete. He was 3 foot laying or standing. Little midget. Used to be a racehorse jockey or some fucking thing.

He's telling me, "The guy you relieved, he always wanted to tie up. He never wanted to steer, so I used to steer. And he'd go dock or undock." And then he didn't want to climb up on the stack. Cuz we had ammo. You had to put that screen up there. He'd say, "He always used to do that." And he didn't want to do this, and he didn't want to do that.

I says, "You know, Pete, at the end of the trip, did he sign for your payoff and take your money, too?"

The guy couldn't do anything. Plus he was hard of hearing. Just useless. Just another useless thing.

So I'm only gonna make one trip on here. You know, I can see this right away. Oh, yeah. I don't need this. And it's a nowhere run: Bremerhaven, Germany. I did the usual. I went over to the seamen's club for the 1 day I got off.

On the way back, we undock, and everybody knew Pete was useless. He's up there steering. I undocked, and we have coffee at three o'clock. We're sitting in the mess hall, and the bosun's there, drinking coffee. I had a half hour yet to do on deck before my relief.

I says, "I have a choice now, don't I, bos'?"

He says, "What's that?"

"Do I go up and relieve Pete, cuz I know he's all fucked up up there, or do I go out on deck?"

The bosun started laughing. He says, "Why don't you go relieve Pete up on the wheel."

He couldn't steer. So I get up there.

Pete says, "What are you doing?"

"I got it, Pete."

He gave me the course. He's five degrees off. So I adjust, bring it over. He starts whining.

I says, "Go see the bosun."

He wanders off.

The captain walks up to me and says, "How many degrees off was he?" This is with the pilot up there, the mate on watch and the captain.

I says, "Five degrees, captain. I got it back on course now."

The captain grabs my arm and says, real sincere, "Thanks."

I says, "Yeah, don't worry about it."

"Do you really have to get off, Ron?"

"Yeah, I gotta go, captain. I gotta go."

I can see this. This is bullshit, and I'm leaving.

American Trader

I was still living in Jacksonville, and the company called me, American Trading. This was when I was gonna miss the pension credit for the year. I was hoping to get a Lykes Brothers ship out of Charleston and make a west coast to South America run, and I was cutting it really, really close. You had to have 195 sailing days in the calendar year to make a full pension credit. I had, like, 193. I had miscalculated or something. I was thinking I was gonna miss the pension credit for this year. The company called and said, "You want an AB job out on the west coast on the *American Trader*?" It used to be the *Sun Trader*, Sun Oil Company out of Philadelphia. They had chartered the ship to American Trading with the contract. This was after the *Valdez*, and everybody was worried about having their name on the TV like Exxon did. Bad PR. They had gotten this contract. It was on the grain run, but they had gotten this run to carry oil down from Valdez. That's when they didn't want their name mentioned. They agreed to let American Trading operate this. They could have the ship for a certain amount of time. All kind of deals to take it.

I says, "If you start my pay today, right now, you fly me out tonight, but my pay starts today, no matter when I get to the ship tonight," I says, "I'll take the job." Because I was calculating ahead of time before they had called what I needed, and if I went to work that day, the day they called, I would have 197 sailing days if I made it to the first of the year, which would have given me the pension credit.

They says, "Fine."

I says, "I only want to stay 60 days, 'til the first of the year."

"Stay as long as you want. We don't care."

They fly me out, I get to the ship. They had gotten pretty cheap. It was kind of a miserable operation, to be honest with you.

Anita Johnson was on there, though. She was on the *Potomac Trader*, really the first woman third mate I had stood watch with. Good mate, good person.

The captain on there was Brown. He only had one eye. He had gotten injured on the ship, and he was one eye, so, you know: One-eyed Brown. He was OK. What had happened was: he was sailing as chief mate, he was checking a tank, and something splashed up into his face and blinded him in the one eye. I believe he took a job for a settlement: "Gimme 50 cents, and I want the next captain's job that comes up." Poor guy. Later on he went under cuz the private company went under, and he had nowhere else to go.

Anyway, I'm there, I'm gonna do the job, I'm gonna put in my time, and I'm bailing outta here.

We had one goofy ordinary seaman. He was not a sociopath but—neurotic. He would buy one carton of Marlboro cigarettes and one carton of Salem, cuz he liked to switch. But rather than smoke through a pack of Marlboro and a pack of Salem, he sat in a room and he took a pack of Marlboro and a pack of Salem, boxes, and he took them all out, and then he would load them back into one pack, Marlboro, Salem, Marlboro, Salem, in that order. So he would smoke one Marlboro, one Salem, one Marlboro, one Salem. When you got time on your hands you do things like that.

We were going up to Valdez and coming back down, going into Richmond, California, and I was up on the bridge. We had the pilot on board. Captain Brown was there. It was foggy, but it had lifted.

The pilot says, "Captain, you wanna take the ship up?"

The captain says, "Let's go. Get this cargo in there." Then he says, "Wait a minute. I gotta go down for something. I'll be right back."

The pilot runs over and calls the pilot's association on the radio and says, "Is it OK to take the ship up?"

Which I thought was kind of strange. You know, *you* make the decision on the ship whether to go in.

The pilot's association says, "Yeah, take the ship up."

What I didn't know at the time was that this pilot had had an accident before, and he was very, very shaky. We're going up, we're getting into the dock, and there's a Texaco tanker docked ahead of us. The bow's sticking out towards us. We're low in the water, cuz we're loaded, and they're high in the water, cuz they just got through discharging. They had their mooring lines out. They got the flagstaff up on the bow of the ship, to run up the flag.

Anita was gonna be the officer on the bow docking. I was up there, and a few of the other crew, and we're getting ready to get the lines ready to put 'em ashore. All of a sudden, Anita yells, "Duck and cover! We're gonna collide!"

I look up, and here I see the bow of the Texaco tanker just coming at us. We're going to hit. The tugs are pulling already, cuz we had tied tugs up. The tugs are blowing horns, they're pulling. Found out later we're trying to go full astern, but the momentum is just driving us ahead.

Instead of ducking and covering like everybody else did, I take off running. I mean, I'm *running*. I ain't about to get crushed. *Fuck that.* You know, no matter what the officer says, you gotta think for yourself. I take off running aft. I stop. I look. I can still see 'em, we're still going. I take off running again toward the house. We were so low in the water, I was actually thinking of jumping over the side of the ship onto the pier. I stop one more time to look around. I stopped twice. The second time I stopped, I looked.

We had wedged in between the pier and the bow of the Texaco tanker. We're wedged in there, V-shaped. Our flagstaff and the bow had hit their mooring line. It *parted* it. The line just snapped; I saw it. We're still going in. We're *wedging* in. The tugs, now they're further back, they're pulling and pulling. We don't part the second line. The second line just bends the staff.

I turn to go again. As I'm running the second time, all of a sudden I'm flying forward but I'm looking aft. The tugs had finally got us and the full astern had finally kicked in and now they're pulling us back out. I'm thinking to myself, you know, I oughta—I've come close before, but this is close.

Make a long story short, what had happened was: the pilot is in charge, but the captain can take it from him. Well, this pilot had a problem before nobody knew about. He had done so much damage to another dock. That's why he had called ahead of time: "You really want me to do this?" He's shaky. When you get old, you get shaky like that. If I ever lose my nerve—I'm going anyway—but if I should lose my nerve within the next 8 months, I'll leave. When you lose your nerve out there, *leave*, cuz you're only gonna get people hurt or killed.

Turn around, we dock, we tie up. Now we got the Coast Guard. We got every fucking body coming down there.

The bow of the ship itself doesn't carry any oil. What we have up there is a storage locker. So much of the bow of the ship when you go down is hollow all the way down, for storage. And it was kind of ironic. This is what Sun Oil was trying to avoid, any problems. We didn't spill any oil, but they felt that the tug was pulling so hard it cracked the plates on the side of the ship. They're welded together. They hold the tanks in. But it was forward of number one tank, which was lucky. No oil's gonna spill. They found that damage. We had everybody down there, insurance company, everybody trying to figure out what the fuck's going on.

They figured we can pump the oil ashore, but we're gonna have to go to a lay berth and get that fixed. We don't have to go to a dry dock because it's well above the water line.

So, alright, now it's gonna be around Christmastime, and they knew we were all wanting to quit.

Basically, the company says, "Hey, just be here, no work."

So we go to a lay berth in San Francisco. We're tied up to the dock. There's no cargo activity from us or the shore. Shipyard workers came from across the street, actually, that was where the ship repair was. They built the scaffolding, and they're repairing this.

They pay us when we get there, but they says, "Don't quit. You don't have to do any work. We just want you guys here. We're gonna get this, and we're gonna get another trip." They didn't want to have to get another crew.

So we agreed to stay, on the ship, and it was really lax, easy. We had all the facilities, food, lodging.

And, you don't really think about where you go when you're there, you know, it's San Francisco, gay capital of the United States. Well, you walked out to the end of the pier, and if you walked across the street that's where the ship repair was. But you made a left and at the other pier was Olive Oyl's Bar. So, I'm thinking: well, it's maritime, Olive Oyl, Popeye.

So we're stopping in there at night for a couple of beers, nobody's really going into town. I see all these women, even women bartenders.

I says, "Man, this is great. There's all these fucking broads here." They're all dykes. Finally took me fucking 2 hours of sitting there to figure this out. Duh.

We get the repairs. We get this black kid, ordinary seaman. His father had shipped and was trying to get him started in the industry. Well, we're gonna go back up one more time to Alaska. I figured, "Well, I gotta make this trip back up there, come back, and I can quit. That's gonna be cool." But, this poor kid gets seasick on the way up, and he just stayed seasick, just all the way up, just throwing up everywhere, falling flat on his face, just all fucked up. Just fucking useless. I thought: this is no way to start. They put him out there and expect us to show him what to do.

By now the system was gone. There's no system anymore. You did—*whatever*. There's no *system* anymore. You turn to, and you don't know what to do, where to go. There's no *system*. Yeah, well, this guy's on watch, this guy ain't on watch. Before, everybody knew what their watches were, they knew what to do, where to go, how to dock, how to undock. Now they don't. The school doesn't show 'em much, and then they put him on board. Well, you can't show him because: how do you show him a system that doesn't exist? This is back in '89. It was like that in the '80s, all through the '80s; as soon as they did away with the subsidies, everything went downhill. But the kid, they're sending him to the doctor and this and that. They finally gave him some patches, but he's still falling all over the place.

We get this one guy, comes on board to make the trip, little black guy, didn't talk much. I thought it was kind of strange, but I didn't care. They had a deal in Alaska where, if you hire somebody from the lower 48, you bring them up to Alaska, and you lay them off or fire them, you gotta return them to the lower 48. Maybe only Seattle. You don't have to return them to Miami, Florida, if that's where they got the job at, but you gotta get them outta there. Well, we get up there, and if they thought you were intoxicated, they wouldn't let you go back onto the *property*, let alone the *ship*. This is after the *Exxon Valdez* incident. You didn't go on the *property* if you were intoxicated. The guards at the gate at Valdez had a room where you could sleep it off or lay down and try to take the test again.

This guy comes back from Valdez gassed up. So they won't let him come through, and they tell him to go to sleep. He goes in there and lays down, and I guess while nobody was looking he jumps up and tries to make it through the gate. He runs for it. Well, they catch him. Now they're not gonna let him come back at all.

So they call the ship, tell the captain, "Hey, this guy appeared intoxicated, and then he tried to breach the gate. That's trespassing. We're placing him under arrest."

The captain says, "He's fired."

Just like that. He's fired. Well, they call the agent from the jail.

The agent comes to the ship. "Captain, you gotta pay his way home."

He says, "No, I don't. There's nothing in the contract about that. He's fired. I don't have to pay his way home."

"Captain, there's a state law here. You brought him here? You fire him? You pay his way back."

The company had to pay his way to Seattle. The captain hated doing it, but he did it. He thought he was just gonna fire him, and that was gonna be the end of it.

We finally got back, and it was 1/13/90 down in Los Angeles.

It's Snow White, and he's looking for dwarves

I caught this out of Charleston. Another break-bulk freighter, west coast to South America. I got a two-trip relief, and it was enjoyable except for that crazy bosun we had. The guy had a lifetime job with Lykes Brothers. He was injured, and part of his settlement was that he had a lifetime job with Lykes as a bosun. He couldn't get fired, and he would use that.

Everybody wanted to kill him, right, and anytime somebody would grab him or threaten him, he'd grab his chest and go, "Oh, I'm having a heart attack, I'm having a heart attack." He was a real fucking cunt. Instead of just making the trip, you know . . . his wife divorced him, he lost everything, and he was a miserable prick. He was living in a house outside of Miami or the Keys or something like that. He was a fucking vagabond.

But it was a good run. Back down to the west coast of South America. You talk about just the idiot's delight again, here we go. Back down to Cartagena, Buenaventura, Panama, down to Lima, this was a great run. Plenty of women, plenty of booze, nobody cared. Money was good, it was the higher rate, cuz these were still subsidized vessels.

I made two trips on there. Very good operation. It was the same insanity that usually went with every trip.

Had a chief mate on there, Billy, from Charleston. Nice guy, young guy. I kind of felt sorry for him, in a way, because these ships were on the way out, the union was on its way out, Masters, Mates and Pilots. They were losing contracts right and left cuz the subsidies were gone, competitiveness, they started these other officer's unions, and, like

Reagan said, *compete*. Well, you get guys that needed jobs, they would take anything—you could form a union with just the leftover people that couldn't get jobs and offer them to these companies that were just starting up or buying ships and just—it's a two- or three-ship operation.

We had a couple of cadets on there, and you kind of break them in. They're gonna be officers. These guys were out of Kings Point, the federally subsidized maritime school.

The chief mate says to me, "Say, Ron, you going over to The Blue Goose when we get to Panama again?"

I says, "Yeah, I'll make a run over there."

He says, "You mind taking the cadets with you? I'll pay."

I says, "Well, yeah."

"I'm serious."

"Yeah, but I don't want to get them AIDS, either, or something. I mean, do they want to go? I mean, if they want to go, yeah, but let's explain this to them."

He says, "I'll pay for the girls for them."

"Fine."

I think it was $20, or $50, some fucking thing, by this time. They got the girls downstairs now. No upstairs anymore. You picked out the girl you wanted, you gave her the money, she gave it to the bartender or whoever, and you went back in a room and you freaked out with her for, like, 20 minutes or a half hour, the bell would ring, and that was it. I'm serious. It only rang in the room. They had changed everything from the upstairs. That was gone. That went when they took off the swinging doors, the old Wild West. They put on those big wooden doors and air-conditioning units, that was the end of that. They still had the old woman there, she was still washing out short-time towels for 50 cents. Like I said, I guess if you cut back on the soap a little bit, you'd probably make a profit on that.

What a fucking job that would be, huh? Washing out short-time towels.

Fucking unreal.

Fucking unreal.

So I took them over there, engine cadet and deck cadet. Two of 'em. Matter of fact, I taught the kid how to make monkey fists. A monkey fist is a knot, it goes on the end of a heaving line, and you throw it ashore, and then you tie on your mooring line, and then they pull the heaving line to get the mooring line.

He was really impressed.

"Oh, man," he says, "if you're ever up in," wherever he was from, he says, "you stop by the house. I'm living with my parents and everything."

I'm thinking, "Boy, your parents are sure gonna appreciate *that*." Yeah. "Mom, Dad, meet Ronnie. Ronnie took me over to The Blue Goose." I'm sure mom and dad would appreciate that.

So, yeah, they were willing to go, and we explained it to them. "Look, don't hold me responsible for any VD or AIDS or herpes or anything else you fucking get, man." It was agreed verbally between all of us, us four. I took them over there, and they had a good time. They enjoyed it. As I remember, the engine cadet was a little: "Well, I do have a girlfriend in the States . . . ." I'm thinking: "Yeah, you're gonna get along with this outfit." I mean, she's waiting for him at *home, pining* away, I'm sure.

When we were in New York, when they came on board, their parents brought them up to the ship, sending him off, mom and dad, the loved ones. They've both got their white uniforms on, officer's white, cadets. I'm on gangway, right? Just a pair of work boots, or my cowboy boots, or some baseball cap, pair of gloves hanging out of my pocket. I'm gangway watch saying, "Can I help you?"

"Cadets reporting for duty on board."

I says, "Why don't you leave your gear down here, and I'll get the mate on watch and he'll take your gear and you can"—you know, with the white outfits.

Later on, after I started working with him, he says, "What did you think when we first came on board?"

I says, "When I first saw you, you reminded me of Snow White, and I thought you were looking for dwarves." I says, "That's the only thing I could think of, with that white uniform." Snow White and he's looking for dwarves.

Almeria Lykes

N ow we come to the *Almeria Lykes*. I was there for awhile. I mean: I was *there*. This was a container ship. I was in Charleston. I was very lucky to get this one, too. I was on here 10/12/90 to 1//11/93.

Lykes Brothers had chartered the ship from States Lines. Everybody was scrambling to get these container ships. They called them seamasters. That was like the trade name. They used to call them the sea *monsters*, because if you lost the plant, that was it. You had one big boiler. You didn't have two. So if you lost one boiler, you always had another one to fall back on. It was like the diesels. If you lost the plant, you were in big trouble. I think if you did like an 8- to 10-degree list, a diesel engine will go. It'll die on you. Well, a steam plant, you can just damn near turn upside down and the steam will keep going. They were very good-running ships.

Anyway, this was going to the Mediterranean, and it even stopped at Piraeus, Greece once or twice. Be about 60-day trips, round trips, from the U.S. east coast. It actually initiated in Galveston, Texas, port outside of Houston. That's where you would payoff and sign on. It would go up the east coast to Charleston, then Norfolk and New Jersey. Or, on the way back, it would go to New Jersey, Norfolk, Charleston, and then Galveston to payoff.

I got on in Charleston, so they agreed to keep letting me come on and off in Charleston even though the payoff was in Galveston. We go over to Livorno, Italy; sometimes Piraeus, Greece; Alexandria, Egypt; Izmir, Turkey. We would stop in Izmir. That was the only place we really got overnight. Container facilities were further away from town.

So Izmir was the place. Everybody took off. They had a place there called The Canal. This was where the women were. I used to go out through the passenger dock terminal, and I always took extra cigarettes with me. They had the port police there. They were regular cops.

I show my pass, and they says, "Yeah, OK, no problem." And, always, four or five packs of cigarettes, I'd give 'em, because I knew that if I got arrested, they're gonna take me there first, and these guys—we could talk, you know? Things are negotiable here.

Then I'd go out and get a taxi, do the little tourist thing, look around. There was really nothing interesting. We could use the airport's PX there, cuz that's basically what we had was cargo for the U.S. Air Force that was stationed somewhere around there.

But, The Canal was the place. Matter of fact, the one time I went there, I'm in the taxi saying, "Canal, Canal"—I used to call it the Kennel. Finally, I'm saying "women."

"Oh . . . . Mademoiselle, mademoiselle."

I says, "Yeah, mademoiselle."

Failure of communication here.

We're driving, and there was a police station in front in the street, and then there was an alley. You walked down the alley, and there was a cop by this barricade. If you had packages, you left your package there. It cost you a buck, and they gave you a chip for your package. You couldn't bring any packages in. The cop would let you in through there.

The girls were in windows in buildings. You just walked around in a little enclosed city area. They had 'em 8 to 80, blind, crippled, and crazy. They had good-looking ones, and they had some real dogs. Girls would come in just to work a window for the night. The way I understand how it started was that these women were sentenced to be prostitutes, and they had to work off their fines there. But I'm sure it just evolved, cuz then I knew girls, I'd see them on the street and they'd be coming in. It wasn't my first time there.

But this one taxi driver, he goes right by it, cuz he used to drop me off by the police station, I'd pay him, then I'd walk in, take care of whatever I was gonna do, come back out, and I'd just start walking like I was going back, hail a taxi.

Unbeknownst to me, two blocks up, there's a taxi station! This guy goes right by The Canal, right by the police station.

I says, "No! No! Here!"

He says, "Wait, wait, wait, wait." He pulls around the corner to the taxi station.

I didn't know it was there. It was a bunch of taxis and the office. He parks the taxi. OK, right.

And he says, "Wait, wait, wait, wait." He goes in. Gives the keys for his taxi to the guy who's there, I guess the boss. We walk over to The Canal *together*. *He's* going there to get laid.

Yeah, I mean, you know, hey, what do I care?

I was there mainly because shipping was tough again, and I was there for years. I would do two trips on, one trip off. And it was great. Sometimes I'd take two trips off, but I always made a point of getting my pension credit in. But I was willing to share. So two guys could get it, they could get their time in, too. I didn't hog the job.

Pay was good, pretty easy going on there. You had the same fucking deadheads. The captain was a good guy. Chief mate was a good guy. At the time there was MEBA engineers on there, and Masters, Mates and Pilots were on there for the captain and mates.

They would eat in the same mess hall, and MEBA had gone on strike to save some jobs. As the subsidies came off the American ships, the companies were registering them under a foreign flag. With the subsidies gone, the companies owned these ships. They could do what they wanted; they had paid for them. But they wanted to get in on the American cargo. I think that's what it was.

Anyway, MEBA went on strike, and Masters, Mates and Pilots accused them of: "Oh, you're ruining what's left." Boy, if you walked into that mess hall, you could cut the tension with a knife. That's how thick it was. They're all just looking at each other.

I wasn't really drinking or getting in any trouble, cuz I had a good, decent job on there. I got along with the mate, I got along with the captain. I got along with everybody. You know, I'd go to my room. It was one man to a room. I just go to my room after my watch. Read books. History, religion. Politically incorrect things.

The only place I could have got in any trouble was in Izmir, Turkey, and I tried. But that was the only shot I gave it. The ship itself, got word we were gonna lay up, and they put us on a North Atlantic run for one trip. We turned around and went through Panama, empty, went to San Diego, and as it worked out, Sealand got the last year of the subsidy with that ship, and I had to get off. Otherwise, that's another one I probably would have still been with.

Seeing the world through a porthole

⚓

By this time, it may appear that I was slowing down. Yeah, I was getting older, and I couldn't drink the way I used to. But, you know, you wanted to get away from the booze every once in awhile, too. I was probably drinking more ashore than I was on the ships. It was good to get away from it. Plus these ports, you knew where to go and what to do and where the action was, depending on what you wanted. I usually went ashore by myself, maybe one other guy.

Containerization was taking over. I was seeing the world through a porthole. Get in and out of port, you're lucky if you're in port 24 hours. You never really get to go ashore, you're so far out. It's all about moving cargo. That was the only thing they cared about. The pay was good on those ships, comparatively. If you got a job, you held onto it. See, with that union at that time, when you got a steady job, you could stay, I think it was up to 120, 150 days, something like that. But then you had to take a vacation, you had to let somebody else work.

If you wanted to ship and you had a steady job, you didn't want to give it up. Shipping was tightening up that much. They always try to play it off, see, cuz the union didn't make money unless you had members working. If they paid their dues or not, if they couldn't work, obviously they're not gonna pay their dues and nobody young is gonna come in. The pension wasn't enough to let the guys go and say, "Hey, give it to somebody else for awhile." The money wasn't there to retire unless you wanted to retire, you were 55, you'd get minimum $350 a month. That's ridiculous.

So you would still have to go to work. The majority of guys figured, "Hey, I might as well stay there until I'm 65." And the container ships were not hard work. You didn't have to wing booms in. The most you had to do was tie up and let go. That was the hardest work you really did. It was pretty much an escape.

I can't speak for everybody else, but for myself, I personally would have preferred going to different ports, but this was the run I had gotten. I still had to make a living so I could keep up my drinking ashore and gambling and carousing. So, you know, I needed it.

Slowing down?

The mind was willing, but the flesh was weak. I knew I had to pick my shots. Like Izmir, Turkey. I knew we were close to town. I knew where to go and what to do and how to do it. The other ports, like Alexandria, Egypt, it wasn't worth it. It wasn't worth going ashore anymore.

I had been there I don't know how many times. You go out there, and you'd buy some souvenirs. You go into town, but what are you gonna see? Unless you wanted to take a tour and got the weekend off, you could go see the pyramids. That was it. You didn't find any real dyed-in-the-wool whorehouses, women hanging on you and shit like that. We're talking different cultures.

It was a lot easier to do it the way I was doing it, I felt. I'm not blowing smoke at myself, but everybody tells me I don't look like I'm 61. I *feel* like I'm 5 years older than God. But if you kind of keep a balance, or you try to, and that's what I tried to do.

When I was ashore, back up in Ohio outside of Cleveland, I was drinking every night. Down in Florida I'd drink every other night or so. But I got on board the ships, and like Dave used to tell me when I go to work for him now, he'd say, "I don't care what you do, just don't go on those 3-day drunks. If you want to go drink, let me know ahead of time, but I need you now for this."

Later on, he would actually be pissed off that I went ashore. I'd have to sneak ashore at some of these good ports that I knew. He would go to the gangway to see if I signed out, and he'd see my name on there. "You went in again, huh? Don't get all fucked up. I need you." And that's the way that worked. Cuz if you knew what you were doing, you stayed halfway sober or three-fourths sober or 99% sober, you had a good chance of getting a good fitness report. They'd want you back.

Those days of—"Oh, you're union, and we don't care how many times we fire you, we'll get you back"—those days were gone. The unions had rolled over. Matter of fact, NMU had started an alcohol and drug rehab program. You know, turn yourself in. So much for laws against self-incrimination, right? Turn yourself in. The Coast Guard was doing drug testing every 6 months. If you took a breathalyzer and were drunk on board, you were looking at a Coast Guard hearing and a suspension.

And with this union now that I'm with, if you're found with alcohol on board the ship, you go to the farm. They've got a farm where they put you into alcohol rehab, and you've gotta go there before you can register to ship with the union again.

Now there's nowhere to go. Before, you had a couple of unions and even non-union companies. You could jump around. They've cut each other's throat down to the point now, it's actually cheaper for the non-union companies to hire union, because they did away with all their personnel. They did away with their personnel in the office that did the employment. They write the union one check a month. They call the union hall for the jobs. It's easier.

Green Ridge

This was a different *Green Ridge* than the old one I was on, but it was Central Gulf Steamship Lines, and it had taken over the run of the *Rover*. The *Rover* had finally gotten scrapped. I got on there, and we had a captain with a real Napoleon complex. Let's call him Bob Smith. If I ever see him ashore, I'm gonna fucking punch him out. Everybody that's ever sailed with him wanted to do the same thing.

Jump ahead a little: I ran into a couple of cadets out in the Med that were coming through one of the ships there. This is like 2000, 2001. They said they had just worked there, they were kind of: "Boy, I hope this ship is OK."

I says, "Yeah, it's not bad."

They says, "Jesus Christ, we just got off a Central Gulf with Smith."

I says, "*Bob* Smith?"

"Yeah."

"If I ever see him I'm gonna punch him right in the fucking head."

"Hey, will you punch him a couple of times for us, too, and kick him?"

He was a miserable prick. That's the only way I can phrase it. He never gave a break. Always fucking with people.

It was from Sunny Point over to Germany again and back with ammo. They have a North Sea pilot you can pick up in Dartmouth, England when you're going by, for the English Channel, the North Sea. You can pick 'em up. The government pays for it. It doesn't cost the company a dime. It's a safety issue. They do it professionally. That's *all* they do. They *know* that run.

But Smith says, "I don't need a pilot. That's what I got mates for."

Instead of giving the mates a break, you know? Miserable fuck.

We had a girl for a mate on there, and she said she'd just come out of the Coast Guard. She had graduated from Texas Maritime with a third mate's license, but couldn't get a job. So she went in the Coast Guard. And she was OK.

We get out to sea, and he just says to her, "If you have any problems, ask Ron. He's been out here a long time."

So, for what they're paying *me*, *now* they want me to stand the third mate's watch, too? I never went for that. I'm there to help, but, I mean, it's just the idea . . . .

What's the Coast Guard gonna say if there's an incident? She's gonna say, "Well, I asked Ron"? Well, how about the captain?

And it wasn't cuz she's a woman. Most every ship I think I had one. We had them as cooks, then they came on as ABs, third mates, engineers. The maritime schools for officers were taking them, the services were taking them. What did I think of it? I didn't think of it. In my opinion, and opinions are like rectums, we all have them, some were better than others. Some were worse. Let's put it this way: If you put all the able seamen, men and women, the thousands that are there, into a paper bag and shook them up, and shook out six for each ship—there's six for every ship—you'd get the same thing.

Anyway, on this *Green Ridge*, I had slipped and fell about 4 feet, and I landed on more or less my heels. I got shooting pains in my feet. After that my feet would hurt. We got back to the States, and I went to the doctor.

The doctor says, "You got heel spurs. I recommend 30 days 'Not Fit for Duty.'"

I got back to the ship, and Smith says, "Well, yeah, it's late tonight, and I'm paying off tomorrow and . . . ."

I says, "Yeah, captain, I don't mind."

"Come up before the payoff, and I'll have everything ready for you."

So I go up before the payoff. One o'clock.

He says, "I don't have your paperwork here. I don't have your money ready yet."

I says, "Just give me the discharge captain, and I'll leave."

"*What?*"

"Give me the discharge. You can mail me a check."

"Well, well, uh . . . ." He didn't know what to say, because usually everybody's snarling, "*Give me that money! I want my money!*" I didn't care.

He couldn't believe it, and he was just being a prick: "Well, come back up in a half hour, and I'll have it for you." One of them deals. "Come back. Call back later."

He chased you around deck, followed you around and all that, seeing if you were working and shit. Yeah, this is the captain, doing shit like that.

Matter of fact, I had a young third mate out of school. Nice guy. He partied all over. His family had a few bucks. He was partying down in South America. The family was down there. But he was making his own way in the world. He was a good guy. He had brought a cup of coffee up to the bridge. I was on 12 to 4 with him. He put the cup of coffee up there, and he went out on the wing to check on something.

Smith comes up, sees this cup of coffee, says, "Is that yours?" I says, "No."

The third mate comes back, and he says, "Oh, hi, captain."

"Is that your coffee?"

He says, "Yeah."

"I don't allow any drinking or eating up here."

He didn't allow any smoking on the bridge, too. If you smoked out on the wing, you had to take the plastic ashtray out there with you. There's no plastic in the ocean, you know, you can't pollute anymore. They started those laws in the '80s, all your plastic has to go ashore. And I try not to, I try to butt 'em, and I try to throw the filters away on board. But, I mean, you go into a harbor around the Mediterranean and it's just *filthy*. Come on.

Anyway, if you took the ashtray up there, put it on the wing of the bridge, and you were smoking and you left it out there cuz you might want to go out for another cigarette, and he found it—no plastic in the ocean, right?—*he* would throw it over the side.

So what I did was, I got an old pop can, and I'd fill it with about a third of water. I'd put it in my shirt pocket. And when I'd go out to smoke, I'd put it in there, and then I'd take it down with me, cuz it was always in my shirt pocket.

He couldn't *stand* that, that I'd found a way around it. No plastic in the ocean, but it's OK for *him* to throw the ashtray in the ocean.

Now, see, that's another thing. The Coast Guard said with these new rules about drinking and everything else . . . fighting on board the ship. Years ago, if you were fighting on board the ship, you got logged for it. There was a Coast Guard hearing. If you were ashore and you got into a fight with a crew member, well, that was ashore. Nobody said anything.

Now, if you get in a fight ashore with one of the crew members, it's a Coast Guard offense. I think it's like 2 days or a day after you get off, if you still have a problem with somebody on that ship and you have it ashore, they can still give you the hearing. Yeah, I mean, they've extended the rules of engagement now.

Anyway, I get off on a medical. They had to operate and cut the ligaments. To make a long story short, this took 9 fucking months.

I was "Not Fit for Duty" from June '93 all the way around to March '94. I was "Not Fit for Duty" for that long.

Just before I'm leaving the captain says, "You didn't notify anybody about this injury when you fell."

I says, "I didn't know I was injured."

He says, "That's a fireable offense."

And I thought: "Do you honestly think I give a fuck?"

You know, he's reading me the riot act, I'm getting off on a medical, and he's not making it any easier on himself. Then I sued him over it. I didn't think I got what I should have for that, but—but I just—fuck 'em. You know? You get to a point where you just don't want to be bothered.

Second trip around the world

I'm "Fit for Duty" again, and I'm going back to ship out of Charleston. This *American Veteran* comes up, and it was the namesake of the first ship I was on. We turn around, I get the ship, and it's going to Germany.

It's what they call a LASH ship. It's a lighter aboard ship, it's a synonym. Basically, it's got a big crane that runs the length of the ship on rails. Everybody lives forward, up on the bow. The back of the ship is broken up into containers. There's two cranes, one for the barges and one for the containers, plus you could carry break-bulk cargo, open cargo. These were built during the height of the Cold War. Theoretically, these ships could go around the world without refueling. Seven or eight thousand miles. They were self-unloaders because they had their cranes on board. You didn't have to worry about going to the dock because some of the cargo was in these barges, and they could float. In other words, you could put them off the stern of the ship and drop it right down to the water's edge, and tugs could pick it up with lines and pull it ashore. This was marvelous, you know, in case there's a war somewhere where they couldn't get to the dock.

Funniest part about it was, commercially, they were a white elephant, because they couldn't carry enough of one cargo. They could carry so many containers, they could carry so much break-bulk cargo, and they could carry so many barges. Any other container ship, the containers go fore and aft. If you ever see a container ship and see the containers on board, sitting out there, they're all going fore and aft. The way they built these was side to side. So, basically, when you went to pick one up, you had to pick it up, turn it, and then turn it again, which was a waste of time, and more things to break down.

Anyway, they were gonna scrap this ship. It was a U.S. Lines ship. It was out of Diego Garcia, and when U.S. Lines went broke, nobody wanted the ship. So they were just gonna take it to India for scrap. I think it was something like $2 million scrap price to take it to India to cut it up. So I get on, and so I have another nowhere run, but I need the job. It had been running for about a year when I got it, and I says, "Well, I'll stay." The bosun was easy going. They were pretty easy going on there, the mates. Everybody's there to make a buck, you know?

We turn around, and we keep making runs from Sunny Point back and forth to Germany. July 22 we go to lay up, and, of all things, this company owes money. Most people don't know this, but if you're a steamship company and you owe money, before you get to leave port, you pay all your bills. They owed the shipyard in New Orleans, cuz that's where the ship went after they tried to get it in running shape. I don't know how many millions of dollars. Well, when the ship was running, they'd pay them so much. If it's in an American port, they would make the payments every month. If it's in an American port and you don't make the payment, they can grab the ship. U.S. Marshals grab it for back payment, right? We go to Freeport in the Bahamas to lay up. If it wasn't in the States, they couldn't grab the ship, see. This is great, right? Freeport's in the Bahamas. They're gonna pay our way back to the States. This is wonderful.

So we do that. That was July 22, '94. So we can stay in the Bahamas for a couple of days, party it up, and then fly back, and they'd call us again. They called and told me to be on the ship August 29. Only about a month off. Come back, we had a charter again. I says, "Hey, that sounds great."

This is gonna be my second trip around the world, same ship, same port, sign on, same port, pay off.

We turn around, and they says, "We gotta pick up military vehicles. You're gonna go near Istanbul, Turkey for a combined Air Force/Army maneuver. You're gonna drop the vehicles off there. You're gonna go to Piraeus, Greece and sit there for 2 to 3 weeks until this exercise is over. Pick their vehicles up and bring them back to the States."

I says, "Whoa, man, here we go." This is gonna be great. They fly us to Freeport, we go into Charleston, we load up. They put some Army guys on board with us, and we got a new chief mate. He liked to drink.

So I'm standing watch with the chief mate, 8 to 12. This is the trip with Greg Cousins, the third mate that was on the *Exxon Valdez*. He'd gotten fired from Exxon. He had got his money, his golden hand-shake, and he'd come in with MEBA to ship.

We treated him good. We didn't talk about it. You know, over the years, even after the incident, "Oh, man, why didn't somebody kill him?" "He's the one that caused all this bullshit now with all that." And, "He's still shipping after what he did?" But it was like: what was he gonna do? Join the Audubon Society and repent? You know what I mean? Come on. He was a good guy.

So, we're gonna do this, and then we're gonna go back to the States. Well, now everybody's figuring, "Oh, man, 3 weeks in Piraeus, Greece?" Oh, we had it all fucking figured out. Oh, we had it figured out. Yeah, we knew. Yeah. Cuz I had been to Piraeus already on that *Almeria Lykes*. You got in Piraeus, and you get off the main drag, and you get all the fucking slop holes. Yeah, here we go. Here we come, honey. You know, get ready. You got enough? You want some more? Here, take it all. You need some, too?

We're on our way, and we had these GIs on board there, techni-cally, to guard the cargo. They were National Guard, they were gonna be part of this. They had nothing to do. I think we were out about a day or two, and I'm up there, we're on automatic, chief mate is sitting in the captain's chair, just leaning back.

He says, "Check the radar, Ron, then I'll check it, then you check it. We're not gonna do too much around here."

"OK."

Here comes this GI, this National Guard, walking up, and neither mate or I say anything to him. He comes wandering in, and he's look-ing around. We're still not saying anything to him. He kind of looks at us, and we aren't saying anything.

He says, "Is it OK if I look around here?"

I says, "Well, yeah, it's OK. But whatever you do, don't touch anything."

"Oh, no, no, I won't."

I says, "We gotta be sure. So just tear your pants pockets out and keep your hands in your pockets. That'll give you something to do while you're up here."

Chief mate started *laughing*, and this kid's looking at us like, "Is he for real?"

I started laughing.

He's looking at us. "Wait a minute, this is like a bridge of a ship that's underway. It's not like anything I've seen in the movies."

The mate says, "I don't care, and you can see that Ron don't care." He says, "Do whatever you want to do. We don't give a fuck what you do up here."

He's looking around. I did show him around a little bit. But I told him, "Really, don't touch this or don't touch that, but you can look."

The chief mate says, "Hey, you wanna steer?"

The kid says, "I can steer the ship?"

"Yeah." The mate says, "Ron is gonna stand there, make sure you don't fuck up. Alright with you, Ron?"

I says, "Sure." I says, "You want to do this?"

"Yeah, I'd like to."

I says, "Basically, we're just trying to hold this course." I says, "Watch this automatic, and see if the course goes to the right, the rudder goes to the left. Goes to the left, goes to the right. I'm just saying you're just going the opposite of the way to hold this course." I says, "I'm very serious about this now. I'm not kidding you."

"Yeah, OK. OK." He had the little wheel, like power steering on a car.

I says, "Alright, when I pull up this switch from auto to hand, you're gonna have it. That rudder is just gonna go right to midships. And *you're* gonna be steering the ship."

He says, "You'll tell me."

"OK." I flip it over for him. "You got it. As soon as that rudder hits midships, start steering."

So it's moving, and he says, "Over here more?"

"Yeah, a little more."

"OK. Back here?"

"Yeah, back there."

This is like: it's so fucking boring it's pathetic.

He says, "Is that all there is to this?"

I says, "That's it, unless you got commands, where you gotta go, if you have to stop."

He says, "Can you put this back on automatic?"

I says, "Yeah, I got it."

That was the last time we saw him on the bridge. Yeah, the romance was gone. We didn't care. Going to sea, here's me and the chief mate, and we don't care. Yeah, this isn't like in the movies and the Navy and, you know, *Mutiny on the Bounty* and all the rest of that shit. What do we care? You want to steer? Sure, kid, we'll let you steer.

So we're on our way to Turkey, and we pick up these Navy Seabees somewhere, just breeze by to pick them up, in Crete. They're Seabees, truck drivers and construction, they're gonna take the vehicles off.

This one black kid, all he kept talking about was, "You guys get laid a lot? Do you guys get laid a lot?"

So I went ashore, and I found a whorehouse there in the little Turkish port. I think it was $15 or $20 for a blow job. We're in this port, and they're still getting the vehicles off. Now this is a slow process because they gotta pick 'em up, take 'em off. It's not like you have a ramp, drive them on, drive them off.

This black Navy Seabee says, "Did you go ashore?"

I says, "Yeah."

"Did you get laid?"

"Yeah, actually, there's a whorehouse up here. I got two blow jobs for 15 bucks."

He says, "You paid $7.50 for a blow job?"

I says, "Yeah, but you had to get two, you know, $15."

"Man, what was it for one?"

"I think it was $10, but you got two for $15."

"Man."

He was amazed.

Anyway, they get the cargo off, and we're waiting to go to Piraeus. Now, we're all, "Hey, we're gonna do this," right?

I ask the captain, "Excuse me, captain, I really never ask for any favors. But, the cargo's almost off, and we're going to Piraeus." I says, "Can I go up to Istanbul? I'll pay my own way, and I'll come back."

He says, "No, no, Ron. No."

I says, "Captain, if I should miss the ship, I'll pay my own way to Piraeus. I'm willing to do that."

"No, no, Ron. No." This is Captain Dan, young guy, 36 years old. If it was that chief mate, he'd a probably went for it.

I'm wondering why the fuck he won't let me do this. Here they had changed our orders without telling us. They told the captain, but they didn't tell us. We're getting ready to sail. The old man puts down Diego Garcia, Indian Ocean. We're going there to load old ammo to bring back to the States.

Our 3 weeks in Piraeus—*gone.* All my dreams, the dreams and hopes of *everybody*, gone! We were ready to mutiny over that one. Three weeks in Piraeus. Oh, we had it all figured out. Oh, we were going to Athens, we were going *everywhere.*

But, here we go. Through the Suez Canal, empty, for Diego Garcia, Indian Ocean, south of India, British Indian Ocean territory. The British ran out all the natives back in the late '60s, early '70s. Then after they ran all the people off, the U.S. Navy or the government rented it, and they said, "Oh, it's an uninhabited island." You know, right? And, "We're gonna rent it." I think it was about 4 or 5 years ago, the islanders finally sued the American government and the British government. Had to give them millions of dollars for evicting them. They went to the United Nations for throwing them off there. It's actually an extinct volcano. It's just a rim. It's not an island, it's the rim of an extinct volcano. They can keep up to 13 ships inside the harbor, which is the extinct volcano itself.

When it first started out, the French had it, they abandoned it, then the British took it over, and they used it as a coaling station. In other words, when you had ships that couldn't go completely around the world like this one could on one tank of fuel, you would get coal there. You would stop there, and they had chickens there, and some little population living there. From what I understand, they even made a little money on the coconut oil. They would sell it to the ships and make a few bucks on it. It was a coaling station is what is was, getting fresh water, stores, provisions.

Now ships travel around the world on one load. But Diego Garcia could take up to 13 ships, and they would stay there prepositioned in case of a war. It's loaded in the States with military cargo, and then it's placed strategically. In other words, say a war started in the Middle East. How long would it take for a ship to load in Charleston, South Carolina and get to Israel? Theory being, troops are there, too. So, the ship is ready to go, automatically, take everything to wherever it's needed, right? They have these in the Mediterranean now: prepositioned ships.

But anyway, they had barges in Diego Garcia. Some of these ships that they hadn't scrapped, they had barges like we had. So it was gonna be trading barges. We were gonna take the old ammo out and leave the new barges there. They were gonna load them with fresh ammo. It was a recycling deal.

We go there, and I says, "Jesus Christ."

There's nothing there for me. They got some Filipinos working on the island on 2-year contracts, some Brits, you're drunk every night, booze is cheap. They got a two-lane bowling alley, one movie theater. I mean, there is fucking nothing there. We end up being there a week or two.

Then we're gonna go back to the States with this old ammo. Port Chicago, San Francisco, California. Here we go. So the old man, instead of taking us—like I did the first round the world, going through the Straits of Malacca between Singapore and Indonesia—he takes us right through Indonesia and Java and Sumatra.

Well, this is the true South Seas. I mean, this is the *true* South Seas. It was beautiful. It was fucking unreal. He's taking us all the way through Indonesia, up and around the Philippines. This is *South Sea Tales* here, really.

We go up to the Philippines, hit a storm. The captain decides he's gonna save a day's pay, he's gonna go north because the storm's gonna subside around Guam, and we go north instead of going south, and we all *know* there's good weather because we're gonna save a day if we go north. We hit the storm. Takes 3 more days. Captain Dan, trying to save some time. He's a nice guy, but, you know, they always wanted to save something for the company.

OK, we get to Port Chicago, California, and they're discharging the ammunition. Get paid off from the foreign voyage.

Captain says, "You want to stay, Ron?"

I says, "Yeah, but, what are we gonna do?"

He says, "We're not sure yet," but, when the government charters the ship, they're supposed to pay it to the port that we originated from.

I says, "Are we going back to Freeport?" Which is OK with me.

"Looks that way, Ron."

"Yeah, I'll go."

Went through Panama, didn't stop at The Blue Goose. Fuck, you know? We turn around, and we went to Freeport in the Bahamas. So now that's completely around the world, original port back to the original port, twice now.

They says, "For insurance purposes, we have to leave somebody from the deck department and somebody from the engine room on here. We gotta leave an engineer, but we can leave an unlicensed here in Freeport for up to a month. We'll give you per diem for food, plus you can eat the food on the ship."

So we're eating the food out of the ship. At one bar I was trading it for booze. We're putting in like 4 hours a day. Rented us a car, myself and the engineer, we're driving on the left side of the road, and he says, "You gotta learn to drive like this."

I says, "Jesus, it's just like driving when I'm drunk, on the wrong side of the road." It's cool when you get into it, you just gotta keep thinking, "Left, left."

We're partying up in the islands, and it was a good 3 weeks of this, living on board, doing anything we wanted to do. Man, those 3 weeks went by.

Then: "Oh, well, that's it. You gotta go. We don't need anybody anymore."

We got off and came back, and they says, "Can we call you if we get another run?"

I says, "Sure. More than happy to. I liked it on there."

Matter of fact, me and Dave left some booze on there. He says, "When we come back, Ron, we'll have something to drink."

"OK."

It was 2 months later they called me back. "Would you like to come back?"

I says, "Yeah."

They says, "Well, we got some bad news. We're gonna scrap the ship after the run."

I says, "That's a shame, but I'll make it."

We went to Galveston, Texas from Freeport.

I should say, too, when we used to lay up in Freeport in the Bahamas, the berth they tied us up to was across from a passenger dock terminal and the passenger ships. They used to come in like every third day. They always came in about, oh, seven o'clock in the morning, be tied up by eight or eight thirty, and then people could go ashore.

They were right across from us, and I used to go up to the bridge, early, say seven o'clock, and I'd bring some coffee, and I'd get the binoculars out, and I'd look at the portholes. I could see the people in the portholes, right?

So I was getting a little show going there, you know, start my day off right. I'd be scanning the portholes, looking for the open porthole, curtains open. You'd be surprised what you saw . . . .

Anyway, Dave comes up there one day and says, "What are you doing up here?"

I says, "The other pair of binoculars are in the locker there. Go ahead and grab them." I says, "Third porthole to the left, go up from the waterline."

"*Why didn't you tell me about this earlier?*"

"I just found out about it myself."

That was our little enjoyment for the day, start the day off right. It was something to do, it broke the monotony of work on board the ship. And, we could do it. I think that's why we did it, really, just cuz we could. A little fringe benefit of having a ship laid up in Freeport.

Anyway, they flew us over there. We went to Galveston, Texas, to load grain, to go to Batumi, Republic of Georgia, in the Black Sea. I'd never been there. And then maybe scrap the ship in India.

I says, "Yeah, this sounds good to me."

Get on there, here's the same bunch coming back. There we all are in Freeport. You know: "Welcome back!" We got plenty of booze here. You know, we're gonna do this. We go over to Galveston, load the grain. Go through the Med, you go through the Bosphorus by Istanbul. It's as far as you can go, Batumi, Republic of Georgia. They had just come out from beneath communism at the time. They were free. We hadn't been the first American ship there, but I don't think they were used to being around Americans.

It looked like Cleveland, Ohio in the '50s. They still had the old rail trolleys with the cable, and if it jumped off the cable, the driver would have to go up with a hook and hook it back up. Remember how you'd see those newspaper articles, how people in Russia stood in breadlines? You know, showing how good *we* had it over here. Like, *we* had all this bread, and *they* had to wait in bread lines. Well, that was the impression it gave. That was the first ex-communist country that I'd been to—not that I've been to a lot of them—but that's how they buy their bread. In the evening, when they go home from work, they buy a fresh loaf of bread. They go to the bread store and stand in line and buy their loaf of bread. That's their bread for dinner. That's their bread for breakfast and lunch the next day, too. *Then* they get another fresh loaf the next evening. It's not like us buying 12 loaves, shove it in the freezer, and we have "fresh" bread every day. You know, we don't have to *stand in lines*, see, cuz we got fresh bread in our *freezer*, even if it's been there for 6 months, it's still good, right? This is the way it was. It was like eight cents a loaf. Very good bread, I liked it, everybody liked it. Matter of fact, it was so cheap, I bought four or five loaves and brought it back to the ship and gave it to everybody.

When we got there, we had unloaded some of the grain into barges, it was the same thing with these evacuators. If they'd used evacuators, we weren't gonna be there any time at all. But they still had the old train setup, and the overhead cranes that would actually come and scoop it out of the hatches. The theory still was: keep people working. So they didn't want to use the evacuators. They wanted to keep people working. The more vodka they gave 'em, the more they worked. Yeah. I mean, eight o'clock in the morning, I'm on gangway security, and they're opening bottles of vodka, these Georgians.

They says, "You like? You like?"

I says, "Yeah, but not at eight o'clock in the morning."

They're all fucked up. We're trying to converse back and forth with them and this and that. They all got something to sell.

It was the old system yet, where you had a gate you had to walk to to get outta there. We got a pass, and we were told: "Don't lose your pass, cuz if you lose your pass you're not going out anymore." If you walked out, showed them your pass, you walked to the right, across the street, there was almost like a park. In there were different stores, buildings and that, and they had one rat hole bar that was run by Georgians. You talk about a hole in the wall. I mean, the wires for the electricity were all outside on the walls. Everybody's trying to get laid or get made up with somebody. They had an Armenian girl there who was a hooker, but she was cross-eyed. We used to go in there and drink, and then some of us would venture into town.

They had sheep and cattle wandering all over. What they were doing was: they would pull the trains up, open boxcars, and then these cranes would come over, scoop the grain out, and put it in. After they filled the boxcar up, they'd have to wait to get those out of the way. And this grain is spilling out. The cattle are coming to eat it, the sheep are coming to eat it, the goats, everybody's coming to eat this, the birds, dogs. Even the Georgians are packing it up, taking it home to feed their chickens. They had some wild chickens that were in this area outside the gate. They couldn't get in the yard like the cows and the goats and the sheep and the dogs. So I used to grab a handful of this stuff. Those chickens were all scrounging around. I'd take it there and throw it out there for them. Oh, they loved me. They remembered me coming every time.

I did wander around the town quite a bit. We had this one kid hanging around us, I guess he was 16 or 17, he spoke Georgian, Russian, English, and Turkish. He spoke these four languages, and some of the guys on the ship barely spoke English. I'd wander around with him, he'd show me around. And it was a common fact that there were more millionaires in the Republic of Georgia under communism than there was now that they were free. Because now they could *leave*.

Under communism, if they wanted to leave, they would have to give the communist party the million dollars, and then they'd let 'em go. Yeah, just how corrupt it was.

Then I ended up with Sylvia. She could understand some words; like, I'd say something to her in English, and she would turn her head to look at me, and that turning of the head was, "I'm trying to understand what he's saying." I met her at that bar.

They did have an international club there, it wasn't a seamen's club. This was a carryover from the commies, too. One woman there, used to call her the Dragon Lady, she was an old Russian woman, used to work for the KGB when they were commies. She didn't get along with everybody, but a lot of the girls would come in because you'd meet foreigners. Everybody would say, "Watch out, they just want to marry you and get to America." I didn't think they actually wanted to get to America. I think they just wanted to get married, you know? Whether it's in Georgia or anywhere else.

One day, the bosun and I took a little tour with the taxi, just going around. At the time you could buy an apartment building from the government for $25,000 American, if you had some venture capital. I happened to mention that to one guy.

I says, "You know, $25,000 for an apartment building. I wonder how that would work."

He says, "You're not married, are you?"

I says, "No, I'm not."

He says, "Families would be bringing their *daughters* over to see you." You know, for *this*.

So, the girls at the international club, they tried to be friendly, but you always got that impression they were gonna be friendly *anyway*. You had local hoodlums come up there for the dealing, too.

I remembered seeing on television in the States, when they finally got their freedom, they showed Batumi, Republic of Georgia, where there's this obelisk going up by the beach, with a bust of Lenin up there. It showed this kid shimmying up, knocking the head of Lenin off. Then they showed this building they were burning, KGB head-quarters. *Now* I'm walking down the road there along the harbor, here I see that. I'm *there*. I'm touching this, what I saw on TV a year or two earlier. I'm actually touching history. It was real.

Like in England, I touched part of Hadrian's Wall. It's like things I've seen on television, I'm actually living now.

Sylvia and I happened to be walking by a building one time. I'm just trying to make conversation, and I see this yellow tape around it, and it's burned down.

I says, "The Georgia people gonna renew this?"

She looked at me strange. She says, "This was KGB headquarters. Why would we want to rebuild this?"

I'd seen this burning on TV, a couple of years before. It was strange.

She was living in two rooms with her son, Gregory. She was from the Ukraine, but like anywhere else, they had traveled in the Soviet Union, and she met a guy and came there, got married, and then they got divorced. She got to know him, got married, *then* she got to know him *better*, and they got divorced. She was looking for a job. She was a masseuse. I'd hate to have to fistfight with her.

That kid I was going around with, we were giving them so much stuff, the police actually got him because they said you're not sup-posed to be going to see the ship. They slapped him around, took the bars of soap away from him that we gave him.

I says, "Why don't you give them half?"

"Give them half?"

I says, "Yeah. Say, 'Hey, whatever they give me, I'll give you guys half.'"

Because one night Sylvia and I were walking down the street, and the plains clothes police had set up a roadblock to stop cars. They were stopping cars and looking for stuff.

I says, "What are they looking for, terrorists, robbers?"

She says, "No, they're looking to see what they can find. If you're not supposed to have it, they'll take it and sell it to somebody else. Or if they find it and you have some money, they take that, then let you go."

"OK."

Round and round we go. Evil web we spin.

We get the grain done there, we're there like 2 weeks. It was interesting to see, like I said, the first communist country, other than Mozambique, where it went from capitalist to communist. This is going from communist to capitalism. And they couldn't quite fathom it.

Now we're waiting, and they're trying to get us a cargo, because if you transit the Suez Canal with cargo, they pay for like three-fourths of the load. Of all things, the company finds a cargo in Mariupol, Ukraine, in the Sea of Azov, the shallowest sea in the world.

Come time to leave, the agent and the Dragon Lady were there. I should point out, too, that the Dragon Lady, when she came on when we first docked there, she said that to have the services of the International Club would be $50 for every crew member, that they could come there and pay the $50, and then they would have the privilege of going there.

The captain says, "Let's work a deal. How much do you want, and all the crew can go there?"

You know, it's always "let's make a deal." So I think it was half, and the captain agreed to pay it out of petty cash, so any of us could go up to the club.

But when we were leaving, we had, of all things—I used to call him Turhan Bey. He stayed on board with us. He was an Indian that was doing the expediting of the cargo. I used to call him Turhan Bey, after an old 1930s actor that I used to see in the movies. The thing was, nobody knew what happened to Turhan Bey. It was like he made 12 movies and disappeared. Nobody ever saw him again. So he's up there. And the Dragon Lady. I don't know how she got in on this, but she was handing him bills. The agent's handing bills to the captain. This all has to be paid, you know.

But this Turhan Bey was wandering around saying, "You are screwing me royally." It was kind of funny the way he was saying it. "You are screwing me royally."

I don't know how many bills they put off on him. This is all just to *leave*.

And I was thinking: here comes capitalism. Here it comes.

Now, the Sea of Azov is the shallowest sea in the world. We were the first American ship to come there since World War II. To get in here, it's a 30-, 32-foot draft. We actually dredged them out a channel cuz, even light in the water, we're still drawing 32 feet. And if you pump out any more water and come above 32 feet, you're taking a chance on stability, no matter how calm it is. If the captain does that, he's got big headaches, if something happens. Matter of fact, they didn't even have charts. We're waiting there to go in, go through the strait.

They came out in the launch. "You got cigarettes? You got cigarettes?"

I says, "No. We need charts. The captain's got me down here to get charts."

"You got American cigarettes?"

"You got charts?"

They sent me up some charts. I had a few Marlboros in a pack, so I threw them down. I took the charts up to the bridge.

The old man says—Captain Dan, old man, 36 years old, you know—"These charts are from fucking World War II! Don't they have any newer?"

So the pilot calls back. "We need newer charts."

So they come back. "You got cigarettes?"

I says, "Yeah, if you give me the right charts, I got some cigarettes."

They got some newer charts out. More cigarettes. So we go in and dock.

The Ukrainian Army came on board along with the agent when we got to the dock, and they said that we had to wait there for the cargo, the chemical fertilizer. They all wanted those cigarettes. If you want something done anywhere, cigarettes are always a good squeeze.

They were independent at the time. But they hadn't changed even *more* than the Georgians.

They issued us our passes, and told us the same thing: don't lose the pass. If you lose the pass, that's it. You don't go ashore anymore. It was Ukrainian Army down on the dock. You showed them the pass when you walked down, and you showed them the pass when you came back. You didn't have the pass when you came back, they called somebody, he'd come down, and that was it. You were restricted after that.

They had what they called the worker's-seamen's club. That's where the girls used to meet after work. They were making a little bit of an effort to get in on capitalism, although they didn't understand it. Their money was coupons, and they had what almost looked like a porta pot on corners of the streets. You went there to exchange foreign money for coupons. These coupons were no good anywhere else but Ukraine. Nobody wanted 'em. But if you wanted to go buy bread or something, they wanted coupons, or somebody would change the money for you. Anybody could make a few bucks on it. The black market used rubles.

We're going to the club, the watering hole, back and forth. Met this girl, Uraina, a tall Ukrainian girl. We're having little meetings there, discussions about America.

She tells me, "I don't like Ukrainian men or Russian men. They drink too much."

I says, "You have seen nothing yet. Wait 'til you see the Americans come in here."

They would ask questions about America. They spoke English, or they would try their English out on us. It was funny. They were trying to adapt to capitalism, and they weren't sure what capitalism was, because they'd only lived under communism.

Uraina asks me, "Is it true in America you can own your own home?"

I says, "Well, yes, you and the bank, about 30 years."

She says, "The bank?"

I says, "Yes, you get a loan from the bank. The bank pays the rest of the money for the house, and you pay the bank back for 20 or 30 years."

"But then the house is yours?"

"Yes, but not the property."

"The property?"

I says, "The ground, the land, the dirt the house sits on. You pay property tax."

"How long do you pay this?"

I says, "As long as you have the house. This pays for your sewers, your water, your police force, your firemen."

She says, "What happens if you do not pay this tax?"

"The sheriff comes, throws you out, and they sell the house to somebody who will pay this tax."

She says, "America's not free!"

I says, "Communism wasn't any good, was it?"

"No! No! Communism no good. No good. No good."

I says, "Wait 'til you see capitalism."

We hung around there, and they discharged the cargo. They came on board, eight o'clock in the morning, with big scoops, and took it out of railroad cars and piled it into the ship. Longshoremen weren't any drunker than anybody else walking around. We had a tendency to get into town and go look around and see the different things, which there really wasn't a whole lot. All the buildings were square, very plain, very level. Very clean town. You didn't see the goats and the herds of cattle walking around that you did in Georgia. We took a taxi ride, the bosun and myself, to look around. Nothing interesting.

But one time, on the way back one night, walking back to the ship, I stopped to urinate around the corner of a building, and a Ukrainian policeman caught me.

The little bit of Slovenian I knew, I could mix it up with the Ukrainian or Russian language.

He's pointing to where I urinated on the building, and I'm going, "Nyet."

About that time a prowl car pulls up and a sergeant jumps out. This young cop is telling the sergeant what I did, and I'm going, "Nyet." Sergeant looks at me, looks at the other copper, like, "We're trying to catch thieves here, not people who urinate on buildings." Looks at me and says, "Bye bye."

So I decide to give the young cop a few rubles, 5 or 10 bucks. Have a drink on me.

He says, "No! No!"

It was like the new regime had come in: no more bribery. I give 'em a little credit for that. He didn't want the money.

But I was running around with Uraina pretty steady, and she says, "Can you do me a favor?"

I says, "Sure, what do you need?"

"I have a hundred dollar bill, American. I would like change for it."

"Would you like tens, twenties, fives?"

"A mixture. I would appreciate it if you did this for me."

"It's not a problem."

She says, "I have small business with Moscow."

You know, *everybody* had "small business" with Moscow. Even in Georgia, everything centered on Moscow. I assume it would be like somebody in Cleveland saying, "I'm dealing with Washington, DC, here."

I says, "You don't have to explain it."

What it amounted to was that whatever she was doing with Moscow, she would probably have to give them the hundred dollar bill, and she would have to take her money in rubles, which were good nowhere else in the world. But if, say, she owed $70 out of that $100, she would get $30 worth of rubles. They wouldn't give her the dollars. But if she could give them $70, she could keep the $30, in case she ever made a run for it.

American money anywhere in the world is good collateral. It's accepted. I'm not saying they're gonna do what you want them to do when you give them the money, but at least you've got a chance. I found that throughout most of my trips. Everybody wanted dollars, marks, pounds, francs.

At the time, Georgia received television 2 hours in the morning and 2 hours at night from Moscow. That's all they could afford. Ukraine got 4 hours in the morning and 4 hours at night. That's all they could afford to buy, cuz the government had to pay for this. It was still government controlled. You didn't really see free enterprise coming into this where anybody was running anything except the government. They were talking about how Ukraine wanted to train their own Army; they were scared of the Soviet Union. The Soviet Union, at the time, said, anybody who's not Russian when they break up communist Russia, or the satellite countries, any troops that are other than Russian that don't want to stay in the Russian Army, you're free to leave. Basically, they did, and they just formed up their own Army with the same uniforms in Ukraine. Georgia was under protectorate of the Soviets at the time. There was a Russian Navy ship in the harbor there, and Russian troops all over. Matter of fact, I tried to take some pictures of one of the engineers in downtown Batumi, near the mayor's office, and a Russian soldier stopped me from taking pictures.

Ukraine had formed their own Army, but the news media was saying that Ukraine wanted to have American troops come over and train with them. They said it's gonna cost Ukraine $5 million to have the American troops come and train with the Ukrainians.

Uraina says, "Five million dollars? Ukraine does not have $5 million dollars."

I says, "You know, America doesn't have $5 million for me. Ukraine doesn't have $5 million for you. But for Army troops they have $5 million dollars." I says, "This is capitalism. This is what you're getting."

I should say, too: she had a real job. That club was the meeting place after work. All of them were secretaries in downtown Mariupol. The square there, they had little stalls where you could buy beer or cigarettes, anything you wanted, really. All the girls would come out of the offices, all the office workers in downtown Mariupol would get on the busses to go home in the evening.

And this is just their way of life. There wasn't a lot of traffic. It wasn't congested. It was like a small town in 1930s or '40s or '50s in the States where you had the small city, like a suburb would be. They took the busses to work, and they would take the busses home, and they would do their shopping along the way. They could buy nylons, beer, soda, cigarettes, lighters, bread.

During our stay, the Ukrainian agent came down with the head officer of the port—it's a very small port, a couple of berths—and says, "You have to shift the ship. Tell the captain."

The captain says, "What for? We're not through loading yet."

They says, "We promised this berth to this other ship. We've got to give them this berth."

The captain says, "Excuse me, there's nothing astern of us here. Why don't they go there? There's enough room for one more ship there."

They says, "No, no, we can't do that. We promised them this berth."

So we go aft 300 feet. Let the lines go, go astern. Tie us up. The other ship leaves, the ship that was promised that berth. Now we have to go back again.

The captain says, "What's this?"

He says, "Captain, this is just the way it's done here. And, oh, by the way, it's $5,000 for the shift."

The old man hit the overhead. "*Five thousand dollars to shift! My crew did all the work, and you're charging us $5,000?*"

Yeah.

Now we gotta pay because you can't leave port. They won't give you a pilot until all the bills are paid.

The old man's livid. "*That's it!* No more cigarettes! I don't care! Don't give out any more cigarettes!"

We load the chemical fertilizer. We're gonna leave. And all the girls at the club are saying, "Oh, when you coming back? When you coming back?"

"Probably never." You know? "Excuse us all to hell, but that's it."

Very late at night in Ukraine at the seamen's club, the prostitutes used to show up. They didn't like the idea of it, but they didn't have much choice in the matter because the head prostitute there, a woman, would bribe the police. The police would pull up in a van, and she'd give them vodka, "wodka"—"You like wodka? You like wodka?" She would piece off the cops, and they'd let them stay.

Nobody appreciated it, cuz it was actually like a little civic center. They still had the Lenin room where all the communist propaganda was, if you wanted it. They were free of communism, but they just couldn't break away completely.

I'd like to report a happy conclusion to that whole thing, but I never did see Uraina again. I hope she made it, you know, that business with Moscow, cuz I got her the change.

We left there with a load of fertilizer to go through the Suez Canal. Went around to Karachi, Pakistan to deliver it, and then we were supposed to go to Alang, India to have the ship scrapped. The majority of us were hoping it wouldn't happen, mainly because we had been on there awhile. This family out of Saint Mary's, Florida owned it, and were very easy to get along with. But they were constantly in debt. Used to have to lay us up in Freeport all the time. You know, they were trying to make money with the ship, but according to them, it just wasn't feasible. So we were going to Alang to scrap it.

I don't think anybody really went ashore except to get a newspaper up at one of the hotels. It was an armed camp. I'm not exaggerating. I didn't even want to go ashore. I was on gangway, 8 to 4, and they put two old Pakistanis on there to help me, like a translation-type thing. You talk about anything that wasn't nailed down they would take. So, basically, we started selling them everything. They would buy anything—you know—at their prices. Like, a couple of the guys had bicycles on board. Rather than get a taxi, they'd ride their bikes into town. We sold the bikes. We sold silverware, dishes, soap, linen, clothes. Everything was for sale because Karachi had nothing.

The captain wanted to get us paid off ahead of time, get it all done, so once we got to Alang, that would be it. We always had the option of cash. I said I wanted cash.

The captain calls me up there, in Karachi, and says, "Ron, you've got down *cash*."

"Yeah, captain, I'd like cash."

"This is no offense to you, Ron, I realize you're a big boy now, but, I really don't like the idea of you wandering around India, and then we're gonna make some stops on the flight back, with that kind of cash in your pocket."

It was three or four thousand dollars. They were gonna fly us back from India.

I says, "Captain, I appreciate that. I do. I'm not trying to cause problems for anyone. But," I says, "I'm entitled to it under federal law."

"Ron, how about if I give you the money, cash, and I'll have the agent take you into town, and you get traveler's checks."

"Alright, captain, if that's the easiest way to do this. If that makes you happy, it makes me happy. We're all happy. I'm not gonna cause any problems."

He's concerned about me getting jumped, robbed, losing it, whatever. I guess the majority of the guys were taking company checks. I just didn't want it. With what little rights I had left: Come on, captain, you said I'm a big boy now. This isn't my first trip.

I guess he felt that if you're traveling, use traveler's checks.

Not a day or two later, the agent comes, and the captain says, "Go with him. Here's the money."

Gives me the money. Takes me to the American Express office in Karachi. You talk about an armed camp. Every building that was any foreign interest, there were at least two Pakistanis with AK-47s and shotguns standing in front. It was ridiculous.

And they were rioting then, there were people getting killed in the streets, in the poorer sections. I believe it was Bhutto's daughter in charge of the operation at the time, and these people didn't even have running water in the area that they were being killed. So she bought four used armored personnel carriers for $100,000 from the United States government to police this area. I mean, don't spend $100,000 giving these people fresh water, you know? Buy these armored personnel carriers to further suppress them.

We're getting ready to leave, go to Alang. The tugs come along to tie up, pull us out, and the one tug wouldn't take the lines. Everybody had heard that the ship is gonna be scrapped, right? The word is out on us already. Everybody's taking everything they can. One of the tugboats refuses to take the lines.

We says, "What's wrong?" You know: we're gonna take your line, pull it up, and put it on us. We're thinking that's the problem, a confusion: they want our line, but we want *their* line.

What it amounted to was they wanted an easy chair from the ship before they would do that. That was gonna be their squeeze, their little extra. It's just constantly going on back and forth, the bartering, the dealing.

Now what are you gonna do? I mean, time is money. We drop it down to them. Yeah. We got them an easy chair. That's what they wanted, and we get outta there. We're empty, and we're going to Alang.

Now, Alang is just ships out at anchor. We don't go all the way in. The process there was that you would anchor out, and you could see these other ships that were literally being taken apart. It was a big area. The Indians would come on there—in a swarm, hundreds of them—and start at the bridge of the ship and start cutting away at the stack. That was how this worked. That's how you scrap a ship. Pakistan and India were the scrappers, and the only way they got away with doing this was, with U.S. government-funded ships, they'd hired an American to be president of the company, a figurehead. This way, you were scrapping the ship to an American company, circumventing the law.

I think the price for any ship was about $2 million, and then whatever fuel you had left on they'd give you extra for that. But we never actually took it all the way in. You'd stay out at anchor, and they came out in a launch to get us, except for like four or five people. Then they would actually get the anchor up and go slow ahead as far as they could go, until the ship had run aground. Beach it. It wasn't actually like a docking pilot. He's a *beaching* pilot. They would actually beach these ships. It really wasn't water, it turned to mud when the ship was actually beached. That's when the Indians would come on and start cutting it. *Hundreds* of Indians were there, cuz they had cheap labor.

Welding and hacksaws. We would see parts of the ships just cut off. The stacks would be missing, part of the bow, they'd be leveling it, going down by decks. And they had to have a way to drag it to what was dry land. So they'd taken a winch off the ship and mounted it on a truck, and when the piece of steel would fall into the mud, other Indians would come out with the cable, literally put the cable on their back, maybe 30 or 40 of 'em, and drag this cable out to the ship, put a shackle or put a hole in it or tie it to it any way they could. Then they'd just winch it ashore on the wire and put it on a truck and take it away.

That's what India and Pakistan were doing when they bought these ships. Old ships of every country ended up there because that was their steel industry: old ships. Anytime you see a steel product that says India or Pakistan on it, that's an old ship. They have no capacity to make steel. It was like Nationalist China during the Vietnam War. Ships that would break down over that way would get sold to Nationalist China, cuz they didn't have a steel industry. They would take it and scrap it, melt the steel down, and make other things out of it.

This was their business. Primitive but effective.

While we're getting on the launch, this deep sea tug, this raggedy thing, they says, "We're gonna put you in a hotel in Alang," or the next city over. "You'll have everything you need. Don't worry about anything."

I've been doing this awhile, right. I'm thinking: it's gonna be a long way in. India ain't got a whole lot. I go back, I'm the last one, cuz we left four or five of our crew on there to actually do the beaching.

So I says, "Wait a minute."

I run back to the rooms. The Indians are already going through everything. They're going through the rooms, taking whatever they can, whatever they can pull out. I run back and get us some life jackets. I get four or five life jackets. I throw them down. I run back again. I get toilet paper this time, whatever I can carry. I get bars of soap. I was throwing it all down at them.

The bosun's yelling up, "What are you doing, Ron? Come on!"

I says, "Wait a minute! Wait a minute!" Chairs: I was putting chairs down. Just so we could have someplace to sit. There was nowhere to sit on the tug! You talk about—no offense to the Indian nation, but it's *filthy*. I knew that we weren't gonna get enough toilet paper. I knew we weren't gonna get enough soap. I knew we weren't gonna get *anything*.

Sure enough, on this tug, there's nowhere to sit. But *now* we got chairs. When they were taking us to the dock area, you could actually see what they were doing to the ships. As soon as we got off on the pier, the Indians just confiscated those chairs. Oh, they went and they sat in them, you know, cuz those were *theirs* now, they belonged to *them*. But we had the soap and the toilet paper.

We're in Customs, they're stamping our passports, and there's some other guy there from Bombay Customs.

They says, "OK, what do you got? You got any money for me?"

The guy has a five dollar bill. He says, "Five dollars OK?"

He says, "Yeah, that's fine."

Next one was the bosun. The bosun shows him his Customs declaration to get off in India.

Guy says, "You have any money for me?"

The bosun wants to give him a five cuz he'd seen the other guy give a five. But the bosun only has a ten, the smallest he has, so he gives him the ten.

"Oh, you got that for me? OK. Matter of fact," he says, "this is enough. You're all cleared."

They don't make a lot of money there, you know.

They put us on the bus, and you talk about a ride. It must have been 2 or 3 hours. They're giving us jugs of recycled water; you could see the plastic jugs had been used once and then sealed again.

They always advertise European cuisine, but they're not big meat eaters there. You get a lot of vegetables, but they would give you a little chicken. I was leery. Terry had done this with a Lykes Brothers ship, scrapped it. When he was at the hotel he got food poisoning. So I'm very leery now. Very leery. I'm eating the bread and drinking the Pepsi-Cola. Then I caught an article in the paper where they found ants in the Pepsi-Cola. But, what are you gonna do?

We got to the town, spent one day at one hotel, then they shifted us to another hotel, which was actually a little nicer. It's smaller, but it's off on a side street. They gave us a lot of vegetables, and I ate that, but I wasn't about to touch any chicken. I'm not eating that meat. I got the bread, the Pepsi-Cola.

When we got to the first hotel, there's about three sheets of toilet paper in the room. The bar of soap was like a mini-bar. But now because of what I brought from the ship, we all had soap.

The bosun says, "You know, Ron, you were right."

I says, "I don't trust these people."

Same thing at the other hotel. Three or four sheets of paper and a little bar of soap. But we got ours.

One interesting thing: everyone thought we were Russians. Everybody's asking, "What are you, Russians? Russians?" Because, I guess Russia and India were still dealing pretty heavily at the time.

"No, we're Americans. We're just getting shipped back to the States."

And, no booze.

Matter of fact, the bosun remarked one morning, "You know, Ron, it's a good thing." We're sitting out on the veranda in the morning, drinking coffee, waiting to get called to get taken up to Bombay. He says, "It's a good thing there's no booze around here." He says, "You see that?" Points to a pagoda-type thing, a statue of a lion. He says, "That woulda been on the other side of the street by now." Woulda wrecked the joint.

Then they call and says, "Get ready, we're coming to pick you up."

They take us up to Bombay.

We aren't supposed to drink. They ordered us. Captain Dan wasn't there, it was the chief mate, and this goofy third mate had just come on for about half the trip. The other third mate had gotten off, I don't know whether it was family trouble or something, they had flown him home. They flew this guy over, and he was pretty much a stickler. You know, he was gonna be *in charge of us*.

So when they get us to Bombay, they have to take us to a restaurant to eat. We start ordering booze, and the third mate, he told one of the other engineers: "Well, I can't do nothing now, they're starting to drink."

We're saying, "Oh, man, fuck you." You know, right? "We'll not only drink, we'll put your fucking head up your ass here." Leave us alone.

The bosun and myself were gonna take off to Faulkner Road, see the girls in the cages. We had it all planned. We tried to sneak out, but Customs is right there.

They're saying, "You guys are getting on a bus, and you're going to the airport."

That's it. No girls in cages, no—that was the end of that little performance. Best laid plans. They caught up to us on that one. We get to the airport, take off, go to France, change planes, fly back to the States. And that was it. That was the end of the ship, and I really was kind of sorry to see it go, I really was. As far as I'm concerned, they were good runs. It was a shame.

It was a shame.

This would have been February of '96. This was kind of a laid back useless year out of my life. I wasn't working much. This was a period when shipping really was slow. The union was falling apart. They couldn't get contracts, and when they could get one, it was, "We'll sign anything to get the membership's money." It was the best they could do for us.

So I had temporary jobs. A few coastwise trips.

Green Ridge redux

Then I finally got lucky, or *not*, as the case may be. It was the *Green Ridge* again. I didn't want to take this because this was the one where I injured my feet a year or so earlier and I was off that 9 months. But shipping was really slow, and I had a chance to grab it steady, and I did. The first thing that Captain Smith asked me was, "How are your feet? Do you have a good pair of shoes on?" I knew it was coming, you know? But it was a job.

We're going to Antwerp, Belgium, Skipper Strassa, Skipper Street. Back in the '60s when I started doing this, we used to stop there, too, on that run with the *American Shipper*. Matter of fact, that's where I got my first two tattoos, Skipper Street. I knew we were going back and having a good time no matter what it was like. They got girls in the windows. Here we go. I'm sure I could fall in love again. Find new loved ones. New loved ones to help me see my way in life. And it was great. It really was. We carried ammunition over, dropped it off, and then we started back-loading military goods, household supplies, things like that, to take back. I loved it. It was back and forth. It was three trips on there.

The last trip I got a young third mate, first trip on his license. He was a good guy. He won the anchor pool that last trip. Everybody puts in two bucks, so it's $120. Everybody gets a minute. The minute we pick up the pilot, as it's officially logged, is what counts. Everybody opens their numbers, and if you have the minute, you win. He won it, and he says, "Hey, look at this, Ron. I got $120 to spend. And I got my own guide. *You*." He says, "We're spending all of this."

That's my kind of third mate.

And we did. We went everywhere. We spent that $120 on beer,

women. He wanted to go on his own there a little later on.

I says, "Sure. I'll meet you back here, though."

He says, "Well, if you want to go back on your own . . . ."

I says, "You know, I don't wanna go back to the ship without you. You go party, but I'll meet you back here at . . ." whatever time we agreed on.

He wanted to go explore on his own after I showed him. Basically, the middle of Skipper Strassa, it's almost like a hub of a spoked wheel, the streets go out in spokes.

I says, "You'll know when it ends. Trust me, you'll know." It's like back in the free world.

It's great. Women in the windows, women in bars, women from all over the world. I ended up with a girl from Finland who's working her way around the world, so to speak.

This was where I got my first tattoos, when I was first shipping on the *American Shipper*, we used to stop in Antwerp. Back in 1967, I was wandering around, half in the bag, down Skipper Street. You know, Skipper Street's been there since 1880 for merchant seamen. I really loved it there. Still do. It's free and easy and liberal and, matter of fact, Antwerp had like three seamen's hotels because all through time, European seamen had the option of getting off of a ship and getting another one. They could stay there and grab another one. So it was oriented to us.

So I'm wandering around, checking out the girls in the windows, having a good time. I happen to walk by a tattoo parlor. I go in, I'm the only one there, and I'm looking at the things.

The tattoo artist says, in English, "What can I get for you?"

I says, "I'm just looking. I'm not really sure yet."

He says, "How about me giving you an eagle on your chest?"

"No, no, I don't want an eagle on my chest." I says, "I want a parrot on my arm." To this day, I don't know why I said that. I was drunk. Knowing me, I *assumed* I was gonna get a tattoo. I wander in. The guy's gonna try and sell you something. Gonna tell *me* what *I* want.

He says, "No, I'll give you an eagle on your arm."

I says, "If you can't give me a parrot on my arm, I don't want it."

He digs through his goodie bag there for a stencil. He finds it, puts it on.

I says, "Is there a lot of color in that?"

"Yeah, I'll give you a lot of color." It's six or eight bucks. *Now* it'd be $300, cuz it cost me that to get it re-colored after 40 years.

I says, "How long is that tattoo gonna last?"

He says, "Longer than you."

It did, but the color went out after 40 years.

I says, "How long is this gonna take?"

He says, "Two days. Come back tomorrow."

"The ship's leaving tomorrow morning. Can you do it?"

"How much pain can you take?"

I says, "Do it."

He starts the stencil, and halfway down from the head and the top of the feathers, it's just blood running, and he's just mopping it up and tattooing, mopping it up and tattooing. He gets it done, puts Vaseline on it, slaps a napkin on it, tapes it, says, "Whatever you do, keep putting Vaseline on it, and don't get it wet."

"OK."

I was drinking, didn't feel a lot. I get back to the ship, and at the time there were three of us in the foc'sle, and I was ordinary seaman. I was up on the top bunk, and we had these curtains in front of the bunk. We used to call them jack off curtains. Technical term.

Anyway, I had the curtain pulled, but there was a bar there, where you slept, so you wouldn't roll out. It was halfway along the bunk. And somehow or another, I had gotten this arm over the curtain and over that metal bar, so the curtain was covering it, you could see there was an arm there, but you couldn't see it clear. That's where the tattoo was.

They come in to wake us up in the morning, turn to at six o'clock in the morning to secure the ship, we're leaving.

The third mate comes in and says, "Hey, Ronnie, get up," and slaps my arm, hits the tattoo.

I scream. "*Ahhh!*"

He pulls the curtain back. It looks like I got stabbed. The blood's just like a stab wound you see in the cartoons, big and then tapering down. The napkin is over it, all bloody.

He says, "Jesus Christ, what'd you do, get stabbed last night?"

I says, "No, it's a tattoo."

"Holy Christ, kid." He says, "Come on, you gotta turn to."

So I ask the bosun, Joe Char, when I get out there on deck, "Bosun, I hate to ask you this, but I need a favor." I says, "I don't mind being hung over and working, but I got this tattoo, and my arm's killing me."

He looks at me like, "What the fuck do I care?" And that's just about what he says. He says, "I didn't tell you to go get that fucking tattoo. Just get out there, Ronnie, start securing."

I says, "Oh, fuck."

And that's where I got my first tattoo, Skipper Street. It was kind of a sentimental journey going back and seeing the same places. I think some of the same girls were there, too.

I highly recommend Antwerp if you just want to go to Skipper Street and go out of your fucking mind, or if you want to visit some cathedrals, which is usually what they show you on the travel logs. Antwerp, to see it, you go from cathedral to cathedral trying to get to Skipper Street. Just beautiful cathedrals. And when I went there the first time in '67, they had a zoo there with stuffed animals.

I told the taxi driver, "Is that zoo still here downtown with the stuffed animals in it from Africa?"

He says, "Yeah, it's still there."

It was in the same spot it was 40 years ago. Still there. You walk in and you see these stuffed wild animals from Africa that had been shot and brought back. I mean, they're just like statues. Belgium used to run the Congo, you know. You just walk through there, and they've got in Belgian and in English, too, the name of the animal.

Anyway, the ship finally went into lay up. The three trips turned out to be 120 days. We laid up in Orange, Texas, and I got off.

That was the end of that. But it was a very, very nice run.

I couldn't afford to go ashore

Shipping was really tough for everybody. I took a one-trip relief to northern Europe. Didn't even bother going ashore, did nothing. I can't even remember the ports. Came back, and I had to get off. This was the only thing I could get.

Matter of fact, an electrician threw in on this because when you registered able seaman, that's what you had to ship as. If you registered ordinary, that's what you shipped as. There were two or three AB jobs. I threw in on it. My card wasn't good enough. They put up an ordinary seaman job. We went by seniority, so if no Group 1 wants it, then it would go to Group 2, even for ABs. If no Group 1 ABs, then Group 2 ABs. It went out to Group 1 ordinary seamen. There was nobody. Shipping was really bad.

So they're asking for any other Group 1 that wants this. I threw my card in as AB. An electrician, who was very high paid, a day worker on the ship, he threw in to get the ordinary job, cuz as long as you had it on the back of your seaman's card, you could ship on it.

I beat him out.

He says, "An AB taking an ordinary job?" Like, "Why are you taking this?" You know, because of the difference in the pay. It's almost like he's trying to get me to say, "Yeah, you're right. I'm not gonna do that. I'm not gonna sail below my station in life."

I says, "What? An *electrician* throwing in for an ordinary job?" I says, "You're losing more money than I am if you took that job."

He didn't like that. He didn't like me. I didn't like him, either.

I wasn't making the kind of money I would as AB, but I was making more as ordinary seaman on this ship than I did as AB on the *Green Ridge*. Figure that one out.

We stopped in Israel. We stopped in Izmir. I didn't go ashore because I needed the money. I couldn't really afford to go ashore. It was getting really tough to ship, and I was concerned about when I would get my next ship. I had to spend money to live when I was ashore.

We came back, and the guy had one trip. He came back in Norfolk, and I had to get off. That's how tough it was. I mean, guys were coming *back*. A lot of times guys wouldn't come back, you know, the job where they'd get off on a medical and never come back or a vacation and never come back. That was actually a good-paying job at the time.

Reduced Operational Status

I'm still in Norfolk, and June 30, '97, I got a bosun job. First time I'd sailed bosun, foreman on the ship. He's the boss.

It was a reserve ship, the *Cape Alexander*. Marine Transport Line was operating it. It was an old freighter that was in reserve status. It was up in Baltimore, and I got it for 30 days.

With a lot of jobs now, we're coming up to these lay up jobs. Ships were in lay up for, like, the first Gulf War, they didn't keep crews on them, and the ships were inoperable when they tried to operate them. These ships now were becoming the norm, where you didn't sail anywhere, you just stayed at port waiting for a war to start or to activate for 5 days to see if the ship would run. That's what I had been catching.

And now, I mean, it was *gone* for the NMU. There were *no* jobs. I stayed there for 30 days, and that was it, I had to get off. The guy came back for the job.

That was it for that ship. Nature of voyage: ROS. Reduced operational status.

And that brings us to my long year of living dangerously.

The long year of living dangerously

I was fighting with the union trying to get my pension ahead of time, trying to get a lump sum. Fighting the union is worse than fighting the government. I took a year off to see if I could make it out in the free world. I assume it would be like doing 32 years in a penitentiary and then trying to come out and work in the free world, where you actually had to produce.

It was terrible.

This was from August '97 to July of '99.

My long year of living dangerously.

Now I was actually faced with working ashore and living there and seeing how people actually did the nine to five. I was trying to figure out how people *lived*. I was offered a number of jobs. I'd get there, and it was ridiculous. Landscraping, bartending. I couldn't believe this is how "normal" people lived. For the last 32 years I had been living on the ships and partying ashore. I wondered how people could do it. And then they'd come home to their loved ones.

I thought: this is ridiculous.

At the time, I was helping out the family in a roundabout way. One or two relationships, too, that really didn't work out. I actually felt that they thought they were trapping me, that they had me where they wanted me. They caught me off guard where I didn't have the safety of running to the Merchant Marine, catching a ship and leaving. Two or three that I was involved with during this time off were very supportive to the point of, "OK, I have you." All three of 'em. It was like, "Yeah, you can stay here, and you can find something to do." The exchange was my freedom. It never started out that way or appeared to be in the relationship because I could find a job, right, or

447

they would find one for me, or I could do *something*. And I could live with them, individually, say 3 or 4 months, and then it broke up, it parted. Maybe I had just too much pride. I don't know. It could have been that. Or I think I just fell back on: no.

"No."

It was like the spider and the fly is the only way I can think of it. Or the devil making his offer to Jesus in the desert: I'll give you all this when it's mine already anyway. I got the same impression from those three girls, that it was, "Yeah, you can stay here, and we can have a relationship, and we'll end up getting married, and you can have *this*." Well, what is *this*? Nothing I ever wanted anyway!

It finally dawned on me that the only place I was gonna be happy was on a ship or in a foreign country. Matter of fact, Ken Bottoms offered: "Why don't you just come on over here and stay for awhile? Stay here." His mom and dad had passed away. "Come on over, appreciate having you." But I didn't think that was an answer. That was like putting a bandage on an artery that had been cut.

Everybody was trying to help me.

And it was like everything else in life: their version of "help." Maybe it was me, but I couldn't blend in, on land. All the offers are good, if you're on land. But, technically, I would be starting from scratch, cuz I was fighting with the union over my pension.

The president of the union and his son later got convicted in federal court of misusing the pension money. The administrator of the pension plan pled guilty to misuse of the pension money. The union itself was in shambles. They were constantly being convicted in court of misuse of something or other, some kind of federal offense. All this time I'm arguing with the trustees of the pension plan, and they're saying I hadn't fulfilled some of the things that needed to get the pension.

I said, "Who appoints you?"

They said, "The president of the union. And some people from the company."

Now it's rule by decree. I mean, are you gonna serve the membership, or are you gonna serve the people who appoint you?

And, to me, it was frightening to see how people actually lived, the façade of being: working, going home, weekends, relationships—"the American dream." Where you had your neighbors running over and saying what you couldn't do. Like you couldn't put your garbage out until six o'clock the night before. The neighbors would actually run over and say, "What are you doing? Why is your garbage out when I can't put mine out?"

"Well, you can put yours out. I mean, are the garbage police gonna come by? Is somebody gonna call the police because you put your garbage out an hour earlier; and the grass police if your grass isn't cut?"

"We have to keep up appearances."

To me, it was a total waste of time even dealing with these people. It's a shame.

I was staying with some relatives at the time. They were having medical problems. I was trying to help them, trying to help myself, and trying to figure out the meaning of life. Is this the golden years? If I had to pick an option—I'm getting married or staying with one of the girls and actually going to work—is this what I was looking at?

And it's scary. It's frightening.

I mean, I'd rather take a ship into a typhoon with a load of bombs on it into a war zone. It was a lot easier. You act as a team fighting fires, repelling borders, abandoning ship. Everybody's got a job to do. Not necessarily they're gonna *do* the job, but on there, I know *I* can get me from point A to point B and back again. And if I don't do it, well, then I'm dead, you know? Nobody knows when you're gonna go.

Well, I take that back. When the doctor gave me a physical years ago when I was still sailing out of Charleston, she says, "If you quit smoking and quit drinking and ate a little better, you'd live longer and be healthier."

I says, "Well, I know when I'm gonna die."

She says, "Nobody knows when they're gonna die."

I says, "Trust me, doctor, I *know* when I'm gonna die."

Eat my gun.

Because I saw retired people who had worked all their life, and that was their biggest thing, that was their claim to fame: work. I'm not saying it's wrong. I don't say things are right or wrong. What I am saying is: is this why we're on this earth? Is it some "ism" that's controlling you, whatever "ism" you take—communism, capitalism, socialism, fascism, Catholicism, Muslimism, whatever you have. It's a control issue.

It seemed to me that the vast majority of people, whether they like it or not, were controlled by numerous "isms," which are human thoughts.

And "isms" hate the individual.

And thinking is dangerous.

And asking "why?"—oh, that's terrible, too, that's dangerous.

That's why I stay scared, because I have to get up and communicate every day with the human race. In my case, in different countries, I'm under different "isms". I'm very careful to only insult America, not the country I happen to be in.

If anybody says, "How can you talk about America like that?"

I say, "It's easy. They tax me."

And there's no free thinking.

"You can't put the garbage out at five o'clock in the evening." And you've got your do-gooder neighbors that will come over and mention that to you. It's just sickening. People have nothing better to do than worry about when you put out your garbage?

This, along with the girls, when I stayed with them, you know, I didn't really want to. With one, it was another control issue. Her problems became my problems, but my problems didn't become her problems. I was just expected to go to work. I had to help out. Plus, I was expected to help out the relations I was staying with when I moved out and moved in with this girl. Well, how much am I supposed to do? Am I supposed to listen to the government and the grass police and the neighbors? How many people are controlling my life? In other words, I don't have control of anything anymore. Everybody else had control of me.

Like my uncle once told me, "A rolling stone gathers no bills." He also said, "Never lose your head trying to save your neck." I was thinking back on all those old clichés he had. You know, they kick in every once in awhile. He himself was trapped. He felt it, too. Later on in life, when I had come up from Florida, I'd stop over, I'd get in a fight with the girlfriend and come up, stay there. He would be very, very cynical. I remember one time, the news was on, and I said something about a politician that got killed in a plane crash, and he said, "Yeah, they should all die."

There's a lot of ways to look at things. I see how people live vicariously through movies, sports, television. It's either an escape, or they wish they were doing that, but they're not. But it's escape from what they *are* doing. Which is nothing. And I'm sorry to say that. I mean, it's not like I'm saying getting your garbage picked up isn't important, having policemen or firemen isn't important, having a government—I mean, you *can't* have anarchy. But has it improved from the Greeks? Has it really improved? I don't think so. It's just more government.

I mean, when the government gets into when you can put your trash out for collection and how high your grass is gonna be, and people complain about the Soviet Union, the KGB, or they complain about Nazi Germany with the Gestapo or the SS, about, "Oh, children are informing on their parents. Oh, what kind of government is that, where children actually go to the schools or the party and say, 'Oh, my parents said *no* to the establishment.'" You have the same thing here, but you're not seeing it. You're looking at that as a totalitarian regime, while you're saying here we have freedom. And you don't have any. You have to get license plates for your cars. You've gotta get a driver's license, you've gotta get insurance, you have to have this and that and the other. But people don't think of it this way. You want to add an addition to your house, you've got to ask. They put sidewalks in with *your* tax money, and then *you* maintain them. It just keeps piling and piling and piling on you.

I'd been away from this for three decades, and coming back to it, *it hadn't changed.* It hadn't changed since my youth. It'd gotten *worse.* And everybody had a million dollars worth of good advice, but nobody had the money. I was trying to make it work, but it was like running into a bulkhead, a brick wall. Anything *I* wanted to do was alien.

And: I would ask why.

I would ask why about my pension. Why don't I have some say-so in my pension? Well, "It's for the good of everybody." You have a minority of "elected" telling you how to live again. I found that very, very strange. I mean, what do we get? We don't have public health here in America. Taxes constantly go up, whether it's the federal government or the state or the county or the city, any municipality, they raise the taxes. And you get nothing in return, or you get less than you had gotten before. I mean, there's less firemen, less policemen, but the taxes go up. How this can be justified—by going to work, coming home, to be with the loved ones? Well, yeah, OK. If that's your security thing. Everybody's different. In reality, there is no such thing as security, because tomorrow's not promised to anyone. No matter how hard I looked, everything was a trap. On land. Everything's a trap.

I'm just gonna jump ahead for a minute. It was after 9/11. I was shipping again. I had just come back from Spain, Ibiza, an island in the western Mediterranean, and 9/11 happened. About 3 days later I was in a bar. I spend a lot of time in bars having a few thousand drinks. The only one there was myself and the barmaid, and a stranger came in, a guy we didn't know.

She asked me, "Ron, do you know this guy?"

I said, "No, I don't."

She said, "Whatever you do, don't leave. I don't want to be here with somebody I don't know."

I thought: *This* is America. "I don't want to be here with somebody I don't know." I never saw that overseas. Never. That's how scary it is here.

Anyway, he tried to start a conversation. I assumed he just got out of work, he appeared to be coming in in his work clothes—didn't want to go home to his loved ones, he'd rather stop in a bar, you know, than go home to the kids and wife screaming and yelling. He gave the impression that he wasn't really happy anyway, that's why he was there. Why go home when he could sit in a bar and drink? My kind of guy.

But anyway, he said, "What do you think about 9/11?"

I said, "I think American foreign policy has finally come home to roost." I mean, you abuse people for 50 years or try to control them . . . . Like I said about the Panama Canal: it finally got to the point where every contract, you would have to give more to the Panamanians. It was *theirs*. It wasn't *ours*. We had built it, but it wasn't statehood. We were a colonial power, like every other colonial power, France, Britain, Germany. Only we hadn't lost our colonies after World War I like Germany did. After World War II, England lost their colonies, France lost theirs, but America was still holding on. Britain and France had given up the Suez Canal. And I just said it to this guy. I don't know how much he knew about anything, but I said, "America's foreign policy has come home to roost. You can't rule by decree for so many years and not think you're gonna have a revolt. This is nothing that's uncommon."

He said, "The way you talk, you shouldn't even live in this country."

I said, "OK. I'll go to Spain."

He didn't know what to say. In other words, he wasn't ready for that answer. In other words, America had been attacked, and whether or not he liked it here, or how it was being run, and he bitched about the taxes, and he bitched about home, and he bitched about the conditions, and he bitched about certain ethnic groups, he still would say, "This is America, I have to defend it."

Well, if you're not getting what you want, why defend what you have? You don't want it anyway, why defend it? It passes for democracy and security, but it really isn't.

Voltaire said it's awfully interesting that a king and his court can go to a farmer in his field and say, "Our honor has been violated, you have to leave your plow, your field, your family, and go in the army and go to—" fill in the name of the country "—and kill them. And this guy's gonna do it." And Voltaire said, "Wouldn't it be simpler just to kill the king and his court?"

And, after, oh, well, over a year of this insanity, I said, "I don't need this. I don't need the constant aggravation, the drama, the soap opera, the bitching, the stress, the abuse, the complaining, the pissing and moaning."

I activated my seaman's card again.

I said, "Well, everybody, thank you very, very much for your offer." I'm saying 99% of the people that offered help, there were strings attached.

And what's my freedom worth? Is it worth a woman and a home? No. Is it worth a job, so I could come to a home and help take care of relatives who needed a hand in life? I'm sorry, but the answer's still *no*. Everybody can say, oh, it's terrible—that "me, me, me" thing—just thinking of yourself. But if you're not happy, if you're no good to yourself, what good are you to anyone else? So you have to be happy before you can help anyone, that's the way I look at it.

It was time to go. After over a year of seeing this charade—

And I hate to say it, I really do, but I think some people were actually jealous that I lived the way I did. I haven't done anything that anybody else couldn't do. To me, what I do is normal. You know, figure out whatever normalcy is. To me, I'm normal. And, I'm sure, to homosexuals, they're normal, but they're a minority. So now we have a case again of a majority trying to tell a minority what to do. It doesn't work. It hasn't worked throughout history. Everybody revolts, whether it be the Panama Canal, the Jews at Masada against the Roman Empire, the Muslims against the Christians, or vice versa. Nobody wants to be told what to do. I think you give up your freedom when you get together with a girl, or you get in a relationship, cuz the priorities become, "Well, we're gonna do this for *everybody*, you know, for *us*." As long as you like that, as long as it's an "us" thing, that's fine. But, outside government and religions, they frown on individuals. It gets to be like profiling: single male. "Watch him."

Even when I travel, even the girls overseas, they say, "Well, you're married, right?"

"No."

"You're not? Why aren't you married?"

"Cuz I'm not."

Like there's something wrong with that? Is there a law?

"Well, everybody gets married."

I says, "I'm not everybody."

I mean, does the government decree this? And it's been so strange that I didn't want the house with the white picket fence, go to work and come home, and watch TV. I *assume* people who did this originally wanted it, and the vast majority of them didn't know anything else to do, and once they were in through their religion or government or it's "cheaper to keep her" or God's gonna strike me dead if I don't do this, they were there, that was it.

Even the girls were, "Well, *everybody's* got to have a boyfriend, and *all* guys gotta have girlfriends."

Well, where is that written? To make somebody's life miserable? If you're not happy, you're not happy. I mean, according to America, it's supposed to be life, liberty, and the pursuit of happiness. If you're not happy, you're not happy. *Do* something about it. Don't sit in a bar and complain about it.

Every time I would say something about "if you don't like it change it" or "stop doing it", I'd get, "Well, I can't. They'll put me in jail if I don't."

Well, then they'll put us *all* in jail.

People look at me like it's strange, but they did even before this year of insanity: "How can you talk like that?"

I says, "It's easy."

It's like they say, if little Johnny jumps in the lake, are you gonna jump in the lake, too? Well, just cuz *everybody* else gets married and goes to work, does that mean I have to?

I've always felt it was a control issue by the powers that be, whether it was your parents, the government, or a girl. And while they couldn't say what to do at work, they couldn't tell anybody what to do, when they got home, they could administer something. This is no offense to people that have pets, but I think that's a control issue, too, where they can tell the pet what to do and the pet does it cuz that's probably the only thing that's gonna do as you ask. Even then it's probably gonna bite you if it got the chance. That's a strange thing, too. If you have a dog, and the master gets his throat cut, the dog will lick the blood. If the dog's throat is cut, the master will run to the vet to try to save it.

That always puzzled me, too: having a dog. It's just one more thing to take care of.

With a couple of those girls I was running around with in that year of insanity, it was like—we were watching TV one night, and I told her, "Is this what old people do?" The other one, she liked to go see movies. At the theaters, they got like six movies playing. We were waiting in line, and there were some young girls there, maybe 17, 18.

She saw a friend of hers and she said, "Oh, which movie are you going to see?"

"Oh, we're going to see *this* one. Oh, you've seen *that*?"

"Oh, we saw *that*. We're going to see *this* one, but then we're gonna get out of *that* one and go see this *other* one—"

These people are actually living vicariously through movies. And again, it dawned on me: I *lived* this. I think *Titanic* was the movie. They were gonna see *Titanic*. Well, they were going to see an action film that I *lived* for 32 years.

I'm looking around at these people, and I'm thinking: What the fuck am I doing here with this bunch? This bunch has done nothing in their life and never will. They've never done anything bright, and they probably never will. They'll scruff through life, living vicariously through others, through movies. And even the movie actors or actresses, they didn't live through this. This is all a movie! This is make believe!

The majority of them were never gonna get further than Columbus, Ohio, or from Jacksonville to New Orleans. I mean, that was gonna be their party. I'm not saying it's wrong. I am not. But when you plan your life like: "Oh, I got 2 weeks vacation. I'm gonna go to New Orleans for the Mardi Gras." That's cool. Or, "I'm gonna go to New York cuz I want to see the Empire State Building." That's cool. But I had already been there and done that. Maybe that sounds egotistical, but it's not. It's just that I'm trying to get a grip on something that really hasn't changed for 32 years. I ran away from it to begin with. And 32 years later, it's gotten *worse*. It hasn't gotten better.

I said, "Well, it's time to go again. I've had it."

I had to get to a different place and time.

It was like I peaked early, and I kept peaking. I mean, there was always another adventure. There was always somewhere else to go, women to meet, drunken brawls to get into. You think that would get out of your system. It's kind of like Voltaire's Zadig, poor guy, after he got beat up all over the fucking world, you're just happy to get back and get married, get abused by the wife. It was so much easier. At least he got laid every once in awhile. Voltaire was well ahead of his time, the things I read by him. But, unlike Zadig, I wasn't ready to let a government or a woman abuse me.

You know, in a relationship the girl's attitude is: "I can do better than you."

I say: "Then please do. Don't let me stand in your way."

Or it was: *I* could be better. They had to change *me*. Well, why did you get together with me if I wasn't good enough and you were gonna change me? *That* doesn't work. I'm *me*. What did you expect?

Did I want to blend in? Did I want to conform? No, when I saw what conformity meant, when I saw what blending in would be.

If you're saying, "OK, I'm an individual." I depend on myself more to be self-sufficient rather than depending on a government or another person to support me. I don't ask anybody to do what I do. I mean, if you want to do what I do, do what I do. I could care less. Other people have. I haven't done anything spectacular. I'm living proof that you can do anything you want with your life.

It was like I had come to an end. The end of my life.

I said to myself, "What am I gonna do? Go to these movies and watch TV? *Old* people do this." This is what old people do: they live vicariously through television and movies, whether they're there with their kids or they're there with their grandkids.

I was getting the same impression that I had in my youth, that I was on the outside looking in. It's funny. Everything I'm looking at, everything's a distance from me. It felt the same way it felt when I was young.

It made we want to run again. And the girls, all of them all over the years have said the same thing, "You're scared of responsibility in a relationship." Yeah, I am. I am. I'm good short term. Like that captain calls me all the time, "Hey, you wanna deliver a load of bombs to Iraq?" Yeah, I'm game. I'm good short term. I'm good at what I do. So why do something I'm not good at? That's the only way I can phrase it.

I mean, I have a different political belief. Like, the Englishman will call me the un-American American. "You're one of the few we've ever heard not waving the flag."

I said, "Well, excuse me, but I lived there. I can say it." *There* I can. If I say it *here*, I'm getting ready for a fistfight.

From what everybody tells me, I have a different political belief. To me, I don't. Like I said about being on the outside looking in. I may just be on the inside looking *out*. There may be more people like me in this world than the people in America see in their little community.

By traveling around the world, I see more people like me who aren't happy with their government or who aren't happy with: "Get married, have 2.3 kids and a house and a mortgage, and everybody does it." Well, maybe your neighbors do it. Maybe people you work with do it, but that doesn't necessarily mean *everyone* does it.

It was time to leave. I mean: what's wrong with this picture? I'm in it. Maybe my political beliefs are different. If, by that, I mean, we're not getting what we're paying for here in America. And by people having blinders on or tunnel vision or locked mentalities, the people that can't think out of the box, I'm sorry, I mean, if I offend them whether I'm sitting in a bar here or anywhere else in the world and somebody says, well, you believe in God don't you?

I said, "I believe in a supreme being." That could be an alien in a flying saucer. *That* is a supreme being. Let's look at it. Hey, scientologists, if that's what you believe, that's what you believe. I got no problem with that.

But when I was told, "Lent's coming up, and you're supposed to give up something for Lent."

The only thing I could think of was—you know—sooner than later I'm gonna have to give up *everything*. So why do it *now*?

"Well, you gotta give up something, cuz you believe in God and this and that."

I said, "Well, what are you giving up? It's got to be something you like."

He said, "I'm not sure yet."

I said, "Well, you like being married, don't you?"

He said, "Yeah."

I said, "Why don't you get divorced?"

He looked at me so strangely.

Now it comes to: I'm gonna give up something I like, but now I'm gonna pick something that I like, but that's not really heavy, you know? Well, why put that off on me? I mean, I'm gonna die, and I'm not gonna be able to drink anymore or run around the world and get blow jobs off Tibetan girls. I'm not saying that's great, and, obviously, some people don't like it. No offense to the human race—but hey, you know—I don't like coming home from work and having to sit there and watch television and watch people getting paid for doing things that I do for practically free.

The whole concept of America is totally beyond me. It really is.

A maiden voyage

So I went back down to Norfolk, Virginia, walked into the other union, the competitors, showed them my seaman's papers, and they said, "Pay your union dues, your initiation fee, we'll give you a job *today*, able-bodied seaman."

"Bless you."

I gave them the money, and they got me on the *USNS Sisler*. This ship was going out on its maiden voyage. It was in Newport News, Virginia, going out for a 5-day sea trial. If it worked out, where they didn't have any problems, we were going down to Charleston, South Carolina to load vehicles. Then we were gonna end up in Diego Garcia, Indian Ocean, somewhere I didn't want to go, but I wanted to get away.

We went to Charleston, and they didn't have enough vehicles for us. They sent us to Antwerp, Belgium. I couldn't believe it. It's like, "Thank you, God. You know what? You do me a favor every once in a while, too, fella. I always give You Your due." It's nice to talk to Him every once in awhile. He's not that bad of a fella. You know, He works it out.

And it was great, it was great to be out at sea again. Out standing watches, it was the old system on there. Two able seamen and an ordinary on a watch. It was like second nature, back up steering. Back in another place and time.

They says, "Are you confident in your steering?"

I says, "Yeah, I'll steer this ship through the eye of a needle."

The chief mate was kind of apprehensive. He was up on the bridge, and they didn't know me. I'm steadying up, and the pilot tells him, "He's doing fine, mate, just leave him alone. Just leave the man alone."

Coming out of Charleston.

We went to Antwerp, and it was like a homecoming. Like I'd died and gone to heaven—or hell. It was Skipper Street again, here we go. Dreams do come true. Three of us went in and went to Skipper Street, and they wanted to get a drink first. We stopped in a place. Peddlers were coming around selling stuff, souvenirs, dumb shit.

I says, "Don't buy any of this junk shit they come around selling. It breaks the next fucking day, and you can't get your money back." We had a beer or two, and I says, "What do you guys wanna do?"

They says, "We're gonna sit here for awhile."

I says, "I'll be back. I gotta get a blow job." So I leave, and I get a blow job. I just walk to the first window. "Hi, how are you?" I think it was $20. Came back walking in the door, and they're sitting there.

They says, "Can we have two more beers?" They see me walk in and say, "Make that *three*." They said they'd never forget that, 'til the day they died, me walking back in.

I says, "Hi guys! I'm back!"

I went in every night, visiting old haunts. Felt right at home again. Matter of fact, the bosun came out. I was sitting in one of the bars, here I see the bosun walking down the street.

I walk out of the bar, and I says, "Hey, bos."

He says, "Ron. I was looking for you." He says, "I knew you were here, but I didn't know which bar you were in."

I says, "Yeah, you know me well."

It was really nice to get back. I was in my domain. I was in the picture that I was meant to be in. The place reeked of freedom. Everybody's acceptable. It stayed open all night. Girls from all over the world in the windows, I didn't know their name, they didn't know mine, two ships passing in the night. I loved it. Twenty minutes of love. Sometimes shorter. Depending on how much I had to drink that night. Bars, you just walk in, you get a drink. "Hi! How are you?" Everybody's happy.

I said, "Jesus."

And this is no offense to America, but I'm thinking, this is like a den of iniquity *here*, and in America, I gotta go to work in the morning so I gotta be asleep by ten o'clock. And if you're hanging around a strip club in America, they think you're defeating America, or the American way of life, you know, because you're not gonna get up and go to work the next day.

Anyway, we still don't have enough vehicles for this ship. They send us back to Charleston. We get just about a full load, and they say, "Just go to Diego Garcia." Now I'm really happy. We're not gonna go through the Med. They don't want to pay for the transit through the Suez Canal, so they're gonna take us by way of South Africa. They want to see how the ship runs. I liked it because I had signed on for 120 days. Whether it went foreign or came back to the States, I signed for 120 days. What do I care? I'm perfectly happy doing it. Back at sea. I'm perfectly happy.

We get there, anchor out with the other ships. There's a few NMU ships there. They still had a couple under contract.

I run into some of the guys, and they're just barely hanging on. They're *totally* pissed off. If they quit those ships, they *knew* they were never gonna get anything else again.

I tell them, "I was off over a year, and it's miserable out there in the free world." I suggest: "Get out of the NMU *now*. Retire with the NMU, even if you're not gonna get a pension, and go over to the SIU and start building your time up with them if you're gonna keep shipping."

But they're scared, you know. They're actually scared to give up that job. It was a shame. I mean, they were hanging on to the bitter end. It's like throwing good money after bad. I tried to explain that to them. Under new federal laws, we're vested after 5 pension credit years. I says, "You're not gonna get anything 'til your 55 *anyway*. Why not start another pension?" But I don't think any of them did it.

Out of the 13 ships that were there, there were only two NMU ships. All the rest were SIU, Seafarers International Union, that I just joined with this *Sisler*.

Nothing really happened, though. It was the usual drunks, everybody went to the seamen's club, and they took the last launch back at midnight. That's when the fistfights started.

To make a long story short, I says, "Thank you very much," and I left. I had money in my pocket again. I was recharged at Antwerp. I was well on my way.

American Merlin

I'd come back, repaid the money I borrowed, got everything straightened out as best I could, and I was off and running again.

I'm in the union hall in Norfolk, and they put this *American Merlin* on the board. This was 20 January 2000. What they put was: "Loading Houston to go to Greece and Croatia."

I took the job, they flew me to Orange, Texas, the shipyard there. This thing's a wreck. I mean, I'm talking a fucking *wreck*. I get to Houston, and they hand me a ticket to Beaumont.

"*Beaumont?*" I says, "These lying sons of bitches. This thing's in the *yard*. You rotten fuckers."

The agent picks me up in Beaumont and takes me to the hotel.

He says, "Somebody will collect you tomorrow morning. Don't worry about it."

I go in the hotel, raggedy ass hotel. I get up in the morning.

"Oh, are you off the ship?"

I says, "Yeah."

"Just sign for your meals."

"OK."

I go back and lay down. I'm waiting for them to call. Noon rolls around, two o'clock rolls around. Nobody calls. I says, "Fuck this." I got the agent's number. I call.

The agent says, "What are you doing at the hotel?"

I says, "Somebody from your office picked me up at the airport and took me here."

He says, "All crew members are now supposed to be taken to the ship."

I says, "You better tell your people about that. Don't tell me!"

"There's been a mistake. We'll come and get you and take you to the ship."

"OK."

I get to this fucking thing, and I'm looking at it, and it's just falling apart. I says, "Aw, fuck." You know? "Why me, God?" You're getting even with me for Antwerp.

They're trying to get the Coast Guard inspection to get this thing out. They're trying to get it running. It's an old French ship. This company was notorious for doing this, I found out later: they'd buy these old wrecks, get American government contracts, and just run them into the ground.

Anyway, we're supposed to go to Houston, Texas, load grain for Greece or Croatia, and then we're supposed to go to Wilmington, North Carolina to load these vehicles for one or the other.

I'm thinking: "Well, it's been a long time since I've been to Greece. I've never been to Croatia. So, I'll do it."

Long story short: from Orange, Texas to Houston to Wilmington, North Carolina, it took 45 days. I quit.

We're breaking down every fucking 20 minutes. It's almost like the entire ship's *warped*. They couldn't get the port engine running. Mooring lines are parting. The wires are all rotten. It was terrible. We finally load in Houston. We come out, we just get to the *sea buoy* and we break down. They gotta send tugs out from Galveston. We're laid up in Galveston. They got people flying in from all over the world trying to figure out what's wrong with this thing.

Finally we get going again, and we get around to Wilmington. I says, "I quit."

And of all things, that captain I know, Dave Dwyer, he was working for this company, here he's gonna come in Wilmington as, like, a port captain, to help out.

He says, "I'd appreciate it if you'd make the trip on here. You're the only one with any experience."

I says, "Dave, this ship ain't gonna make it." I says, "This is not gonna make it. It's a wreck, Dave. They have nothing. The wires are all rotten. They're parting. The mooring lines are all rotten. Winches ain't working right. The electrician's a fucking idiot." I says, "I'm getting off, Dave."

Dave says, "Well, keep in touch."

"Yeah. You get something else, give me a call." I says, "I'm more than happy to sail with you."

I got off February 29, 2000 in Wilmington, North Carolina.

Tanabata

I go back to the union hall in Norfolk, and I says, "I need a job." They put this *Tanabata* up on the board. This is a car carrier, strictly cars. In a roundabout way, he tries to talk me out of it, it was down in Georgia, and I had never been on a car carrier.

I says, "I don't care. I want it."

He says, "Well, the good thing about this is they say you only need 60 days to get a vacation check, not 120."

Plus, I could put this 45 days on the *Merlin* with the 60 and get a vacation check.

I says, "I'll take it."

Thirty days round-trip from Baltimore to somewhere else, then Brunswick, Georgia, and then across to Bremerhaven, Germany, where you got overnight, and Southampton, England, where you picked up some commercial cargo and some military cargo.

Jesus Christ, you talk about insane. It was nonstop on there. This new chief mate, first time he was trying to do this: "Ron, can you help me with this? Ron, can you give me a hand with that? Ron, can you—"

I says, "What the fuck are you doing on here, mate?"

Everybody's working 12, 15 hours a day, violating international watch standards. We get to Bremerhaven. The only place we got overnight was Bremerhaven. I go to the windows, checking out the girls. The crew wasn't that bad. Everybody knew they were getting beat. It was very low pay and a lot of work. I made one trip, and then I figured I had to make another one, so I made one more, same deal. Stopped in Southampton. We were there a matter of hours. I used to get off at noon, and I'd walk to the gate and then across the way there was a park. To the left was a seamen's club. I'd go over there and have a beer or two and a sandwich.

I called the Englishman, let him know I'm there. He can't, obviously, come down and see me.

When I got back to Baltimore I had exactly 120 days, and I fucking quit.

When I told the chief mate, he says, "What are you gonna do?"

"After seeing this, I should have retired." I says, "This is fucking ridiculous the way this is run."

When I got off, one of the ABs on there, Tom, was getting off, too. Our reliefs weren't there yet.

The captain calls me in. "Your relief is here for you, and Tom, too. I'm giving 'em the paperwork, kind of fill 'em in on what's going on, and when they give the paperwork back, I'll give you your pay, and you can go."

One is a Filipino, doesn't speak much English. The other one's a Cuban, speaks worse than the Filipino. They couldn't fill out their paperwork, didn't know how. I got their paperwork and filled it out for them.

They says, "Make a lot of money?"

I says, "You'll make a ton of money, partner. Don't worry, it's a good job." I says, "The only reason I'm getting off is I got family trouble, you know, sick. That's the only reason I'm going."

But the captain doesn't know that these guys can't speak English, or very little. And I'm thinking: man, if the old man sees them, and he rejects them, me and Tom are stuck. They won't give us our money. So I fill out all their paperwork for them. I says, "You guys just stay here. I'll take it in to the captain."

I go to the captain and say, "Here's their paperwork, captain. I'm filling them in on what's going on, and they're going on the ship right now."

He says, "Where's Tom?"

"Oh, he's here somewhere, captain."

"Here's your money, Ron. Good luck."

"Thank you, captain. I appreciate it." I felt like saying, "I wouldn't even take a captain job on this."

I'm gone. I'm in the wind. I'm down the ramp, cuz we had a ramp on there for the vehicles. Here comes Tom.

I says, "Tom."

"What's up? Did you get paid?"

"Yeah. Our reliefs are here. You better get up there."

He says, "No. I got time now. Me and this other guy are renting a car, and we're gonna drive home."

I says, "You better get up there."

He says, "Why is that?"

"I had to fill out the paperwork for these two guys."

"*What?*"

"A Filipino and a Cuban guy. Neither one of them speak English. I filled the paperwork out for them. The captain hasn't met 'em yet." I says, "If he talks to these guys, he's liable not to give you your money, might not accept them."

He says, "Thanks. Thanks, Ron."

I says, "OK, Tom. I'll see you. I'm getting outta here before they call me back."

I got off May 2, 2000.

Harry L. Martin

$\qquad$

Dave Dwyer called me. Captain Dave. He'd just been assigned to the *American Merlin* in France. He's calling me from France. He says, "You doing anything?"

I says, "No."

"You gotta come out here and give me a hand."

"How bad is it?"

He says, "You were right. It's fucking terrible. It broke down. They had to tow it in to Gibraltar. They repaired it again. They took it, dropped all the cargo off to transport it to Croatia. They got it back here. The crew is gone. The chief mate just fell down in a cargo hatch; he's all busted up. They're sending me Filipinos to work on here. I'm calling the company and telling them to call you and send you out here." He says, "You willing to come?"

I says, "Yeah, Dave, I'll give you a hand."

The company calls me. Jane somebody: "We have a request from Captain Dwyer for you to come over to the *Merlin*, to fly you over to France." Marseilles, France.

I'm thinking: that's a nice place. Never been there, but I've been to France, and I like it there. That's going through the back of my head.

She says, "We don't know if we're gonna get cargo for that ship, so how about if we assign you to the *Harry L. Martin* down in Jacksonville, Florida?"

I says, "What?" I says, "I agreed to work for Captain Dwyer. I'm not agreeing to any of this, flying to Jacksonville, working on the *Martin*." I says, "I'm sorry, but you can check with Captain Dwyer. I'm pretty sure he wants me over there."

She says, "I'll check with Captain Dwyer, but we don't know if we're gonna get cargo for that ship, and we really need an able seaman down there in Jacksonville on this *Harry L. Martin*."

"You better check with Captain Dwyer."

So Dave calls me. Dave says, "Where the fuck are you?"

"I'm still here."

"Why aren't you flying over here?"

I says, "You gotta talk to the company."

Jane, better known as Shanghai Jane—fucking broad would lie to you about anything to get you where she wanted you. I used to call her that: Shanghai Jane. She used to laugh about it. I'd say, "Who are you Shanghaiing, Jane?"

She says: "Oh, the food's real good on the *Martin*, they have a real good crew, and I'm sure . . . ."

I says, "Well, I know Captain Dwyer personally."

"Oh, you'll like this captain." She says, "I was on there. It was great."

What a liar.

Finally, she's just bugging me to the point of—I says, "Look. You pay my way from Cleveland to Jacksonville, you take me over to the union hall, and I only do 60 to 80 days." I needed 80 days for a vacation check or something.

She says, "It's 60 or 120, and we need you for 120."

I says, "I'll do 80. You sign me on for 80 days," cuz it's gonna go to the Mediterranean, stay there in the Med—it's a prepositioned ship—and then I can fly home. I'm making up all these fucking rules.

She agrees to it! I can't believe it!

So then Dave calls and says, "What do you mean you're going to the *Martin*?"

I says, "Dave, it ain't *me*! She says you're not getting cargo. You're liable not to go anywhere. I made up all these fucking rules. *She agreed to them!*"

He says, "I don't care. I need you on here as a bosun."

I says, "Dave, she ain't gonna send me. It's that simple."

"Goddamn help over there. You ask for something, they don't want to give it to you."

"Alright, I'll keep in touch."

They fly me down to Jacksonville on June 9, 2000. I'm off about a month. I get to the *Harry L. Martin*, and it's getting ready to leave the shipyard. It's a vehicle carrier for the military. We're getting ready to leave to go to the Med, and nobody's signed us on yet to go foreign. I'm thinking: what the hell is this? We go out past the sea buoy. We stop. Let the pilot off. The captain stops the ship and calls us up there to sign on. See, it was some kind of federal law that they had to pay us more in the United States than they did when we got out to sea. Once you're out to the sea buoy, you're international, *technically*. So they could actually sign us on for *less* once we hit the sea buoy, or you could just say, "No, I'm not signing." Then they'd have to get you off the ship. It was actually *cheaper* to sign us on once we got outside the sea buoy, in international waters. What a fucking company.

I says, "This cheap ass fucking outfit."

I sign. Cuz I was going to the Med.

It was beautiful going across. We go through the South Atlantic up to Gibraltar. Beautiful big pond. You're talking June, July. It's really great. August is when it starts picking up. Get over to Gibraltar. We go to Rota for stores. Then you go through the straits.

All of a sudden, they turn around, and they said we're getting British security for gangway. I mean, they're just pulling all this on us. So the Brits come on, and we're getting along with them. First week they were taking our jobs away from us. You know, we're all getting shafted. But they're a good bunch; we all gotta eat.

So we get into the Med, and we're gonna make some good ports. I mean, we're going to Ibiza, Mallorca, Barcelona, Benidorm. Oh, this is great! This is fucking great! We went to Sardinia. We went to Sicily. We went to Naples. I mean, this is like the Spanish Riviera, the French Riviera. This is fucking great!

But we don't go to dock. We anchor out. I'll never forgive the chief mate on there for that.

He says, "We're going on day watch."

I says, "Mate, this ain't my first trip. There's no such thing as day watch. It's day *work*."

"No, no. You guys are still on watches, but you're gonna be working eight to five. That's your watch, eight to five. It's day watch."

And no weekends, unless you want to work overtime. Nine dollars an hour for an able seaman to work on a weekend.

You know, OK, I'm not saying anything. The bosun on there's a nice guy. He's taking it easy on us. The only time they set watches is when we go from one port to another. Then we stay 2 weeks.

Now, I'm a tourist. I'm doing enough to get things done, keeping everybody off my ass. Weekends, I'm *gone*. Friday at five o'clock, I'm outta there.

We got a cut-down crew of six able seamen, four engineers, the captain, chief mate, second mate, third mate. Three in the steward department. There was *no one*, to speak of. I mean, if a fire broke out or we really were attacked…. So the chief mate's wanting us to work to make up for it, 4 hours overtime a day. But you gotta work from six at night 'til ten o'clock. Well, the last launch goes out at ten o'clock. So you can't go ashore. I'm thinking: you rotten mothers. Then you can't come back 'til the morning, see? They got the morning launch at six o'clock. The mate denies it, and he can deny it to this day, but he'd be lying. He set it up like that. He was thoroughly convinced that the ship was gonna be attacked. Whether he had privileged information, I don't know. But we got the British security, like, six of them. Anyway, he wants to give out that six in the evening 'til ten, as overtime.

He says, "Ron, you gotta work some of this overtime."

I says, "Thanks, mate, but I don't need the money that fucking bad."

I'm *gone* on the weekends. Friday, I take the six o'clock launch, I'm out there partying. If I did come back, it was only cuz I needed money or a change of clothes. I might come back Sunday night for day work Monday morning.

Mate says, "You know, Ron, you could stay on here on the weekends and work and actually make some money."

I says, "Mate, I think we've been there on this." I says, "Nine dollars an hour? I don't need it that fucking bad."

"But, you know, you might be sitting in a bar over there and those

Basque separatists—" at the time, the Basque separatists were the big thing there, this was before 9/11— "they don't know that you're an American, and they might just blow that place up, and that'd be terrible. You could be here making money."

He had that corn-pone, Andy-Griffith kind of logic, you know?

I says, "Well, mate, that's not really good for me. I understand what you're saying." I says, "It's OK if I'm on here working for $9 an hour, and the terrorists come on here and blow me up? That's OK. Right?" I says, "Look, mate, it's the Spanish Riviera. You think I'm gonna stay on here when I can go over there, the topless beaches, hang with women?"

He didn't like that.

Anyway, now we're gonna get anti-terrorist training. We're running with another ship. It has larger facilities, meeting rooms. We're gonna go over there, and they take nine of us. And the chief mate's gonna be in charge.

He he he. Fucking idiot.

We go over there, eight o'clock in the morning, for 2 days, two 8-hour classes, and we're gonna be anti-terrorist trained. They got these two: one guy's retired Navy Seal, the other one's some kind of retired federal police. In other words, they're double dipping. They're getting their pensions, plus they're doing this. First thing they do is get our names right, cuz they're printing up our certificates that we passed.

That's telling you something.

The first day is what to do if terrorists come and how to make friends with them. Like if they think you're friends with them, they won't kill you.

I'm not really paying attention.

He says, "If somebody comes in here with an AK-47, tells you to lay down on the floor—" He points at me cuz I'm sitting at a table in the front: "You! Spread out! Put your arms out on the table and put your face down there!"

To be honest with you, I'm kind of daydreaming.

One of the engineers off the other ship says, "Look, we're merchant seamen. Come on. We don't know anything."

"Oh, we can train you."

In 16 hours? They're gonna make trained killers out of us? Come on.

They says, "Are there any questions?"

I can't pass. I raise my hand.

He says, "Yes?"

I says, "Excuse me, too. Not only are we just merchant seamen, we're all like engineers or able seamen. I myself am an able seaman." I says, "We've had training to be like professional firemen with these firemen suits, and we're getting professional fireman training, and we're not getting paid any more for it." I says, "*Now* you want us to be policemen or security guards, but we're not getting paid for it."

"Well, I don't have anything to do with that. You've got to take that up with the union and the company."

I just figured I'd throw that in, because I just didn't like those two guys.

It's about 6 hours into this, he says, "OK. Terrorists just came through the door with AK-47s and told everybody to lay down." He points at me. Cuz I'm sitting at this table up front. "What are you gonna do?"

I says, "Kill him."

"*No, no, no.* You're supposed to stretch out on the table!"

I'm looking at him, and I says, "I'm gonna kill this guy, or this guy's gonna kill me."

He says, "You're supposed to lay down and do like we showed you."

I says, "OK."

The next day we're gonna search the ship with our toy guns—our fingers. They don't give us real guns. I don't blame them much. They're gonna show us how to look for *bombs* and *wires*. *Fucking idiots!*

So, we're wandering . . . .

They want us to set up like the police do, all bunched up together and hunched until they all go in to a room together at once. The chief mate's in front, this short AB is in front of me, there's me, and then this other AB is behind me. We're hunched up together, and we got our little guns, our fingers. I shot the AB and the chief mate in the head, with my finger.

This guy behind me says, "What'd you do that for?"

I says, "I just saved our lives, cuz these two will get us killed."

So then we're taking turns doing this, we're searching, I'm rear guard now, and I figure they're gonna sneak up behind us. I figure if they sneak up on me, I'm gonna nail 'em. They didn't.

But this trainer says, "You, rear guard, you're doing a helluva good job."

I says, "Yeah, I want to stay alive. I got money to spend, women to meet."

We get through this training, and they give us our certificates. Now this mate honestly believed something was gonna happen to us.

At the end of this, these two guys are giving him the big story, "Yeah, you got a good bunch here. These guys are really—"

Come on, you're gonna tell *everybody* that.

The chief mate says, "Yeah, but what happens when these guys start rotating out? You guys gonna come back and train some more?"

They says, "Well, we got a schedule to meet, but when somebody rotates out, you'll have to replace him and hope they know what's going on 'til we can get back and train some more."

He points at me and says, "When you rotating out?"

I says, "August 30."

This guy looks at the mate and says, "Well, mate, if anything happens, you better hope it happens before August 30."

I wasn't about to defend that ship.

When my time's up I says, "It's my 80 days, I'm outta here." So they fly me home.

But I did like the run. It was very nice, all the ports we hit. If you ever get a chance to see that, please do. It's expensive now, cuz then it was a dollar in changing against pesos and lira and that. But now it's all the euro, and the dollar took a beating. But I would highly recommend it. Just to go to the beach and sit there. Just go to the beach, nude beaches, topless beaches, whatever you want. You don't have any, "Oh, that's nudity. Oh, we'll have to call the police on you." Nobody cares. They don't care when you put your trash out or when you cut your grass.

So I was back in the States, seeing how much I could stand it. Got back end of August. So it's September, October, all of November, December 1, they call me to go back. I get a call from Shanghai Jane to go back on there. Same ship, back to the *Harry L. Martin*. It's still in the Mediterranean. I take a good look around at the free world again. I've been ashore 3 months. I says, "Yeah, time for me to go again." Spain beckons. Party time here we come. A good bunch on there. Some of the people there had a little more live-and-let-live attitude, but you still had some hard asses on there.

They flew me to Tenerife, Canary Islands. That's where the ship's at. Tenerife was beautiful. This is where I slid down the light pole.

When I got there the guys were all telling me, "We take the launch in." You went right to the port authority building. They had a little restaurant in there, different agents for the shipping companies, and off to the right was facilities for containers.

We were down at the bottom of a hill, and you could walk up through the terminal, two or three levels. Then you would walk out and go across to the street. There was a bridge that went across this hill. If you decided to walk on the road, you would have to walk up, to the right, up to the top of the hill by a streetlight. Then make a left to get to all the bars and restaurants and souvenir stores.

I get there, and the guys are filling me in on what's going on. If you got back before ten o'clock at night, you can go through the terminal. You would come across the street, a four-lane highway. It's all very modern. You would come through the terminal and walk back down and get the launch and go back at whatever the launch time was. If you didn't make it by ten o'clock, they locked the doors to the terminal. So what they were doing was: they were climbing over the barricade there, the railing that led to the grassy knoll on the side of the hill. There was a big brick retaining wall there. They were walking down this to the bushes and grass. There was a big light post, brushed aluminum, with a big fluorescent light. You could jump out to that pole and slide down, then walk across the street to where the launch came by the containers pier. Or you would have to do the long walk around down the road.

I says, "Why do any of it? What are we talking in a taxi, five bucks?"

They says, "Yeah, whatever you want to do."

One night I decide to go ashore and have a few thousand drinks. Next thing you know, it's twelve o'clock. Instead of getting a taxi like I told everybody to do, I wander back, and sure enough the doors are locked on the passenger dock terminal. So I'm gonna walk up to the corner, walk down and around, or I'm gonna grab a taxi. But I'm thinking—you know—everybody else is doing it, I can do it, too.

I climb over the railing. Now I'm in the dirt and the bushes going down to this concrete embankment that's holding up the wall. I'm up maybe 20, 30 feet, standing on top of the concrete wall, and I'm looking at this brushed aluminum pole with the light. I look down on the sidewalk, and I see that there's a pillar that this brushed aluminum pole is bolted into. So it's about another 2, 3 feet before you get to the sidewalk.

I'm hemming and hawing, you know, right, and: oh, you know, it just don't pay to go back up again now, does it? I'm looking, and I'm thinking: gee, when I jump on this, I'm gonna have to turn a little bit, to the right or to the left, because if you'd a went down straight between the wall and the pole, you'd probably got wedged in there as it narrowed.

So I says, "Well, everybody else is doing it. I can do it, too." I'm a big boy.

I jump on this pole.

I go down like a ton of bricks.

I'm laying there, in the bag, drunk. The only thing I could think of is: "Gee, Ronnie, you're a big boy now. You better be able to get yourself up." I pull myself up by the base.

I'm scared to look at any damage I did. I'm not even looking for blood. I get up and stumble across the road, along the side of the passenger dock terminal. As I'm walking, I pass these benches. I'm close to the launch area. It's a Friday night, and I don't have to work Saturday. I says, "You know what? I don't need this." I lay down on the bench.

Next thing I know, two of the young guys from the ship are grabbing me. "Hey, Ron! Ron, get up!"

I says, "Oh, man, just leave me here."

"No, man, we can't leave you here. Those Spanish kids, they get up to the top of the hill and throw matches and empty beer bottles down here. We gotta get you out of here. You got too much sea time."

They get me up. I made it under my own steam to the launch with all the rest of the heavy drinkers. I passed out on the launch. Get back to the ship. I go to my foc'sle, pass out. Next day I get up around noon. Now I figure I better take inventory and see what's wrong besides the headache.

I look all over. I get in the shower. I look. The only thing I have wrong is my jeans on my left knee are scuffed. I got a small bruise on the knee. I look at the watch I was wearing, you could actually see the brushed aluminum on there where it had ground into the watch face, cuz I wear my watch inside out, on the inside of my wrist. I'm thinking: Is that all?

I can't believe it.

Then I stop and talk to the guys, tell them what happened; and I'm the one that tells everybody: what's five bucks in a taxi.

But we stopped at some very good places this trip. That's the first time I had been to the island of Ibiza, pronounced "Ebeetha." I was saying "I-beeza" until I was corrected numerous times. What had happened was, we're making these different ports, like 2 weeks in every port.

One of the British security guards asked me, "Have you ever been to Ibiza?"

I says, "No."

He says, "I've got some free passes for the clubs there." At the time it'd saved you about $20 to get in. He says, "Would you like to go?"

"Sure, I'll go with you."

"One thing I gotta tell you now, though. Ibiza's the gay capital of Europe." He says, "But if that doesn't bother you . . . ."

"No, no, I got no problem."

You had to start out at ten o'clock at night, like everything else in Spain. Everything starts happening at ten and goes around to six or seven in the morning. I says, "Hey, this is great!"

It's one big party. It's another place everybody should see once in their life. The night life there is live and let live. We stopped at one place, The Blue Rose, exotic dance club. Girls from all over the world, guys from all over the world, gays, straights, bis, nobody cared.

I met a girl there and we started talking—well, they all try to get a conversation, cuz that's how they make a living. But anyway, she says, "You're not gay are you?"

I says, "No."

She says, "You're not bisexual, either, are you?"

I says, "No."

"You're straight."

"Yeah."

She says, "You're a commodity here." For the girls. You are a *commodity*.

So, my time's up on this. Now we're working different ports. Naples, Italy. The naked lady of Capri, which is just an island off the coast of Naples, it looks like a woman laying down is what it looks like. Back and forth, we're having a pretty good time. Not making any money.

We came back to Tenerife, and that's where I get off, and I flew up to England to see the Englishman, just to say hello. I spent a week up there, wandering around, doing the tourist thing. Nothing exceptional happened. He's pretty well retired now. He's seen his better days from sitting around jail in Saudi Arabia.

I flew back after wandering around London for about a week with Ken. I was just seeing some of the sights, doing the tourist thing.

LTC Calvin P. Titus

I'm back in the States. The company calls again, first part of April 2001: "We need someone for the *Lieutenant Calvin P. Titus.*"

I says, "No. I'm not interested if it's not going to the Mediterranean." Cuz now I'm really getting into the Med. I want to go back.

They says, "Oh, please do this." Shanghai Jane again, you know, promise you anything.

It's going to West Africa. I wasn't interested at all.

She says, "It's only gonna be 45 days. You'll be here in the States loading, go over, hit maybe two, three ports, and come back all in 45 days."

I says, "OK, if it's 45 days, and I get the next AB job on the *Harry L. Martin.*" I says, "I'll do a deal with you. You guarantee me that I get that job," which really isn't hard to do, they couldn't find anybody, the pay was so low. But I says, "You get me back on the *Harry L. Martin* for 60 days."

"Oh, no, no, 120, Ron."

"I'll do it. You give me 60 days, though, and I'll make this run for you to West Africa." I only wanted 60 cuz I could get off quicker so I could party faster. If I stayed for 120 days, I would have been getting off towards the end of the season. The season ends there late October or November. Then everything shuts down in Ibiza until May, so you only have the people that live there hanging around.

They says, "OK. That'll work out. We're gonna need an AB relief in the first week in June."

I says, "That's fine. I do the *Titus* for 45 days, then I'm on the *Martin.*"

I get to the *Titus.* They were firing all the able seamen, but they wouldn't fire them until they could get reliefs. They wouldn't pay them off. That's the way it was when I got there. We were loading ammunition and water buffalos, which are nothing but trailers with water tanks on them for somebody's West African army. America's goodwill gesture. You know, give them some ammunition and then some water.

There's a real crew on there. Nobody wanted to be there, and for most guys it was their first trip into the union, where they had come from other unions and they needed a job.

I says, "Yeah, I'm glad I only decided to do the 45 days and didn't sign for anything more so they couldn't hold me against my will."

We go there, and it hasn't changed at all from the '80s. It's even worse. Armed guards everywhere. I can't even remember the names of the ports. You don't want to remember things like that. It's just armed guards, security guards, whatever army happened to be in charge at the time. They have patrol boats guarding us. All this is before 9/11. It's a zoo. Probably still is. Nobody went ashore.

I can't remember the first two ports we hit, but it was like a period of 8 hours and we were outta there. We just got there, unloaded whatever cargo we had, and got outta there. I think Lagos, Nigeria was the last port, and we ended up staying there like 18 hours, and they kept us all on security. We got like 6 hours off out of a 24-hour period. Everybody was on security. They were scared of stowaways, robberies. Glad to leave.

Came back to Norfolk, Virginia. My time was up.

They says, "You can stay here or—"

I says, "Wait a minute! The deal was that I do this 45 days and I get to go to the *Harry L. Martin*, you know, first week in June." I says, "That's it. You're good for your word or I'll never do this again." I tell Jane that. She agreed. I got off May 23 in Newport News.

Harry L. Martin, 2001

⚓

They flew me out to the *Martin*. I joined in Rota, Spain, the U.S. Navy base. Well, it's a NATO base now. We're going to these same wonderful places. You're talking June in the Mediterranean. June, July, and August I was there. Stopped in Ibiza again. So, on one hand I have America and my loved ones, and on the other hand I have Ibiza and insanity, a different way of life, anti-social behavior.

I get off August 13 in Cagliari, Sardinia with a ticket back to the States. I walk into the airport and says, "Can I change this ticket?"

They says, "What do you want to do?"

"I either want go to London tonight or Ibiza."

"We can't get you to London tonight, maybe tomorrow. But we can have you in Ibiza tonight."

It's $100 to change the ticket.

I says, "OK. Here's $100." We're on our way.

I go back to Ibiza. I get a room. It was wonderful. Unbelievable. I spent about 10 days there. I'm burning out again. Ten days of very little sleep. You always keep a hotel room, you know, as a safe house. I didn't come back for 3 days, and when I came back to the hotel, the guy at the desk says, "We were worried about you. Where you been?"

I says, "Don't wake me. Just let me sleep."

Yeah, it was 3 wild days. I was with a girl, got a tour of the topless beaches, the nude beach up in the mountains, then you come down into a valley, and there's a little restaurant there, looks like something you see in the South Pacific. You know, palm leaves over the roof, and there's a little picnic area. That's the nude beach, as far as you can walk down. It's secluded. I got a complete tour of the island, just the different areas, just the way of doing things. Totally, totally great.

So, now, I was meeting different people. It was like Florida: nobody was from there. Everybody was from somewhere else. Also, Ibiza is an old hippie colony from the '60s. There were actually Americans there that had gone there in the '60s and just stayed. I believe the ones I did meet were financially pretty well set in life. You had some Americans, too, coming through there that the only thing they went back to the States for was to renew their passport every 10 years. That was basically what they did, and they were just living there. As long as you didn't cause any trouble, Spaniards gave you no trouble. When I started running over there, it was to the point where during the season the people that actually live on the island were given the first jobs. If you lived on the island and were Ibizan, you had the first choice of the jobs. They had to get hired if they wanted to work in any of the restaurants, bars, hotels, or anything. Then you had the Spanish. They had their choice. Then you had people from the European Union, then anybody after that. But you had people from all over the world.

I stayed 10 days, which would have made it the 23rd of August, 2001. Then I went to England to recuperate, more than anything else, to go see the Englishman, see what he was up to. That would have put me back in the States just about September 1, 2001.

And that girl calls me and says, "Are you coming back?" She had just broken up with her boyfriend. I fell into the break up part, and I was next on the hit parade. So she calls me in the States and says, "Can you come back?"

"I can't right now. But I'll be back."

That was September 6.

September 11th, boy, that put a kibosh on everything. Fifty years of American foreign policy coming home to roost. I says, this is gonna be a tough nut to crack here now, to even get back there under these conditions.

Harry L. Martin, 2002

Of all things, May 31, 2002, the company called. "Would you like to go back on the *Harry L. Martin*? It's still in the Med."

I says, "Sure. Sounds good to me."

I'm back on the *Martin*, and we're still gonna make these ports. I got a 60-day job again. We're making the same run, but now we're coming out of the Med. They didn't want to keep the ship in the Mediterranean the complete time. They wanted to send it up to Europe, up to England, even going as far as Poland. They wanted to get it out of the Med. They were scared to death. Security.

So, same ports, same style. It was great to be back again.

Now they're gonna take us up to Torquay, England. I slipped and hurt my knee. Jammed it. They sent me to an English doctor.

He says, "I'm gonna give you 7 days 'Not Fit for Duty.' Is that alright with you?"

I says, "Sure. Not a problem."

They get me off in Torquay. This is like an emergency. They have to get me a flight back to the States.

So the captain says, "The agent's gonna get your ticket. They're taking you to London, to Heathrow, and you're gonna fly outta there later on today."

So I get off, and they gotta drive me to Heathrow. And I knew Ken Bottoms was in London.

The agent gets me and says, "OK, I'm driving. Let's go." It's a long drive. Got to see Stonehenge on the way.

We get to Heathrow, and he says, "I'll watch your bag. Go see if your ticket's alright. You'll be leaving in about 6 hours."

"OK." I go up to the ticket counter to check my ticket.

"Oh, yeah, you're fine."

I says, "Is there any possible way I can change this ticket?"

Ticket guy says, "Yeah. You paid full price for this."

I'm thinking: that's right, friend, I sure did, huh? I says, "I'd like to change it." I says, "And I'll probably want to change it again after that."

He says, "You can do anything you want with this. I can give you the cash if you'd like."

"Oh no, don't do that. I'd like to have the ticket. Can you give me 2 or 3 months?"

"Two or three months?"

I says, "I'll probably want to come back after, but I'd like enough time."

He says, "I'll give you 60 days, but you can change this back and forth. Whenever you want. If it's within the 60 days, you can just call and say, 'Hey, I changed my mind. I'd like to leave a little earlier.'"

"That's cool."

He changes the ticket for me. No money of my own changes hands in this. I go back to the agent, and the agent says, "You all set? Ready to go?"

"Yeah, I got everything."

He says, "You got about 5 hours now. You don't need me here, do you?"

"Of course not. I can take this. I'm a big boy now."

"OK. Good luck."

I says, "Thank you very, very much."

He leaves.

I call Ken Bottoms. I says, "Keep a light in the window, I'm on my way," right? I've got a 7-day pass to stay in the UK as an emergency deal. I didn't get checked in. I never saw Customs.

I go to Ken. Ken says, "Wait a minute. What are you gonna do after 7 days with that ticket?" He says, "You'll get stopped anywhere you go."

I says, "Let's do it the old-fashioned way." I says, "I'm flying to Ibiza, right? Then I'll come back, and I'll get 6 months." I got off on a medical, I got 7 days to stay in the UK, just to transit the UK, technically, to go back to the States. I wasn't allowed to work or anything. I wasn't coming as a tourist, I was coming in as an injured merchant seaman. I stayed in England 6 days, but I made the flight down to Ibiza. I had to pay for that. But when I left Ibiza, I checked through with my passport, and they just stamped me out of the UK. They didn't know where I was leaving for. They just knew I had 7 days, and it was OK. I was there less than 7 days. They didn't care where I was going. I get to Ibiza, they stamped me there for 60 days, right? "Transit." Technically, I'm going from one EU country to another.

I get down there, I enjoy Ibiza for another week or so. That's about as long as I could keep any kind of a relationship going. Then I fly back up to the UK, and they give me 6 months. I'm entering from Spain, technically. So I'm good for 6 months now. So I spent another week or so in London, then flew back to the States.

Yeah.

You can do things like that if you really look at it, if you really, really look at it.

Cape John

The captain called me on this one. He says, "Hey, Ron, Captain Dwyer. You wanna go bomb Iraq?"

I says, "Sounds cool to me, Dave."

He says, "I need you on here. I'm captain on the *Cape John*."

This was an older freighter from the '60s, '70s, one of those self-unloaders with booms, and it's in Orange, Texas. It's being put into commission—you know—even though it's been laid up and it's been maintained, now you have to do the little things to it to get it together. We go up to New Jersey to load November 30, 2002, and we're getting ready to go across to the Middle East.

I get internal blockage from an old wound, scar tissue had built up, from when I had my appendix removed. They take me off the ship, and I go to the hospital in Red Bank, New Jersey. They perform surgery on me. I'm off thirty days. I get back on the *Cape John*. 'Fit for duty' again.

We're on our way with a load of bombs. Going across, the crew isn't that bad: personalities, conflicts, the usual thing you find if you ever make a trip to sea with people. I mean, literally, we're all in the same boat, and the personalities start coming out, you know, "I'm doing more than that one," or "This one's not doing enough," and "This one's getting paid more."

During the Vietnam War, McNamara was Secretary of Defense, and there was so much trouble on these merchant ships, taking ammunition over to the war, that he said—they give all servicemen mental tests—they're gonna give *all* merchant seaman mental tests. The presidents of the unions got together and said, "If you give these guys mental tests, you won't have *anybody* to sail your ships."

Like I say, even among the officers you don't have rocket scientists going out. You don't have NASA engineers. You have people that want to do this for a living, and then they're stuck, or they think it's an adventure, and then they quit doing it. Everybody's got their own little agenda.

We go to Sicily, take on some fuel and some deck cargo that they want us to have. I should mention, the last thing we put on board in New Jersey was a load of lumber—two by fours and planks and stuff—on the deck.

Everywhere we stop they want this lumber. "Can we have that lumber?"

"No, you can't have it because it's for some general in Kuwait or Iraq that wants this to build his house."

In Sicily they're asking, "Can we have that lumber?" The Navy, everybody, "Can we have that lumber?"

I says, "If it was up to me, I'd give it to you, but it belongs to some general in Kuwait or Iraq that needs it. It's going over to him." Rank does have its privileges.

Now, part of the crew decides to go home. It's not *their* war, and I don't blame them. So it's back and forth to the doctors. Everybody's trying to talk the doctor into letting them off, except me. I get some kind of an infection, but I just want some medication, cuz I'm gonna *do* this. You know, here's another adventure to get into, some kind of trouble.

We get orders to go up to some port in Norway—something like Goodensnot, or Jackuoff, or something like that, Norway. This is near the Arctic Circle. Back in the '60s and '70s we're storing ammunition in caves up there in case of a war with the Soviet Union.

We come back out of the Med, stop in Rota for more food and fuel. Everybody's kind of relieved that we're not going into the war zone just yet. We're going to a sideshow to what's gonna happen later.

In Rota we pick up some Navy guys that're gonna do the shoring of the ammunition when we get up to Norway. So now it's up through the English Channel, up to Norway. You talk about lousy weather. We're getting beat to death. It's very close to the Arctic Circle. We go into the fjord, a secure area, and it was six or eight hours to get where we're going. A Norwegian tug is breaking the ice up ahead of us.

Now we anchor out, and we take eight hundred feet of anchor chain. Eight shots. One shot is about a hundred feet. We have eight shots out to hold us. You know how deep those fjords are? I mean, Russian submarines used to hide in there. That's how deep they are. They got a barge, and the tug takes the barge to the shore and gets the ammunition, trucks it in. They're bringing it to the ship. As they push the barge alongside, only one barge at a time, the tug has to go around us breaking up the ice cuz we'd freeze in there.

We're there 2 or 3 days with this operation, getting all these bombs on board. We let the Navy guys off before going through the channel. And now we hit *another* storm. Now the ammo's shifted. These big five hundred-pound bombs that they shored up with lumber are shifting. So now we've got to go down there and shore it up again. Everybody's pissing bricks, you know, "Goddamn this," and "This is bullshit," and "Gotta do all this fucking work."

But we get it done, and shoot through again. Now we stop in Crete. We just stopped there for a matter of, like, 12 hours, and we go ashore and have a few drinks and pick up the Greek national cigarettes. Stopped in Souda Bay, Crete. I picked up a carton of cigarettes to bring back, as I usually did. The Greek national cigarette, Assos— say it like "assoles." They went over big with the girls in the States. They really did.

"Would you like a pack of Assos?"

Giggling: "Oh, yeah, OK, Assos."

Yeah, they loved it. I take them all Assos.

Giggling: "The Greek National cigarette."

They used to take them to work with them.

"He he he. Look what I got. Assos. He he he."

You can imagine the crowd I run around with at the bar, huh?

OK. We stopped there for about 12 hours. We pick up Marine guards, security, they're gonna stay with us in case we're attacked. Through the Suez Canal, all the way around, they stay with us. Good bunch of guys, they believed in what they were doing, which was more than I could say for myself and half the crew on that ship already.

We go around, into the Gulf of Aden, then the Gulf of Oman and then into the Persian Gulf. We stop in Kuwait. There's three bases there, port facilities. That's where we're gonna discharge the ammunition.

I get a toothache. It's killing me.

So the Navy doctor comes to the ship and says, "Yeah, you need dental, but we don't have a dentist here. The only dentist we've got is up about a hundred miles from the Iraqi border, waiting to go in with the Marines. Do you want to go?"

I'm thinking about it now. How bad does this hurt? I says, "You know, I'd rather take my chances than have this toothache."

President Bush is still screaming about the line in the sand, and we got a week or something before the war starts.

A Marine sergeant and a corporal come and get me in the lieutenant's Wagoneer. Sergeant says, "Now we gotta get these other Marines. Cuz everybody needs dental work. We're taking you all up."

Now this was interesting. We had to go through Kuwait City. I mean, he's driving sixty, eighty miles an hour. I can still see some damage in Kuwait City from Gulf War One. This is Gulf War Two coming up.

Then they says, "Alright, now we're gonna go the tourist route. We're gonna go on Dead Sheep Highway."

I says, "OK."

They says, "By the way, have you had your anthrax shot?"

I didn't have the shots yet. They were getting ready to give 'em to us on the ship. I says, "No, I haven't."

Then I'm seeing these water wells that are dry now, and there's big signs by them, "Don't drink." I see all these dead sheep: Dead Sheep Highway.

I says, "Excuse me. These sheep: are these road kills?"

They says, "No, this is from the last war." Poisoned wells, and the water gone into the ground, and now the anthrax is coming back up and the sheep eating the grass.

I says, "Oh, that's nice."

We get up to the base, and I get to the dentist. I mean, I'm talking they got *generators* for electricity.

I get a young Navy dentist, Oriental-American, and he says, "We have to pull that."

I says, "I hope so, after I've gone through all this. Don't try to drill this thing." I says, "One thing, if you would, please, I'd like to have the tooth after you pull it."

He says, "Oh, I can't, because after I take it out of your mouth, it's contaminated."

The only thing I could think of was, "It was contaminated when it was *in there*. If you'd seen some of my girlfriends." Now that it's *out*, it's contaminated? I want to save the tooth because I bury them. All the teeth I've had pulled, I bury all over the world, or throw in the ocean, different spots, everywhere.

It's a sentimental thing. Once I threw a tooth into the ocean halfway between New Zealand and Panama. I just threw it in the ocean. I left blood and sperm all over the world. Why not my teeth, too?

I explain this to the Navy dentist.

He looks at me a little strange. He's young, doesn't understand the ways of the world yet. But now I get in an argument with him.

I says, "I gotta have it."

"No, you can't have it, it's contaminated."

"Look, friend . . . ."

He says, "I'll tell you what. I'll pull it and save it, and then we'll ask the captain if you can have the tooth."

I says, "Yeah, go ahead and do it."

He pulls it, then I'm waiting, cuz the other Marines need dental work. Then here comes the captain.

The Navy dentist says, "Captain, we have a problem here. This gentleman's a merchant seaman, and he's up from a ship in Kuwait. He needed a tooth pulled. I pulled it, but he has some religious thing about burying his own teeth. He wants to take it with him, but it's contaminated."

The captain's looking at him like, "You know, we're less than 100 miles from the Iraqi border, there's gonna be a *war* here, we're all going up to the front lines in less than a week! Give this guy his tooth!"

So the dentist, he puts it in alcohol in a little plastic container and gives it to me. I thank him. I wanted to thank the captain for siding with me on that.

Now I have to wander around the base with the Marines, cuz we can't find the sergeant or the corporal. So they drop me off at the company headquarters, this tent. It has a wooden deck, not sand. So I'm sitting there, and guys are in there on the internet complaining to their wives and girlfriends. There's homing pigeons in there, too, and I'm looking at these.

One of the Marines comes by and says, "It's my job to take care of these things."

I says, "That's nice." You know, we're talking World War I here.

Finally, somebody with authority comes in, this warrant officer. He's got his hands in his pockets, and they're all coming up to him with their problems.

One of the Marines says, "Somebody said this was stolen."

This officer looks at him and says, "There's nothing stolen in the Marine Corps." He says, "It was appropriated."

He gave me the impression like, "Do I really need any of this?" My kind of guy.

We're kind of drawn to each other because I have coffee.

He walks right over to me and says, "You being helped? Is there something we can get you?"

I explain to him why I'm there. It's like he finally found somebody he could communicate with.

He says, "I got 2 more years, and I'll be getting out."

I says, "Where you gonna retire? I'm planning on retiring, too."

He says, "Well, I'm dual citizenship, Brazil and America. One of the officers I've been with actually retired to the Canary Islands, and he'd like me to come over there. You know, we keep in touch, he's retired over there, and I'm really thinking about it." He mentions a golf course.

I says, "The golf course that you fly over when you land there?"

"You've been there?"

I says, "Yeah!"

He says, "Man, come sit down here a minute. You know, we could—"

Now he's got somebody he can bond with here. We're talking about the Canary Islands and Spain and this and that. And about that time, the pigeons start acting up.

"Look," he says, "I'm requesting everything I can, and what do they send me? *Pigeons! Carrier* pigeons. In case we lose communication, we can use these pigeons."

I says, "You better be careful. The Iraqis will eat them if they get a chance."

I'm there 2 or 3 hours talking.

He says, "Well, it's getting late. You wanna stay here?"

"Stay here?"

He says, "Yeah. We'll get you something to eat. We'll get you a bunk. You can stay here. Just stay here with us. We might pull out tomorrow or the next day. But you can go with us."

"Go with *you*?" I says, "Look," I says, "no offense, me and you are OK, but I'm going back to that ship one way or another, even if I gotta thumb my way back. I *seen* sand."

By then the sergeant and corporal are back. It's dark already.

He says, "You come on back anytime, we'll be more than happy to take care of you, help you out, just come up."

To this day I don't know the guy's name, and he don't know mine.

I get back to the ship and give Dave the paperwork.

Dave says, "What the hell took you so long?"

I says, "They wanted me to stay there. They wanted to give me a bunk, and I could sleep there for the night."

He says, "I don't believe it."

"Neither do I."

OK, now the war's supposed to start, the line in the sand thing, George Bush gives them two more days. We know the war's gonna start because they send us away. They says, "This is it. Stop discharging ammo. Secure your ship and go out to sea." They don't want us alongside the dock for the war.

And everybody's really confident. Guys are having their picture taken on the bombs, on the dock. The Navy's doing the discharging.

They says, "Come on, Ron, we'll go down on the dock and have our picture taken on the bombs."

I says, "No. I don't think so."

"You don't think Saddam Hussein's gonna win, do you?"

I says, "I don't want my picture taken. It's OK. I rarely have my picture taken. It's a personal thing."

"Well, you don't think Saddam Hussein's gonna win this, do you?"

I says, "We're gonna win the war, and we're gonna lose the peace." I says, "America's never gonna get outta here."

They look at me like, "How can you even talk like that?"

I says, "Trust me. Trust me on this."

Just before we leave we get Navy reservists who are gonna do unloading at sea. The *Cape John* has that capability, to get bombs moved from ship to ship. So now they're gonna use us as a floating warehouse.

We basically do grids in the Persian Gulf. We have a certain area we stay in for the entire war—OK, for the entire *23 days*. We got Marine security, we got Navy reserves who are gonna do this replenishment at sea with other ships. And I'm thinking, "Oh, God, all these bodies on a ship. There's too many people on here now!" These Navy reservists, they had firemen and policemen and some guys that were run-of-the-mill people that just had jobs and stayed in the Navy reserve, you know?

Give me a break. They got no finesse. They're wandering around the ship all hours of the day and night, coming up to the bridge. One of them wants to have a photo op, so he tries to get one of the Marine's M16s and have the other Navy guy take pictures of him like he was actually standing guard on the wing of the bridge. The Marine wouldn't give it to him.

So he goes and gets the Marine captain, and the Marine captain comes up there and says, "Humor these assholes. Give him your rifle. Take the clip out, but give him a rifle."

This guy puts on the flak jacket and the helmet. The other Navy reserve takes pictures of him, like he's actually doing this.

One of the Marines walks by me and says, "What do you think?"

I says, "Hey, you know, more heroes. Everybody's a hero."

It's all bullshit. I got along better with the Marines. The Navy tolerated me, and I tolerated the Navy.

We do these replenishments until the end of the war. Then they send us back into the dock.

We have two sandstorms. First time I've been in a real good sandstorm, other than like in Egypt. But this is a good one, I mean, *blinding*. One, we're alongside the dock, and one out in the Persian Gulf where the sand is actually coming out. It's just like you see in the movies. Your eyes burn, your throat chokes.

They had the PX in Kuwait, but you couldn't even get rubbing alcohol. There's all the Cuban cigars you want, though.

There's women in the Navy, these replenishment crews that come on. I assume I could have talked one or two of them into something. But you get to the point where you just don't need it anymore, you know? You just don't need the bullshit anymore. It all ends up being the same thing. I don't bother them, and they don't bother me. Well, one of them gives me a piece of candy.

We're at dock, and I'm out there on gangway. One of the Navy girls comes out, gives me a piece of candy. Just walks by and says, "Oh, here."

I says, "Thank you."

I should have asked her name or said, "Hey, I'm Ron." But the only thing I'm thinking about is getting this fucking over with and getting back to Ibiza.

I mean, really. I'm very plain about that. I'm getting off of there. I don't want to stay, although the money's good, plus we get the war bonus, and hazardous duty pay from the time we hit Crete. And I'm making extra overtime because of the crew reduction. So it's actually pretty profitable.

So Dave gets me one day and says, "Hey, we're leaving sometime the first week in May. Alright with you?"

I says, "Yeah. You go, I go."

He says, "Would you like to stay?"

I says, "No. You go, I go."

We get off in Jebel Ali, United Arab Emirates. UAE. It's a small country. You've heard of the Dubai Open, Tiger Woods. They use all their oil money to build things up. They're gonna have the largest air-conditioned mall in the world. There are signs there that say "Fastest growing city in the world." I mean, girls from all over the world are coming there. Women and booze are wide open. No restrictions on that. I end up with a Russian girl for 2 days, I don't remember her name. She probably don't remember mine.

And the UAE is all very progressive, very open-minded. It's nice, if you can stand the heat. We're stuck there for 3 more days. We do a desert tour. We sign up for it at the hotel when we find out it was gonna be at least three more days before they can get a flight out for us, because they took us from Jebel Ali, on the coast, into Dubai.

So an agent explains we're flying from UAE to London.

I says, "Here we go again." So I ask the agent, "What happens if I get off in London?"

He says, "Just explain to them that you want to get off in London. Don't put your luggage on there, and then when you get off in London, tell them you'd like to have the ticket changed again."

So from the hotel I call Ken Bottoms. He answers the phone.

I says, "I'm on my way."

He says, "I'm here. You know where the key is, in case I'm not."

So I knew I had a safe house in London.

I get off there, turn around, and he's getting ready to go back to work on the dredge. So we get together and do a little wandering around. We do the tours, Jack the Ripper walk, the London Eye, that big Ferris wheel. We do it all. The Ten Bells where Jack the Ripper's victims used to drink, before he cannibalized them or whatever he did to them.

Then I decide to fly down to Ibiza.

Yeah.

So I fly down there for a week. Then back up to England. Then back to the States.

Oh. And the tooth. I buried that in the Persian Gulf. Flipped it overboard. I just wanted—you know—blood, sperm, and teeth, all over the world.

Cape Farewell

Captain Dave calls me and says, "I just got a captain's job on this *Cape Farewell.*" This is a LASH ship, lighter aboard ship. They brought it out of lay up, and they're gonna load ammunition on the west coast and take it over to the Far East. He says, "I'll hire you if you want to go."

I says, "Yes, I'd like that."

About a week later, Dave calls and says, "The company said I can hire. Just fly out here, save your receipts, and I'll reimburse you."

I says, "Fine."

This is March 2004. I get out there to Indian Island, north of Seattle near the Canadian border, where the ammo pier is. Everybody's loading, getting ready to make the trip. It's gonna be a run to the Far East, we're discharging ammunition for the U.S. Army and the Korean Army. This is a chance to get back to Jinhae, Korea, somewhere I'd been in '77, see what it was like again.

Got a good ordinary seaman on there, Brett Younginger, first trip to sea, he'd come out of the school. I got on watch with him. It was really good having an ordinary there that was in tune with the way a watch should be stood, or the way I feel a watch should be stood. And I'm gonna say "aggressively," for lack of a better word. Everybody relieves each other on time, if not before, gives each other breaks. Just take care of the watch. So, basically, the other gentlemen on the watch, the other able seaman, we'd take care of each other. When we give the watch over, we're right, you know, when we take the watch, we make sure things are right before we take the watch. If I'm on board, it's dead serious. I do expect other people to be that way on my watch. But once I'm ashore, that's it. I separate the ship from shore.

My time off is my time off. I'm entitled to do anything I want with it.

I felt this way since I started. That's the way I learned. You know, old habits are hard to break. So I try to pass them along to anybody that's willing to learn. I'm not saying it's right. I'm just saying that it makes it a lot easier on all of us if the watch knows what they're thinking, all three of us know we're on the same page.

I could care less what the other watches do.

Somebody'll say, "The other watch does it this way."

I'll say, "Well, that's the other watch." When I take the watch, I take the watch. It's right, and when we turn it over it's right. When we go to dock or undock, the easiest, safest way to do things is: everybody gets a job, everybody does their job. If you have people that don't know their job or how to do it or the way it's to be done, it just adds more work.

You know, people will say the captain's word is law. In reality, the captain has the least say-so of anybody. I mean, you got the agent, the government, somebody else's government, the Coast Guard, the Navy, you got everybody involved in this. It's pretty ridiculous: master's word is law. I mean, captains end up going crazy is what it amounts to, trying to take care of everything. Putting the pressure on the captain to perform, ordering around decisions that are made elsewhere. The people ashore who make these decisions don't suffer. The crew and the captain suffer. The only way I can phrase it is: "captain's word is law" or "the buck stops here" is ridiculous anymore. The captain might as well be an overpaid taxi cab driver. I mean, that's as simple as it is. I'm not taking anything away from captains, but to say "Oh, *captain*" is kind of ridiculous in this day and age. I've got people tell me, "Oh, the captain told you to do this. You've gotta do it." In reality, you *don't*. You can just wander off. What are they gonna do, argue with you? I mean, that's as simple as it is. You get your orders, and if you don't know what you're doing, well, then, you don't know what you're doing. I mean, the Coast Guard says you're an able-bodied seaman, or the Coast Guard says you're qualified to do this. The union sends you out, unless you trip over your own feet too many times. I mean, you do get warnings. The third warning is dismissal. But everybody learns it a different way, and the way they learn at these schools leaves a lot to be desired. Matter of fact, at the unlicensed school, I believe it's only 5% even bother go to sea. I mean, they get there, and they're totally disillusioned: "They didn't show me this at the school." A lot of it's common sense, docking, undocking, standing a watch. "I didn't learn that at the school."

I'll say, "Well, that was the school, and this is here."

There's no set rule of thumb anymore, how the watches are gonna operate. This is when I say, you know, how the watch is run. There's no system to it anymore, because it varies from ship to ship. You kind of get the ground rules started as soon as you get on board, and you see what you've got. Then you try to establish how it's gonna go.

But I try and run it where you learn something, or somebody learns that this is the way it was done 40 years ago. I'm not saying anybody's gonna make a career out of this anymore, or a lifestyle. But it does help to communicate a system of how we, on the watch, know what to do. It sounds very simple to tie up or let go of a ship. But when somebody doesn't know how to do it, or know what lines go where, it's ridiculous that they even come out there with no hands-on experience. They learned everything out of a book. It's not that hard. There's nothing that hard out there. It's not hard to steer a ship if you apply yourself. Some people just don't want to apply themselves. Some able seamen like day work. They prefer the eight to five, just like they're ashore. I prefer the watch. I prefer to be up on the bridge. That's just a preference. But why not? If you're gonna be there, why not try to do something correct or learn a little something that you might be able to carry over to the next ship, rather than if you do it wrong once, why keep doing it wrong all the time?

And you get guys that say, "Well, that's the easy way to do it, we should do it this way. Why do it the hard way?"

I've been on ships where the crew will be back on the stern, and I'll have to ask the mate on the stern, "Why are we doing it this way?"

He says, "I don't know. That's the hard way to do it."

I says, "Well, why don't you take charge, and why don't we do it *this* way?"

There's a lot of that where people don't want to get involved, even the mate on watch. You know, the mate that comes back to tie up and let go doesn't want to get involved in it because somebody will say, "Oh, I like the way we did it on the last ship." Well, that's the *last* ship. Maybe it was right and maybe it was wrong, but it's *this* ship now—you know—and *this* is the way we're gonna do this. Hopefully it's the right way *and* the easiest way.

Anyway, we get going on the foreign voyage. First port is Guam, where we discharge the ammo. Then we turn around and made a quick trip up to Japan, didn't get a chance to go ashore. Came back down and went to Okinawa. Never did get over to see the Sapphire Bar. Wanted to, but just couldn't make it.

Now this was the interesting part of the entire trip. We got back to Guam, and this is a case of how much it's changed. We're tying up on the stern, and the bow was still tying up. What it amounted to was you had a small pier, just the length for the ammo to be taken off. Then you had what we call dolphins; they're a permanent fixture in the ocean, just on a block of concrete supported by steel pillars. The lines have to be taken there by a small boat or drug over and put on.

We managed to get those over there on the stern and the bow. The bow was still tying up. They're having a little harder time than us. We walked forward to get to the gangway. Now we had all the Guamanians who don't do anything for a living but come to the ships, and they all gotta have everything done. Well, they lower the gangway a little bit ahead of time. Now they all gotta go see the captain.

"We have to see the captain."

I just want to punch them all out. I mean, don't I take enough orders? Now I got these shore-side people telling me what to do?

Anyway, I get them up there.

Captain Dave is looking at me like, "What the fuck is this? We're still docking."

So I try to explain that to him, but can't explain that to people who are ashore and have a job to do, because all their paperwork has to be done right *now*, nothing can *wait*. You know: "This paperwork has to be *done*, and I *have* to see the captain!"

One day before I quit, I probably will punch somebody out.

I says to Dave, "You know, Dave, you oughta really tell everyone on this ship not to even lower that gangway 'til the ship is secured alongside the dock."

You have to imagine this: There are 15, 20 people, agents, people from the government, cargo superintendents, harbor people, on the dock yelling, "Lower the gangway! We need to come on!"

Then you've got the line handler standing down there, looking at you, smiling, the native Guamanians, they've got that Oriental in them, they smile when they're embarrassed. You just want to grenade the whole crew, you know?

So we're discharging ammo, self-unloading. As a matter of fact, Brett Younginger is running the overhead crane to get the ammo off. He's running the crane eight to four while the other AB and myself are security, signing people in, signing them off, escorting them, for safety.

Turn around, they want us to work 4 hours overtime, from 4 to 8 at night. I don't like the idea, but I says, OK, it's overtime, and I could use it, but I want to go ashore, too.

One evening, eight o'clock, we're done, I didn't even bother going to shower. Money's in my pocket. I'm gonna stay on the base, they use American money, obviously, in Guam, it's an American possession. At the gangway I sign the logbook, 2000, my time of leaving. I walk down through the pier, and I go out to the gate, and there's a bus stop there where the van would come to get you at the time, the eight o'clock van.

Now a stores truck pulls up to the area by the bus stop where I'm standing right outside the gate. We're talking a 100-yard walk from the ship. He's not allowed to come through. They need to come out and OK him coming in. Well, the bosun comes out to OK the truck.

He sees me and says, "What are you doing standing out here?"

I says, "I'm going ashore."

He says, "We got stores. You gotta come back and help take stores on board."

I says, "Bos', I just put in 12 hours today. I'm entitled to a 6-hour rest period." That's standard for watch. I'm entitled to 6 hours off after 12. If not, it's a violation of federal law.

"Well, if you don't come back, you're gonna have to see the mate tomorrow morning. I'll take you to the mate."

I felt like saying, "You know, you can take me to the mate, the second coming of Christ, anybody you want to take me to, and as soon as he opens his mouth, I'm gonna say, 'Yeah, I wanna go see the doctor cuz I'm going home.'" I refrain from saying it. I says, "You gotta do what you gotta do, bos', but I'm going to get a drink. You do as you please."

I come back about midnight. Next morning I'm going out to stand the 8 to 4 gangway with the other able seaman, and I see Brett getting ready to go in the crane.

Brett says, "You know what happened yesterday?"

I says, "What? About me?"

He says, "No, about me." He says, "The second mate told me that I wasn't working hard enough. He was telling me how to do something, but I said it wouldn't work out that way. He said, 'If you don't do it, I'll charge you with insubordination and take you to the captain.'"

This is about 10 minutes to 8.

I tell Brett, "You know, Brett, if they come and get us at eight o'clock, bosun's gonna take me to the mate, second mate's gonna take you to the captain, we'll just go see the captain ourselves and tell him we're getting off."

Never did take us to the captain.

You know, this is ridiculous in this day and age: "insubordination."

We're there about 3 days, and now a typhoon's coming. So all these assholes that gotta have the gangway down, cuz they *gotta* see the captain, all come on board, they have a big meeting on whether we're gonna leave or not to avoid this storm.

Well, they need this ammo in Guam, and they don't want us to leave, and they feel that the storm's gonna bypass us. This is about three o'clock in the afternoon. They all come back down, and they're all smiles. "You're not gonna leave. That storm's gonna miss us."

Eight o'clock next morning, turn to to secure the ship, the storm's coming, right? *Buckets* of rain are pouring on us. We're out there try-ing to secure the ship because the rain that wasn't coming, that the United States Navy and all the people that just *have* to come down to the ship, you know, to make sure these *papers* are signed and *every-*thing has to be done right—well, you know, *they* don't go there to se-cure the ship. *We* do. So we're out there in this rain, trying to secure the ship, get it ready to go to sea.

We get it ready. We're all set to go.

Well, now the sea is too rough. The line handlers can't go over on the dolphins and let our lines off. They can't do that. It's too rough for them, see. These are the same ones who are demanding, for the paperwork, lower the gangway, and "Why aren't you doing this?" and "Why aren't you doing that?" These are the same fucking people. Love to give orders. I should have punched four or five of 'em out.

The only thing we could do is let our lines go that were tied to the ship, and we let them stay on their dolphins. So we let our mooring line go, just to get out of there.

Captain tells them, "Soon as that storm subsides, get our lines out of the water. We don't want 'em in the water." The idea is: get them dry, at least get them on the dock so they're not floating in the water getting *bloated.*

We're out there for 3 days in the storm, trying to outrun it. Three days of rolling around. Not that bad, but every day the captain's send-ing the same message, "Please get our lines out as soon as possible."

They're saying "yes," right? The harbor master—everybody. "As soon as we can."

We get back 3 days later to dock. The lines are in the water . . . .

And the Guamanians are just standing there smiling at us, the people that *have* to *have* the papers. They're just: "Oh. You're back."

You know, you get the urge to kill. You really do.

So we still gotta get our lines. We can put out the lines that we have, but the ship's not secure yet. Well, we're trying to get them to pull our mooring lines in. They can finally get to them from those dolphins. They get on the dolphins, and they're trying to pull them in. The two stern lines aren't bad. They hadn't wrapped around each other. The three head lines had wrapped around each other. It's just a mess. Wet lines. It's like you see in the movies when they tie somebody's hands up with rope, and they pour water on them, and then try to get the knots out when they're wet. That's what you've got.

And I'm thinking all this time: You motherfuckers. Somebody ought to kill all of you.

We end up doing it. We put the gangway down, and we go down there and separate the lines. We get them set on board, right, we free them up. We get one of the eyes, they throw it on the heaving line, we tie it up. They put it on the winch to pull it up, hoping the line doesn't break. We're pulling up two lines. Some of them are unraveling, some of them aren't, cuz we've got to get these lines free so they're not wrapped around each other.

All this time the Guamanians are standing there looking at us. They don't know how to do any of this. You know, it's not rocket science, it really isn't. We get it done, and I'm up near the bow of the ship, cuz we all went up there to do it after we got the stern taken care of.

Now here they come again, all the pencil pushers, the number crunchers, the have-to-be-signed paperwork people. They're coming on board. The captain asks for the head of the port authority there.

Here's this guy: "Yeah, I'm the one you want to see. I'm in charge of all this."

Captain says, "Why weren't those lines taken in?"

"We didn't have time. You came back, and the storm had just subsided. We didn't have time."

You know, they were thinking of the safety issue, but it's OK for *us* to go do it.

Then they wonder why nobody wants to do this for a living.

We finally leave, go to Jinhae, Korea. I haven't been there in 25 years. And it's changed. It really has. Very much an improvement, but when we would take the bus or the van to go into town, we would go by the old whorehouse. It was still there. Out of business, but it was still there. It was interesting to go back and just see what's transpired. Basically, everybody's moved on. You know, you move on. Time stands still for no one. It was nice, though. Nice, friendly people. Same as it was in '77.

We turn around, we do a little time there, and I did stop at one bar. Met a very nice Korean girl. I spent some time with her at the Crown Bar near the U.S. Navy base.

She owned the bar. She liked to drink. I found a match. My kind of woman. At least for a couple of days.

I says, "Can I use the phone to call the States?" I meant the phone at the bar.

She says, "Sure."

I says, "I was only kidding."

She says, "Little bit. Little money. Small money."

"Are you sure?"

"Yeah, you just buy me drink." She liked to drink. *Liked* to drink. She had imported a couple of Russian girls. I should say that the Russian girls and Eastern European girls have invaded Korea, trying to get sex work, or they worked in the bars. And if sex happened, then sex happened. I mean, if you're negotiating a price, you're negotiating a price.

It's like, "Oh, I got laid for free." Now some of these guys couldn't get laid for free in a women's prison if they had a fistful of pardons. But it was never free to the point where you always felt obligated to leave them something or give them something. But even Spain, England, all the communist block countries, it was just a massive invasion of girls. UAE was loaded with European girls. *Loaded*. Once they got their freedom, that they could get out of the country, they were *gone*. Korea's loaded with Russian girls, Polish girls, Eastern Europeans. That had changed because there were only Korean girls working there back in the '70s.

We leave. I leave Jinhae again. It was getting good to me, especially at my age. I was thinking, gee, I could say a mind is a terrible thing to waste. I was thinking, gee, in my case, a mind's a terrible thing to have.

South Korea is another case of: it's easy to get along. I mean, the women, booze, nobody bothers you too much. And when you know you're going back to the States to go back under the rules, "how good we have it here"—I was leaving the carefreeness of it all, and when I'm leaving any place, any port that I ever liked, I get melancholy about it. And I wonder, gee, I'm going back to. . . . I've used different expressions for America . . . . I don't know if I want to get into that, but you come back to the perceived land of plenty, and to me and a lot of other people, it's really not the land of plenty.

Everybody says, "Well, yeah, *everybody* comes to America. We're growing all the time."

Well, yeah, but there's a lot of people that *don't* come to America. There's a lot of people that left Eastern Europe for *better* opportunities that stayed in the European Union or that went to England or Canada or Australia for a better life.

Sure, I know: how many people immigrate to China, or Vietnam, or Cambodia? People want to *leave* these countries and go somewhere, *anywhere* other than there. But they live just like they lived in the country they left, they carry their way of life with them rather than become part of the place they moved to. It's like, "Well, OK, I want to live in this country under their laws, but I want to keep a tie with the country that abused me." Yeah, it's really strange, and I run into that kind of thing. The majority of people that come to America that I've run across in my travels basically never break their ties to the old country. And the majority of them are sending money to the old country, planning to go back. They're using the American dollar to go back even though they are citizens of this country.

People say everybody comes here because it's so great. No—everybody doesn't come here because it's so great. Everybody comes here so they can make money or try to save some money or try to work here and live just at a basic scale and then go back to their home for whatever reason, no matter what conditions they put up with. They can save the money, or even if they buy a house, they can sell the house, get the equity out of it, and move back to their country. It's not that hard to give up your citizenship.

One guy on a ship, just lately, he was a Kurd from Syria, and he says, "If you ever come to Syria, my family is very wealthy, you're more than welcome to come to the house."

I says, "Thanks." I says, "But if you had it so good, why are you here? Why don't you stay there?"

"Well," he says, "my political beliefs—they caught me and broke my fingernails."

I says, "Does Syria have national health?"

"Oh, yeah, I went there after they let me out, and I got my fingertips taken care of."

"Wow." I says, "You actually have it better than you do here in the States, because here in the States if they break your fingernails, you have to go to the hospital and pay for it yourself."

He thought that was hilariously funny, but it's probably the truth.

Anyway, we leave there, and we're gonna come back to the States with a load of ammunition. We loaded some old ammunition in Okinawa to bring back to the States. Went to Port Chicago, California to discharge, and then it was just the point of waiting to see if we were gonna get another run or not, but the captain was getting off, and I just didn't want to stay if he went. So I bailed out, too.

The tourist thing

December 25, 2004. This is the *William Baugh*, another prepositioned ship in the Mediterranean. When I took this out of the union
hall it was an able seaman job for 120 days, and they were gonna fly
me to Cagliari, Sardinia.

Back in the Med. Few things had changed from when I was running over the last time. But I still wanted to get there. The cost of going over to the euro had really risen. But it's still a nice area, and this
is gonna be Christmastime, so I'd be getting off late April and just at
the party time. So I felt this would be great.

One of the most interesting things we did was go to Malta. Had 2
weeks there. This is another very nice place to visit, historically. Val-
letta, Malta. It's a walled city, an old crusader's stronghold. They had
the old churches there, they had the excavations, the original hospital,
it was a museum. Very well kept up. They found buildings on Malta
that were older than the pyramids. The older I got, the more of a tourist I became. I mean, I was *always* a tourist. I worked on a ship and
anytime I could get off, I went ashore. But the boozing and women
of the night were fading. As I got older, I didn't have the steam I used
to have. But, just to go to these places and see these historical things,
I want to say from about the mid '90s on, it was interesting. When I
was younger, there were times I wouldn't stop to see anything, you
know, besides hit the nearest bar and go partying. And now it really
kicks in on you where you can actually travel and see these things
on purpose, like when I'm standing by that obelisk, where that kid
knocked the head of Lenin off, and here's the building that was the
KGB's, it's burnt out. I'm actually touching these things. England, the
same thing. Every time I went I did the tours at Windsor Castle. It's

really, really interesting.

When I got off on this one, I was gonna go back to Ibiza. We had stopped twice in Palma de Mallorca, Spain. The place *drips* wealth. I'd been there before. That's where they had Cowboy's Bar. Everybody would stop in to see Cowboy and say hello. He's a retired British seaman.

I had gotten off there, and I said, "Well, I'm gonna spend a couple of days there." I wanted to go back to Ibiza, and for reasons out of my control, I didn't. I flew back up to England, and I went there to stay with Ken. There's so many things to see, British Museum of Natural History, and all that. Just places to go, things to do, just wander around, do the tourist thing. After that, in London, I was gonna go back down to Ibiza, but nothing was working in my favor there, so I came back to the States.

After a 3-month layover, nobody's calling to give me a job. So I figured I better go down to the union hall in Norfolk and look for one. I was there about a week in the hall, and a ship came up, the *American Turn*. This is my old friends with the *Harry L. Martin* and Shanghai Jane, who is now gone. She burned out, or couldn't hire anybody else anymore cuz they knew she was lying to them.

I especially was interested because they said the ship is prepositioned in the South China Sea. It's in Sattahip, Thailand, which is in the Gulf of Thailand. From Sattahip it's not that far to Kata Beach. This is what they call "naked by noon, dead by dawn." Guys in their 60s, 70s, 80s go there to die. I mean, they got the blow job bars, all the drugs you can do—the Thai police just take the dead bodies out. You don't even have to be rich to go to Thailand and end your life there. It's very accommodating, I'll phrase it that way. It'd make any seaman blush. The place is unreal. They've got all kinds of shows they put on there. It's a different lifestyle, and if you don't like it, well, then, you don't like it.

Anyway, I see Sattahip, Thailand, and I said, "Hey, maybe gonna stay in Sattahip 2 weeks." I could see this coming, right? I mean, I could really be a tourist now, you know? I take the job, and they fly me out, and I get to the ship. I get to Bangkok.

The guy who's hired help with the agent, he takes me to the hotel and says, "Just stay here in Bangkok until we come and get you." Room, food, you know.

"Room and food," that's all I had to hear. I get in at eleven o'clock at night, and I'm dead tired from the flight over. They flew me from Norfolk, Virginia, to Detroit, across the top of Alaska to Japan, changed planes and go to Bangkok. I says, "I know what it's like, the nightlife in Bangkok." I says, "You know what I'm gonna do? I'm gonna get a decent night's sleep." Got up in the morning, had breakfast, went to the desk. No one called for me.

So I'm gonna walk around and see what it's like in Bangkok. Traffic's crowded. Every third place is a massage parlor. Gotta be careful you don't get run over. I wander around in that heat for about 2 hours. I was gonna pick up a few souvenirs, and I says, "You know what?" I says, "I'll come back later."

I go back to the hotel, eat lunch, go up to the room, and here they call and they says, "You go ship. You go ship."

I says, "Oh, Christ. I was just gonna lay down and then go party."

I came down there, and here's more of the crew members. They had just flown in, and they're gonna put us in a van, take us to the ship in Sattahip, which is about a 2-hour run, because this is the first time I came back since '71, you know, in that Mexican bus ride. It was a lot better now, and the roads had really improved. They even had places along the way you could get gas and eat.

We get to Sattahip, and as soon as I get there I go up and see the captain, and the captain says, "You're gonna relieve the guy that's on the gangway now. I'm sure he wants to go home."

I says, "That's fine, captain."

So I get off at eight o'clock at night, and I'm gonna see what's going on. The taxis were charging different prices. If you caught them inside the gate there, they'd charge you like 5 or 10 bucks. But to bring you back, they wanted 30. You know, we all gotta make a living.

So I says, "Ah, we're gonna be here awhile. Why rush it?" I still had a little bit of jet lag. So I get up in the morning, eight o'clock, I go in.

The captain says, "Come on up. I'd like to see you to sign you on."

He says, "You work for this company on the *Harry L. Martin*, didn't you?"

I says, "Yeah, captain."

He says, "Glad to have you. I got a good report from you from the company."

I says, "Thank you, captain, it's nice to be back in this area for 120 days."

He looks at me. He says, "Ron, we're leaving tomorrow. We're going back to the States empty."

You talk about how your heart falls. I'm awestruck, pissed off, you name it.

I says, "The only reason I did this was to get back over here."

So, here we go. We're gonna go back to the States empty. We go down to Singapore, stop there for about 3 hours, just pick up some spare parts. We go around to Singapore. I'm already thinking: oh, Singapore, man, we could, you know—

It was 3 hours and we're gone. No shore leave.

We come around. We stop to pick up Navy security to take us through the Suez Canal. Stopped at UAE. So we get there, spend 3 days there. Allegedly, we're too far out for launch service, right? But, it's funny, they can bring workers out to work on the ship. They can bring parts *out* to us. But they couldn't get us launch service to go *in*. In reality, they were using deep sea tugs to come out. We were too far out, but we were there 3 days. No shore leave, and now I'm really pissed.

I says, "This is gonna be a long trip for nothing."

We get through the Suez Canal. We stop in Crete for about 6 hours. No shore leave again.

But now they says, "Stop in Livorno, Italy." Just a small port there. It's a weekend resort area for Rome. Couples come to spend the weekend, to get away. Not a bad place. They're bringing old ammunition down on barges, from Livorno, and we're loading it for the States. We're there 2 weeks, and I get ashore one day. Another toothache. I always manage to get a toothache when I'm ashore, cuz they can't deny you that, see? I have over the years if I needed time off. I don't have many teeth left. So they take me from the one town to the other, and I get the tooth taken care of.

They drill it and fill it. The agent's real nice.

I says, "You know, if I have to pay to have it drilled, I have to pay, but if it's pulled, the company pays."

He says, "Alright, tell the dentist that they pulled it, and the company will pay."

I says, "You're a nice guy."

A taxi takes me over to the next town, and we get this done. So I got some time off. Some of the guys want to go to Rome. They ask me if I was interested, and I says, "No, not really." You had to take the bus at six o'clock in the morning, you got to Rome 2 or 3 hours later, you wandered around Rome, then you had to catch the bus at six o'clock at night to bring you back. Not my style, you know?

Well, we do the 2 weeks there, then we load up. We still have Navy security on board. They're kind of wandering around in a daze. We get to Rota, drop them off, and we go to Sunny Point, North Carolina, the old ammo dump. I'd been going there since the '60s. We're dropping the ammo off. I go and tell the captain I want to quit.

He says, "When do you want to quit?"

I says, "Captain, where are we going from here?"

He says, "We're going to Norfolk to lay berth, for about 2 or 3 weeks, and then we're gonna go up to Thule, Greenland, Arctic Circle."

I says, "Well, captain, I'm definitely gonna wanna get off before we go to Thule."

"Fine."

So we take it up to Norfolk to this lay berth. There's really nothing to do. I'm standing gangway security.

To make a long story short, I did a deal. I went, after all. See, it was gonna be a short trip, like 30 days. I had never seen an iceberg. I'd been up near the Arctic Circle, but I had never seen an iceberg. All through the years I had heard how nothing was there in Thule, it was godforsaken. I mean, even the U.S. Air Force base, they sent all the gays up there—you know—they were the only ones that got along with each other.

I says, "You know what? I'm gonna do it just because it's a short trip."

As soon as we reached the Arctic Circle we started seeing the icebergs. A Canadian icebreaker took us up, guiding us through.

I saw big ones, like 10 stories. *Monsters*. But there's smaller ones that came by. You have to avoid those, too, they weigh a ton or two. Called them "growlers."

I says, "Why do you call them growlers?"

They said if you get close to them, you can hear the ice cracking and breaking, it sounds like they're growling. We avoided those, too, because they're scared of hitting one even though the ship has an icebreaker bow on it. You really don't want to hit one.

But something like that, I mean, really, you gotta like it because you can see that on National Geographic. I mean, you can't see Ibiza on National Geographic. Trust me. You can't. You can't *fathom* the place. You can't *fathom* Panama, The Blue Goose. But to take a trip up to Thule, Greenland and the icebergs, I mean, come on. It's nice to see.

I get up there, and we get to the dock. It's raining, and it's about 35 degrees. The pier itself is just a couple of barges that they've welded to pilings, and then there's dirt. There's three shacks. The largest one is owned by Denmark. They've got Danes working there and Inuit Eskimos. I see a sign on the shack: "Greenland Consortium Company. Welcome to Thule, northernmost deep water port in the world."

It's 3 days before I even go ashore. This is the only time of year you can get up to Thule. It's 6 months of sun and 6 months of dark. Up in the Arctic Circle, it's 24 hours a day of sun, it just goes from horizon to horizon, back and forth. That's all it did. So we're there, it's raining, about 35 degrees, and I says, "Jesus Christ, is it gonna be like this the whole time we're up here?" Third day, the sun comes out, it stops raining. The temperature goes up to *almost* 50 degrees. I'm standing gangway watch, layered in clothes, freezing. The Danes and the Inuits are in shorts and t-shirts. This is like heaven to them, and I'm thinking, God, if they ever go anywhere else, they'll never come back here.

We could walk outside the base, but they do have polar bear attacks. The Eskimos can kill anything they want. All the seals, all the polar bears. So for all you environmentalists and nature lovers who are trying to save the whales or save the polar bears, Denmark allows them to kill anything they want, and then they sell it at the Danish post office on the base. They've got a freezer there with caribou meat, whale meat, seal meat.

I didn't want any. I don't believe in it—buying things that they're killing the animal for the sake of the killing. Matter of fact, I was looking at the polar bear claws, and they wanted something like $200 for a polar bear claw with a little silver tip on it. Just an inch long of the claw. I almost bought it. I thought about it, you know, and I said, "Well, so the polar bears come too close to the camp and they gotta kill them." I don't know. By me buying a polar bear claw, or polar bear meat or—I'm not saying they don't kill it and eat it themselves, but I'm just encouraging this. They had boots, too. They wanted $300 or $400 for a pair of boots made out of reindeer skin. But I didn't buy any of it. I mailed some postcards from there with a Danish stamp.

When you came to the harbor, to the right is where you docked, and that was where the pier was where they were discharging and loading. To the left there was a mountain jutting right into the middle of the harbor. So the harbor is almost like a heart shape. On the left were buildings propped up, everything was 2 or 3 feet off the ground, even on the base itself. Even the Quonset huts were built up, or the trailers were built up to keep you off the ground. This was where the U.S. Air Force had built this for the Inuits. They still used it. Some of them that worked on the base would go there overnight. During the Cold War, for security reasons, they moved them 100 miles further north, if you can imagine that. If you ever look at a map and you see Thule, Greenland at the left hand corner there in the Arctic Circle, figure 100 miles north of that. I don't know what those people did. But some of them would come down and work on the dock or on the ships. Then they'd stay overnight at these huts, rather than go all the way 100 miles further north.

The base had a library and a PX. They had the Danish post office that sold souvenirs. You had the Danish club with a little TV set. The only thing they really got was CNN at the Top of the World Club, which was an air force club.

We were there 10 days. Nobody could believe we had such good weather. I was just praying, "Just hold until we leave." We had brought up containers and vehicles, stuff for the air force base and the PX. There were a bunch of vehicles that had been wrecked or motors burned out from the cold. We loaded them to bring them back.

We came back to Norfolk, Virginia. That was summer 2006. We got back, and I quit.

Captain says, "It was nice having you."

I says, "Thanks, captain. I appreciate that."

He says, "About October or November, we'll be going down to Antarctica." This ship made a run to Antarctica. "If you'd be interested, you could see penguins."

"Thank you, captain, I'll keep it in mind." No offense, it's just not my thing. If you wanna see penguins, see National Geographic. It's like icebergs: you've seen one, you've seen them all.

Final voyages

So, I'll be leaving soon. For good. I have no complaints. It's given me what I wanted: no responsibility or temporary responsibility. Like I say, it's not good for everybody, or it's not what everybody wants. And seeing the world from the late '60s up into 2000 and later, I've seen the changes. But people are still the same. Even in my youth, everybody else was worried about getting a girlfriend, or a girl getting a boyfriend, or the prom, or being important, or the social structure. But I'm not a competitor. I don't think I've ever competed. I could care less. I never had to have the prettiest girl, the prettiest hooker. While everybody else was thinking about where they were gonna go to college, I was thinking about different places I could see in the world. I had made a list, and I've pretty much seen everything I've wanted to see.

Everybody was so against it. You have to remember that it was—for lack of a better term—a Depression-era mentality. You weren't encouraged to think out of the box. You were supposed to just want a job. And I would watch television, which was the only escape I had, besides books, from a pretty mundane life with mundane people, who were stuck in their ways, who had never done anything bright in their life. That's all they did was go to school and then go to work. You married the girl who lived across the street, bought a house two blocks away, and every Saturday and Sunday the families would come over and help you with the house.

I'm not saying there's anything wrong with that. But when I would watch television or read a book, it was always adventure. And I was always told: "People really don't live like that. That's just on television or in a book." Well, who was telling me this but people who had never done anything before in their life?

No offense, you know, different people like different things. But it was so programmed. They used to talk about the communist countries: "you have no freedom," "they're suppressing Christians." And the only thing I could think of is: well, wait a minute, what do I have here? I'm being programmed into this.

Remember how girls used to pull that old bullshit? "My girlfriend likes you."

What the fuck do I care?

I used to try to explain to them: it's not *them*, it's *me*! Look, I don't need anybody telling me what the fuck to do, and I don't want to tell you what to do, either.

It was always that: you had to have a girlfriend, or you didn't count, or you had to have a boyfriend, or you didn't count.

Who leveled out this playing field with everything I'm "supposed" to do?

And the worst word in all the languages, besides "no," is "why?"

To me, it was escape. The great escape. It was during the late '60s and early '70s; it was escape from conformity. Groups have a tendency to form, it's always "birds of a feather". Well, you had the most popular together, then the jocks would be together, and you had the nerds together, and then you had some people that didn't care. Well, you had them together, too, but once you get an "ism," then it's conformity again in its own sense of the word. I really never kept in touch except with a few people. If they did what they wanted with their life, that's fine. I'm happy with mine. I did what I wanted to do. I couldn't let too many laws get in my way. I preferred countries that were very lax on law.

Maybe it's a "me" thing. I felt that way years ago: me, me, me. But what about "me"? How many people am I supposed to please? Or am I supposed to please an "ism"? "Isms" come and "isms" go. I still have to be me.

I don't think I've changed. Every time I get back to the free world, I see the same insanity. I'd see the same thing, whether it was Ohio, Florida, wherever. I haven't changed. This is once in never out. I mean, this is it. It's a lifestyle. No conformity of any kind, no stress, no drama. A number of guys on the ships ended up marrying foreign girls and send their money there. Then they're gonna retire to the different places, you know, where they have a little business going or something. If they feel that's correct, then that's correct. I don't feel I need a female partner to tell me what to do. I mean, come on, I'm gonna marry a Filipino girl? Or I'm gonna take over a family and raise the kids? Like my uncle used to say about kids and dogs: Dogs are easier to train, and they don't last as long. He told me that all the time. Then he'd look at me.

People have the tendency to feel that they've accomplished something. And that's great. It's self-satisfaction. Ego. "I did this," or "I did that." I don't even talk about what I've done with people. I don't even talk about where I've been.

And talk about the future? Well, the future's *now*.

Let's face facts. I don't want to hold anybody back, either. I can't deal with the "look at what I've done for you." I mean, come on. Like the United States government, all we've done for you, or you owe allegiance to us. What it all breaks down to is control under an "ism."

For me, the sea was escape. It was an escape from the grind. I'd come back, and I'd see the guys that got married, with children and homes and "Well, yeah, I just bought a new couch," or "I got another car," or "I've got another kid." The ones I kept in touch with over the years, some had made it, some haven't. Some are better off, some aren't.

Would I want to change it? No.

I won't work. I'm perfectly honest in every relationship I was ever in. I won't work. It's that simple.

And, you know, governments and jobs—you always hear the phrase "That's a good job," or "That's a good place to work." When, in reality, the job has *you.* You don't *have* the job. You *need* the job cuz you're usually so far in debt or the wife wants more or the kids want more or the government wants more.

I'm less than a year to retirement, and one of the main reasons I want to stop is I'm running out of things to do. I want to collect my Social Security. I don't want to leave it in there for "everyone else." I mean, I love that term. It's for "everybody." Really, it's not for everybody. It's *mine.* That's a me thing again. And I should be able to do with it anything I feel like doing with it, without being told.

And what I want to do is absolutely nothing. I want to do nothing. I very seldom have done anything unless I was forced to do it, you know, earning a living or something. I just want to be left alone now. In Central America somewhere. I'm sure there's other people like me bouncing around. If there's a woman, anywhere from 18 to 50, you know, I mean, hey—I can handle a part-time relationship. A weekend's a long relationship for me.

But it would have to be two people of the same mind. And it's hard because people have a tendency to change. You know, they want to change the rules in the middle of the game. I really don't do that. If I'm in, I'm in. And change occurs constantly . . . . But for me, change *what?* Why? What am I trading? I'm trading my freedom for somebody else's security. It's ridiculous.

I'm looking forward to oblivion. Just oblivion. That way I won't have to get up anymore.

I hate to say this, and I don't want to sound egotistical, but there is really nothing left. The adventure's gone now. Everything's becoming a job. The ships are becoming a job. It's time to go. One should always know when it's time to go. You know, you get what you want and leave. Is that terribly wrong? I can't see that it's wrong. Or: "I'm staying here because I'm staying here for the kids," or "I'm staying here because I have so much time into this." It's like bondage. And bondage was done away with years ago in the States; or they changed the name of it maybe to Social Security—from bondage to Social Security, where you've got to work so long to get so much.

But no, I've done damn near everything I wanted to do anytime I felt like doing it. I never believed in restriction. Restriction, whether it be school, state, county, city—"You can't do this. You can't do that." Guardians, the same thing. Self-appointed guardians who feel that they know better than I do. Well, it becomes the old thing: walk a mile in my shoes. I mean, I don't care to walk in your shoes. You do what you want with your life, and I'll do what I want with my life.

I've seen it happen in different places where somebody's getting ready to retire, and all of a sudden they get to the widow, who's got a house, and say, "Gee, let's get together, we can make it and take care of the house." Give me a break. I'm sitting in a bar, having a good time, somewhere where there's sunshine and the weather's warm.

You take a partner, allegedly to help you out. That's in anything. Partners in anything. Either they're gonna help you out, or you're gonna help each other out. When, in reality, one becomes a burden to the other. And then: "Well, I gotta stay, I've been here so long. I'm scared of the unknown." What's unknown? The future? Yeah, well, do you want the future you've got, or are you willing to take a chance and go the other way? It's like they call it Arab luck: "I'll get rid of this one, I'll get another one just as bad." Most people just decide to stay where they're at. It's a security issue. "Well, I've got a house in the suburbs, the kids are grown, and maybe I don't get along with her the way I used to, but, you know, we've been there so long. We might as well just keep abusing each other now." That's what it amounts to.

To me, there is no such thing as the American Dream. Being in so many countries, seeing so many different people . . . .

When I was with that Korean girl, she was listening to the Voice of Reunification, in South Korea, back in '77, broadcast in English from the South. Propaganda.

I says, "Oh. North Korea number 10, huh?"

She says, in her broken English, "Same people, different mind."

And pretty much that's it, people are still people, wherever you go.

No matter what you do, they're looking for security. Whether it be a government, a religion, or their mate. People are always looking for security. Depending on what religion you're born into, or you convert to, because it answers your needs, or whatever government you want to live under because it answers your needs. And this is no offense to people who get married, but it's a power-sharing deal. I really believe it becomes one using the other one. Giving up so much to getting so much. Or: is this the best I can do? Later on in life it becomes the mid-life crisis: is this what I *really* wanted?

I've seen incidents off the ship where it's basically the same thing. People are looking for security. There's no such animal. It doesn't exist. And when they can't have security, it has a tendency to go over to control. And when it gets into control, it can be very dangerous, because now you're getting into other people's lives, which can be easily led. And once you're easily led . . . .

The human race puzzles me, with striving for freedom, and then basically just giving it away.

I'm the biggest coward you'll ever run across in your life. I fear everything. I stay scared. I think that's why I stayed alive so long. Dumb luck's played a hand in keeping me going, sure. Some of the dumb, ignorant, stupid shit I did, you know, maybe I should be dead. But I'm not. Whether that's just a case of it wasn't my time, I don't know. But if you stay scared or you stop and think—I was once told that you can think your way out of anything if you just stop and think. Don't panic. Don't hit the panic button. Stop and think your way through, and it's really worked out for me.

And every once in awhile, you have to turn around and snarl at the government, or the establishment, or the "ism" you happen to be forced to live under. If you turn around and snarl at it every once in awhile . . . .

And it helps me to say "no."

You'd be surprised what the establishment or the "ism" thinks they can get away with, when, in reality, you can say "no" and they'll back off when they're not sure. You can slide around, circumvent laws. It's pretty much rule by decree, but there are ways out that they haven't found to tighten it up yet.

And if you're willing to do—well, more than once I've been told that I use more brain power trying to get out of work than if I just went to work. Maybe I do. But the people who said this to me are now dead, and I'm still here. Does that make it right? I don't know. But did they get anything more from working harder than I did? It's why I like working for Captain Dwyer. When push comes to shove, Dave just tells me, "Look, Ron. Get it done. I don't care how you do it. Whatever it takes. Get it done." I love that attitude: "Hey, get it done. I don't care what you gotta do. Get it done." That's why he likes me to work for him. And I don't mind it at all, because I know what he wants, and it's a lot easier to work for somebody that knows what they want.

Even in a relationship with a woman, you never know what they want. Whatever they say they want, obviously, isn't gonna be right. And I'm sure there's women that say the same thing about their husbands or their boyfriends. It's always the few relationships that I've really been in, it all changed, or I'm supposed to do this, or I'm supposed to do that. Well, wait a minute, I never signed on for this. Didn't we say it was gonna be free and easy? You were the one that said, "Hey, look, I'm an exotic dancer, and you're a merchant seaman. Let's not ever forget that."

And that's fine with me.

Picking out a partner would be like the drunken brother I never had. You know, how much can you drink? That's all I'm interested in.

And, looking back, up until about the mid '80s, you got into port, you didn't have to work on the weekends unless you had gangway. We used to call the guys "tourists", who would take off all the time and didn't work a lot of overtime, right? Trust me, I was president of the club. At five o'clock Friday afternoon—if we were gonna be in for the weekend, they would post it on the sailing board by the gangway—I was standing there, waiting to see what they were gonna put on the board. And if they didn't put that we were sailing, I was gone for the weekend. The only time I would come back would be to change clothes or get money. I did it constantly, to everybody's chagrin, because the officers hated it. I mean, any company I worked with: "You're young. You're a big, strong guy. You should be out there working overtime."

I would say, "You go out there and work overtime. I'll go have a good time with my life." I'm not here for the money. I'm not trying to support a wife and 12 kids. I'm just going out here for a good time.

The surprising part about it was I always got a rehire. I couldn't believe it. I mean, they couldn't get me to work overtime, but when we had to work, I *worked*.

You know, "The guy don't work any overtime, but he *works*."

Cuz it was a lot of work to secure those old ones. You had to pull tarps, wing in booms, secure guides. It was a lot of work. And I always did it. In the beginning, after that first trip to Hamburg when I was on the deck department, that bosun said, "We work hard now, Ronnie." He says, "You can have all the time you want off when we get to these ports." He used to give me time off. So I was really fucking gone then. He'd find me in some fucking hellhole I'd be in, you know?

We used to call those guys tourists. "That guy's a tourist," you know, right? I mean, he's never here. And I was president of the club. I was *gone*. I didn't need anybody to run with. I would take off on my own and go exploring, finding different women and abusing myself, and them, too. The surprising part is they liked it as much as I did.

And I could give you more, too, if I could remember it all. It was just constantly dumb, stupid shit we did.

But it was great.

It was fucking great.

The End

"Life is either a daring adventure, or nothing."

~Helen Keller

CPSIA information can be obtained at www.ICGtesting.com
Printed in the USA
LVOW040315211211

260314LV00001B/54/P